INTELLIGE

INTELLIGENT DATABASES

Object-Oriented, Deductive Hypermedia Technologies

Kamran Parsaye

Mark Chignell

Setrag Khoshafian

Harry Wong

WILEY

John Wiley & Sons, Inc.
New York · Chichester · Brisbane · Toronto · Singapore

Library of Congress Cataloging-in-Publication Data:

Intelligent databases.

Bibliography: p.
1. Data base management. 2. Expert systems (Computer science) I. Parsaye, Kamran.
QA76.9.D3I548 1989   005.74   88-33948
ISBN 0–471–50346–0
ISBN 0–471–50345–2 (pbk.)

PREFACE

Anthropologists have argued over whether humans became smart because they walked upright, because they had to kill other animals without having the powerful jaws and claws needed for the job, or because they learned how to communicate using a complex form of articulation and vocalization. However, lurking behind our definitions of humans as tool users and language users is the prior concept of humans as information users. Information and its use allow us to build and use tools and to express ourselves in language.

It is often remarked that we are living in the information age, yet we are struck by the fact that many existing technologies (1) are under-utilized and (2) tend to be treated in isolation. In the past few years, major advances have been made in several fields of critical relevance to information technology. These advances have been significant, but fragmented. Bringing these separate technical leaps into a unified framework will benefit people involved in all of the contributing disciplines by facilitating cross-disciplinary activity and by pointing out new avenues for both research and application.

This book is about the emerging intelligent database technology that will have a dramatic impact on the way we think and work. Intelligent databases will greatly expand our capabilities as information users. The phenomenon of the shrinking world is reaching its natural conclusion (i.e., McLuhan's global village), and intelligent databases are the means by which we may store and retrieve the information and expertise of this global village.

We may have to discard some familiar intellectual habits and presuppositions along the way. For instance, we are accustomed to thinking about information as passive, residing in books and documents. Similarly, we often use libraries because we want to get at the information contained in their books, and we use databases as retrieval systems to find "answers." These "answers" are not always predefined in the system and may have to be created "on the fly," depending on the particular characteristics of the user and his or her current interests. Intelligent databases will change how we do research, how we look for ideas, how we make decisions, and how knowledge is transmitted.

In writing this book, we began with the premise that the database is at the heart of any information system and then sought to combine databases with a variety of tools that would make them more intelligent. In so doing, we have developed the model for intelligent databases that is described in this book.

The intelligent database model is based on five information technologies:

- Databases
- Object-Oriented Programming
- Expert Systems
- Hypermedia
- Text Management

Each of the four authors of this book has expertise in one or more of these areas. The book represents a balance between the need to provide sufficient background in each of the five technologies while also including new material on intelligent databases.

Databases and expert systems have been extensively discussed elsewhere, but the material in Chapters 2 and 4 distills the key concepts, thus allowing this book to be a self-contained treatment of intelligent databases. Although many texts on databases and expert systems are available, none relates them to the other technologies discussed here.

We also felt the need to provide clear expositions of object-oriented programming, hypertext, and text management. In addition to covering the major points made elsewhere in a number of scattered texts and journals, our treatment of these topics extends them where necessary so as to provide the tools for constructing intelligent databases.

The eight chapters of the book provide a complete and self-contained exposition of intelligent databases. Chapter 1 begins by defining intelligent databases and places them in the context of evolving information technology. The next five chapters present the key concepts for each of the five contributing technologies. In its discussion of databases, Chapter 2 focuses on relational and semantic data models in particular. Chapter 3 discusses the major issues of object orientation, including encapsulation, inheritance, and object identity; it also reviews existing object-oriented languages and databases. Chapter 4 introduces the expert-system building blocks of knowledge representation and inference, and describes the process of building expert systems. The chapter concludes with a discussion of how expert systems and databases may be combined to form deductive retrieval systems.

Chapter 5 provides a thorough introduction to hypertext, relating it to the knowledge representation methods described in Chapter 4 and showing how hypertext networks may be linked to conventional databases. Chapter 6 reviews the extensive topic of text management, focusing on these elements most relevant to the construction of intelligent databases. Chapter 7 elaborates on the themes developed in Chapters 1 through 6. A formal model for intelligent databases is described that incorporates the five technologies described earlier. The main points of the earlier chapters are summarized in Chapter 8.

While writing this book, we constructed a prototype of the Fortune Finder intelligent database described in Chapter 7, thus demonstrating the viability of our intelligent database model. The material presented in this book represents the fruits of research and development that have been carried out by universities and industry over the past few years. In particular, we would like to acknowledge the contribution of Project Jefferson at the University of Southern California in demonstrating how hypermedia can be used for information management.

We write the book with several types of readers in mind. Those who want to master the topic of intelligent databases in its entirety should read all the chapters of the book in the order they are written. Database specialists who want to update their technical knowledge should skim Chapter 2 before focusing on Chapters 3, 4, 5, and 7. Administrators and managers should begin by reading Chapters 1 and 6, followed by Chapter 7. They should then return to the more technical material provided in such chapters as 4 and 5. Readers who have a good grasp on topics such as object orientation and expert systems, but who want to know what intelligent databases are, should concentrate, at least initially, on Chapters 1 and 7. Conversely, the book can also be used to review individual topics such as expert systems or hypertext. We see it being used in this way, for instance, in graduate-level college seminars on information technology or expert system applications.

All of the techniques described in this book can be implemented on a microcomputer such as a Macintosh II or a 286 or 386 class machine, and most of the techniques have already been implemented. In many ways, this books describes what is needed to build a shell for intelligent databases, much like the shells that are used to construct expert systems. In the same way that knowledge engineering of expert systems can be a difficult task, even when one has the expert system shell, so our experience has shown us that intelligent database engineering is a difficult task. However, we have no doubt that the benefits of intelligent databases will lead to them becoming a firmly established information technology.

We would like to thank those people who have helped us in preparing this book: Jenny Ghielmetti, Sandra Chignell, Silva Khoshafian, Linda Wong, Bob Blum, Bob Fraser, Joe Goguen, Lee Jaffe, Rei-Chi Lee, Diana Lin, Phil Smith, David Thompson and Gio Wiederhold. In preparing this book, we also benefited from discussion and interactions with a wide variety of colleagues, including the members of the Project Jefferson Team at USC.

KAMRAN PARSAYE
MARK CHIGNELL
SETRAG KHOSHAFIAN
HARRY WONG

Los Angeles and Walnut Creek, California
January, 1989

CONTENTS

1.

INTRODUCTION

1

2.

DATABASE SYSTEMS

35

3.

OBJECT ORIENTATION

97

4.

EXPERT SYSTEMS

5.
HYPERMEDIA

223

6.

TEXT MANAGEMENT AND RETRIEVAL 293

7.

INTELLIGENT DATABASES   367

8.
SUMMARY
435

BIBLIOGRAPHY
449

INDEX
469

ABOUT THE AUTHORS
479

1

INTRODUCTION

■ 1.1 **INTRODUCTION**

This book is about intelligent databases, which can be loosely defined as *databases that manage information in a natural way, making that information easy to store, access, and use*. We use the term *information* rather than *data* here since the intelligent databases discussed in this book deal not only with traditional applications such as inventory management, but also with knowledge bases, automatic discovery systems, textual data, images, and so on.

The concepts of "ease" and "naturalness" are so well accepted that it is hard to argue with their worth. However, while the definition above is rather general, in Section 1.5 we provide detailed criteria for what makes a database intelligent. These criteria establish that by using intelligent databases users can perform tasks involving large amounts of information that otherwise could not possibly be performed. This relies on defining three levels of database intelligence.

    i. Intelligence of the high-level tools provided by the database.
    ii. Intelligence at the user-interface level.
    iii. Intelligence of the underlying database engine.

These are illustrated in Figure 1.1.

Intelligent databases represent a new technology for information management that has evolved as a result of the integration of traditional approaches to databases with more recent fields such as

1

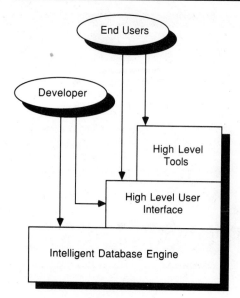

Figure 1.1 Three levels of database intelligence.

- Object-oriented programming
- Expert systems
- Hypermedia
- Online information retrieval

The merger of these technologies is illustrated in Figure 1.2.

Intelligent databases thus represent the evolution of a number of distinct paths of technological development. As Figure 1.3 suggests, traditional database systems were developed in the mainframe environments of the early 1960s. They were typically applied to numeric and record-based data (e.g., employee records or parts inventories) and soon began to spread throughout industry. In the early 1970s, online information systems became available as a specialization of database technology, and they began dealing with textual databases. In the mid-1970s the technology of expert systems developed and had become prominent by the late 1970s. Similarly, in the late 1970s and early 1980s, techniques relating to *object-oriented programming* grew out of work in software engineering, user interfaces, and high-level programming languages. Finally, in the mid-1980s practical hypermedia systems, which dealt with information in a variety of forms such as text, images, and sound, became available.

Until recently, these technologies were treated in isolation, with each technology being only *weakly linked* to others. For instance, in the early days expert systems relied on little more than file-transfer protocols to gather data from databases. This was partly

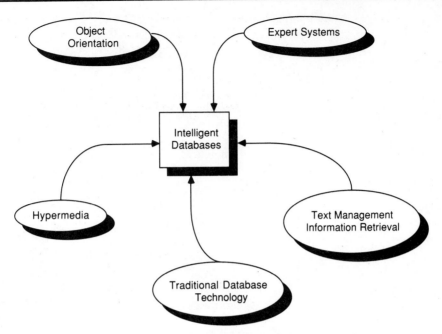

Figure 1.2 The merging of technologies into intelligent databases.

due to the fact that because of the phenomenal growth in each field, the connections and correspondences to the other fields did not have time to form. Now that these technologies have reached a stage of maturity on their own, it is possible to define an overall unifying structure for viewing all these fields as parts of a blueprint for intelligent databases. Intelligent databases provide a common approach to the access and use of information for analysis and decision making.

Although intelligent databases are intellectually appealing as frameworks for integrating diverse technologies and approaches, their importance may also be justified on practical grounds. To answer the question "Why are intelligent databases better?" we need to consider what we mean by "better" in a given context (i.e., "better for what?"). The essential characteristics of an intelligent database are that it (1) is easy and natural to use, (2) can handle large amounts of information in a seamless and transparent fashion, and (3) allows people to carry out their tasks using an appropriate set of information management tools.

Today, we live in a world of information glut. To simply survive in today's society, we need to access and use information, and by using an intelligent database more people can have better access to, and use of, more kinds of information than they could otherwise. This means that intelligent databases should

- Provide high-level intelligent tools (e.g., automated discovery) that provide new insights into the contents of a database by extracting knowledge from data.

- Make information available to larger numbers of people because more people can now utilize the system due to its ease of use.
- Improve the decision-making process involved in using information after it has been retrieved by using higher-level information models (from this perspective, intelligent databases serve as decision support systems).
- Interrelate information from different sources using different media (e.g., images, text, numbers, etc.) so that the information is more easily absorbed and utilized by the user.
- Use knowledge and inference, making it easier to retrieve, view, and make decisions with information.

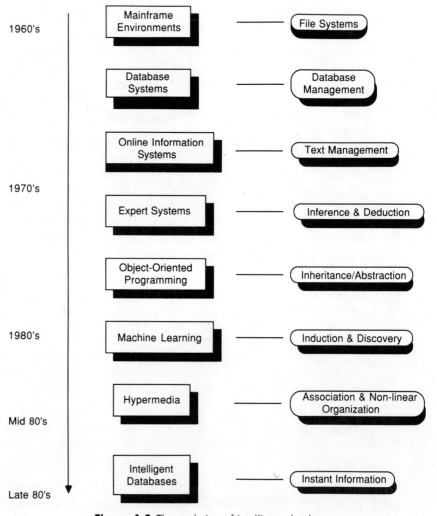

Figure 1.3 The evolution of intelligent databases.

Thus, an intelligent database caters to the needs of the user for information that is relevant, easy to obtain, and helpful in making decisions.

The top-level architecture of the intelligent database consists of three levels.

> high-level tools
> high-level user interface
> intelligent database engine

As Figure 1.4 shows, this is a staircase layered architecture, that is, users and developers may independently access different layers at different times.

The first of these levels is the *high-level tools* level. These tools provide the user with a number of facilities such as intelligent search, data quality and integrity control, and automated discovery. These high-level tools represent an external library of powerful tools that some users may find useful, but not others. Most of these tools may be broadly classified as information management techniques. They look and work much as their stand-alone equivalents, such as spreadsheets and graphic representation tools, but they are modified so as to be compatible with the intelligent database model. Thus they are object-oriented, and their basic structure mirrors the object representation methods of the intelligent database model.

The second level is the *high-level user interface*. This is the level that users directly interact with. This level creates the model of the task and database environment that

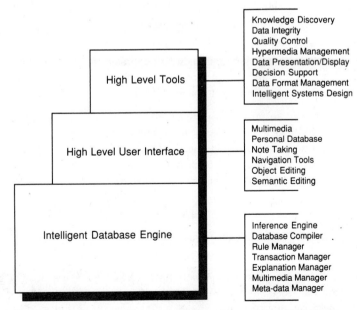

Figure 1.4 The top level architecture of an intelligent database.

users interact with. As such, it has to deal as much with how the user wants to think about databases and information management as it has to do with how the database engine actually operates. Associated with this level are a set of representation tools that enhance the functionality of the intelligent database.

The user interface is presented in two aspects. There is a core model that is presented to the user. This core model consists of the object-oriented representation of information along with a set of integrated tools for creating new object types, browsing, searching, and asking questions. In addition, there are a set of high-level tools, which although not an essential part of the core model, nevertheless enhance the functionality of the intelligent database system for certain classes of user.

The base level of the system is the *intelligent database engine*. The intelligent database engine incorporates a model that allows for a deductive object-oriented representation of information that can be expressed and operated on in a variety of ways. The engine includes backward and forward chaining inference procedures as well as drivers for the external media devices, version handlers, optimizing compilers, and the like. Many of the features of this integrated engine will depend on the specifics of the hardware and software environment in which an intelligent database is implemented.

In this book, we outline an architecture for intelligent databases. This architecture includes the major components of hypermedia, databases, expert systems, object-oriented programming, and online databases. To understand the technology of intelligent databases, however, we have to understand the essentials of databases and data modeling, object orientation, expert systems, hypertext, and information management, and it is these topics that we address in the next five chapters.

Chapters 2, 3, 4, 5, and 6 thus discuss a range of technologies for conceptualizing and processing information. Although generally considered to be distinct in the past, these diverse technologies can be integrated into a methodological framework for the construction and use of intelligent databases. We shall describe a formal model for implementing intelligent databases using these technologies in Chapter 7.

However, to provide a perspective on the information society and to know how we have gotten where we are, in the rest of this chapter, we first discuss the concept of information and then present a brief history of information and its use. This historical discussion is designed to provide a foundation of basic concepts that will assist in interpreting the material covered in later chapters.

■ 1.2 INFORMATION AND INFORMATION GLUT

One of the reasons for using intelligent databases is that we live in a state of information glut. This is definitely a case of too much of a good thing being bad for us, since anytime we want specific information we are forced to wade through a large amount of mostly irrelevant information to find it.

One might think that electronic access would answer the problem of ready access to information, but like the invention of printing, this only shifts the problem. Making information widely available still does not answer the question of how to get to what one needs to know. Having billions of words of text is not much use to one if there is no way of knowing which particular documents address the current information need.

We are constantly bombarded by data that demands our attention. This data ranges from the information provided in newspapers, magazines, and television broadcasts to stock market reports, economic projections, census data, and other items that are used in a variety of applications and analyses. Collectively, we are approaching, and have probably exceeded, the point of information glut, where we can no longer assimilate and utilize more than a small fraction of the available data. Symptoms of this general malaise are plentiful. People begin to cancel their magazine subscriptions because they no longer have time to read all the issues. Managers insist on executive summaries of the data because they don't have time to deal with all the details.

An old joke once implied that the United States would eventually collapse and sink into the sea under the accumulated weight of back issues of *National Geographic*. Although physical scientists dispute that prediction, information scientists may find in it a useful metaphor for the mounting problems caused by the growing glut of information and data.

In some cases, the electronic availability of information may serve more as a distractor, preventing one from finding what is really relevant, much as a needle gets lost in a haystack. Thus, the challenge is to organize and index information in a form that allows ready access to specific subtopics.

It is no longer possible to stop the printing presses, word processors, and wire services and go back to a simpler time. We must deal with the information glut by adapting to it and creating technologies that distill the most essential information for subsequent human consumption. This ability to separate the informational wheat from the surrounding chaff is one of the features that distinguishes intelligent databases from databases in general.

Part of the solution to information glut is to make information less amorphous and more easily interpreted as an answer to a potential question. Too frequently, information is treated as an unanalyzable document that can only be indirectly accessed. Yet people want information to answer questions and to make decisions with. In most situations, people don't just want information, they want to update their knowledge about a particular topic. Bell (1979) has characterized the distinction between information and knowledge as follows:

> By information I mean data processing in the broadest sense; the storage, retrieval, and processing of data becomes the essential resource for all economic and social exchanges. . . . By knowledge, I mean an organized set of statements of fact or ideas, presenting a reasoned judgment or an experimental result, which is transmitted to others through some communication medium in some systematic form.

If we accept this distinction, it would appear that many people who use information retrieval systems to answer questions or make decisions are really seeking knowledge rather than information per se.

1.2.1 Precursors of the Information Society

The modern information society has arisen out of the ability to store information and data in electronic databases. The concept of a database is a modern one, but it had its beginnings in the earliest attempts to archive and retain information past the fleeting thoughts of a single human observer. The first step toward the modern database was the representation of information in written form. Until recently, representations of information consisted of marks made on physical objects. Prior to the electronic information revolution, there was a slower, but just as important, series of revolutions in hard-copy information technology, which are summarized in Figure 1.5.

1.2.2 The Hard-Copy Information Revolution

Initially, the written form was iconic, a visual representation of what was being described, as in pictograms and hieroglyphs. These iconic languages were used by a variety of cultures, including the ancient Egyptians and the Aztecs. Early iconic languages tended to use a large number of pictorial forms that were not well standardized. Consequently, they often required a great deal of interpretation on the part of the reader.

As the symbology of communication became more standardized and restricted, the modern alphabet developed. The alphabet is a restricted set of standard symbols that has acoustic (sound), but not lexical (meaning) interpretations. Thus, these alphabetic symbols do not by themselves represent objects, but form the building blocks for words that then represent objects and concepts. The alphabet is a form of coding where linguistic concepts are coded into a restricted alphabet of letters. It may be argued that modern alphabets have a certain size (e.g., 26 letters) and structure (vowels and consonants) that correspond to psychological principles of memorability and usefulness, but the computer revolution has demonstrated that concepts of arbitrary complexity may be conveyed by the simplest set of coding symbols (on-off bits). At the other extreme, the extensive set of characters used in modern Asian languages also provides the same coding function even though they contain a much larger alphabet and there is a closer relationship between single characters and objects.

The use of alphanumeric coding systems was a critical precursor to the development of science and technology. In Greece, for instance, the preceding Homeric oral tradition was largely replaced by written philosophy in the golden age of Athens and the Greek city-states. The medium of spoken language used by the orators and poets was transformed into stories and written arguments that were stored verbatim outside the mind of the speaker. To some extent, the transition from the spoken to the written word created a greater emphasis on the form rather than the content of language. Issues of spelling and grammar assumed greater importance. However,

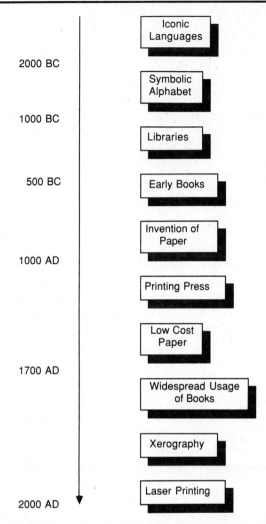

Figure 1.5 Revolutions in hard-copy information technology.

writing also allowed arguments and discussions to be archived, and this led to greater attention to the definition and use of words as discrepancies between the usages of different writers became apparent in the cumulative written record. Thus, Socrates and other philosophers concentrated on the definition of single words in clarifying and standardizing philosophical argument. This early emphasis on the definition of words was then replaced by the employment of abstract concepts in chains of discursive reasoning. Aristotle converted the dialectic method of Plato and others into a formal analysis (propositional logic), which forms the basis of modern symbolic logic (see Parsaye and Chignell, 1988, Chapter 3 for further discussion of formal logic and its use in inference).

Invention of the book was necessitated by the demands of large-scale classifying, storing, and retrieving of information. Previously, manuscript rolls had been of varying lengths. Sometimes a roll would hold one short work only; sometimes the writings of several authors in sequence. The maintenance of a half-million such manuscript rolls must have been a nightmare. A new information-processing technology was clearly necessary, and a simple, but effective, technique was developed. Books were constructed out of manuscript rolls cut into standardized lengths and bound together. The thin-leafed pages of the book made information much more readily manipulable and browsable than had been possible with rolled-up knowledge.

In addition to being storehouses of knowledge, books were also objects that embodied and represented knowledge. Thus scholars would routinely refer to knowledge by the authors and titles of books. Books began to be collected, classified, stored, and retrieved. Even in early times, the collection and storage of books was big business. Over two thousand years ago, the Library and Museum in Alexandria held more than a half-million books. The acquisition of all these books was not achieved without some effort. It is said that every ship entering the harbor was carefully searched and all books had to be given up long enough for the library scribes to make (handwritten!) copies of them. Presumably, the additional knowledge provided by each of the books in a ship must have more than compensated for the effects of extended shore leave for her sailors on the host city.

The evolving written tradition was available to relatively few people in early societies. Only a tiny fraction of the inhabitants of Athens, for instance, would have read Plato's *Republic* at the time that it was written. Although standardized symbolic languages were in use, there were still obstacles to the widespread dissemination of information. The first problem was expense. Books had to be laboriously hand copied and were definitely a luxury item. Not only were books not readily available, but few people could read them anyway, since illiteracy was widespread. The information technology of the time had relatively little impact outside of scholarly circles. Thus, early knowledge was tenuous and the "lore" of previously accumulated knowledge was continuously threatened by societal upheaval and conflict.

Even when illiteracy was not a problem, it was sometimes difficult to get physical access to certain books. Barriers were raised by the church, for instance, which at different times regarded certain scientific works as heretical. Paradoxically, the increasing availability of books also raised barriers to the efficient diffusion of knowledge. As books became cheaper they also became more plentiful. Even though it was cheaper to acquire each individual book, it was still impossible for a single individual or institution to purchase or read all the books that were being written on more than a narrow range of topics.

The language in which books were written sometimes constituted another type of barrier. As recently as the late nineteenth and early twentieth century, for instance, language had a huge impact on the development of psychology as a science. The majority of psychological works of the time were written in two languages, German and English, and separate schools and theories tended to be associated with each language. Today, even when books are widely available in English and in other languages, the language and style in which some books are written may still discourage readers. E.D. Hirsch (1987), for instance, has coined the term *cultural literacy* to refer to concepts that readers have to know in order to understand much of what is written in a particular society. Thus, a book may make a reference to Faust, but this won't be understandable unless the reader already knows that Faust was a fictional character who sold his soul to the devil.

For many countries, there are also continuing problems with mathematical and scientific literacy. The writings of modern physics, for instance, are accessible to only a tiny fraction of the population, just as much as were the writings of the early Greek philosophers in their time. This has led to a phenomenon where difficult technical works are popularized and translated into a form that typical readers can understand. As an example of this phenomenon, there are a number of books that try to explain the scientific work of Einstein into everyday language. There are some, however, who claim that at least some of the essential information is lost in this type of translation.

In historical terms, today's books are ridiculously cheap, and many millions of people are literate. However, the process of gaining access to information is no longer a solitary process. It used to be that one could find information by going to the appropriate book and reading it. When there was only one recognized authority on the geography of the world or the history of Greece, this was a straightforward matter. As books and authorities multiplied, it became more difficult to know where to find the appropriate information. Information access became a cooperative process that included editors, reference librarians, book reviewers, and a host of people involved in the regulation and documentation of information as an abstract quantity. By the middle of the twentieth century, it was recognized that information was both a commodity and a resource and that the development of tools for efficiently handling information would have a major impact on productivity. In fact, the concept of information and its use has become so prevalent in our society that it is often asserted that we are living in the *information age*. But what is this information age, and how did modern information technology evolve?

1.2.3   The Evolution of Information Technology

Historians tend to divide time up into ages, epochs, and periods. Collections of these divisions, often running in parallel across different geographical locations, form timelines that we use to chart our progress as a species. Figure 1.6 shows one timeline indicating the major technological ages of the human race. There are, of course, many other timelines that could be constructed for such overarching concepts as political and ethical development, literature and art, and so on, but we will focus here on the development of technology and knowledge.

Figure 1.6 shows three major ages, namely, the agricultural age, the industrial age, and the information age, that followed the earlier extended period of hunting and gathering that characterized our species. The agricultural age began with the control of crops, the creation of metal tools, and irrigation in the great river valleys of the

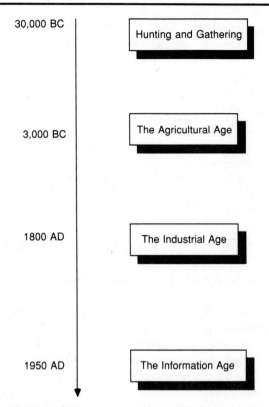

Figure 1.6 Technological ages of the human race.

Tigris, Euphrates, Indus, Yanghtze, and so on. One of the fundamental changes of the agricultural age was that people began to exercise a degree of control on their environment that allowed them to stay in one place. Often this control was in the form of prediction and adaptation rather than the more modern notion of creating structures and systems that actually modified the environment. Although it was not possible at that time, for instance, to cause the Nile to flood at a particular time, the use of fairly precise calendars allowed the Egyptians to predict the annual flooding of the Nile and plan their crop plantings accordingly.

The mass production of food allowed a portion of the citizens in the agricultural societies to focus their energies on other pursuits such as the arts and sciences. The nomadic life of the hunter and gatherer was replaced by the more stable environment of the city and the town. As was also true for the later ages, the surplus wealth created in the agricultural age allowed the development of technological innovations that led to the next age.

Depending on which part of the world one studies, and how one defines it, the agricultural age lasted for two or three thousand years. Although it was interspersed with other ages such as the age of discovery, agriculture continued to be the key technology until the beginning of the industrial age in the eighteenth century. Why did the agricultural age last so long? Well in fact, two to three thousand years was a surprisingly short time for this type of era, considering that the age of hunting and gathering had lasted many thousands of years.

The accumulation of knowledge and technology appears to be accelerating the rate at which new ages occur. Thus, the industrial age that supplanted the agricultural age lasted only about two hundred years. The industrial age began as the age of steam. The steam engine, which was originally developed to pump water out of coal mines, was adapted to move machinery in factories and to provide power to traction engines and trains. The wide availability of power encouraged the invention of a number of machines that were specialized to produce particular goods. Economies of scale led to the construction of factories as places where a relatively few items were mass produced. These factories were able to produce goods cheaply, and the cottage industries and job shops of the agricultural age were unable to compete. The new factories needed labor, and plenty of it. This led to the development of the working class. The new factories also required a large amount of capital investment and a high degree of planning and management. Thus, the industrial age produced new social structures as well as new increments of surplus wealth.

The industrial age greatly increased the complexity of society. The organization of labor, the purchase of parts and supplies, the maintenance of inventories and customer records; all required large amounts of record keeping. The growth of competition among different industrial concerns also placed a high premium on efficiency, quality, cost effectiveness, and technological innovation. Jacquard's use of the punched card to "program" patterns in looms, for instance, revolutionized the textile industry. Similarly, the development of precision machine tools by Babbage and others gave British manufacturing a competitive advantage in the nineteenth century.

The pace of technological innovation in the industrial age quickened as competitive pressures forced individuals and companies to look for new solutions. Those who relied on the efficient adaptation of older technologies were quickly overwhelmed by the accelerating pace of technical change as the organizers of the pony express found out when the wire telegraph became available shortly after the introduction of their service. As the pace of industrialization quickened, social and economic conditions produced a need for powerful information technologies that could match the advances in industrial technology.

Throughout the frenetic developments of the industrial age we find hints and precursors of the age that was to follow. Jacquard, with his punched cards, used information to program the activity of large looms. Babbage, with his analytical engine, developed the architecture of the modern computer in the nineteenth century in an attempt to develop a machine for mathematical computing. Samuel Morse developed his code to permit the concepts of human language to be transmitted down a wire. Although it was not generally appreciated, *the world of concrete objects was being controlled more and more by a parallel, but separate, world of abstract objects and concepts.* Using the new methods of coding and control, intangibles could move tons of machinery and thousands of men. Electrical impulses in a wire could make armies move, and holes in punched cards could signify census data or textile patterns.

One can argue, in fact, that the information age evolved slowly through a set of key inventions such as the alphabet, books, printing, coding, symbolic logic, and ultimately the computer. However, the invention of the modern computer stands out as a watershed in the information age. For the first time, a device was available that could represent and process information on a large scale with almost complete generality. Although echoes of the industrial age remain even today, modern society has, since the invention of the computer, come to be more and more dominated by information, and thus we place the beginning of the information age as 1945.

It is, of course, possible for different societies to exist in different ages around the world. Thus, there are some societies that are only beginning to emerge out of the Stone Age, while other societies are currently in the agricultural age. However, as geographical barriers break down and global communications continue to improve, these discrepancies are becoming less and less clear-cut. Similarly, the transition from the industrial age to the information age in a society is often accompanied by a high degree of inertia. This is largely because social structures tend to lag behind developing technologies.

In spite of the inertial forces, information is coming to supplant machines as the engine of change in our society. In one sense, all ages are information ages. But the special sense in which ours is a new kind of information society refers to the fact that nearly all basic social functions are strongly influenced by electronic archival, information processing, and knowledge processing technologies. We now consider how electronic information processing has been made possible by the computer.

1.2.4 The Evolution of Early Computers and Databases

The identity and builder of the first modern computer is a matter of some debate, although it is generally ascribed to ENIAC (Electrical Numerical Integrator and Computer), built by Eckert (an electrical engineer), Mauchly (a physicist), and a small army of helpers. It is hard to believe that this early monster, equipped with 18,000 vacuum tubes and weighing 30 tons, was the forerunner of today's workstations.

However, the earliest digital (manually operated) computer was the abacus, invented over two thousand years ago and still widely used in many parts of the world. With the abacus, the human operator had to perform all the machine operations. Semiautomatic mechanical calculators appeared in the seventeenth century, when Pascal (the son of a tax collector) invented a calculator to assist in adding and subtracting the columns of figures associated with the assessment and collection of taxes. Although there were problems with Pascal's machine, the toothed-wheel mechanism that he invented was the basis for modern mechanical adding machines. Other mechanical calculators were developed by Leibnitz and Napier. In the 1830s, Babbage proposed and partially built a *Difference Engine* to calculate mathematical and astronomical tables. This machine was never built in its entirety. In the 1840s, Babbage designed his *Analytical Engine* which embodied many of the fundamental principles found in the modern computer. Punched-card accounting began in 1890 when Hollerith used punched cards to tabulate data from the 1890 U.S. census. Concurrent developments in electronics (most notably the invention of the vacuum tube) then set the stage for ENIAC and the computers that were to follow.

Since the development of ENIAC, there have been a number of major changes in computing technology. A few of the most significant include:

1. Stored programming—implemented in 1948.
2. The invention of the transistor in 1949 at Bell Labs.
3. The introduction of the first microprocessor chip (the Intel 4004) in 1971.

The pace of technological development in computing has been nothing short of incredible. Noyce (1977) compared the microcomputer of that time to ENIAC in the following words:

> It is twenty times faster, has a larger memory, is thousands of times more reliable, consumes the power of a light bulb rather than that of a locomotive, occupies 1/30,000 the volume and costs 1/10,000 as much.

Or as Forester (1987, p.18) has picturesquely put it

> . . . if the automobile and airplane businesses had developed like the computer business, a Rolls Royce would cost $2.75 and run for 3 million miles on one gallon of gas. And a Boeing 767 would cost just $500 and would circle the globe in 20 minutes on five gallons of gas.

Each of the components of the computer has undergone rapid technological change. The earliest input device was the toggle switch, which was replaced by paper tape and card readers. Currently, there are a wide variety of input devices available, including touchscreens, digitizing tablets, keyboards, lightpens, trackballs, joysticks, and mice. Similar advances have occurred in all phases of computer hardware.

Early thinking on computers was dominated by the hardware, which was massive and omnipresent. However, it soon became clear that there was more to computers and computing than just hardware. Programs, procedures, and documentation were needed to effectively use computer hardware. There are many paths that can be traced relating to the development of software technology, programming languages, efficient compilers, and the like. We will focus here on the representation of information and the transition from data to databases.

Characters can be handled in binary notation by arbitrarily defining certain codes as corresponding to specific characters. The most common alphanumeric coding system in use is the ASCII (American Standard Code for Information Interchange) system. This code allows the representation of 128 alphabetic (upper and lower case), numeric, special symbol, and control characters in a 7-bit byte.

The use of the ASCII character coding system and floating point arithmetic allows computers, using binary representation, to represent any type of textual data. The same principles of digitization and coding can also be applied to sounds, pictures, and other forms of data. Pictures, for instance, are generally represented by dividing them up into a large number of individual points (pixels). Each pixel is then coded using a binary coding system. Thus, in gray-level monochrome graphics, sixteen levels of gray may be coded using four binary digits (bits). With a large enough

SATURDAY, SUNDAY AND HOLIDAY SCHEDULE
SATURDAY SCHEDULE WILL BE OPERATED ON SUNDAY, NEW YEAR'S DAY, MEMORIAL DAY, INDEPENDENCE DAY, LABOR DAY, THANKSGIVING DAY AND CHRISTMAS DAY.

W	E	S	T	B	O	U	N	D	
Lv Fullerton (Park-Ride Lot)	Lv Buena Park (Manchester Av. & Beach Bl.)	Lv Cerritos (Artesia Bl. & Carmenita Rd.)	(183rd St. at Sears Entry)	Lv Bellflower (Artesia & Lakewood Bls.)	Lv North Long Beach (Artesia Bl. & Atlantic Av.)	Lv Compton (Walnut St. & Wilmington Av.)	Lv Artesia Bl. & Vermont Av.	Lv Artesia & Hawthorne Bls.	Lv Hermosa Beach (Pacific Coast Hwy. & Pier Av.)	Ar Redondo Beach (Torrance Bl. & Catalina Av.)
♿ 619AM	624AM	632AM	641AM	651AM	658AM	705AM	717AM	728AM	739AM	747AM
♿ 715	720	728	737	747	754	802	814	826	839	847
♿ 815	820	828	837	847	854	902	914	926	939	947
♿ 915	920	928	937	947	954	1002	1014	1026	1039	1047
♿ 1015	1020	1028	1037	1047	1054	1102	1114	1126	1139	1147
♿ 1115	1120	1128	1137	1147	1154	1202PM	1214PM	1226PM	1239PM	1247PM
♿ 1215PM	1220PM	1228PM	1237PM	1247PM	1254PM	102	114	126	139	147
♿ 115	120	128	137	147	154	202	214	226	239	247
♿ 215	220	228	237	247	254	302	314	326	339	347
♿ 315	320	328	337	347	354	402	414	426	439	447
♿ 415	420	428	437	447	454	502	514	526	539	547
♿ 515	520	528	537	547	554	602	614	626	639	647
♿ 615	620	628	637	647	654	702	712	722	733	741
♿ 715	720	728	737	747	754	802	812	822	833	841

♿ — BUS ASSIGNED IS SCHEDULED TO BE ACCESSIBLE TO THE DISABLED.

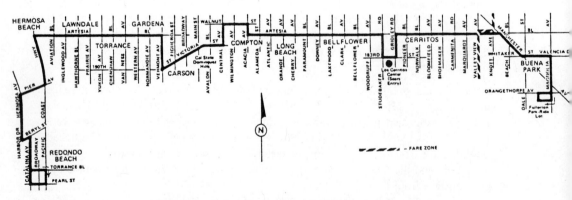

Figure 1.7 A bus timetable with accompanying map.

number of pixels and many gray levels per pixel, it is possible to provide high-quality pictures using digitization. Using such digital coding, pictures from planets in the farthest reaches of the solar system have been sent back to earth.

The principles of digitization and coding allow information of any form to be electronically represented. However, coding is not enough. Data models (see Chapter 2) are needed to structure and organize data. Data correspond to the discrete, recorded facts about phenomena from which we gain information about the world. Data may be considered independently of its interpretation. Thus, a bus timetable (e.g., Figure 1.7) provides data, with its interpretation typically being given in terms of maps showing the locations of the stops represented by each column of data.

Stored programs allowed people to store and modify programs. In similar fashion, databases provide flexibility in modifying and manipulating data. The original motivation for databases came from computer programmers who wanted a convenient way of handling the data that was being used in their programs. In some applications, the data became so important that specialized programs were developed to manage and update the data.

In addition to the databases that grew out of the programmer's need to handle data in computer programs, another type of database developed to store large amounts of text information. These textual databases evolved somewhat independently of the databases based on fields and records that held numerical and factual information (e.g., customer accounts, inventories, address lists, etc.). These textual databases typically represent documents through citations, abstracts, and index terms. Thus, an

```
AN 00645 60-1.
AU FRAZIER-SHERVERT-H.
IN MCLEAN HOSP, BELMONT, MA.
TI MASS MEDIA AND PSYCHIATRIC DISTURBANCE.
SO PSYCHIATRIC JOURNAL OF THE UNIVERSITY OF OTTAWA.  1976 DEC VOL 1(4)
   171-172.
LG EN.
YR 76
CC 2700 2800.
PT 10.
MJ TELEVISION-VIEWING.  VIOLENCE.  AGGRESSIVE-BEHAVIOR.  CHILDREN.
   LITERATURE-REVIEW.
AB EXAMINES THE RELATIONSHIP BETWEEN TV AND VIOLENCE, AS REPORTED BY THE
   SURGEON GENERAL'S SCIENTIFIC ADVISORY COMMITTEE ON TELEVISION AND SOCIAL
   BEHAVIOR (1972) AND BY OTHER STUDIES.  IT IS SUGGESTED THAT THE IMPACT
   OF NEWS COVERAGE ON CHILDREN IS MORE SHATTERING AND BEWILDERING THAN
   THEIR SO-CALLED "FORBIDDEN PROGRAMS," BECAUSE NEWS PROGRAMS (A) INVOLVE
   REAL PEOPLE AND VIOLENCE, (B) OFTEN TAKE PLACE IN SETTINGS SIMILAR TO THE
   VIEWER'S OWN SETTING, AND (C) DO NOT SHOW THE AGGRESSOR BEING PUNISHED
   (AS GENERALLY IS DONE IN SERIES PROGRAMS).  THE AUTHOR CITES E. FROMM'S
   (1968) 3 CLASSES OF AGGRESSIVENESS AND OBSERVES THAT SUCH TYPES ARE NOT
   MUTUALLY EXCLUSIVE BUT OFTEN OCCUR IN COMBINATIONS.  (17 REF).
ID TV NEWS VS OTHER PROGRAMS, INSTIGATION OF VIOLENCE & AGGRESSIVE BEHAVIOR,
   CHILDREN, LITERATURE REVIEW.
```

Figure 1.8 An article about television and violence as represented in psychological abstracts and accessed through Bibliographic Retrieval Service (BRS).

article about television and violence might be represented in a text database as shown in Figure 1.8.

Text databases represent a new direction in information technology. First, and most obviously, they provide text in online form. In contrast to a conventional book, a single electronic copy of a text source may be downloaded from many different locations in the same day. This overcomes some of the frustration that library users feel when the book that they want is currently checked out. The second effect of textual databases is that they provide a very flexible way of organizing information. In a library, the books are typically ordered by subject in a linear sequence of stacks. However, with index terms, the same text may be accessed in a number of different ways.

■ 1.3 CURRENT TRENDS IN INFORMATION TECHNOLOGY

The field of information technology is driven largely by computing technology. The ability to create networks of computers makes vast distributed databases possible. In principle, this has removed all physical barriers to information. All one needs is a terminal and connect time. Although costs are still significant, the remaining barriers to information appear to be logical and conceptual, and it is the removal of these barriers that forms the motivation for this book.

What are the implications of the new computing technologies for information retrieval? Consider four of the major technologies

Mass Storage—In recent years, there has been an exponential increase in the amount of storage available. Evolution in disk technology has replaced the few memory registers of early computers with gigabytes of information available at high speed on optical media. This has led to the development of massive databases.

Optical Scanning and Electronic Publishing—One barrier to the development of large databases has been the difficulty of transferring from print versions of text to corresponding electronic versions. This difficulty is being overcome by two technologies. First, optical scanning enables printed text to be translated into electronic media very quickly. Furthermore, much of what is being published today is electronically published, using word processors, so that the electronic versions of documents typically precede the corresponding print versions. Thus, a database can grow by electronically transferring document files from the publisher to the database producer.

Networking—One of the most significant developments in databases and information retrieval in general has been the connection of computing systems through local and wide area networks. Connectivity and data sharing among computing systems have evolved from electronic mail and file servers in local networks to heterogeneous databases spanning multiple platforms and data models.

Online Databases—For over two thousand years, books have represented the major technology for archiving the world's knowledge. However, as the capabilities for building text databases have evolved along with relatively cheap mass storage, large online databases have been developed that collectively contain many millions of documents of various types. These online databases represent a vast storehouse of information.

These three technologies provide the prerequisite infrastructure that makes intelligent databases possible on a large scale. We shall consider each of them in turn in the following sections.

1.3.1 Large-Scale Computing and Mass Storage

Mass storage has engendered a whole new way of thinking about text, data, and their manipulation. One is reminded of the effect that expanding working memory (RAM) capacity has had on the development of applications for personal computers. In early 64K microcomputers, a large program might take up 32K of working memory. Then, as the availability of RAM increased, programmers felt less constrained about having to fit their programs into a certain size. This has led to the development of information intensive applications (such as the hypermedia applications discussed in later chapters) that may take up megabytes of working memory. One sees the same effect with mass storage devices, where the same people who used to make do with 360K disks are now finding it necessary to work with Winchester or optical disks that may hold hundreds of megabytes of information.

The removal of memory limitations in mass storage allows one to store a great deal of information in ways that make it easy to use, even if they are fairly profligate in terms of the space that they consume on the storage device. Thus, it is conceivable to have multiple representations of information at different points in information networks or hierarchies. Similarly, these multiple representations of information can be linked to each other in a variety of ways. In one type of application (hypertext), associative links are constructed that allow one to browse through information in a highly flexible fashion.

Getting all this information into memory in the first place is made possible on a grand scale because of optical scanning and electronic publishing. Optical scanning and electronic publishing provide data in a machine-readable form. Without these technologies, text and data must be input through the keyboard. This creates a bottleneck where it is almost impossible for new information to be added to a database as fast as it is produced.

Optical scanners typically read a printed page by passing a light-sensitive grid over it. This grid is made up of elements, each of which records an area of the reflected light. This process creates a pattern of pixels that are converted to a bit value based on the intensity of the reflected light at that point. This process produces a string of bits that is commonly referred to as a *bit-mapped image*. The more pixels and bits that this image contains, the more closely it will match the original.

Optical character readers work in similar fashion to optical scanners, except that software is used to interpret the bit-mapped image in terms of alphanumeric characters. This can be a difficult process because of the variety of fonts and styles that text can appear in. The output of an optical character reader frequently requires further processing to edit any errors that occurred during the scanning process.

The availability of mass storage on optical media has been particularly critical in the development of multimedia information systems. Alternate media, such as digitized images and voice data, require relatively large amounts of storage text. In terms of storage requirements, a picture is usually worth thousands of words, since there may be millions of bits of information in a high-resolution color or black-and-white (with gray levels) image, whereas a typical word will typically require fewer than 100 bits for its representation.

Voice, like pictures, is surprisingly information intensive. A standard page of characters stored as ASCII text requires about 2000 bytes of storage (2K). A scanned image (pictorial representation) of the same page would require approximately half a megabyte of storage (500K), while if someone took two minutes to read the same page of text, the corresponding voice data might require a megabyte of storage to be stored in its entirety. Naturally, there is a great deal of interest in data compression techniques that can reduce these heavy information storage requirements. However, even with data compression, the storage requirements of alternate media are still proportionately much higher than those of text.

The storage demands of multimedia information are exacerbated when that information is linked into hypermedia systems that may include versioning or retention of the previous history of the database (Copeland and Khoshafian, 1987). Fortunately, the availability of mass storage has kept pace with the demand, largely due to the impact of optical storage. However, as discussed in Chapter 7, version management can help with other issues such as concurrency control and recovery when suitable algorithms (e.g. Minoura and Parsaye, 1984) are used.

Optical disks provide cost effective media for the storage of large volumes of data such as those encountered in hypermedia applications. Compared with magnetic media, the characteristics of optical disks can be summarized as follows:

    a. *Removability and Transportability.* Although some magnetic media such as floppy disks and magnetic tapes share these characteristics, optical disks are more rugged and possess the additional benefits of the features described in (b) and (c) below.

    b. *Higher Storage Densities.* Compared to magnetic technologies, optical disks are much denser. Magnetic bit densities, measured in bits per square inch (bpsi), are about 4×10^7 bpsi. In comparison, optical (write once) bit densities are two orders of magnitude greater at better than 10^9 bpsi.

    c. *Lower Cost.* One of the results of the higher density of optical disks is their lower storage costs. Optical disks are orders of magnitude cheaper in bit per dollar terms than magnetic disks. This ratio will continue to improve in favor of optical disks in the future.

    d. *Longer Archival Life.* Archival life of magnetic media is about 2 to 3 years. In comparison, the archival life of optical media is more than 10 years.

However, optical disks have some drawbacks, such as

    e. *Slower Access Times.* Although it depends upon the particular drive and technology, optical disk drive seek times may be significantly slower than magnetic disks.

    f. *Higher Error Rates.* Another problem with optical media is the high error rates encountered. This necessitates the incorporation of special error detection and correction mechanisms to improve data quality.

Variants of optical disks include digital videodisks and CD-ROMS. Digital videodisks and CD-ROMs differ in terms of their size, storage capacities, seek times, standardization, and implementation cost. The technology of optical disks is progressing very rapidly, making them an integral part of all information-processing systems.

Early trends have favored the storage of large image files on videodisks and text (or mixed text and image files) on CD-ROM. Examples of CD-ROM products include Grolier's Electronic Encyclopedia which comes on a single disk and contains all the text of Grolier's 20 volume *Academic American Encyclopedia,* and *Compact Disclosure,* a disk that contains a large amount of business information on prominent U.S. companies. Nelson (1987) has listed several hundred CD-ROM publications, with more publications being added every month.

1.3.2   Computer Networks

Satellite communications, high-speed networks (e.g., ethernet), and the enhancement of hardware compatibility and standardization enables information to be distributed and transmitted across networks. One of the first manifestations of this trend was the development of electronic mail (e.g., Arpanet), which enabled scientists around the world to communicate with one another. Telephone lines have also been used for data networks as in Fax technology. Today, there are many forms of electronic network for transferring information, including computer bulletin boards and large online databases.

Centralized computing is being replaced by distributed computing where individual computers are connected across networks to one another and to large mainframes, which become *file servers*. File servers act as central repositories for information, data, and programs. We can illustrate the concept of the centralized file server and the distributed computer network with an analogy to the way that libraries work.

The library is a facility that acquires, processes, stores, retrieves, and disseminates information. These five functions are also performed by computers that, from the perspective of information management act as archival machines, providing that they are linked to appropriate mass-storage capabilities. Individual librarians participate in a collective structure that manages the massive amount of information available in a large library. The success of this endeavor depends on ensuring that the mass of individuals works within well-prescribed procedures. This may explain why large libraries tend to have strongly hierarchical administrative structures.

Each individual librarian constitutes an entity that typically has access to personal information and expertise and to larger information available in the library. The librarian with expertise about chemistry, for instance, can directly answer questions about chemistry, or he can use standard references within walking distance of his desk. The librarian who specializes in the acquisition of books will generally work autonomously, but on occasion he will communicate with other librarians or with a central database (the online catalog) in order to find information such as whether or not a particular book is already available within the library. We can pursue the analogy by considering how the individual processors (librarians) are linked to one another and to centralized file servers. Links will include verbal communication, telephones, and computer workstations. This example illustrates the essential function that occurs in the successful operation of a network—the storage and transfer of information.

The modern library provides an example of a mixed human-computer network where a computer network is augmented with a corresponding human network that uses and supplements the computer network. A second example of the operation of a network is electronic conferencing. Electronic conferencing typically consists of two primary modes of communication: text and dialog. Here again, the characteristics of the network can be observed (i.e., transfer of information, distributed processing, and the distinction between local and global databases).

1.3.3 Online Databases

Ideally, information is electronically published and is then immediately available online. This removes the need for a keyboarding or scanning process, although difficulties associated with copyrights and royalties may still arise. Many publishers now have electronic versions of books and journals, even if the final result appears in hardcopy or book form. These electronic versions can then be indexed and input directly into text databases.

Many online databases only include summary information such as citations to documents. However, the increasing availability of information in electronic form is leading to the development of a number of full-text databases where complete information, and not just citations, is available online. Some full-text databases already exist, and the use of full-text databases should increase as their capabilities are more fully exploited.

One of the major motivations for developing intelligent databases is to make full use of the vast information resources that are now available and that are being added to daily. The explosive growth in the amount of information stored in various institutions and databases has become an accepted fact of life. For example, between 1900 and 1970, the eighty-five major American universities were doubling the number of books in their libraries every seventeen years, for an annual growth rate of 4.1 percent (Bell, 1979, p.189).

Millions of scientific and other writings are published each year, and the number appears to be increasing. Many of these documents are being added to online databases. Williams (1987) estimated the worldwide number of online documents as of 1985 at 1.7 billion and growing rapidly.

In 1979 there were four hundred online databases worldwide. By 1988 there were well over three thousand. Recent growth in the number of online databases is summarized in Figure 1.9. Many more databases exist but are proprietary, containing company records and the like. In addition, text documents are not the only form of information being added to online databases. Chemical Abstracts Services, for instance, has a file of all known chemical substances, as well as a file of indexed representations of articles, books, and reports on chemistry and related fields. Companies and corporations also keep massive amounts of data relating to prices, yields, inventories, accounts, payrolls, and so on.

This vast body of information is only useful if there are adequate methods of information retrieval. Glossbrenner (1987, p. 5) gives the example of someone who wants to know how wind power compares to the cost of traditional methods of generating electricity. The answer is certainly available online, but finding the right source can be challenging. As it turns out, the information (as of 1981) can be found in the May 13, 1981 issue of *Chemical Week* which is one of 660 different magazines and journals covered by a single database:

> Cost estimates of wind power range from 3.25c/kwh (cents/kilowatt hour) to 10c/kwh. The installed cost of wind turbines is estimated to be $1,000–2,500/kw as compared to $800/kw for fossil fuel plants and $1,050/kw for a nuclear plant.

This rather succinct statement turns out to be just the tip of the iceberg on this topic. An example of additional information on wind power is

> In 1983 California led the country in wind power production with over 1,400 commercial windfarms in four locations, with a total capacity of 72,000 kilowatts. Most of these were financed through limited partnerships made attractive by federal and state tax credits and rapid depreciation schedules. (*Dun's Business Month*, July 1983)

Now, if we wanted to know about solar power, where would we look? The challenge for information science is constantly growing as more and more diverse information is stored online. Traditional indexing policies may not be able to deal with the organization and description of all this information. Finally, even with adequate indexing, knowing where to find information and how to access it using current retrieval systems is a difficult task. Today's online databases have grown out of the

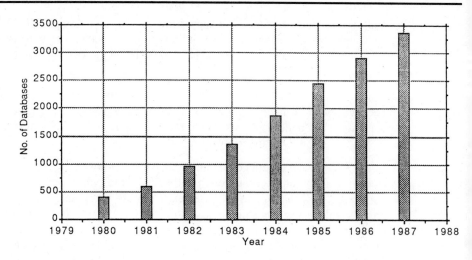

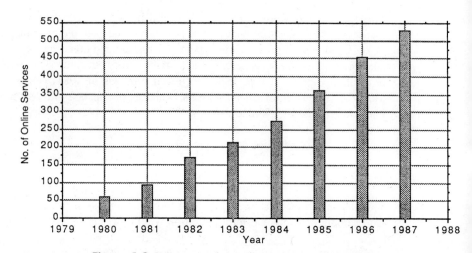

Figure 1.9 Recent growth in online services and databases.

technology of mainframe computing and lack many of the interface features and help facilities that the users of personal computers have come to expect. Conceptually, at least, the solution to this problem is simple. Build intelligent databases that take the load off the user. Ideally users should be able to say what they want without having to worry about having to supervise the search process for that information. It would also help if the retrieval system took into account who the user was and what they were looking for so that the retrieved information was focused to their needs. Conceptually we can see what to do, but the creation of intelligent database functionality turns out to be a complex topic.

■ 1.4 THE EVOLUTION OF INTELLIGENT DATABASES

As discussed above, the world today is approaching, if it has not already exceeded, the point of information overload. This is not to say that information isn't still being effectively used, but that the effective use of information today is just a small fraction of what it potentially could be given the appropriate storage and retrieval mechanisms.

The wide availability of online text databases is both attractive and frustrating. Attractive, because it becomes possible for any combination of textual materials to be retrieved, reorganized, redisplayed and redisseminated in totally new ways. Frustrating, because our methods of retrieving all this information are primitive and prevent the full utilization of this information.

Imagine for a moment an ideal (intelligent) information retrieval workstation that permits intelligent access to, and recombination of, online information. A market analyst who was designing an investment portfolio could order up a completely new set of electronic data merely by selecting menu items from relevant databases. The creation of financial reports, investment strategies, and so on would be enormously facilitated by this type of information retrieval capability. Similarly, a marketing consultant might use a variety of text databases to form a sales strategy tailored to a particularly demographic segment. On a limited scale, this type of usage is already occurring. For instance, Pacific Bell (*Hypercard Update,* April, 1988, p.4) is using a hypertext interface to a variety of databases to support its advertising sales efforts. In one application developed by Pacific Bell

> after selecting any of 5000 Yellow Pages headings, the sales rep can use a pop-up window to identify related headings. The rep can quickly reach HyperCard stacks with testimonials or information on consumer usage or co-op advertising programs. Prior to the sales call, this information helps sales representatives inform advertisers about the benefits of Yellow Pages advertising and helps managers to formulate sales tactics and marketing strategies.

Three features that allow intelligent databases to achieve this type of performance are that an intelligent database

1. Provides high-level tools for data analysis, discovery, and integrity control, allowing users to both extract knowledge from, and apply knowledge to, data.
2. Allows users to interact directly with information as naturally as if they were flipping through the pages of a standard text on the topic or talking with a helpful human expert.
3. Retrieves knowledge as opposed to data and uses inference to determine what a user needs to know.

Intelligent databases represent the latest step in the evolution of database technology. Databases typically include a data model, an indexing system, and a querying language among other components. However, conventional databases are generally static in the sense that they are updated with new information from time to time, and this updating process is externally carried out, instead of being an intrinsic task carried out by the database system itself.

From another perspective, the evolution of database languages may be linked to the evolution of programming languages. Early database languages used the procedural control structures usually found in traditional programming languages such as FORTRAN and Pascal. As discussed by Parsaye and Chignell (1988), expert system technology represents a new set of paradigms for programming that enhances the components of

- new data structures
- new control structures.

Thus, the ever increasing need for more and more semantics in database languages is satisfied by using expert system technology.

Hypertext (hypermedia) represents an important step towards more dynamic databases. In programming circles, dynamic databases represent a type of working memory where new facts or data are recorded during the process of computation. But there is also a different sense of dynamism where information can be added in a free form fashion without concern for the prior structure of the database. This is somewhat antithetical to the traditional and highly structured approach that has been used with static databases. Thus, one of the challenges of the intelligent database formulation that we present in this book is how to combine the dynamism of hypertext with the structure and efficiency of relational databases and similar structures.

Knowledge-based systems further enhance the dynamism of databases by providing the capability for reasoning and inferring new information on the fly. This creates the capability for self-modifying databases (metastorage), as well as the ability to reason about what information a user might be interested in, even if the user's information need was not originally expressed that way.

Online databases represent the ultimate challenge for the intelligent database technique. As we will show in this book, it is possible to construct small examples of intelligent databases, but the transformation of large mainframe databases into a more intelligent form raises serious difficulties. Perhaps the major difficulty is the required indexing process. One of the secrets to improving the intelligence of a database is to use a thorough indexing process that is based on concepts rather than keyword labels. We will explore the relationship between intelligent databases and large online databases in Chapter 6.

■ 1.5 WHAT IS AN INTELLIGENT DATABASE?

There are three components that make a database intelligent.

1. Intelligence at the high-level tools level.
2. Intelligence at the user-interface level.
3. Intelligence at the database engine level.

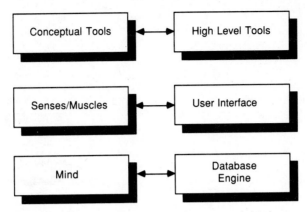

Figure 1.10 An analogy between humans and databases.

Figure 1.10 shows an analogy that can be drawn between humans and databases. Most human behavior can be interpreted in terms of people processing information in order to select activities and achieve their goals. In fact, this analogy between human and computer information processing has been well known since the 1950s. Humans use their senses to input information, their muscles to carry out activities that further their goals, and their minds to store (memorize) and retrieve (recall) information as well as to reason and make decisions. Thus, we can distinguish between the senses and muscles, which act as a person's interface with the outside world, and the mind, which internally processes information and accordingly plans actions. This distinction between senses and muscles on the one hand and the mind on the other hand is analogous to the user interface level and database-support level of information systems. The extent to which this analogy seems surprising may indicate the potential for making databases intelligent and providing them with powerful interfaces. We now consider the nature of intelligence within the two main components of intelligent databases.

1.5.1 Intelligence at the High-Level Tools Level

One of the characteristic features of intelligent databases is that they are an aggregation of a number of technologies that have previously been considered in isolation. In addition to the technologies that are integrated within the basic intelligent database architecture, there will be other high-level tools that will supplement and complement the intelligent database functionality. These tools may be used by database users and developers. They provide a toolbox consisting of distinct tools, reflecting the facts that different applications have different needs and it is unnecessary to burden all applications and users with tools that they may not need.

As shown in Figure 1.11, we distinguish seven types of high-level tools.

1. Knowledge discovery tools.
2. Data integrity and quality-control tools.
3. Hypermedia management tools.

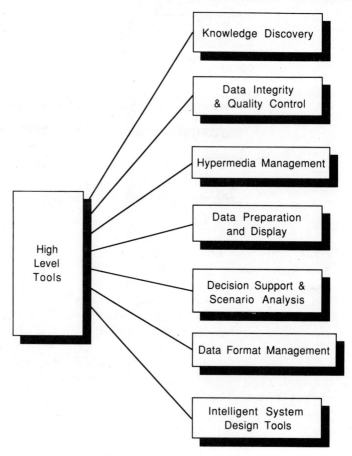

Figure 1.11 High-level tools.

4. Data presentation and display tools.
5. Decision support and scenario analysis tools.
6. Data format management tools (reformat data, etc.).
7. Intelligent-system design tools.

We now sketch the features of each category of tool to supply an overall feeling of what each type of tool provides.

1. *Knowledge discovery tools.* This category includes tools for data analysis, machine learning, and statistical analysis. These tools represent a new and exciting frontier in intelligent database technology that allows us to extract knowledge from data. They allow a user to automatically discover hidden (and often totally unexpected) relationships that exist in a large database. For instance, by using the machine-learning tool IXL (Parsaye and Hanson, 1988; Parsaye, 1987) on a database of car trouble reports, a car manufacturer discovered the

reasons for wiring problems, while a computer manufacturer discovered that a large number of disk-drive problems were due to one specific error repeatedly performed by one operator in one process. Thus, these tools discover relationships that users would not have even expected. Since today's oceans of data are abundant with these relationships, these tools will dramatically increase our ability to distill knowledge from databases.

2. *Data integrity and quality control tools.* The tools in category 2 are needed due to the unwanted side effects of the increasing number and size of databases. In particular, two conflicting side effects are

   a. We are becoming extremely dependent on data stored in databases.

   b. There is an increasing number of errors appearing in databases.

It is thus imperative to have tools that automatically detect or signal errors in databases. These range from tools that use the encoded knowledge of an expert to detect errors in data to tools that signal statistically deviant records.

3. *Hypermedia management tools.* Category 3 tools allow developers and users to build hypermedia information systems that combine free-form linked text, data, images, sounds, and so on. This category reflects the fact that information may be expressed in many different forms or media and that methods are needed for organizing and accessing these different forms of information.

4. *Data presentation and display tools.* Given a large database, most users wish to see and display some of the data (or summaries thereof). Thus, the presentation and display tools in category 4 provide graphics, forms, and other types of data presentation. Although this category is logically separate from the previous one, in practice the display tools will often be an extension of the hypermedia management tools.

5. *Decision support and scenario analysis tools.* Tools in category 5 allow for a uniform merger between spreadsheets, databases, financial-modeling systems, and so on. This stems from a view of decision support as a special kind of information management, retrieval, and utilization, where the information is tailored towards particular decision-making activities.

6. *Data format management tools.* Data never seems to be in the format that it is needed in. The tools in category 6 allow users to transform data between formats, for example, to merge an ASCII file with data in dBASE format and data obtained from IBM's DB2 with an automatically generated SQL query. These tools are indispensable for applications that rely on the analysis of real data.

7. *Intelligent system design tools.* Category 7 tools provide facilities for designing intelligent databases. Although the fields of database design, information-system design, and expert-system design have maintained a separate existence in the past, their integration in an intelligent database is essential. Thus, these tools allow system developers and administrators to better design and maintain intelligent databases.

Although these high-level tools may seem somewhat peripheral to the central idea and functioning of intelligent databases, one or a number of them are needed to make intelligent databases work in particular applications. Not only should intelligent databases be things of intellectual beauty, they should also be things of practical use.

1.5.2 Intelligence at the User-Interface Level

The user interface is the part of a software system that a user interacts with. Normally, we can distinguish between two levels of the user interface.

- The physical level
- The cognitive level

The physical level of the interface is typically more obvious, consisting of input and output devices such as the mouse, keyboard, and video monitor. In contrast, the cognitive level of the interface is harder to describe, consisting of the underlying model used to present the information, the interpretation that the user then makes, and the intentions that the user then formulates.

Early computer interfaces seemed to confuse *intelligent* with *esoteric*. One not only had to be smart to use early interfaces, one also had to learn a complex and somewhat arbitrary syntax. This led to a situation where the interface was fairly dumb and the intelligence resided in the ingenuity of the user who worked around the undesirable aspects of the interface. Some users adapted to this situation while others either avoided computers or persisted while voicing their complaints. It became apparent that existing computer interfaces were shutting out a large number of potential users. The solution is to make interfaces less esoteric and more forgiving. If a typical user can sit down at the computer to perform a task and at each stage of the program it is obvious what to do next (within the context of the task), then the interface is satisfactory.

When it becomes obvious what to do next throughout a program or application, the interface recedes from consciousness and is replaced by a fuller concentration on the task itself. Ideally, an interface is transparent, in the same way that when we look through a clear window we are not aware of the intervening glass as we observe the view. Needless to say, this ultimate form of transparency is difficult, if not impossible, to achieve. Instead, interface designers aim for a related goal of ease of use and naturalness that carries with it much of the same positive aspects as "transparency." An interface that is easy to use and natural is sometimes referred to by interface designers as *cognitively compatible*. Compatibility is a concept that has evolved from the fields of human factors and engineering psychology. Cognitive compatibility can briefly be defined as the degree to which the model of the task presented by the input and output characteristics of the interface conforms to the corresponding expectations of the user. Interface design technology seeks to make interfaces more natural and compatible using sounds and pictures, voice input and output, associative and deductive retrieval, etc.

We use the word "natural" here in the old-fashioned sense, prior to the phenomena of artificial sweeteners and nude beaches. In the usage used in this book, natural means that the intelligent database behaves the way "we do" as much as possible. In this sense, naturalness is not a single characteristic, but rather a collection of attributes that jointly enhance the naturalness of an interface. Some strategies for increasing the naturalness of interfaces are to

- Use sounds and other media as well as text. People often like to see diagrams along with the text.
- Allow users to switch between broad and narrow views (zoom-in and zoom-out) of topics.
- Allow users to carry out an associative search if they are looking at one topic and they would like to be able to look at related topics.
- Where possible, design the interface so that it contains familiar objects and concepts.
- Don't just give raw information. People generally want information (answers) summarized according to their needs and interests.
- Allow people to operate on objects represented in the interface directly, rather than indirectly through some type of command language.

We should not confuse naturalness with weakness or simplicity. One may take a powerful functionality and embed it within a natural interface or an esoteric one and yet retain the same functionality. One example of this is the Unix operating system. Although Unix is recognized as a powerful multi-tasking operating system, it is notoriously difficult to use when compared to other operating systems. However, by transforming the appearance of Unix, it is possible to make it much more palatable to users while retaining the main functionality. This is reflected in the NextStep operating system.

Naturalness is one aspect of intelligence within an interface. An interface can also be intelligent over and above the extent to which it is easy or natural to use. In this case, the interface uses reasoning to interpret what the user is really after or to deduce information that cannot be directly obtained. For instance, using deductive retrieval, the system would find who someone's grandfather is from knowing only father relations (i.e., who is the father of whom) using rule-based reasoning.

1.5.3 Intelligence at the Database Engine Level

The user interface is supported by a set of database capabilities. These database capabilities are the mechanisms that allow a database management system or information management application to function as it does. Examples of database support capabilities include query processing and the ability to carry out deductive reasoning.

The intelligence of the user interface is to a great extent determined by the intelligence of the underlying application. There are a number of features of a database system at this support level that enhance the overall intelligence of the system.

- Knowledge-based, object-oriented data model.
- Integrated database and inference engine.
- Context-sensitive or structure-sensitive search.
- Support of multiple storage media (such as videodisks, etc.).
- Intelligent version management, recovery, and resilience.
- Concurrency and transaction support.
- Query optimization.

A knowledge-based and object-oriented data model allows the representation of information in a form which most readily reflects the user's perception of the real world. Once formulated, it could then serve as the knowledge base for an expert system.

Integrated databases and inference engines follow from the use of knowledge-based data models. They allow deductive retrieval to be carried out in an environment where information search and inference are integrated.

Structure-sensitive search involves knowledge retrieval based on *shape*. Context-sensitive search involves knowing where to look for relevant information based on *content*. In online retrieval, a search is context sensitive if it is directed to the retrieval systems that are most relevant for the search topic.

Multiple storage media allow information of varying types (e.g., maps, paintings, graphs, sounds, etc.) to be efficiently stored and retrieved within the database.

Intelligent version management ensures that current and previous versions of evolving databases are retrieved efficiently. Recovery and resilience are issues that address the extent to which the database handles the operational demands it experiences, including simultaneous access by many users and equipment failures. Thus, like most conventional databases, intelligent databases also support concurrent atomic transactions. In addition, the underlying engine of an intelligent database performs extensive query optimization to provide adequate real-time response for complex queries involving object-oriented knowledge bases.

■ 1.6 SUMMARY

We are now immersed in an information age where technological capability has, up until now, exceeded our capability to build systems that will effectively retrieve the information. As our ability to store information exceeds our ability to retrieve that information we become mired in an information glut of global proportions. The problem of information glut affects both textual and record-oriented databases.

The solution to the problem of information glut requires the development of intelligent databases. Intelligent databases represent a convergence between databases that evolved out of computer programming and text databases that have evolved from traditional text sources such as books and journals.

In this chapter, we have described some of the intellectual movements that have led to the current information age and the need that society as a whole now has for the intelligent storage and retrieval of information. As we define and elaborate the model of intelligent databases throughout this book, however, we will be driven by several goals.

- To manage large volumes of information.
- To make information easily and meaningfully available.
- To provide mechanisms that will augment human capabilities.
- To make the information in online databases almost as available as if it were already inside the memory of the user.

Now that we understand what it is that intelligent databases are intended to do, we need to address the issue of how these goals are going to be achieved. The next five chapters address some of the critical technologies that form the foundation of intelligent databases.

2

DATABASE SYSTEMS

Database systems represent a complex and evolving discipline. Although our focus in this book is on the development of intelligent databases, we will need to consider general issues in the development and use of databases. This will serve as a firm foundation for introducing and describing the properties and uses of intelligent databases.

■ 2.1 INTRODUCTION

We begin by considering the history and evolution of databases from the early development of files structures on mainframe computers. The hierarchical, network, and relational data models are introduced, along with a distinction between the conceptual, logical, and physical levels of database architecture.

Because of the relational model's theoretical purity, popularity, and the close relationship to logic, the focus of this chapter is on relational DBMS's (Database Management Systems). Object-oriented databases are covered in Chapter 3, and inference is covered in Chapter 4.

Methods of querying relational databases are examined, with emphasis on the SQL and QBE querying languages. A practical database design methodology based on forms specification techniques is then outlined with a simple example, generating a relational database definition along with other information that is useful for application development. A separate section is devoted to a discussion concerning the precise definition of what makes a database system *relational*, the so-called *relational fidelity* issue. The chapter ends with a discussion of some extensions to relational systems.

■ 2.2 HISTORY AND EVOLUTION OF DATABASES

The original motivation for databases came from computer programmers who wanted a convenient way of handling the data that was used in their programs. In some applications, the data became so important that specialized programs were developed to manage and update the data. Today, we are seeing a convergence between databases that evolved out of computer programming and text databases that have evolved from traditional text sources such as books and journals. We shall explore this convergence later in this book. In the remainder of this chapter, however, we will look at the data structuring and management techniques that have been developed.

Early computers had little storage capability and programmers had to take great pains to handle and manipulate data using the few memory registers that were available. Subsequent advances in computing technology have produced ever greater storage capabilities with the transition from punched cards to disks, magnetic tapes, and optical media. Data-structuring techniques have also generally kept pace with the evolving storage capability. Primitive data structures include integers, real numbers, and characters. At a slightly higher level is the character string, which was the basic data type of the PL/I language and which continues to be prominently featured in many of today's programming languages. More advanced data types can be distinguished as either linear or nonlinear. Stacks and queues are important linear data types for controlling the operation of a computer, but from the perspective of databases, the most important nonprimitive data structures are arrays, lists, and files.

Like most technologies, the directions that computing pursued were determined not only by improving hardware and software capability, but also by the socioeconomic needs of the organizations that used computers. In the 1960s, the use of mainframes became widespread in many companies. These companies often had a great deal of data that they stored on disks. To access this data, they began writing programs in languages such as FORTRAN, COBOL, and PL/I. Initially, these programs were developed for specialized applications such as parts management systems and marketing information systems. However, it soon became apparent that a large amount of information was common to different applications and that there was a need to share access to data. As a result, scattered files and data were integrated into centralized databases that provided a number of benefits.

    a. Shared access to data for diverse users.

    b. Security.

    c. Improved ease and efficiency in providing maintenance updates.

Large centralized databases required methods of structuring and managing large amounts of data. Data was generally structured in terms of files (collections) of records. Files contained objects referred to as records, which were described by fields (attributes).

The task of managing data consisted of three subtasks.

1. General structure of the data was defined using a Data Definition Language (DDL).

2. The data was changed and updated using a Database Manipulation Language (DML).

3. Methods for retrieving subsets of the data based on specific queries were provided in a Database Query Language (DQL).

A system that handled all three of these subtasks was referred to as a Database Management System (DBMS).

The forerunners of database management systems were Generalized File Management Systems (GFMS). File management systems grew out of the COBOL programming language and were designed to supplement the weaknesses of COBOL in the areas of storage, retrieval, and report writing. They also included sort packages and a number of file handling systems.

COBOL was developed by CODASYL (Conference On DAta SYstems and Languages) in 1960. Based on experience gained with COBOL implementations of the early 1960s, there was a need to add sorting capabilities and report writers. Report writers performed the tasks required to generate reports such as editing, summarizing, and formatting data. Report writing languages were developed, most notably RPG (Report Program Generator), which added report writing and file management facilities to a stripped-down version of COBOL. By the early 1970s, organizations were constructing large databases and the systems required to manage these databases began to evolve. The Data Base Task Group (DBTG) report presented by CODASYL in 1971 formed a basis for subsequent systems.

In the 1970s, the DBMS known as IMS (Information Management System) was developed. It was the result of a project that began in the 1960s in response to the massive information handling needs generated by the Apollo moon program. Earlier, General Electric's IDS (Integrated Data Store) system had introduced a number of new concepts and facilities, including the first implementation of a network model of data.

Codd (1970) published a seminal paper on the relational database model. This model offers the simple notion of tables as the only data structure for user interaction. Its close relationship to set theory and first-order logic allows the relational model to inherit many elegant properties and operators. Many experimental relational DBMS's were implemented in the 1970s with the first introduction of commercial systems in the late 70s and early 1980s. Now there are over a hundred relational DBMS's, even though many of them are stretching the definition of the relational system.

The proliferation of large databases had to be managed and administered in some way. Although the DBMS's that developed handled the storage and retrieval aspects of data, organizational structures and educational disciplines adapted to the new technology. It was soon realized that the initial form of data did not in itself determine the optimal structure of a database. Instead, a database had to be designed in accordance with the functionality and usage that was desired. In addition to database designers, database administrators were needed to supervise the design, development, and maintenance of the increasingly large databases. As the maintenance and use of databases became critical to the operation of large organizations, larger investments were made in providing support staff and facilities. Thus, the new discipline of MIS (Management Information Systems) was formed, which was responsible for providing the functionality of ready access to information throughout organizations. The growing importance of MIS is reflected in the fact that many large corporations now have a Vice President of MIS.

The relational model of data has attracted tremendous attention in both the research and the vendor community. Relational DBMS's have become the dominant data-processing software in the 1980s, and thus will be emphasized the relational database model in the remainder of this chapter.

■ 2.3 MODELING DATA

The functionality of DBMS and information systems rests on a well-established technology. The basis of this technology consists of methods for structuring and organizing data. Data needs to be organized if it is to be useful. Data models specify how separate pieces of information are related in a database. Information is broken down into data structures. The most basic of these structures are records and fields.

A record can be simply defined as a collection of fields or attributes, as illustrated in Figure 2.1. In a payroll file, for instance, a record may correspond to a person and may contain fields such as name, social security number, birthdate, salary, and address. At the logical (file) level, records are the basic units of data storage.

Fields, such as Social Security number and birthdate, are the elementary data items. A field can be defined both in terms of its syntax and its semantics. Syntactically, the information that a field contains conforms to a certain type, such as a real, an integer, a character or a string. Semantically, the meaning of information within a field should correspond to the concept represented by the field. Thus, if a field refers to an age, the number in that field should represent a realistic age.

Although one can define arbitrarily complex data models, at the heart of every data

Name	Age	Social Security No.	Telephone
Smith, John	27	213-45-1212	765-4321

Figure 2.1 A database record.

model lie structures that are equivalent to records and fields, whether or not they are referred to by those names.

2.3.1 The Hierarchical Model

A number of data models have been proposed for organizing data records. The first considered here is the hierarchical model.

A hierarchy (or tree) is a network in which nodes are connected by links such that all links point in the direction from child to parent. Another way of saying this is that nodes in a hierarchy are strictly nested, that is, every node has a parent node except for the single root (top) node of the hierarchy.

The basic operation in a hierarchy is the tree search. Given a query to a hierarchical database, the hierarchy will be searched and nodes that meet the conditions of the query will be returned.

In a hierarchical database, the nodes of the hierarchy consist of records which are connected to each other via links. Figure 2.2 shows a small example of a hierarchical database representing information about employees in a company. There are two record types: employee and department. The employee record type might consist of four fields: name, Social Security number, salary, and telephone number, with the department record consisting of three fields: department name, department manager, and location. Figure 2.3 shows a sample database schema for employees. In this example, the set of employees and their departments is organized as a tree. A hierarchical database is a collection of such trees.

Data has to be strictly nested in hierarchies (i.e., each node has only one parent), but real-world data does not always conform to this requirement. One piece of data may need to be repeated in several different locations of the database. This repetition may occur in the same database tree or in several different trees. Virtual records are used to achieve a situation where data appears to be repeated within the hierarchies without

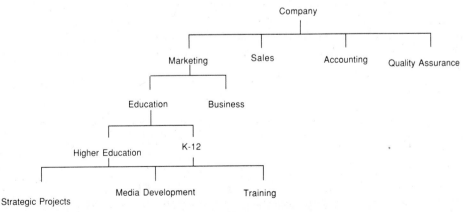

Figure 2.2 A hierarchical database representing information about company employees.

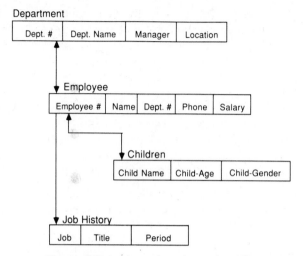

Figure 2.3 A schema for a hierarchical file.

having to waste storage or increase the difficulty of updating the database. Instead of data, a virtual record contains a logical pointer to a physical record. Records can be repeated by keeping a single copy of the actual record in a tree and then creating repetitions of that record as virtual records that point to the actual physical record. This has the desirable property of allowing us to update all the virtual records simply by updating the one physical record that those virtual records point to.

Maintenance of a hierarchical database requires that we have flexible methods for changing and updating records. Each change is equivalent to deleting the old version of a record and inserting the new version. The type of insertion and deletion that is possible depends on the way that pointers are used to create virtual records. In general, a pointer to a hierarchical database record consists of (a) the address of the first block of the database record, and (b) the value of the key field or fields for the record in question.

Consider how we might update one of the records in the database. It is found that the name of one employee has been misspelled and should be changed from Lockwood to Lockward. In this case, the record is retrieved, the name field of the employee is found, and then the old record is replaced by a new one that has the corrected spelling for the name field.

Hierarchical databases often exhibit poor flexibility, but because of the "hardwired" access paths, they often provide very good performance for preconceived applications. Many "classical" programs and applications (accounting, payroll, etc.) have been written in hierarchical DBMS's such as IBM's DL/1. Consequently, hierarchical DBMS's continue to be used although many new database applications are migrating to relational environments.

2.3.2 The Network Model

The network model uses additional pointers to add flexibility to the hierarchical model. In its most general form, a network is a collection of nodes with links possible between any of the nodes. These links can be assigned meanings and the creation of links between nodes can be constrained in various ways. The hierarchical model, for instance, is a special case of the network model where each node is linked to a parent node. In a pure hierarchy, each node may have only one parent although it may itself be the parent of more than one lower-level node. In a hierarchy, there is only one path between any two nodes, whereas in a network, there may be a number of paths.

The DBTG data definition language is a formal notation for networks that was proposed by the Data Base Task Group (DBTG) of the Conference on Data Systems

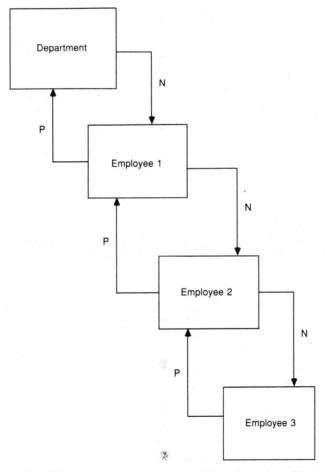

Figure 2.4 A CODASYL dataset showing how next (N) and previous (P) pointers connect owner record (department) and member records (employees) into a linked list.

Languages (CODASYL). In this model owner and member records are linked by pointers as in Figure 2.4.

Links are referred to as sets in the DBTG data definition language. Each link (set) and the record that it points to is referred to as a set occurrence. Figure 2.5 shows the schema of an employee database. Declarations for record types and DBTG sets are made in the DBTG data definition language (DDL).

In the DBTG model, only one-to-one and many-to-one links between items are allowed. Each DBTG set has one owner and zero or more member records. The DBTG model also provides for repeating groups, where fields may have sets of values associated with them. An employee, for instance, may have several addresses.

Networks may be implemented in different ways, depending on the way in which records and pointers are organized. One method utilizes a multilist structure. In a multilist organization, each record has a pointer for each link that it is involved with. Search through the database is handled by the DBTG data-retrieval, data-manipulation language. This consists of a number of commands that are embedded within a host language such as COBOL or Pascal.

The *Find* and *Get* commands allow one to navigate within the database. The find command locates a record in the database. Modifiers to the find command (these are keywords that follow the word find) distinguish specific find operations. Some of the versions of the find command are as follows

> Find any—finds the first record in the ordering that has the specified value.
> Find duplicate—finds the next record that matches the value.
> Find next—finds the next element within a particular set.

Other DBTG facilities provide for updating a database. To store a new record of type <record-type> into the database, we create the record *r* in the template for record type <record-type> and then add this new record to the database with the command

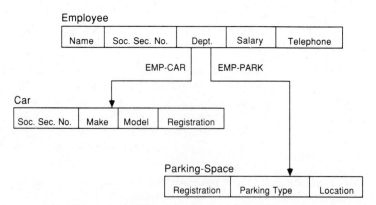

Figure 2.5 An employee-car-parking space DBTG Database.

store <record type>

Other commands for updating the database include the modify command, which modifies existing records, and the erase command, which deletes existing records.

The rise of the relational model has also had a strong impact on network DBMS's. Companies such as Cullinet, which sold the IDMS system, have added relational capabilities to existing network systems. Thus, the IDMS/R system adds relational capabilities to the IDMS system while remaining upwardly compatible with the prior nonrelational versions. For further discussion of the DBTG data model, see Date (1986) and Cardenas (1979).

2.3.3 The Relational Model

Large databases were stored on mainframes in the 1960s and 1970s. Early mainframe systems such as IMS and CODASYL continued to be popular in the late 1970s and early 1980s. Since there were no personal computers prior to the mid-1970s, the database world consisted of mainframe applications written in COBOL, IMS, and similar languages.

At first, mainframe database applications were dominated by the network and hierarchical models. In the mid-1970s, however, the relational model gradually began to gain acceptance. IBM at San Jose implemented the first working version of the relational model in their System/R (Astrahan, et al., 1976). Another early system, which is still prominent today, is INGRES, developed at UC Berkeley (Stonebreaker, Wong, Kreps, and Held, 1976).

By the early 1980s, with the proliferation of personal computers, commercial relational database management systems began to appear. On micro-computers, dBASE was a partial realization of the relational model and was followed by other systems such as rBASE.

A relational database is a database consisting of a set of tables. Figure 2.6 shows a small example of a relational database. Each row in a relation represents a relationship between a set of values. One reason for the widespread acceptance of the relational model may be that it is based on this straightforward and easily understood conceptual model. The model can be summarized as follows

A relational database consists of tables. Each table bears the name of a relation and contains rows and columns. We can define a relation scheme as the set of attribute names for a relation. New tables can be constructed from these tables by cutting and pasting rows and columns from the existing tables. The process of constructing new tables in the relational model is governed by the operations of the relational algebra (Section 2.5).

Once we attach attribute names to the columns of a relational table, the order of the columns (attributes) becomes unimportant. Conceptually, operations on this relational

Employee

Name	Age	Dept. No.
Timpson	41	7
Starr	31	7
Hurst	19	4

Department

Dept. No.	Manager	Phone
7	Timpson	2938
4	Sondquist	4068

Figure 2.6 An employee relational database.

database consist of cutting and pasting portions of the existing tables to create new relational tables that satisfy certain criteria.

Besides the three major data models (the hierarchical, network, and relational), there have been active research and experiments in the research community on adding more semantics to data models. For the remaining part of this section, we will provide two representative examples of adding semantics to data modeling: the *entity relationship* data model and the *semantic data* model. Both of these models implicitly introduced early concepts which later also appeared in object-oriented systems, as discussed in the next chapter.

2.3.4 Entity-Relationship Data Model

The entity-relationship approach is a widely accepted technique for data modeling (Chen, 1976). In the entity-relationship (ER) model, an entity is an object or thing that exists and can be distinguished from other entities. An entity might be a person, an institution, a flight, and so on. Entities are described in terms of attributes or properties. In terms of the regular database constructs, entities generally conform to records while their attributes are represented as the fields of those records.

A relationship is defined as an ordered list of entity sets. In a family database, for instance, *sister-of* represents a relationship between one set of entities and their sisters. In terms of the relational data model, the relationship corresponds to the name of the table, while the different entity sets correspond to columns in the table. This correspondence is shown in Figure 2.7.

Entities and relationships can also be used as a diagramming technique in conceptual design of databases. The standard notation for such diagrams is as follows:

a. Rectangles represent entities.

b. Circles represent attributes.

c. Diamonds represent relationships.

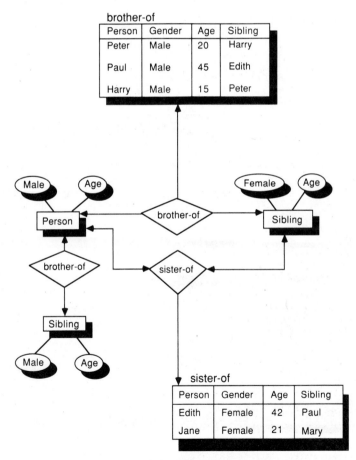

Figure 2.7 The correspondence between an entity-relationship diagram and a relational table.

Relationships are generally described by verbs such as:

    supplier <u>supplies</u> customer

or,

    customer <u>is-supplied-by</u> supplier

Figure 2.8 shows an entity-relationship diagram for a manufacturing process. This process has to deal with the following data

        numerical-controlled machine data
        work-in-progress
        assembly structure
        vendor
        master parts
        customer
        finished-goods inventory

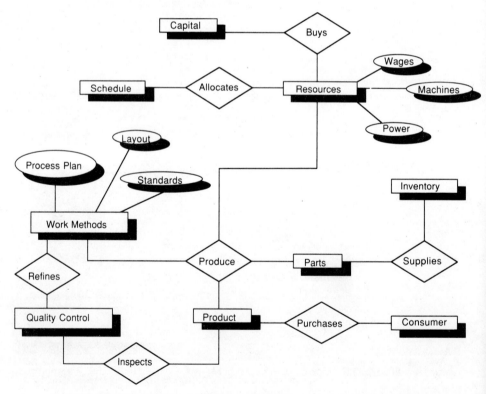

Figure 2.8 An entity-relationship diagram for a manufacturing process.

raw-materials inventory

orders

accounts receivable

Departments that use this information would include:

purchasing—to determine parts needs and vendor data

marketing—to determine the availability of product in the finished-goods inventory

production control—to update work-in-progress

inventory control

facilities planning

engineering

Although there is a close analogy between the relational data model and the entity-relationship model, there are also important differences. The entity-relationship model is a conceptual description of the data that does not determine which relations are necessary and which relations can or should be omitted. In spite of these differences, the entity-relationship conceptualization can be a useful starting point for building a relational database. The graphic representation shows the relations that exist within the data. This must then be supplemented with constraints and relationships that are added to the data dictionary.

2.3.5 Semantic Data Models

At present, most databases only have a limited understanding of what the data that they contain really means. This is a major motivation behind the development of intelligent and active databases. Semantic data models are designed to overcome the problem of limited understanding by incorporating more meaning into the database.

One approach to semantic data models breaks the problem of adding meaning to a database into four stages.

1. Identify a set of semantic concepts that describe relevant information and meaning. This set of concepts might, for instance, include entities, properties, and associations. These concepts may then be linked in a descriptive formalism where the world is described in terms of entities, which are described by properties and linked together by associations.

2. Represent the semantic concepts identified in stage 1 in terms of a set of corresponding symbolic objects, such as those provided in the entity-relationship model.

3. Devise a set of integrity rules that govern the description of the semantic concepts in terms of the symbolic objects.

4. Develop a set of operators for manipulating the symbolic objects.

At present, the incorporation of semantic models within databases remains a research

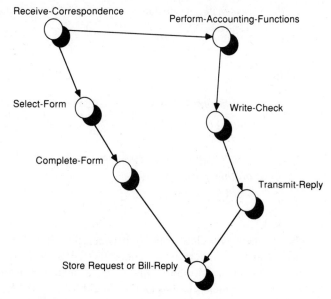

Figure 2.9 Communication paths within a semantic model of an office system application.

issue that is actively being explored. A number of semantic data models have been proposed, including models that deal with activities as well as with data. One such model is the event model discussed by King and McLeod (1984). This semantic model is built around the ideas of process events and function links. Applications within the database are modeled as process events, while function links model the organization (e.g., hierarchy) of process events. Database activities are modeled by means of directed communication links, which indicate the flow of information among process events. Sequences of communication links are formed into communication paths.

Figure 2.9 illustrates a communication path within this model when applied to an office-system application. In this example, an item of correspondence is received. If the correspondence is a bill, an accounting task is carried out and a check is written. If the correspondence is a request for information, a form is filled out and a response is then transmitted, with a copy of the response being archived along with a copy of the incoming correspondence that initiated the activity. The semantic concepts used in the King and McLeod model are shown below.

Objects	Application Events
Accounts	Process-Correspondence
Checks	Write-Check
Correspondence	Select-Form
Bills	Complete-Form
Forms	Transmit-Response

Other approaches to semantic data models attempt to bridge the worldviews of AI, object orientation, and data modeling (Mylopoulos et al., 1980). For example, the concepts of semantic networks, procedural attachments, and frames from AI are finding their way into semantic data models. Similarly, the concepts of encapsulation, inheritance, and so on from programming languages are also gaining popularity in the newer experimental data models. The subject of enhancing data models with more powerful features is the focus of the object-oriented approach described in Chapter 3.

▪ 2.4 LEVELS OF DATABASE ARCHITECTURE

Architecture and structure are critical issues in building databases and database management systems. There are three levels of architecture that need to be considered, as illustrated in Figure 2.10. We shall consider each of these levels in turn.

2.4.1 The Conceptual Level

The defining of structuring principles (such as files, pointers, networks, and relational tables) for databases did not solve the problem of formulating real information and data in terms of those principles. The initial stages of database design required a process of conceptual design.

The conceptual view of a database is a somewhat abstract representation of the physical data and the way that it is stored. The conceptual view is defined through conceptual schema, written in a conceptual DDL. In general, these conceptual schema only describe the information content and structure of the database, avoiding issues concerned with specific storage structures and retrieval strategies. This allows the same conceptual model of the database to apply to a variety of different physical implementations.

In general, as databases became more complex, the development of a conceptual database preceded the definition and implementation of logical and physical databases.

A conceptual database is an abstraction of the real world that focuses on the elements of information that are relevant to the users of the database.

The representation of the conceptual schema can be expressed in many forms. For example, it may be expressed as a semantic data model where the key object types, events, and constraints are identified and modeled. The realization of conceptual schema can also be achieved by mapping the constraints in the semantic data model into definitions, procedures, and constraints in a particular data model, such as the relational model.

Another method of representing conceptual schema is to use a combination of narrative descriptions and formal data structures to capture the important entities and their activities. However, the realization of these descriptions into logical schema will be more difficult due to the use of less constrained narrative descriptions.

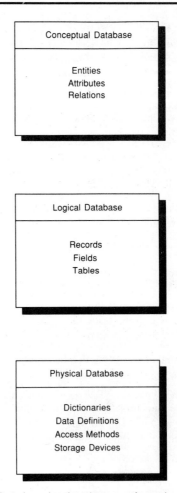

Figure 2.10 A three-level architecture for a database system.

2.4.2 The Logical Level

The logical level of database description consists of the definition of the logical structure of a database, written as logical schemas within a data definition language. The purpose behind defining database schemas is to specify those properties of the database that are permanently true regardless of the particular situation that happens to apply at a given point in time.

2.4.2.1 Schemas and Data Dictionaries

At the logical level, the structure of a database is defined in terms of schemas. The schema includes a description of the various record types and of the ways in which these record types are related. The schema is usually defined in terms of a data definition language (DDL). A subschema is a logical subset of the schema that applies to a subset of record types and relations.

Once they are identified, relations and attributes can be cataloged in the data dictionary. The data dictionary is itself a database consisting of the critical concepts that the user should know about when working with the DBMS.

Functions provided by the data dictionary include

1. Definition of fields and files.
2. Definition of relationships.
3. Definition of external schemas or subschemas (this might include information about files that can be accessed, lists of fields within each file, lists of relationships accessible to a particular user, and access type).
4. Definition of important physical schema concepts such as data locations and volumes.
5. Definition of views.

Originally, data dictionaries were static, requiring complete revisions after each update of data definitions. In recent years, dynamic data dictionaries have become available. Dynamic data dictionaries can be updated at any time because they use an interpreted mode of operation within the DBMS. Each access request results in a check of the current description of the data in the data dictionary by the DBMS. Access locking occurs only for the few seconds that it takes to update definitions.

However, as we shall see in later discussion on intelligent databases, traditional notions of specification through scenarios and documentation with data dictionaries will need to be extended as we deal with dynamic processes where there are few repetitive queries, and where the same data may be used in a variety of different ways for querying, decision making, simulation, and communication.

2.4.2.2 *Hierarchical and Network Schemas*

A network database holds records that are connected by links. In a hierarchical database, these links are constrained so that a tree structure is formed. We illustrate the logical description of hierarchical and network models with two well-known systems. The IMS (Information Management System) model is used to illustrate the hierarchical model and the DBTG proposal is used to illustrate the network model.

IMS was one of the first database systems to become commercially available. The first version of the system was released in 1968, and it remains one of the most widely used mainframe database systems as of this writing.

An IMS database consists of a hierarchy of records, with each record described as a collection of fields. The two major data definition constructs in IMS are the database description (DBD) and the program communication block (PCB). User views of the data are handled by the PCB.

Similar data definition methods are used in network databases. In the DBTG DDL, for instance, the schema description includes four types of declaration.

    a. The declaration of the schema name.

    b. One or more declarations of record types.

    c. One or more declarations of sets that define the relationships between the record types.

    d. One or more declarations defining the physical areas in which records will be stored.

DBTG record type descriptions look similar to COBOL type descriptions. Several network database management systems were based on the DBTG proposal. One of these is IDMS (Integrated Database Management System).

In the IDMS schema DDL, a database schema defines records, the fields contained in those records, and the sets in which they participate. The schema is compiled by the schema DDL compiler and the output form of this compilation is then stored in the IDMS data dictionary. For further information on the network data model, see Wiederhold (1983), Date (1986) and Cardenas (1979).

2.4.2.3 *Relational Schemas*

The relational data model provides a simple yet rigorous model of viewing data. The basic concept underlying the relational model is a table template with a set of fields, called a schema. Each schema may have a set of records, which define a table. By use of the relational algebra, tables may be joined, projected, selected from, and so on.

A relational database consists of a set of tables. Each table consists of columns (also referred to as attributes or fields) and rows of data records. A row in a table represents a relationship among a set of attributes. For example, consider Figure 2.11. Note that customer numbers are used to uniquely identify customers in the figure. In each table there will generally be one attribute that is referred to as the primary key. For instance, Social Security numbers are used to distinguish people since names cannot be guaranteed to be unique.

We will refer to each row in a table as a record. In relational databases, each record usually describes a single object. The attributes that describe records (i.e., the columns

Cust-Address

Name	Cust #	Street	City
Hughes	1712	Sepulveda	Culver
Aamco	2487	Washington	Venice
MGM	1464	La Brea	Hollywd
Gucci	3577	Rodeo	Bev Hls
SAG	2667	Stone Cnyn	Bev Hls

Figure 2.11 A customer database.

in the table) are referred to as fields. The fields of the table shown above are *Name*, *Cust #*, *Street*, and *City*.

Each field has a domain, or set of possible values, for example, *Cust#* must be an integer between 0 and 999999999. Domains may also be less strictly defined. For instance, we could define *Cust#* as an integer, with no specification of upper and lower bounds.

The definition of a table's fields and domains is called the database schema. The particular table shown above and many others of the same type are called database instances. For most purposes, the schema of a database is all a database designer may be concerned with from a logical point of view.

2.4.3 The Physical Level

The physical level of database description addresses specific implementation issues. These include the data accessing and management methods that are used (e.g., sequential, indexed sequential, or direct) as well as higher-level file organization. The physical level of description is essential since at some point the database must be physically organized on storage devices. Issues relating to this physical organization include data layout and access, and higher-level organization such as inverted files.

The physical schema describes the structure of the database at the physical level, as it would be seen by the operating system. It contains descriptions of the physical files in the database, including the sizes and layouts of the fields. Issues addressed by the physical schema and the physical level of database description include the handling of physical storage areas such as segments, blocks, and buffers (i.e., file space allocation), the utilization of links and pointers, and file structuring using techniques such as sequential files and indexed files.

Since databases are frequently large and unwieldy, physical database design is driven by the need to increase the efficiency of data storage and retrieval. In addition to the file structuring techniques covered in the following sections, there is coding information that may further speed processing. One example of data coding is sometimes referred to as packing. One simple example of packing uses frequency of usage to determine the coding strategy by carrying out the following steps:

1. Place all the words in a file.
2. Count the frequency of occurrence for each word.
3. Code the words according to their frequency of usage.

Packing is typically used in data compression for communications, such as may occur across a relatively low-speed telephone-line transmission. However, similar methods for coding and structuring data are central issues in physical database design. Packing and other data compression techniques become particularly important considerations in distributed databases, where the performance of the database is determined in large part by speed and reliability of network communications.

Record	Name	Age	Soc. Sec. No.
1	Hurst	19	282-43-6821
2	Timpson	41	776-15-0029
3	Richards	23	432-90-7461
4	Murray	27	439-47-8270
5	Sondquist	45	361-44-7221
6	Lewin	38	125-41-3094
7	Starr	31	901-75-1228

Figure 2.12 A sequential file.

2.4.3.1   Sequential Files

In sequential files, data records are ordered into specific sequences. Attributes are categorized so that records are described by attributes that appear in the same order. Figure 2.12 gives an example of employee information represented in a sequential file. All records in a sequential file are structurally identical. The entire file has to be reorganized whenever a new attribute has to be added to a record. This makes sequential files difficult to update and maintain in complex database applications.

Records are typically retrieved from a sequential file by carrying out a serial search of the file. Access to a sequential file can be improved by adding an indexing scheme. Indexed sequential files provide better random access to records along with an overflow area that handles additions to the file.

The index consists of a collection of entries, one for each record. These entries contain the value of a key-attribute (such as Social Security number) and a pointer that provides immediate access to the record. While the index entry adds to the storage allocation of a record, it is generally much smaller than the record itself. In a large database, the index may itself be indexed to reduce search time. In our employee example, this might mean that groups of Social Security numbers starting with the same three digits might be indexed as subsets of the main index.

2.4.3.2   Indexed Files

Files can be indexed without being sequential. In an indexed file, sequential search is eliminated and the records can only be accessed through the index. In indexed files, there is no restriction on the placement of a record as long as a pointer exists to a relevant index.

Indexed files provide more flexibility since the physical placement of records is no longer determined by sequential constraints and files may be defined with variable-length records. Indexing on multiple attributes greatly increases the potential for flexible information retrieval.

Indexed files are sometimes referred to as inverted files, particularly in the domain of information science and online retrieval. The term fully inverted is generally used to describe files where all the attributes have indexes.

Indexed files have many benefits, but one problem arises when records need to be updated. The indexes that refer to a record also have to be updated whenever a record is added, deleted, or modified. Indexed files are used when rapid retrieval of information is required. Examples include online retrieval systems and airline reservation systems.

2.4.3.3   *Directly Accessed Files*

Directly accessed files rely on the ability to directly access any block of known address on disk units and other external storage media. In direct addressing, the key of the record is used to locate the record in the file (as illustrated in Figure 2.13). Direct-access methods are fast, but they require records to be located on the basis of a single key-attribute.

Directly addressed files differ from indexed files in that they use a computation to find the address for a key, whereas indexes are used in indexed files to identify the record corresponding to a particular key.

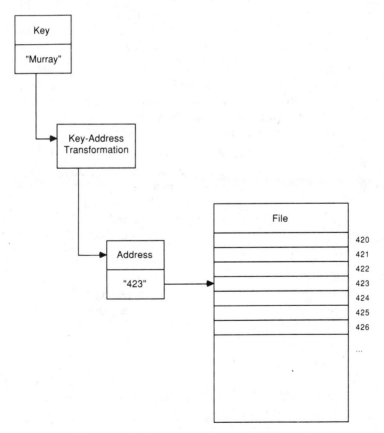

Figure 2.13 A directly accessed file.

One method of implementing directly accessed files is to use direct file addressing. In this case, the key of a record corresponds to its location. Thus we might have an employee whose key is 29748 and whose record is also stored at location 29748. Problems arise in this method because it enforces a correlation between physical locations and the keys assigned to records. This makes it difficult to optimize the physical structure of the file or to assign a meaningful basis to the construction of keys.

It is generally preferable to define keys and locations separately, and then use computational procedures to translate key-attribute values into relative addresses within the file space. These computations are referred to as key-to-address transformations. Construction of these transformations can be difficult. Deterministic transformations seek to construct a unique relative address for each key-attribute value. This technique becomes unmanageable with large numbers of distinct key-attribute values and is generally not used in the physical design of large databases. Randomizing transformations represent an alternative method where randomizing algorithms are used. The purpose of randomizing is to provide a uniform distribution of addresses, so that the available address space is used efficiently. Randomizing techniques that tend to maintain the order of the records are referred to as sequence-maintaining methods. In contrast, hashing techniques attempt to maximize the uniqueness of the assigned addresses.

The problem of collisions occurs in key-to-address transformations when different records are assigned the same location. This occurs because hashing and other randomizing methods do not ensure that unique relative addresses will be chosen. Linear hashing (Litwin, 1980) is a method designed to avoid the problem of increasing frequency of collisions as the size of the directly addressed file grows. In linear hashing, the size of the address space is increased, with new blocks of addresses being added to the hash space as the size of the file grows. Overflow blocks are used to handle the remaining collisions that occur under this scheme. There are a number of formulas for deciding when to add new blocks to the address space. In general, these formulas depend on the number of collisions that occur. Thus, a new block might be assigned after n collisions occur. This type of address allocation strategy, based as it is on performance feedback, ensures a roughly constant collision rate over the long term. The increasing address space also requires modifications to the hashing function. In general, as the address space doubles, the hashing function grows by one bit.

There are a number of hashing methods of which we describe only one, the remainder of division method. In this method, a pseudorandom number is generated and that number is then divided by a large prime number. The remainder of this division then serves as the hashing address. The pseudorandom numbers for the records are created by assigning a uniform distribution based on the key-attribute values. This is referred to as a distribution-dependent method because it relies on knowledge of the expected distribution of key-attribute values.

Many choices exist for transforming record keys to relative addresses, of which only a few are considered above. Satisfactory results have been obtained with these methods and attempts to fine-tune and optimize them sometimes lead to costly failures when conditions change, for example, the distribution of key-attribute values deviates from expectations.

Although directly addressed files have some desirable properties, they also impose limitations. For the methods discussed above, only one attribute of a record can be used for retrieval, and data records have to be of fixed length. Although these problems can be solved, the solutions themselves generate additional access costs.

Directly addressed files can be extremely efficient, but their limitations make them unsuitable for complex data retrieval. They work best in applications where fast access is essential, simple access is sufficient, and where record sizes are small and fixed. Examples of such applications include directories and name lists.

2.4.3.4   *Hybrid File Organizations*

Physical database design is a complex topic. In general, we favor the use of indexed files because this allows flexible access based on the type of complex queries that will be generated and considered in intelligent databases. However, at the physical level, it is possible to develop hybrid file structures that combine the benefits of techniques such as indexing and direct addressing. There is often a tradeoff between retrieval flexibility and space requirements. As computing technology advances, however, it is likely that considerations of retrieval flexibility and overall functionality will come to outweigh computational and storage issues.

In later sections of this book, we will assume the existence of indexed files that may be linked in a variety of hierarchical and relational structures. Although our approach assumes that basic performance will rest on efficient storage and access tools such as hashing at the physical level, it is possible if not extremely likely, that neural networks, parallel-processing architectures, and advanced database machines may revolutionize the process of physical database design in the future.

■   2.5   RELATIONAL DATA MANIPULATION LANGUAGES

The relational model of data used in relational databases is based on a well-defined logical structure, namely, the relational algebra. Formally, the representation of a relational data consists of lists of relations and their attributes, along with the description of existence constraints. Data retrieval within the relational model is handled by using the relational algebra to manipulate relations.

2.5.1   The Relational Algebra

The relational algebra is a method for operating on relations. Relations are often considered as sets of records, with each record being described in terms of key fields or attributes. However, the link between a record and one of its attributes can itself be considered an elementary relation.

When two relations share an attribute, there is a functional dependence, or relationship, between them. Thus, we might have the relations

EMPLOYEE (employee-number, department, employee-name . . .)
REPORT (department, due-date, topic)

These relations both have the department attribute in common and the functional dependence or relationship implied by them can be expressed as a 1-to-N relationship where a department is responsible for writing N reports.

Vacation time represents a 1-to-1 relationship where each employee has a certain amount of accumulated vacation time. This relationship is implied in the following two relations:

EMPLOYEE (employee-number, department, employee-name . . .)
VACATION-TIME (employee-number, accumulated-vacation-time)

Records were referred to as tuples in the original formulation of the relational model (Codd, 1970), to distinguish their more formal nature from the rather fuzzy and informal way in which the term *record* had been used in database terminology up to that point. We shall treat the terms *tuple* and *record* as equivalent for the purposes of this book. Both terms in our usage refer to what is sometimes known as a flat record instance.

The five fundamental operations in the relational algebra are

Selection
Projection
Product
Union
Set difference

In addition, the join is another operation that may be defined in terms of the Cartesian product and selection operations.

The selection and projection operations are unary operations, since they operate on one relation. The other three relations operate on pairs of relations and are therefore called binary operations. Joins can be performed on two or more tables.

2.5.1.1 Selection

Selection involves taking a table and selecting the rows that satisfy a predicate. For example, you can select all customers in Beverly Hills from the Cust-address table. The selection operator takes a table (Figure 2.11) and a predicate (in this case, City = BevHls) as input and returns another table as output.

Name	Cust#	Street	City
Gucci	3577	Rodeo	BevHls
SAG	2667	Stone Cnyn	BevHls

2.5.1.2 Projection

Projection removes certain columns from a table. For example, you might want to see just the Name, Customer number, and City fields from the Cust-address table. The projection operator takes a table and a set of field names as input and returns another table as output. The resulting table contains the same number of rows but fewer columns. Thus

Project Name, Cust#, City (Cust-address)

produces the following table where only the columns referred to in the projection are included.

Name	Cust#	City
Hughes	1712	Culver
Aamco	2487	Venice
Shell	3445	WHlwd
MGM	1464	Hollywd
Gucci	3577	BevHls
SAG	2667	BevHls

2.5.1.3 Product

The third basic operator is the product. The product multiplies two tables so that if one table has N rows and I columns, and the other has M rows and J columns, the product table will contain (N*M) rows, with I + J columns. Thus, if we take the product of the following two tables:

Cust-address

Name	Cust#	City
Gucci	3577	BevHls
SAG	2667	BevHls

Cust-credit

Name	Credit
Gucci	Good
SAG	Average

we obtain a table with $2 \times 2 = 4$ rows, where the first three columns are from the first table and the last two columns, from the second table:

Name	Cust#	City	Name	Credit
Gucci	3577	BevHls	Gucci	Good
SAG	2667	BevHls	Gucci	Good
Gucci	3577	BevHls	SAG	Average
SAG	2667	BevHls	SAG	Average

This new table does not look right as it stands. Why should we have a record that refers both to Gucci's location and SAG's credit record, for instance?

We can clean up the table by selecting those rows where the names in columns 1 and 4 match to obtain the following table.

Name	Cust#	City	Name	Credit
Gucci	3577	BevHls	Gucci	Good
SAG	2667	BevHls	SAG	Average

We can then project out one of the Name fields to get

Name	Cust#	City	Credit
Gucci	3577	BevHls	Good
SAG	2667	BevHls	Average

2.5.1.4   Union and Difference

The union of two tables with N and M rows, respectively, is obtained by concatenating them into one table with a total of (N + M) rows. Union will generally make sense only if the schemes of the two tables match, that is, if they have the same number of fields with matching attributes in each field.

The difference operator can be used to find records that are in one relation, but not in another. The difference between A and B is often denoted by A - B. As an example of set difference, we can find all the part-names in the product-composition table below that are parts of the fastener but not of the adapter by specifying the following query:

```
Project Part-name ((Select Product = fastener (Product-composition)) -
(Select Product = adapter (Product-composition)))
```

Product	Part-name	Part#	Qty
fastener	lever	2021	1
fastener	sprocket	2197	3
fastener	cog	2876	4
fastener	spring	2346	6
adapter	spring	2346	5
adapter	pulley	2477	5
adapter	rivet	2498	21
transformer	pulley	2477	3
transformer	lever	2021	1
transformer	cam	2655	3
transformer	rivet	2498	12
processor	cpu1	9876	1
processor	8k-chip	9801	4
processor	led	9701	4

The result of this query is then

Part-name
Lever
Sprocket
Cog

Additional operators can be defined to simplify the process of building queries, but the essential elements of the relational algebra consist of the operators defined above along with intersection, which can be expressed by using differences and unions. The intersection between two relations A and B can be expressed as

$$A-(A-B)$$

and contains all records in A that are also in B.

2.5.1.5 Joining Tables

The join operator allows us to join several tables together. Although the join is not one of the basic five relational operators, it can often be very useful.

Given two tables, A and B, the join operator allows one to apply a predicate to all rows that are formed by concatenating rows from A and rows from B. Those rows satisfying the predicate are returned. For example, if we have 3 rows in A and 7 rows in B, we can form 21 possible rows to apply the predicate to (this is simply the product of the two tables).

Only some of the rows have any meaning. For example, if both tables contain data about customers, we must include in our predicate a test that the *Cust#* fields in A and B are equivalent. Thus, the join operator is equivalent to a product followed by a selection that ensures that all the rows in the new table are meaningful. For example, a manufacturer may have a database containing the following data:

Cust-address:
> Cust#, Name, Street, City, Amount

Suppliers:
> Sup-name, Part#

Product-composition:
> Product, Part-name, Part#, Qty

Orders:
> Order#, Cust#, Product, Qty, Status

How can we derive a table that includes all customers who returned products that contained parts manufactured by the Ace Supply Company? We will need to use selection, projection, and the join to find the desired table. Such a table, constructed out of one or more tables by the application of the operators, is called a view.

To get the view, we need to do a number of operations. We need to join the Supplier and Product-composition tables (shown below) together to obtain a table (W shown below) that relates products to parts-suppliers (we need to use a predicate that ensures that *Part#* is equal). Then we will select only those products that contain parts made by Ace Supply Company.

Product-composition

Product	Part-name	Part#	Qty
fastener	lever	2021	1
fastener	sprocket	2197	3
fastener	cog	2876	4
fastener	spring	2346	6
adapter	spring	2346	5
adapter	pulley	2477	5
adapter	rivet	2498	21
transformer	pulley	2477	3
transformer	lever	2021	1
transformer	cam	2655	3
transformer	rivet	2498	12
processor	cpul	9876	1
processor	8k-chip	9801	4
processor	led	9701	4
•	•	•	•
•	•	•	•

Suppliers

Sup-name	Part#
Ace	2021
Ace	2346
Ace	2477
Jackson	2197
Campbell	2876
Truman	2498
•	•
•	•

After projecting out the important fields and eliminating duplicate records, we need to join the resultant table to the Orders table (after selecting only the returned products) to find the returned orders that contain Ace parts. The following table W shows the first step in the process, where W = Join (Product-composition, suppliers, Part#).

The relational algebra provides a concise language for representing queries. However, database system products require query languages that may be easily used and interfaced to programs. There are many similarities between the processes of querying and programming. Both querying and programming follow the general process of input, computation, and output. Both querying and programming require syntactic conventions and debugging. Querying is in fact a high level form of programming that is specialized for the problem of data or information retrieval.

Relational databases require efficient and usable query languages. Two major approaches are based on the languages SQL (Chamberlin, Astrahan, Eswaran,

W

Product	Part-name	Part#	Qty	Sup-Name
fastener	lever	2021	1	Ace
fastener	sprocket	2197	3	Jackson
fastener	cog	2876	4	Campbell
fastener	spring	2346	6	Ace
adapter	spring	2346	5	Ace
adapter	pulley	2477	5	Ace
adapter	rivet	2498	21	Truman
transformer	pulley	2477	3	Ace
transformer	lever	2021	1	Ace
transformer	cam	2655	3	Bitstream
transformer	rivet	2498	12	Truman
processor	cpul	9876	1	Bitstream
processor	8k-chip	9801	4	Electra
processor	led	9701	4	Electra
•	•	•	•	•
•	•	•	•	•

Griffiths, Lorie, Mehl, Reisner, and Wade, 1976) and QUEL (Stonebraker, Wong, Kreps, and Held, 1976). Another innovative query language was known as Query-By-Example (QBE, Zloof, 1977). In the next section, we review the language SQL (Structured Query Language), which is the most widely used relational query language.

2.5.2 SQL

SQL, pronounced Sequel, was developed in the mid 1970s by IBM as the command language for a prototype relational database system, System R. Since its introduction, SQL has been extensively studied and has been used as the basis for a number of products, including two from IBM, DB2 and SQL/DS. SQL is rapidly emerging as the standard database language for all platforms and has been adopted as an ANSI standard. SQL is, in fact, more than merely a database query language. It includes features for defining the structure of the data, modifying the data, and specifying security constraints within the database. We shall present a generic version of SQL, whose specific features may vary between different implementations.

SQL expressions are made up of three clauses: *select, from,* and *where*. A query in SQL has the form

select Attribute$_1$, Attribute$_2$, . . . , Attribute$_n$
from Relation$_1$, Relation$_2$, . . . , Relation$_m$
where Predicate

In this notation, the list of attributes may be replaced with a star (*) to select all attributes of all relations appearing in the *from* clause.

The *select* clause in SQL (confusingly) corresponds to the projection operation described above for the relational algebra. In SQL, a *select* is used to list the attributes desired in the table produced by a query. The *from* clause specifies a list of relations to be used in executing the query. Finally, the *where* clause corresponds to the selection predicate of the relational algebra. If the *where* clause is present it consists of a predicate involving attributes of the relations that appear in the *from* clause.

The result of an SQL query is a relation. SQL acts as follows:

a. It forms the product of the relations named in the *from* clause.

b. It performs a relational selection using the *where* clause predicate.

c. It projects the result onto the attributes of the *select* (in the SQL sense) clause.

SQL can thus be viewed as an outgrowth of the relational algebra. It includes the basic relational algebra operators that we discussed earlier. Selection is represented in SQL's *where* clause, while projection is performed in SQL's *select* clause. Product is represented by the *from* clause of SQL. SQL also handles set operations including the union, intersection, and set difference, and the logical connectives AND, OR, and NOT.

Some features of SQL are not available in the relational algebra. For instance, aggregate operators such as avg (average) operate on aggregates of records, providing statistical and related information, while sorting procedures can be used to order records according to their attributes. The flexibility of SQL can be further enhanced by linking it with general-purpose languages such as Pascal and C. This allows the development of customized routines to manipulate the database and makes the SQL language extensible.

2.5.2.1 Simple SQL Statements

Consider the relation shown earlier in Figure 2.11. The query "Find the names of all the customers in the Cust-address table" can be expressed in SQL as

> *select* Name
> *from* Cust-address

The result of this query will be a list of all the customer names in the table, that is, Hughes, Aamco, Shell, MGM, Gucci, and SAG. In this example, each customer name appeared only once in the table. However, if there had been more than one record for a customer name, that name would have appeared as many times as there were relevant records in response to the query. In such cases, the duplication can be avoided by using the keyword *distinct* after the select instruction, as in

> *Select distinct* Name
> *From* Cust-address

We identify the customers located in Beverly Hills using the query

> *Select* Name
> *from* Cust-address
> *where* City = "BevHls"

To find those customers in Beverly Hills owing more than $5000, we then pose the following query:

> *Select* Name
> *from* Cust-address
> *where* City = "BevHls" and
> *amount* > 5000

In addition to the relational predicates (<, >, =, etc.), there are other built-in predicates to express more elaborate retrieval conditions. They include *between* (for range specification), *in* (for membership), *like* (for text pattern matching). To retrieve all people who live in a city with the second letter being "e," we use the following query:

Select Name
from cust-name
where City like '_e%'

where,

_e Means any one character can go here for a match
% Means any number of characters can go here for a match.

In SQL, the order in which the result of retrieval is returned can be controlled by an *order by* clause. For example, to display the table Cust-address in the order of City

Select Name, City
from Cust-address
where City = "BevHls" and
amount > 5000
order by City

The last two clauses of SQL, *group by* and *having,* allow us to arrange rows into groups and then perform operations on those groups. For example,

Select City, Sum(Amount)
from Cust-address
group by City

This query groups the rows in the table Cust-address so that each group has the same city value, and for each group, applies the aggregate function Sum over the field Amount. There are five aggregate functions in SQL: sum, avg, max, min, and count.

The *having* clause is to groups what the *where* clause is to rows. It imposes a retrieval condition on groups. For example, to display the same information as previous query except that each group should have more than 100 customer accounts

Select City, Sum(Amount)
from Cust-address
group by City
having count(∗) > 100

The "∗" in the having clause refers to each group. The aggregate function count computes the size of the group.

SQL can be used to update data in the database. For instance, the command *Insert* adds new records to a table.

For example, the following instructions add an IBM record to the Cust-account table:

Insert
into Cust-address (name, cust#, street, city, amount)
values ("IBM", 1234, "Corry Street", "San Jose", 5000)

It is also possible to insert more than one new row at a time. This can be done by using the *Insert* statement with a *select* statement, as in

Insert
into New-customers
    select *
    from Cust-address
    where Cust# > 10000

where New-customers is a newly defined relation.

Similar commands are available in SQL to perform deletion (the *Delete* command), and updating of rows values (the *Update* command).

2.5.2.2 *Multitable SQL Queries and Subqueries*

SQL can be used to perform the so-called join operation. For example, given the following tables in the manufacturer database introduced in Section 2.5.1:

Cust-address(Cust#, Name, Street, City, Amount)
Orders(Orders#, Cust#, Product, Qty, Status)

the following query retrieves all orders whose customers are located in San Jose:

Select Order#, Cust-address.Cust#
from Cust-address, Orders
where Cust-address.city = "San Jose"
and Cust-address.Cust# = Orders.Cust#

The last condition in the *where* clause of the previous example is the "join condition." In general, SQL allows any number of join conditions involving tables in the *from* clause, including joining with itself, the "self-join." The clauses *Group-by, Order-by,* and *Having* can also be used in queries that have join operations.

Just as we can use joins to combine tables in a query, we can use subqueries to combine one query with another. The simplest kind of subquery is one that returns a single value.

We can use the results of a subquery in place of a constant in a SQL statement. Here is an example that selects Orders whose customer's name is "IBM."

Select Order#, Cust#
from Orders
where Cust# =

> *Select* Cust#
> *from* Cust-address
> *where* name = "IBM"

This query has two parts. The inner part returns the value Cust#associated with IBM. The outer part uses that Cust#of IBM to retrieve the Orders records.

Subqueries can themselves contain subqueries. There is no theoretical limit to the level of nesting. Subqueries can take on many advanced variations, such as subqueries returning more than one value, subqueries that reference the outer tables (the so-called correlated queries), subqueries with special predicates such as Exists, Any, and All.

2.5.2.3 *Using SQL in a Host Language*

SQL is not a complete language in the sense that there are no control structures, screen and form manipulation facilities, and so on that would be needed to put an application program together. However, these capabilities can be provided by embedding SQL within a conventional programming language. Languages such as PL/I, COBOL, and C are referred to as *host languages* when SQL is embedded in them.

Because these host languages typically do not have the set-at-a-time type of operation that SQL does, special commands within SQL are provided to process the SQL retrieval result in a record-at-a-time fashion. The key concept is the so-called cursor. A cursor is a name given to a query. When a cursor is *opened,* the corresponding query is executed. Any subsequent *fetch* command on the cursor will produce a row to be returned to the host environment. When the cursor is *closed,* the corresponding query and its result are no longer available to the host language. An example below will be sufficient to illustrate the concept of embedding SQL statements in a general-purpose programming language. We use all CAPS notation in the following example to indicate the use of SQL within a host language.

```
EXEC SQL       DECLARE X CURSOR FOR
                   select S#, SNAME
                   from S
                   where CITY = :Y ;
EXEC SQL       OPEN X;
               DO WHILE (more)
                   EXEC SQL FETCH X INTO :S#, :SN
                       . . .
               END; /* DO WHILE */
EXEC SQL       CLOSE X ;
```

This example contains a definition of a simple cursor, an iteration over the result of the cursor, and finally closing of the cursor.

Note that each SQL statement has to be flagged with the keywords EXEC SQL so that the host language processor is notified. Within a SQL statement, host language

Staff	Staff_Id	Last_Name	First_Name	Title	Supervisor
—					

Figure 2.14 A section of the skeleton for a table.

variables can be referred to anywhere a constant is expected. In the example above, the variable :Y is a PL/1 variable providing the City value to the cursor definition.

The result of SQL retrieval can also be passed into the host language variables. Consider the fetch command in the example above. In the middle of the do while loop, the cursor is returning a row whose attributes are to be deposited in the host variables :S#, :SN, etc.

Other special commands within SQL available in the embedded mode include the transaction processing features (begin transaction, end transaction, rollback, etc.), dynamic SQL (which allows the generation of SQL statements dynamically based on the interaction with end-users during terminal interactions, for example), and authorization control (which allows the definition of who can do what to which part of the database.)

2.5.3 QBE

Query-by-example (QBE) is a query language that was developed at IBM (Zloof, 1975). Although it incorporates a number of the features of the relational model and is expressed in a table format, it does not conform as closely to the relational model as do the SQL and Quel query languages. QBE is designed to build queries interactively and contains a number of features not found in other relational query languages. The idea of querying by example is that instead of describing the procedure to be followed in obtaining the desired information, the user gives an example of what is required.

The basic idea of QBE is to draw an example of the query or update you want to perform. For example, to display the column Last_name in the table Staff, we first ask the system to display the skeleton of the table Staff, (Figure 2.14 shows a section of the skeleton), we then enter the command "P." under the column of Last_name (Figure 2.15). This is equivalent to the following SQL query:

select Last name
from Staff;

Staff	Staff_Id	Last_Name	First_Name	Title	Supervisor
		P. —			

Figure 2.15 Selecting the last name from a table in QBE.

Staff	Staff_Id	Last_Name	First_Name	Title	Supervisor
P.			.	'writer'	

Figure 2.16 A QBE query to find all rows with staff title of 'writer'.

To select specific rows, conditions can be specified on the columns. For example, Figure 2.16 contains a QBE query to find all the rows in Staff where title is *writer*.

Multiple conditions using all the predicates and operators as in SQL can be specified on the Table skeleton. For example, Figure 2.17 specifies a QBE query that finds all the orders that have been returned and have between 25,000 and 75,000 in quantity.

Commands are also available in QBE for specifying the output order. For example, the QBE query in Figure 2.18 is equivalent to the following SQL query:

select Order#, Qty, Status
from Orders
order by Qty, Status;

Expressions involving built-in operators such as arithmetic operators, data functions, and aggregate functions can be specified in QBE, as well as in SQL. For example, the QBE query in Figure 2.19*a* finds the minimum and maximum of orders quantities from Orders. Note that the symbol "_r" is referred as an example. The newly created columns contain the needed expressions.

The use of examples in QBE is very convenient in expressing complex queries in an easy-to-understand manner. For example, to find all customers who returned products that contained parts manufactured by the Ace Supply Company, we can create a QBE query to express the relationship of joins between the tables Orders, Cust-address, and Suppliers (see Section 2.5.1.5). Figure 2.19*b* contains such a query. The use of the same example (_123) in the Cust-address and Orders table skeletons tells the QBE system that there should be an equal join relationship. Similarly, relationships are also established between Orders, Product-composition, and Suppliers.

Orders	Order #	Quantity	Status
P.		> 25000 < 75000	'returned'

Figure 2.17 Using multiple conditions within a QBE query.

Orders	Order #	Quantity	Status
P.		AO(1)	AO(2)

Figure 2.18 A QBE query that specifies output order.

Orders	Order #	Quantity	Status	Max	Min
P.		_r		max._r	min._r

Figure 2.19a Using a QBE query to find the minimum and maximum order quantities.

Commands to insert, delete, update, specifying arbitrary complex conditions across tables, and so on are also available to the user. The major advantages of QBE can be summarized as follows:

- The table skeletons are displayed, thereby relieving the user from having to memorize the table names, column names, etc.
- The interaction is through a two-dimensional user interface where the order of entering commands, examples, etc., is immaterial and the user has the overall picture of the entire query displayed on the screen.
- The amount of language syntax is much smaller using QBE, compared to SQL.
- The linking of tables using examples is intuitive in the sense that it is very similar to how people handle data retrieval in a manual paper system.

Many relational DBMS's are now offering some versions of SQL and QBE.

Cust address	Cust #	Name	Street	City	Amount
	123	P.			

Suppliers	Sup name	Part #
	'Ace'	456

Product composition	Product	Part-Name	Part #	Qty
	hammer		456	

Orders	Order #	Cust #	Product	Qty	Status
		123	hammer		'returned'

Figure 2.19b A QBE query that expresses the relationship of joins between tables.

■ **2.6 RELATIONAL DATABASE DESIGN**

During the past decade, we have seen a dramatic advancement in the development and applications of database management systems. Today, not only the databases themselves have become very large, but the applications on databases have become very complex.

A good database design is a prerequisite for producing successful applications. Designing a database involves three major, typically iterative, activities; requirements capturing, logical database design, and physical database design. In this section, a simple yet powerful method of database design is outlined to illustrate some of the issues involved in these activities. This design method emphasizes the importance of requirements capturing using the intuitive data structure of forms. Forms can be used to generate normalized relational schema, SQL programs, and statistics. These generated objects can be used as a backbone for a prototype database application as well as a validation for requirement studies.

2.6.1 Capturing Requirements for Database Design

There are two major groups of information needed for database design. The first group deals with data and integrity constraints on data. Integrity constraints define "legal states" of a database that have to be maintained. This type of information is important for the derivation of the database structure (schema). The second type of information is the anticipated processes that use, modify, or produce the data. They are important for efficiency considerations of the application.

2.6.1.1 *Forms Approach*

The method we are proposing is based on forms. The forms approach is a natural interface between an end user and data because a large number of end users employ forms (e.g., purchase-order forms, expense report-forms, etc.) or versions of forms (e.g., reports, memos, etc.) in their daily work activities as well as in their personal lives (e.g., tax forms, employment application forms, etc.).

A *form* is an information-holding object consisting of two parts: (1) a form heading that describes form name, form structure, and component names; and (2) one or more form instances (or form occurrences). The form heading assumes a role that is commonly known as data-structure definition or schema definition.

As an example, Figure 2.20 shows the heading of a PRODUCT form. The top line contains the form name. Components of the form are represented by their names. The

(PRODUCT)						
PROD_NO	PNAME	TYPE	(SUPPLIER)	(STORAGE)		PRICE
			VNAME	BIN_NO	LOC	

Figure 2.20 The heading of a PRODUCT form.

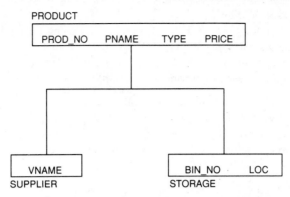

Figure 2.21 The information in Figure 2.20 represented as a hierarchy graph.

form structure is represented as follows: field names are represented in the columns, groups names are placed on top of their components, parentheses are used to denote repeating components. A corresponding hierarchy graph is also included in Figure 2.21. Forms are a natural way to represent hierarchies.

The collection of all form instances belonging to a particular form is known as a file of that name (e.g., collection of all instances of EMPLOYEE form is referred to as the EMPLOYEE file).

A basic concept underlying our approach to database design is the premise that most common data-processing applications (including the manual ones) can be viewed as manipulations of forms. An application may consist of one or more processes. Each process produces or modifies one form. Thus, specification of an application involves capturing information about the forms that are being manipulated. Very often the information on form processing is embedded in the manual office procedure and/or partially implemented computer systems. The actions (processes) on these forms can themselves be described using forms by specifying the effect (output) they have on forms. Therefore, to describe a process involves three parts.

1. A form heading that defines the form name, form structure, and its components.

2. A description of the data that constitutes the form, including statistical information (such as data types, data volume and value distribution) as well as integrity constraints on the data (such as value constraints, etc.).

3. A description of the operation that produces or modifies the form, including the type of operation (such as insert, delete, update, print, or query), the mode (online or batch), and frequency of the operation, as well as the cost-bearing characteristics of the operation such as the necessity of accessing more than one file to produce an output, testing for conditions, aggregation that requires accessing of many records, (e.g., sum, max, etc.), the need of sorting to meet the ordering or grouping requirements, and so on.

2.6.1.2 Data Specifications

Information about data can be captured using an intuitive notation associated with the form heading. Figure 2.22 specifies a data specification for the PRODUCT form. Underneath the form heading, there are clauses describing statistics and constraints. Below, we will describe the meaning of these clauses.

A *Key* denotes an item or collection of items whose value uniquely identifies an instance within a group. Thus, when applied to the top-level item(s) of a form, the value of the key uniquely identifies a form instance. When applied to the item(s) of a repeating group at lower level, it uniquely identifies an instance of the group under the parent instance.

In Figure 2.22, an "*" under PROD_NO in the KEY row specifies that PROD_NO is the unique identifier of PRODUCT form instances. The example also shows that for a given instance of PRODUCT, VNAME uniquely identifies an instance of SUPPLIER, while BIN_NO uniquely identifies an instance of STORAGE.

In each determinacy row, the item(s) marked with "*" determines the item(s) marked with "_>." In our PRODUCT form example, BIN_NO determines LOC. Therefore, given a bin number, location can be decided.

The *Occurrence* clause is used to provide data volume information. When applied to a top-level item, the specified number represents the number of instances in the file. When applied to an item in a repeating group, the specified number represents the

DESCRIPTION	PROD_NO	PNAME	TYPE	(SUPPLIER) VNAME	(STORAGE) BIN_NO	(STORAGE) LOC	PRICE
KEY	*			*	*		
UNIQUENESS	*				*		
DETERMINACY					*	➔	
OCCURRENCE	1000						
DATA TYPE	9(4)	X(6)	99	X(8)	99	XXX	9999v99
VALUE	10%(<100) 10%(>999)					SJC SFO	
NULL		*	*				
SET INCLUSION				VENDOR_INFO			
SET EXCLUSION	OUTDATED_PROD						
AUTHORITY LEVEL (WRITE)							>5

Figure 2.22 A data specification for the product form.

(PRODUCT)							
			(SUPPLIER)	(STORAGE)			
PROD_NO	PNAME	TYPE	VNAME	BIN_NO	LOC	PRICE	
SOURCE				——			
CONDITION	PROD_NO = ___						
FREQUENCY	5/DAY						
MODE	ON_LINE						

Figure 2.23 Augmenting the form heading with a process description.

average number of occurrences within a parent instance. The example in Figure 2.22 shows that there are 1000 occurrences of products, and there are, on the average, 16 instances of VNAME and 10 instances of BIN_NO for each occurrence of PRODUCT. For a more complete discussion on data specification in the forms approach, see Shu, Wong, and Lum (1983).

2.6.1.3 *Process Specifications*

To define a process, the first step is to formulate the form heading for the target (output) form. The form heading is then augmented with process descriptions. Figure 2.23 specifies a process that inserts a new instance of VNAME for a specified PROD_NO into the PRODUCT form. The clauses describing a process are: insert, delete,

	(ORDERLIST)					
		(ORDER)				
INSERT	CUST_NO				(PROD)	
		ORDER_NO	CADDRESS	DATE	PROD_NO	QTY
SOURCE	NEW ORDER FORM					
FREQUENCY	1000/DAY					
MODE	ON_LINE					

Figure 2.24 An example of how a source may be another form.

(INVOICE)						
PRINT	CNAME	CADDRESS	(ORDER)				TOTAL
			PROD_NO	QTY	PRICE	SUBTOTAL	
SOURCE	CUST_INFO FORM	PICKUP FORM	PICKUP FORM		PRODUCT FORM	QTY * PRICE	SUM (SUBTOTAL)
CONDITION	CUST_INFO.CUST_NO = PICK.CUST_NO AND PICKUP.PROD_NO = PRODUCT.PROD_NO						
FREQUENCY	1000/DAY						
MODE	ON_LINE						

Figure 2.25 An example of how a source may be an expression.

update, print, and query. The underscore under VNAME in the Source row represents an input to be supplied by the user.

The clause source specifies how or where to obtain the records relevant to the operation. A source could be another form that generates a list of orders from the existing form (Figure 2.24), several forms, as in a complex process that generates invoices (Figure 2.25), or a user's input (Figure 2.26).

The *condition* clause is to provide criteria for selecting instances out of a form. It is equivalent to the where clause of an SQL query. In Figure 2.25 it expresses the required relationship between the Cust_info, Pickup, and Product Forms.

(ORDERLIST)						
INSERT	CUST_NO	ORDER_NO	CADDRESS	DATE	(PROD)	
					PROD_NO	QTY
SOURCE	—	—	—	—	—	—
FREQUENCY	1000/DAY					
MODE	ON_LINE					

Figure 2.26 An example of how a source may be a user's input.

(VENDOR REPORT)				
PRINT	PROD_NO	(SUPPLIERS)		
		VNAME	ADDRESS	VPRICE
ORDER	DES	ASC		
NODUP		*	*	
SOURCE	VENDOR_INFO FORM			
MODE	OFF_LINE			
FREQUENCY	1 / 365 DAY			

Figure 2.27 Description of a process that generates a report.

The *order* clause appears in the example shown in Figure 2.27. Figure 2.27 describes a process that generates a report, (i.e., a new form named VENDOR_PRODUCT), using PRODUCT form as input. This report lists for each VNAME (of vendor), the group of products (in terms of PROD_NO, TYPE and PNAME) supplied by the particular vendor. The NODUP clause specifies that VNAME and CADDRESS should be unique for a given PROD_NO in the report.

Other process information is supplied by the environment. For instance, the process environment supplies information such as Mode (on-line or batch), execution frequency and time constraints (Response time). This information is important to establish priority of resource allocation for processes.

Note that the forms oriented application specifications capture information on data, processes, and constraints in a manner independent of the data model. Database schema design, however, by nature is highly dependent on the underlying data model. In the next section, we describe how the information presented in forms is translated into relational inputs: a relational schema, a set of processes in SQL syntax, and relevant statistics for performance tuning. These objects can be used to form a prototype quickly for demonstration and validation of requirements. In actual experience using this methodology, we found that a large part of the structure and programs can be used in the eventual production system of the application.

2.6.2 Generation of Relational Structures and Normalization

Given the collection of forms describing the application, a relational schema can be generated. There are guidelines in the relational theory for database design that govern the "well-formedness" of relation schema, the so-called normal forms. These normal forms are designed to prevent data duplication, inconsistency, and update anomalies.

Normalization is a step-by-step process for converting data structures into a standard form (relational tables). This standard form then satisfies the following constraints:

1. Each entry in a table represents one data item (no repeating groups).
2. All items within each column are of the same kind.
3. Each column has a unique name.
4. All rows are unique (no duplicates).
5. The order of viewing the rows and columns does not affect the semantics of any function using the table.

There are several types of normalization that differ in the extent to which the resulting standard table is constrained. Fifth normal form is the most restrictive, whereas first normal form is the least-constrained normal form. Only the first three normal forms will be discussed here, for a discussion on other less-common normal forms, refer to Date (1986).

2.6.2.1 *First Normal Form*

First normal form restricts the values in each record to be *atomic*. In other words, a table is in first normal form if there is no variable-length or repeating group in any of the fields of the table. A first normal form table always contains the same number of fields. All relational theory assumes that all tables are in first normal form. An example of removing a repeating group from a table is shown in Figure 2.22.

To derive a relational schema containing first normal form tables from the collection of forms discussed above, we can decompose the forms so that for each hierarchy branch of a form, a table is derived whose key is the concatenation of the keys of the ancestors in the branch. For example, in the form of PRODUCT above, the hierarchies of SUPPLIER and STORAGE will be "split" away to form two extra tables whose keys are respectively PROD_NO, VNAME and PROD_NO, BIN_NO. The keys from the ancestors are needed to form the table for each hierarchy in order to uniquely identify each member of the hierarchy. After the splitting, all fields remaining will be "nonrepeating" and they form a separate table.

The PRODUCT form above will produce the following tables:

```
PRODUCT(PROD_NO, PNAME, TYPE, PRICE)
SUPPLIER(PROD_NO, VNAME)
STORAGE(PROD_NO, BIN_NO, LOC)
```

All three tables are in first normal form.

2.6.2.2 *Second Normal Form*

Second normal form is violated when a field that is not part of a key is a fact of a subset of a key. For example, the table STORAGE above in addition to having

PROD_NO, BIN_NO as composite key, also has the property that given a BIN_NO alone, the LOC value is decided (refer to the Determinacy clause in the PRODUCT form). The basic problems with this record design of STORAGE, even though it is in first normal form, are

- The bin's location value is repeated in every record that refers to a product in that bin.
- If the bin's location changes, every record referring to a product stored in that bin needs to be updated.
- Data inconsistency might occur because data is redundantly stored due to the relationship between bins and their locations.
- If there are no products stored in a bin, there will be no place to keep the location of the bin.

To satisfy second normal form and to remedy the problems mentioned above, the table STORAGE should be decomposed into two tables

STORAGE(PROD_NO, BIN_NO)
LOCATION(BIN_NO, LOC)

which would then satisfy the second normal form definition.

2.6.2.3 Third Normal Form

Third normal form is violated when a non-key field is a fact about another non-key field. For example, suppose that table PRODUCT has the property that all products with the same type have the same price. The problems with this record design are the same as those when second normal form is violated.

- The price is repeated in the record of every product of the same type.
- If the price of a product type changes, every record referring to products of the type needs to change.
- Because of the redundancy of the relationship between types and prices, there might be inconsistency.
- If there is no product of a particular type, there will be no record to keep the price information for that type.

Similar to second normalization, the record PRODUCT should be decomposed into two tables.

PRODUCT(PROD_NO, PNAME, TYPE)
PRICES(TYPE, PRICE)

To summarize, a table is in second and third normal forms if every field is either part of the composite key or provides a nonrepeating fact about the whole key and nothing else.

2.6.3 Process Transformation

From the collection of form processes, we will give some guidelines to derive relational processes (in our case, SQL statements). We will first deal with flat-form processes and then move on to processes with hierarchies and processes with embedded aggregate functions.

2.6.3.1 Flat-Form Processes

The transformation observes the following mapping:

FORMSQL

UPDATE	*UPDATE*
INSERT	*INSERT*
DELETE	*DELETE*
PRINT/QUERY	*SELECT*
SOURCE	*FROM* clause
CONDITION	*WHERE* clause

For example, a process that finds products having PROD_NO > 500 and their prices might generate the following query.

select PROD_NO, PRICE
from PRODUCT
where PROD_NO > 500;

Only relation PRODUCT is needed in this case because PROD_NO and PRICE are contained in it. The process in Figure 2.28 (where the BIN_NO field has been added to the process referred to previously), on the other hand, involves a join operation in the following SQL query:

select PROD_NO, BIN_NO, PRICE
from PRODUCT, STORAGE
where PROD_NO > 500 AND
PRODUCT.PROD_NO = STORAGE.PROD_NO;

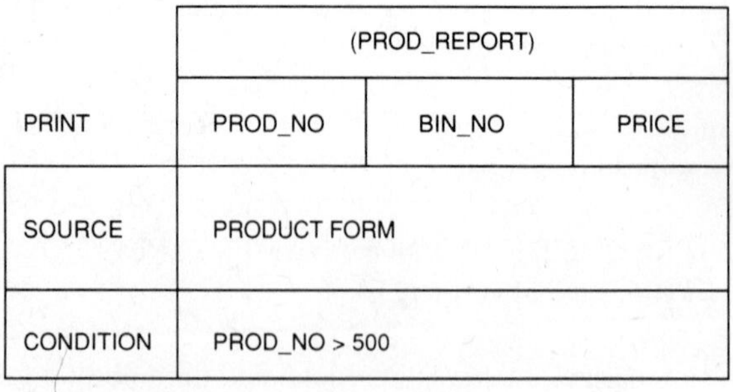

	(PROD_REPORT)		
PRINT	PROD_NO	BIN_NO	PRICE
SOURCE	PRODUCT FORM		
CONDITION	PROD_NO > 500		

Figure 2.28 A process involving a join operation.

The joining of PRODUCT and STORAGE is needed because the form PRODUCT has been decomposed into several relations and the items requested span more than one relation.

Updates on a form that is decomposed into several relations present no additional problems because of the straightforward decomposition scheme we employ. An example is the process that inserts an instance into the PRODUCT form. Depending on what is to be inserted, this may correspond to one or more SQL statements that insert into relations PRODUCT, SUPPLIER, STORAGE and LOC.

2.6.3.2 *Form Processes with Hierarchies*

We need the *order by* clause in SQL to produce the effect of a repeating group in forms. For each hierarchy branch in the form process, we derive a SQL statement with an *order by* clause that names the keys of the ancestors as the control fields. An example will illustrate the point. The VENDOR_PRODUCT process (see Figure 2.29) corresponds to the following SQL statement

> *select* VNAME, PROD_NO, TYPE, PNAME
> *from* PRODUCT, SUPPLIER
> *where* PRODUCT.PROD_NO = SUPPLIER.PROD_NO
> *order by* VNAME;

Suppose that the aggregate function MAX is used to find the maximum price that a vendor is charging. The following SQL statement would then be generated.

> *select* VNAME, MAX (PRICE)
> *from* PRODUCT, SUPPLIER
> *where* PRODUCT.PROD_NO = SUPPLIER.PROD_NO
> *group by* VNAME;

			VENDOR_PRODUCT		
PRINT		VNAME	(PROD)		
			PROD_NO	TYPE	PNAME
	SOURCE	PRODUCT FORM			
	FREQUENCY	1000/DAY			
	MODE	ON_LINE			

Figure 2.29 Producing the effect of a repeating group in a form.

2.6.3.3 *Form Processes with Aggregate Functions*

An aggregate function requires the *group by* operation to produce the desired effect. Consider the example shown in Figure 2.29. The aggregate function SUM in the TOTAL column has the semantics that for each unique CUST_NO, the value of the summation is produced. This requires the *group by* clause in SQL.

2.6.4 Statistical Transformation

Coupled with the decomposition scheme, statistical expressions can be derived quite easily. First, the clauses that are associated with columns on a form are applicable to columns of the derived relations. Among these clauses are VALUE, DATA TYPE and OCCURRENCE. For example, in the PRODUCT form, the distribution of PROD_NO value is specified. Ten percent of the PROD_NO value is less than 100, 10% is larger than 999, and the other 80% is assumed to have the remaining values. The distribution of PROD_NO value is propagated to PRODUCT, SUPPLIER, and STORAGE.

Second, from the OCCURRENCE clause in the form, the volume (i.e., number of tuples) of the relations can be derived by the following method. For each derived relation R corresponding to a hierarchy branch of a form, the volume of R is equal to the product of the values of the OCCURRENCE clause in the branch. The volume of PROD2 is 16000, for example, because PROD_NO has OCCURRENCE 1000 and VENDOR _NO has 16. The volumes of relations PROD1 and PROD3 are similarly derived.

RELATION	VOLUME
PRODUCT	1000
SUPPLIER	16000
STORAGE	10000

Statistics are vital for performance tuning, especially in the physical database design where indices and sorting order of records have to be decided.

First, the ordering requirement of storing the records can be decided from the most frequently executed processes. A process is considered to have an ordering requirement if there is an *order by, group by,* or *join* clause present. Ordering requirement of a table should be incorporated in favor of important processes, that is, those processes that are the most frequently executed and read, and that produce large results. The ordering requirement of other, less dominating processes can be satisfied by generating indices on the tables. Because of the presence of relevant statistics, the number and size of the indices can be estimated.

2.6.5 Normal Forms and Performance Tradeoff

For a very frequently performed join between two (or more) tables, it may be more efficient to duplicate the fields in the tables so that the join is not necessary. The consequence may be a violation of the normal forms that we discussed in the previous section. For example, in the following database:

PRODUCT(PROD_NO, PRICE)
ORDER(CUSTOMER, PROD_NO, QTY)

The second table describes the quantity that each customer orders. In order to generate an invoice, we need to pick up the price via a join between the tables on PROD_NO. If this is a frequently executed process, we may want to consider forming a table to replace ORDER.

ORDER'(CUSTOMER, PROD_NO, QTY, PRICE).

This new table is not normalized (not even in second normal form). As we recall, this introduces all kinds of update anomalies. But if the prices of products are very stable, then ORDER' is a perfectly acceptable table because of the savings of the join. In other words, there is a tradeoff between well-formedness and performance in database design. If the requirements are captured adequately, the database designer will have all the information necessary to make a reasonable tradeoff.

■ **2.7 WHEN IS A DBMS RELATIONAL?**

The relational model, backed by an extensive theoretical foundation, swept the computer science community during the 1970s, and led, during the late 1970s to the development of the first commercial products based upon the model. Because of its elegant, yet real-world appeal, the model has gained widespread user acceptance, and hence led to a rush among vendors to claim that their product is in some way "relational." In particular, some traditional vendors of DBMS products based upon network and inverted list models of data have implemented a few relational features to fend off competition from newer relational DBMS offerings.

In a related event, a collection of management information products whose origins lie in the file management and report generation system of the late 1960s came to the market under the name of *Fourth Generation Languages*. These products claim to make end-users into programmers and to improve application programmer productivity by orders of magnitude.

Concerned that the full power and implications of the relational approach were being watered down, Codd (1985) has offered 12 rules (13 with Rule 0, the foundational rule) defining what really constitutes a relational DBMS. This baker's dozen of rules forms a yardstick against which the "real" relational DBMS products can stand up and be counted.

The twelve rules are a helpful tool in database product evaluation. If a DBMS does not implement a significant fraction of the rules, it is probably not worth further examination on grounds of performance. If a particular DBMS scores poorly in implementing the rules, complete revision of applications is generally necessary because of the shaky foundation of the underlying data model.

Codd's rules have caused a great deal of controversy. Some have tried to argue that these rules are nothing more than an academic exercise. Some have tried to claim that their products already satisfy most, if not all, rules. The end result of the heated discussion that was generated by the rules is an increasing awareness within the user and vendor communities of the essential properties that a true relational DBMS should have. This has led the ANSI committee on SQL to add and expand on their initial standard to include many of the concerns contained in the rules discussed in this section.

The remainder of this section is organized as follows. We first discuss the twelve rules themselves, reorganized into functional classifications of

> Foundational rules
>
> Structural rules
>
> Integrity rules
>
> Data manipulation rules
>
> Date independence rules

This organization enables us to see the broad implication of each functional group. We then discuss the advantages of a DBMS observing the rules, followed by a consideration of how to use the rules to evaluate DBMS's, carefully explaining those areas where most existing DBMS products fail to implement one or more of the rules. Finally, we close with a discussion of the problem areas inherent in the so-called Fourth Generation Languages.

2.7.1 Foundational Rules (Rule 0 and Rule 12)

Rules 0 and 12 provide a litmus test to assess whether or not a system is a relational DBMS. If these rules are violated by any DBMS, that product should not be considered relational.

> *Rule Zero:* For any system that is advertised as, or claimed to be, a relational database management system, that system must be able to manage databases entirely through its relational capabilities.

This rule means that the DBMS should not have to resort to any nonrelational facilities to achieve any of its data management capabilities, including data definition, data manipulation, query, integrity, security, and performance enhancement. All the management capabilities of the system must be subsumed by its relational interface. The "relational interface" in this context means a set-at-a-time operational language, of which SQL is an example.

A number of so-called relational products can only achieve part of this rule (for example SIR/DBMS can only do queries with SQL, not updates or data dictionary manipulation) and hence would be rejected out of hand as inadequate.

This restriction is also reflected in the following rule:

> *Rule Twelve:* If a relational system has a low-level (single-record-at-a-time) language, that low level cannot be used to subvert or bypass the integrity rules and constraints expressed in the higher-level relational language.

This rule removes from consideration products that claim to have a relational interface but provide the user ("for performance reasons") with a pre-existing, low-level, record-at-a-time interface, trapping the user into the belief that such an interface will maintain the same integrity constraints imposed by the set-at-a-time relational interface. By going to the record-at-a-time interface, the integrity of the database can be compromised without the knowledge of either the user or the database administrator.

If such products cannot satisfy this auxiliary foundation rule, Codd says they are not truly relational, and should not be considered further in a product selection. Many network-based or hierarchical-based DBMSs offering a relational front-end typically fail to satisfy this rule.

2.7.2 Structural Rules (Rule 1 and Rule 6)

The fundamental structural concept of the relational model is the table. A relation is a two-dimensional table of values where the columns of the table are called attributes and the rows are called tuples. Classical data-processing terms are similar, substituting data elements for attributes, records for rows, and flat files for relations. In Codd's view, a relational database must support several structural features. The first is relations of degree n, that is tables with some arbitrary number n attributes, in which the ordering of rows or columns is not relevant to the model.

Tables are of four types.

> Base Tables
> Query Tables
> View Tables
> Snapshot Tables

Base tables are the actual data stored in the database, while *query tables* are the result of any query, which may at the user's option be saved in the database for further operation. (Note that a relational database is thus a mathematically closed system, i.e., all operations on relations in the database produce more relations.) *View tables* are the dynamic result of one or more relational commands operating on the base tables to produce another table, called the *view*. These are "virtual tables" that don't actually exist in the database (although their definitions are stored in the system catalog tables) but are produced upon request by a particular user, at the time of request.

Snapshot tables are the resultant evaluation of view table invocation frozen and materialized at any particular time, which are physically stored away into the database, together with a catalog entry specifying time of creation as well as accompanying descriptive information.

Another structural concept is the *domain,* which is the set of values from which individual columns (attributes) can be defined. The domain concept is important because it allows the user to define in a central place the meaning and source of values that attributes can take on. As a result, more information is available to the system when it undertakes the execution of a relational operation, and operations that are semantically meaningless can be excluded. An example of a nonsensical operation is a join between the weight of a ship and the age of a person.

Another fundamental structural concept is the key, which provides associative access to records (tuples) in a relation without specifying the actual method by which such access is physically accomplished. The primary key is a combination of attributes (fields) whose values uniquely address each record in a relation. There should be a primary key for each relation in the database. Most existing products do not support the primary key concept. DB2, for example, allows the user to create an index based upon the primary key idea, but thus implements a physical instantiation of access, compromising data independence (because application of programs have to refer to this specific index rather than a primary key independent of index).

A foreign key is an attribute in one relation (table) which can serve as a primary key into another table. Support for these key concepts allows for all the associativity of the network data model independent of implementation.

With these structural features identified, we can apply the following structural rules:

> *Rule One:* All information in a relational database is represented explicitly at the logical level and in exactly one way—by values in tables.

This rule, subtitled the *Information Rule,* asserts that all information, even system catalog information, must be storable as relations, manipulable by the same operational features as would be used to maintain data. Thus, all information on table names, column names, domain names, view definitions, security, and integrity constraints are stored in the system catalog as tables themselves.

> *Rule Six:* All views that are theoretically updateable are also updateable by the system.

This rule deals explicitly with view tables. It has been know for some time that updating view tables that depend upon multiple base tables can produce inconsistent results. This rule states that if a rule is theoretically updateable, then the DBMS should actually be able to perform the update. No system truly supports this feature, because conditions haven't been found yet to identify all theoretical updateable views. DB2 supports a tiny subset of theoretically updateable views. Even though certain views are clearly updateable, DB2 has no algorithms for recognizing such views.

2.7.3 Integrity Rules (Rule 3 and Rule 10)

Codd specifies two rules to address system capabilities to guarantee data integrity. In the view of most information managers, data integrity is of eminent importance in database management, and the more facilities that can be embedded in the DBMS product (rather than add-on products such as screen generators or data dictionaries), the better the guarantee of good data quality. There are three kinds of integrity.

> Entity Integrity
> Referential Integrity
> User-defined Integrity Constraints

Entity integrity guarantees the existence of a primary key for each record in a table. For example, if Social Security number is a primary key in a personnel record, there cannot be a record without a value for the Social Security number.

Referential integrity guarantees the existence of references to any foreign key. For example, if in a personnel record, the employee works in the payroll department, there must be a payroll department record in the table of departments.

User-defined integrity constraints are those specified by the users or database administrators of the database. For example, if a personnel ceiling of 20 employees has been placed upon the payroll department, then the user must be able to specify it and expect the DBMS to enforce it, such that a new employee cannot be added to the personnel file or the payroll department if the number of employees currently in the payroll department is 20. Another example might be that in an inventory file that contains information on uniforms in stock, the number of uniforms would not be allowed to go negative by any application that tracked issuance of uniforms.

> *Rule Ten:* Integrity constraints specific to a particular relational database must be definable in the relational data sublanguage and storable in the catalog, not in the application programs.

Codd makes a specific point that integrity constraints must be stored in the DBMS data catalog, rather than encapsulated in particular application programs or user interfaces.

Having the constraints stored in the DBMS catalog has the advantage of centralized control and enforcement. In the event of a constraint change (an example is the personnel ceiling on the payroll department is being lifted), the change and enforcement will be performed in the catalog, without having to rewrite any of the application programs. Also, because all constraints are stored only once, there will be no chance of having multiple versions of constraints, each enforced by different application programs. The insulation of application programs having to change in the event of the integrity constraints changing is referred to as *integrity independence*.

The situation is even worse with those systems not based upon the relational model in which user-defined integrity constraints are built into the database schema definition. Changing those constraints may require a complete reload of the entire database, as well as a rewrite of every application that interfaces to the old schema to conform to the new schema.

> *Rule Three:* Null values (distinct from the empty character string or a string of blank characters) are supported in fully relational DBMS for representing missing information and inapplicable information in a systematic way, independent of data type.

The concept that an attribute (field) may assume a null (nonexistent) value is essential to support the ideas of entity and referential integrity (e.g., the requirements that primary keys must be non-null), and various kinds of statistical analysis (for example a survey questionnaire where the respondent does not answer a particular question). Support for nulls must be a concept independent of attribute type.

For example, suppose you wish to obtain the average salary of all employees in a department and further suppose some of those salaries are null (either missing or possibly unavailable for privacy reasons). Do you treat these nulls as zero, or are you going to ignore the records will null values? Implementation of null handling in full generality will require the development of three-valued logic as a theoretical foundation.

2.7.4 Data Manipulation Rules

There are 18 manipulation features that an ideal relational DBMS should support. These features delineate the completeness of the query language (where, in this sense, query includes update, append, and insertion capabilities). These can be organized into *relational operators* and *set operations*. Some of these key operators were introduced earlier in Section 2.5.

The data manipulation rules guide the application of the 18 manipulative features.

> *Rule Five:* A relational system may support several languages and various modes of terminal use (for example, the fill-in-the-blanks mode). However, there must be at least one language whose statements are expressible, per some well-defined syntax, as character strings and that is comprehensive in supporting all of the following items:
>
> Date definition
> View definition
> Data manipulation (interactive and by program)

Integrity constraints

Authorization

Transaction boundaries (begin, commit, and rollback)

This rule requires that the query language used by the system must be high-level in the sense that it should be a set-at-a-time statements, as opposed to a single-record navigational language.

> *Rule Two:* Each and every datum (atomic value) in a relational database is guaranteed to be logically accessible by resorting to a combination of table name, primary key value, and column name.

This completeness rule guarantees that the query language allows the user to get to every single piece of data in the database. You cannot say that some part of the database cannot be touched by the query language.

> *Rule Seven:* The capability of handling a base relation or a derived relation as a single operand applies not only to the retrieval of data but also to the insertion, update, and deletion of data.

This also says that operations which change the contents of the database should also be set-at-a-time operations.

> *Rule Four:* The database description is presented at the logical level in the same way as ordinary data, so that authorized users can apply the same relational language to its interrogation as they apply to the regular data.

This rule specifies that there is not a different language for manipulating metadata as well as data, and moreover that there is only one logical structure (relations or tables) used to store system information for manipulation.

2.7.5 Data Independence

Codd provides three rules to specify the independence of data from the applications that use the data to accomplish tasks. In physical data independence, we have the important notion of separation of the physical storage and performance aspects from the logical structures of data that an application sees.

> *Rule Eight:* Application programs and terminal activities remain logically unimpaired whenever any changes are made in either storage representations or access methods.

If, for example, the database administrator decides to drop an index on a column in a table, computer programs that access that table should continue to run without recompilation or any modification whatsoever. In many non-relational systems, a change in physical structure brings to a halt the working of applications programs that operate on the data. Thus, database modifications on such systems to tune performance cause enormous overhead in requiring consequent application modification to adjust to the changes.

Adherence to this rule allows the database administrator full freedom to tune the performance of the relational DBMS and to rearrange the physical organization such as clustering tables or creating different kinds of indexes, different data sort orders, or relational tuples without affecting running applications. SQL achieves full physical database independence by specifically excluding access to low-level database structures.

2.7.6 Logical Data Independence

Logical data independence provides yet another level of insulation of application programs from the structuring of data. Under this concept, even the logical structure of the database may be altered, if done in such ways as to preserve all information, without affecting the running of applications. Key to this concept is the view structure which hides the logical structure alteration. For example, if two tables are combined without information loss, views can be defined which are projections of the combined table, leaving the appearance to the user (or application program) with the impression that no change has taken place.

> *Rule Nine:* Application programs and terminal activities remain logically unimpaired when information-preserving changes of any kind that theoretically permit unimpairment are made to the base tables.

2.7.7 Distribution Independence

Distribution independence means that an application program which accesses the DBMS on a single computer should also work without modification, even if the data is moved about from computer-to-computer, in a network environment.

> *Rule Eleven:* A relational DBMS has distribution independence.

In other words, the end-user should be given the illusion that the data is centralized on a single machine, and the responsibility of locating the data from (possibly) multiple sites and recomposing it should always reside with the system.

2.7.8 Advantages of Conforming to Strict Relational Criteria

Relational database management systems that play by the rules offer the following advantages:

1. A complete high-level query language that insulates the user and application programs from the physical and logical mechanisms that implement the data management capabilities.

2. The same language for data and metadata with all the benefits of the high-level query language, as well as greater flexibility in database restructuring.

3. Longevity of applications is achieved through the mechanisms supplied for data independence. Both users and developers are guaranteed against having to change running programs in the event of low-level reorganizations of the database.

4. Additional correctness of data is guaranteed through the mechanisms implementing integrity constraints.

5. Ease of distribution is achieved because neither the users nor the application programs need to know where the data is physically located.

■ 2.8 THE FUTURE OF RELATIONAL SYSTEMS

At present, the relational model of data is dominant in database technology. Although ongoing research in neural networks has interesting implications for databases in the future, the relational model appears to represent the existing state of the art. However, as we discuss in Chapters 3 through 5, the relational approach to databases should be combined with object-oriented, deductive, and hypermedia approaches.

Thus, there are four major forces having an impact on the future of database systems:

> integration with expert systems
> object orientation
> hypermedia technology
> distributed-database technology

The impact of three of these technologies on database systems are considered in later chapters. Consequently, we concentrate here on the fourth issue of distributed databases.

2.8.1 Distributed Databases

In this section we will address some of the major problems that must be solved during the process of designing a Distributed Database Management System (DDBMS) that make it different from a simple collection of local databases or a distributed implementation of a centralized database. First, a definition adapted from Cerri and Pellagatti (1984).

> A distributed database system is a collection of data which is distributed across many computers possibly at different sites. The computers are connected by a communication network. The system must support local applications at each computer as well as global applications in which more than one computer is involved.

As in the case of a centralized system, the purpose of a DDBMS is to let users specify high-level queries stating what they want rather than how they want to get it. The user must be shielded to the maximum extent possible from the effects of distribution so that he may operate under the impression that he is using a single centralized database.

Examples of some transparencies we would like to have are

> *Location transparencies*—After a user presents a query to the system, the system must determine an efficient strategy for obtaining the data from various sites and combining them to answer the query.

> *Fragmentation transparencies*—Data may be stored in a fragmented way, for example, records in the file may be stored in multiple locations in the distributed network. The user need not be aware that the fragmentation occurs when using the system.

> *Transaction transparencies*—The users must be protected from side effects of interference between their own transactions and other transactions currently in the system.

> *Failure transparency*—Site or communication-link failures should affect only applications that currently use these resources and should be transparent to all other applications in the system.

Below we will present some examples illustrating the concept behind some of these transparencies.

Suppose that we have three sites in our network. The table SUPPLIER is fragmented into three relations SUPP1, SUPP2, and SUPP3, and they are stored in Site 1, Site 2, and Site 3 respectively. Suppose that we want to retrieve the name of a supplier whose supplier number is 1234. If the database system allows us to use the following query to retrieve the answer, then fragmentation transparency is achieved.

> *Select* NAME
> *from* SUPPLIER
> *where* SNUM = 1234;

The reason is the fact that the user needs not be concerned that SUPPLIER is fragmented into three separate relations.

If, on the other hand, we have to use the following interaction

> *Select Name* NAME
> *from* SUPP1
> *where* SNUM = 1234;
>
> if not #found

Select NAME
from SUPP2
Where SNUM = 1234

if not #found

Select NAME
from SUPP2
Where SNUM = 1234;

then fragmentation transparency is not achieved, but location transparency is present because the user does not have to specify the location of the tables.

In order to achieve high degree of transparency, the system must automatically record and maintain information about the location of the data in the database, status of transactions, failure of different sites and communication links in the network optimization algorithms, protocols for ensuring transaction atomicity property, commit and recovery mechanisms, and so on. In the remainder of this section, we will state in more detail important design issues that will affect the degree to which a system can support all the above requirements.

Site Autonomy—Most distributed database designers agree that each site should maintain local privacy and control of its own data. The question is whether to allow some central dependencies in the network such as central catalogs, central scheduler, central deadlock detector, and so on. The answer to this question in System R* is definitely negative. That means that local applications in a given site are not affected by any external factors to that site.

Support of fragmentation and transparency level—We assume that the data is stored as tables (relations). Different fragmentations among the sites such as vertical, horizontal or combination are possible. Data also may be replicated or dispersed.

The reason for fragmentation and replications may be external such as geographical and organizational constraints or as a result of some data distribution strategy to enhance performance. If all this must be supported, we have to decide about the degree of fragmentation transparency to the user. Based on that decision, code must be written for data consistency, reassembly of relations and access of remote data. We assume only homogeneous databases at this stage. Allowing heterogeneous databases will, of course, introduce many more complications at all levels of the design ᴄ mappings between different data models and languages must be provided.

Object naming and distributed catalogues—Object naming must ensure unique system names without restricting user choice of names.

This seems a relatively simple issue and there are various ways of handling it. The approach in System R* is that the catalog itself is a relation therefore it can be fragmented and replicated just as any other relation. Ingres distinguishes between global and local relations. For the former type, a global catalog is maintained restricting site autonomy (this seems to be the case also in SDD1). System R* uses a distributed catalog implementing a primary site principle for each object. As the catalog is used later on in the compilation process of queries its structure and maintenance can affect performance significantly.

> *Query execution and optimization*—This is a very large topic as dozens of research papers have been written on it. Basically it involves global and local optimization plans, selection of access paths, etc.

There are two major additional features that add to the complexity of query processing in a distributed database system as compared to a centralized one. The first is that cost of communication between different sites must be taken into account in developing a query execution plan. The second is that the opportunity for parallelism of execution in multiple sites must be taken into account in developing an overall strategy. The objective of the optimizer is to minimize response time to the query, which consists of transmission time between sites and local processing.

There are many different approaches in the literature to find an optimal or a close to optimal strategy. The idea behind most of these algorithms is to decompose the query into a sequence of serial and parallel operations that yield the correct result. This decomposition can be represented as a query tree. Typically, there are many different ways in which a feasible query tree can be constructed from a given query.

The next step consists of grouping together operations that can be performed on the same site and constructing a query processing graph in which each node represents the execution of a group of operations at a single site and arcs represent transmission of information from one site to the other. Again, many different alternatives are possible at this stage and their cost must be evaluated using some exact or estimated information about transmission costs, sizes of base relations and intermediate results, and various selectivity factors.

In general, the number of possible alternatives is too large to permit exhaustive evaluation. For that reason, it is important to have heuristics that eliminate some bad alternatives from consideration as early as possible during the optimization process. Mathematical programming techniques such as dynamic programming and branch-and-bound methods are used for that purpose.

Another source of complexity in the design of efficient query-processing strategies arises because of the dynamic nature of a distributed system. Each local processor has its own workload to deal with in addition to processing multisite queries. This workload, which varies with time, may affect the time for local processing of a subquery. Also, statistics that are used for devising a query plan, such as transmission costs, may vary with time as a result of patterns of traffic and bottlenecks in the network. In some recent research papers, there has been an attempt to incorporate these dynamic elements in the query optimizer.

The above discussion also relates to whether queries embedded in some kind of host language should be precompiled or interpreted. Compilation has a great performance advantage with respect to queries that are repetitively executed. A potential problem with this is that optimal query execution plans may change because of a change in location or characteristics of the data involved.

The following example illustrates the importance of a good query optimizer in a distributed database environment. Suppose we have the following tables:

> S(s#,city) - 10,000 tuples stored at site A
> P(p#, color) - 100,000 tuples stored at site B
> SP(s#, p#) - 1,000,000 tuples stored at site A

For the query "get all supplier numbers for Suppliers in London who supply red parts," the following SQL query is needed:

> select S.S#
> from S,SP,P
> where S.city = "London"
> and S.s# = SP.s#
> and SP.p# = P.p#
> and P.color = "red"

Assume the following statistical distributions:

1. Number of red parts = 10.
2. Number of shipments of London Suppliers = 100,000.
3. Data rate = 10,000 bits per second.
4. Access delay = 1 second per message.
5. Total time = number of messages + number of bits/10000.

The following is a list of possible strategies of retrieval by a distributed database system and their estimated processing time given the above assumptions:

I. Move P to A and process at A.
time taken = 16.7 minutes.

II. Move S and SP to B and process at B.
time = 2.8 hours.

III. Join S and SP at A, select from the results for which city is London. For each, check if part is red at site B.
time = 2.3 days.

IV. Select parts that are red from P at site B; for each of these check site A to see whether there is a related London shipment.
time = 20 seconds.

V. Select red parts from P in B, ship this to A, and complete processing there.
Total time = 1 second.

This example demonstrates the dramatic performance difference a query optimizer can make to the same query in a distributed database.

Transaction management protocols—These protocols must be provided by the system to ensure that a distributed transaction either commits or aborts at all sites visited by the transaction.

In general, protocols for logging, recovery, commit, deadlock detection, and prevention are all needed.

Support of views and snapshots—This issue also exists in nondistributed databases, only that now view component objects may be in different sites. Again, issues similar to query processing are involved here in querying and maintaining the view. A snapshot is a relation that is a copy of another relation but it is not necessarily up-to-date.

System R* supports snapshot maintenance (refresh) and queries against snapshots. Performance is enhanced for queries that do not require a totally up-to-date database.

■ 2.9 SUMMARY

One of the early evolutionary steps in computing technology was the clear separation between programs and data. In this chapter, we have reviewed some of the steps by which early views of data as disconnected numbers and strings of text have developed into sophisticated database management issues. In this chapter, we have touched on a few of the most important issues pertaining to database systems. Yet, in spite of the impact of the relational database model, database systems continue to evolve. In Chapter 3, we will consider a new philosophy and implementation for storing information and data, that is, object-oriented databases. We would like to stress, however, that the development of object-oriented systems does not invalidate the relational database approach that has proven its validity over a number of years. Instead, the object-oriented approach supplements the relational approach, and well-designed object-oriented systems may be integrated with more conventional relational databases.

This theme of integrating relational databases with newer technologies continues in Sections 4.5 and 4.6 when we consider how relational databases may be integrated into expert system environments, so that the relational data from an external relational database can be effectively imported into the knowledge base of an expert system. However, we now turn to object-oriented systems that will provide another essential element in the intelligent database technology.

3

OBJECT ORIENTATION

■ 3.1 INTRODUCTION

In Chapter 1 we summarized some of the main properties of intelligent databases. In Chapter 2 we traced the history of database data models and demonstrated that the general direction in data model design today is towards higher level, more declarative, more expressive primitives. We gave particular emphasis to the main features of the relational model.

One fundamental feature of an intelligent database is that the user is provided with an abstract data model of the database that closely resembles the user's model of the real world. In this chapter we introduce, explain, and illustrate the elements of object orientation and object-oriented databases.

We first discuss the fundamental concepts of object orientation. Section 3.3 introduces the notion of abstract data typing or encapsulation; Section 3.4 explains inheritance; and Section 3.5 elucidates object identity. When these concepts are coupled with persistency and transaction support, the result is extremely powerful systems referred to as object-oriented databases. An object is said to persist after program activation and termination if the object remains accessible in subsequent programs. For example, files accessed and manipulated within programs usually remain accessible after the program terminates. The program might read or modify some elements in the file, but the file itself is a persistent object. Transactions are programs that are executed atomically (i.e., in their entirety or not at all). Transactions manipulate persistent object spaces. Classical transactions include debit and credit in banks, which everyone is familiar with. Object-oriented databases are described in Section 3.6.

Section 3.7 presents three main applications of object orientation in addition to knowledge representation; discrete-event simulation, design engineering, and software engineering. However, to begin with, we trace back the history of object-oriented databases by reviewing the evolution of object orientation.

3.1.1 The History and Evolution of Object Orientation

Since the introduction of digital computers, programmers have been searching for higher-level languages. The roots of object-oriented programming can be traced back to the gradual attempts of programming language designers to develop language constructs, disciplines, and programming philosophies that would help write software more quickly, either by individual programmers or programming teams, and would help maintain software after it had been written.

In the late 1950s one of the problems that had existed in developing large FORTRAN programs was that variable names would conflict in different parts of a program. Thus, the designers of the language Algol decided to provide "barriers" to separate variable names within program segments. This gave birth to the Begin . . . End *blocks* in Algol 60. Since the variable names appearing within a block are local, their use will not conflict with the use of the same variable name elsewhere in the program. This was thus a first attempt at providing protection or *encapsulation* within a programming language. Block structures are now widely used in a variety of languages such as C, Pascal, and Ada.

In the early 1960s the designers of the language Simula-67 (Dahl and Nygaard, 1966; Dahl, Myhrhaug and Nygaard, 1970) took the block concept of Algol one step further and introduced the concept of an *object*. Although Simula's roots were in Algol, it was mainly intended as a simulation language. Thus, Simula objects had "an existence of their own" and can in some sense communicate with each other during a simulation. This was the beginning of the use of *data encapsulation* within programming languages (see Section 3.7.1 for more on Simula). In retrospect, if the Simula compiler had had better "marketing," it could have become a more widespread language and would have introduced the concept of data abstraction. However, in the late 1960s the $20,000 price tag for the Simula compiler was perhaps too high.

In the early 1970s the concept of data abstraction was pursued by a number of language designers, with a view to managing large programs (Parnas 1972). Languages such as Alphard (Wulf, London and Shaw, 1976) began to use data abstraction. On another, more visual programming front, the language Smalltalk began to use objects, classes, and inheritance of properties (Kay, 1977).

At the same time, a good deal of the foundational and mathematical theory for *abstract data types* began to be developed. This helped establish the concept of abstract data types by providing a rigorous mathematical basis for using object orientation (Goguen, Thatcher, Wegner and Wright, 1975; Guttag, 1977; Burstall and Goguen, 1977). This theory was then developed further for applications to specifications (Ehrig, Kreowski and Padawiz 1978), and for higher order abstract data types (Parsaye, 1982). These extensions to the theory provide a solid foundation for data abstraction.

Similarly, the concept of data abstraction and inheritance within database languages was emerging with languages such as Taxis (Mylopoulos and Wong 1980). This also provided a bridge to the emerging concept of "inheritance" which had been popular in artificial intelligence programs based on the early work on semantic nets (Quillian, 1968; Norman and Rumelhart, 1975) and frames (Minsky, 1975).

In the early 1980s these concepts began to merge together towards a uniform concept structure for encapsulating data, inheriting properties and having active data elements. In fact Rentsch (1982) predicted that "object-oriented programming will be in the 1980's what structured programming was in the 1970's. . . ."

In 1986 OOPSLA (Object-Oriented Programming Systems and Languages) became the first major conference entirely dedicated to object orientation. Additionally, in the past few years several object-oriented languages such as C + + (Stroustrup, 1986), Objective-C (Cox, 1986), Smalltalk-80 (Goldberg and Robson, 1983), as well as object-oriented databases such as GemStone (Maier and Stein, 1986), became commercially available. Several major computer companies started pursuing object-oriented styles of programming for developing their own software. A notable example is the decision to use C + + by the joint distributed workstation venture of SUN micro-systems and AT&T. Other companies are attempting to extend their existing platforms and languages with object orientation. An interesting example here is the commitment of Microsoft to extend BASIC with object-oriented constructs.

■ 3.2 INTRODUCTION TO OBJECT ORIENTATION

In recent years, we have seen significant changes and evolution in software engineering as a whole. Some of these changes were caused by significant improvements in the bandwidth of computation, as well as by the proliferation of affordable high capacity primary and secondary storage systems. High-speed, high-capacity systems enabled the development of more sophisticated and advanced CPU, and space-intensive software systems and applications.

However, software engineering as a whole and data modeling more specifically have also progressed as self-contained disciplines. Although some of these changes were due to the availability of high-performance hardware components, software engineering science is starting to acquire its own characteristics and is progressing at a rapid pace. In fact, we are seeing more and more decoupling of the hardware and software components of computation. The support of the same language, operating system, or application on different platforms is a simple example of this.

In fact, we have identified four areas in database data modeling and programming in general that have progressed towards more expressive paradigms.

1. *Representation of the Object Space.* Database data models such as IMS, CODASYL, and SQL allow the direct representation and manipulation of certain types of objects. For example, in IMS one manipulates trees. In CODASYL,

the object space is a directed acyclic graph. In SQL, the object space consists of a collection of *flat* (normalized) tables. Needless to say, the most general structure is an arbitrary graph, which could include cycles. Some more recent database data models and languages such as FAD (Bancilhon et al., 1987) have this general capability to model and access arbitrary graph structured object spaces.

2. *Declarative vs Navigational.* One basic difference between IMS and CODA-SYL on one hand and SQL is that the former database languages are *navigational*. SQL on the other hand is more *declarative*. In other words, in SQL the user specifies what he wants from the database in a high-level declarative style of programming. In contrast, in IMS and CODASYL, the user opens a database and scans its contents record-by-record. Both styles of database programming are useful. In some applications, it is more natural to scan and navigate through the database than to ask declarative queries. However, the trend is to have more power in the declarative style and more generality in the navigational style of programming. For example, SQL is not expressive enough to evaluate the transitive closure of a relation. It is less powerful than, say, predicate calculus. In Chapter 4, we demonstrate the power and flexibility of a query language that incorporates logic programming.

3. *Abstraction and Modularization.* Another trend both in database languages and programming in general is towards modularization and abstraction. Even the SQL standard (ANSI) is trying to incorporate the notion of *modules* to generate independent compilation units and provide better abstraction than embedded SQL statements (i.e., SQL embedded in a programming language such as Pascal, C, or Ada). The main concept behind the notion of modules in Modula (Wirth, 1984) or packages in Ada (Buzzard and Mudge, 1985) is the idea of abstract data typing, where the language allows the separation of an interface to the outside world and an internal implementation. This allows better reusability and extensibility.

4. *Inheritance.* The understanding that inheritance is useful in organizing information has been around for some time, especially in semantic networks (Minsky, 1968). Similarly, in database data modeling, semantic models incorporate the same notion. More recently, inheritance has also been used to share code among computation units (modules). The trend is to use inheritance both to organize an object space and share and reuse code.

As we shall see, object orientation contributes to (1), (3), and (4). In Chapter 4, we shall discuss the declarative style of programming in more detail.

3.2.1 What Is Object Orientation?

Despite its popularity, there is a certain amount of confusion and controversy regarding the overloaded term *object oriented*. Several attempts from both the programming language and database side have been made to define, and categorize object orientation (Wegner, 1987; Cox, 1984; Diettrich, 1986).

In this chapter, we present a particular characterization of object orientation. The emphasis in characterizing object orientation will be through what we believe to be the three most fundamental aspects of this paradigm: abstract data typing (encapsulation), inheritance, and object identity.

These concepts will be explained in much detail in subsequent sections. Here, we use a simple example from production factories to illustrate these three elements. Assume a factory produces a number of items with common subparts. Consider Figure 3.1, where a hierarchy of Ford Mustang models including base, LX, and GT models is illustrated. A car model has typically several submodels that have common features and subparts with the base model. Also, each car model has a dashboard. The switch gear on the dashboard together with the pedals constitute the interface to the car. Each car model has a particular collection of switch gear depending on model, year, luxury items (e.g., air conditioning), and so on. To drive the car, the driver needs to interact only with the switch gear and the pedals. In fact, the operation of the car does not in-

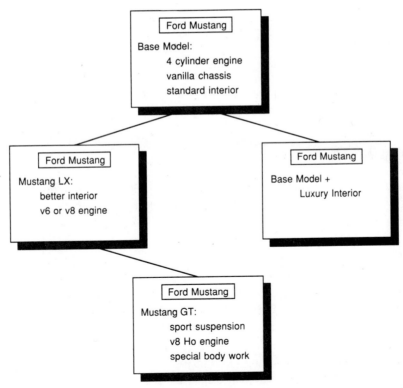

Figure 3.1 A hierarchy of Ford Mustang models.

volve any knowledge of interior engineering design or structure. This basically captures the notion of abstract data typing or encapsulation. A language supporting abstract data typing will allow the instances of the data type to be manipulated only through a prescribed collection associated with the type.

This example also shows a hierarchy of Ford Mustang models. The LX for example, "inherits" most of the features and subparts of the base model, but "specializes" the interior and parts of the engine. Similarly, the GT inherits for the LX but has a better interior and engine. This is the essence of inheritance hierarchies, where object types inherit most of their attributes from generic or less-specialized types.

Each car consists of subparts: an engine and a body. The engine itself consists of (is a composite of) a steering system, a propulsion system, and a braking system. The subparts are attached to each other through wires and other hardware. For example, the chassis is shared and accessed by the front and rear suspension systems. Thus, the conceptualization of the car is a graph where subparts are accessed or referenced by other subparts. In object-oriented languages, this graph-structured object-space representation is made possible through the notion of object identity.

In addition, numerous concepts and constructs associated with object orientation will be discussed below. We shall elucidate these concepts through several illustrative examples. However, we encourage our readers to concentrate on the explanation of these concepts rather than the taxonomy itself.

More importantly, we believe these features (encapsulation, object identity, and inheritance) provide the essential building blocks for modeling intelligent databases. As demonstrated in subsequent chapters (Chapters 4, 5, and 6), the inference and hypermedia capabilities of intelligent databases are mapped onto object-oriented data spaces.

3.2.2 Model of Reality

Why has object orientation become so popular? The intuitive appeal of object orientation is that it provides better concepts and tools to model and represent the real world as closely as possible. The advantages of this direct representation capability in programming and data modeling are obvious. As pointed out by Ledbetter and Cox (1985),

> object (oriented) programming allows a more direct representation of the real-world model in the code. The result is that the normal radical transformation from system requirements (defined in user's terms) to system specification (defined in computer terms) is greatly reduced.

Figure 3.2 illustrates this. Using conventional techniques, the code generated for a real-world problem consists of the encoding of the problem and the transformation to express the problem in terms of a Von Neumann computer language. Following object-oriented disciplines and techniques, the bulk of the code just encodes the problem and the transformation is minimized. In fact, when compared to more conventional (procedural) styles of programming, code reductions ranging from 40 to 90 percent

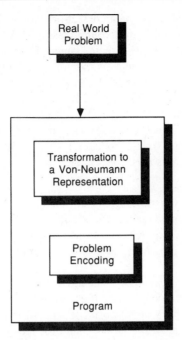

Figure 3.2 The process of converting real world problems into program coding.

have been reported for a number of problems, after adopting an object-oriented style of programming.

As far as the representation of the object space is concerned, the goal of knowledge representation in AI and database data modeling is exactly the same. In Chapter 2, we described the evolution of database data models incorporating increasingly semantically rich constructs to model the real world. In AI, the popular frame-based representations (Minsky, 1975), as discussed in Chapter 4, are very similar in structure and organization to the object spaces in object-oriented languages such as Smalltalk-80. However, while AI and database data models provide powerful and expressive representations for the data in the universe of discourse, object-oriented languages provide, in addition, expressive programming or manipulation primitives.

The nodes and links of hypermedia documents can also be easily mapped onto graph-structured-object spaces. In addition, the "actions" associated with links or nodes of hypermedia documents can be associated with object-oriented node and link types (classes). Thus object-oriented models provide a natural representation for hypermedia systems (discussed in Chapter 5).

Another aspect of the real world that is at least theoretically captured in an object-oriented model is concurrency. For example, in an office environment secretaries, managers, and other employees function concurrently and independently. They communicate with each other through conversations, memos, electronic mail messages, and so on. Similarly in an object-oriented model of the world, everything is an active object communicating through messages. We used the word "theoretically" because although some object-oriented languages such as Smalltalk-80 use terms such as "messages" to describe the activation of a method by the object, the underlying semantics and execution model of the language is purely sequential and these messages are nothing but procedure calls. However, there have been some attempts to incorporate parallelism and to design concurrent object-oriented languages (Agha and Hewitt, 1987; Yonezewa et al., 1987), which provide parallel models for dynamic object manipulations. In Section 3.7.1, we describe one such concurrent object-oriented language that is used for discrete-event simulation.

3.2.3 Approaches to Object-Oriented Programming

It is important to realize that one does not need an object-oriented language (concurrent or otherwise) to have an object-oriented program! In fact, object orientation is permeating programming in general through three different approaches.

1. *Novel Languages.* The most radical approach is the introduction of entirely new object-oriented languages. The most popular example is Smalltalk, which takes a uniform approach in treating all data in a program as *objects*. Much of the hoopla, of the newly found (or rather, rejuvenated) object-oriented "religion" is due to the Smalltalk culture. Other examples include Eiffel (Meyer, 1988) and Trellis/Owl (Shaffert et al., 1986).

2. *Language Extensions.* A less controversial approach is to extend an existing popular language by adding object-oriented capabilities. C++ and Objective-C, as well as lesser-known extensions such as Object Pascal and Flavors, are examples of this approach. The advantages of extending an existing language are many.

   a. Many users will be familiar with the syntax of the language and would feel more comfortable using it.
   b. All the tools, such as editors and libraries, developed for the underlying language become accessible or extensible for the extended language.
   c. Linking new code developed with the extended language with existing code for the underlying language is rather straightforward.

As indicated earlier, the main disadvantage of this approach is that if the extended language is fully compatible with the underlying base language, then "hackers" in the base language will ignore the object-oriented principles to use it as the conventional language. Thus, some programmers will ignore, say, the encapsulation provided by C++ and continue to use their programming skills with the basic functionality provided by C: casting, pointer chasing, function parameters. However, some of these low-level (bit-wise) data manipulation skills have to be abandoned to make good use of the semantically rich extended languages. Avoiding these well-practised techniques a familiar context could in be harder than learning an entirely new language that enforces disciplined programming.

3. *Object-oriented Style.* This brings us to the third approach, namely, that the object-oriented style of programming is above all a discipline. Hence, it is perfectly feasible to do some object-oriented style of programming in a conventional language such as C (or even in an assembly language!). For example, for each structure or record type defined in the conventional language, enforce the discipline that all manipulations of instances of the structure or record type be done through a pre-defined collection of functions associated with the type, and never directly. Other "hacks" could be used to simulate inheritance and identity. It should be emphasized, though, that an object-oriented language facilitates the enforcement of the object-oriented style and discipline.

▪ 3.3 ABSTRACT DATA TYPES

One of the most important features of object orientation is the support of abstract data types, which define sets of similar objects with an associated collection of operators. A language supporting abstract data types must satisfy the following:

1. *Object Classes.* Every datum (object) must be the element of an abstract data type (the object's class).

2. *Information Hiding.* Furthermore an object is accessed and modified only through the external interface routines and operations defined for its abstract data type. The internal implementation details, data structures, and storage elements used to implement the objects of an abstract data type and its operations are not visible to the clients accessing and manipulating the objects.

Similar to many conventional programming languages, the built-in types of the language (e.g., integers, characters, etc.) also satisfy the following:

3. *Completeness.* The operations associated with an abstract data type correctly and fully define the behavior of the abstract data type as intended by the programmer.

In fact, (1) and (2) will be enforced if the language supports abstract data typing. The principle of completeness is impossible to enforce and is left to the user.

The contrast between conventional systems and object-oriented systems using abstract data typing is illustrated in Figure 3.3. In conventional languages, programs are collections of procedures or subroutines that pass parameters. Each procedure manipulates its parameters, sometimes updating them, and possibly returns a value. Thus, the execution units (i.e., the procedures) are central.

In object-oriented systems the universe is viewed as a collection of independent objects

CONVENTIONAL

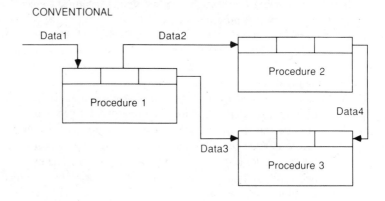

ENCAPSULATION

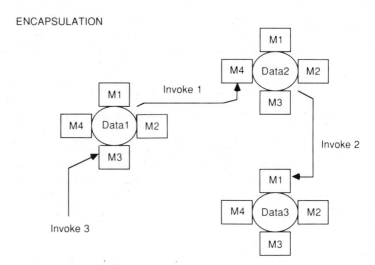

Figure 3.3 Conventional and object-oriented systems.

that communicate with each other through procedures, often called *messages* in the object-oriented jargon. In fact as we said earlier, the objects are the active entities and the procedures (messages) are passive entities that together with their arguments, are passed from one object to another. An object investigates the requests (i.e., procedures or messages) presented to it and acts upon them. Thus, the data (i.e., the objects) are central.

The information-hiding feature of abstract data typing means that objects have *public* interfaces and *private* (hidden) representations and implementations of their interfaces. The basic idea of this type of abstraction is rather simple. Consider a base type such as integer in a conventional programming language like C or Pascal. The language provides a finite number of operations such as +, *, and − that represent addition, multiplication, and subtraction operators of integers. Some additional operations are *remainder* and *quotient*, which, respectively evaluate the remainder and quotient of integer division (for example, 15 remainder 4 is 3, 15 quotient 7 is 1). These operators have well-defined associative, commutative, and distributive properties, which fully define the behavior of integer objects. Most sane users simply invoke these operators to manipulate integers (although some "lower-level" languages like C allow the bitwise manipulation of base types). In fact, in some languages such as Pascal, these are the only operations that are permitted on objects that are of type integers. Furthermore, the internal bit-string representation of an integer (e.g., using 32-bit two's complement) is completely hidden. Programs manipulating integers can easily be ported and compiled on systems using entirely different internal representations for integers. This is illustrated in Figure 3.4.

A language incorporating abstract data types extends these notions to every object or datum in a program. The abstraction mechanism that enforces the access and update of objects with user-defined types is encapsulated and hence can only be performed

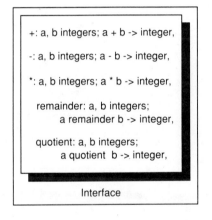

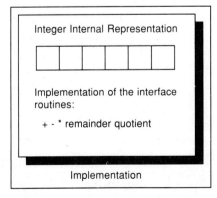

Figure 3.4 Class for manipulating integers.

through the interface operations defined for the particular type. Contrast this with conventional programming languages like C or Pascal where, for example, a set of integers defined through

```
type SetOfIntegers  =  ^ListElem;
        ListElem  =  record
                        Element:integer;
                        Next: ListElem
                end;
```

can be manipulated by any function or procedure within the scope of the record's type. In other words, we can traverse an object that is a SetOfIntegers as a list, and we can directly retrieve or update one of its elements. This is illustrated in Figure 3.5 where the function Find traverses the linked list to see if a given element is in the linked list. If the representation of a set of integers is changed (for example implemented through an array of integers), the function Find and all other functions that depend on the data structures used to manipulate the object type have to be modified.

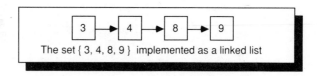

The set { 3, 4, 8, 9 } implemented as a linked list

```
Procedure Find:     (X: integer, L: SetOfIntegers)

            /* returns true if and only if X is in L */



begin

            while L is not Nil do
            begin
                    if X  = L^.Element
                            return True
                    else L := L^.Next
            end /* while */
end /* find */
```

Figure 3.5 List representation and traversal.

With abstract data typing, a number of set operations will be defined for sets and manipulations of sets will be done only through these "external" operations. These operations will (hopefully) completely capture the behavior of sets of integers. Internally, a set of integers can be stored and implemented as a linked list of records as indicated, or as an array of integers, or by any other representation. As far as the users of sets of integers are concerned, it will make absolutely no difference. Thus a function, such as Find, that depends on the internal representation of sets will either be part of the interface of the abstract data types, or invoke operators on the object to perform particular tasks (e.g., get the next element).

3.3.1 Classes

The most commonly used language construct to define abstract data types in most object-oriented programming languages is the *class*, which incorporates the definition of the structure as well as the operations of the abstract data type. Thus, a class defines an abstract data type and elements pertaining to the collection of objects described by a class are called *instances* of the class. This is illustrated in Figure 3.6 for the class representing companies. The notions of instance variables and methods are discussed and explained in more detail in Sections 3.3.1.1 and 3.3.1.3 respectively.

Figure 3.7 shows a number of instances for this class: IBM, AT&T, and so on. In Figure 3.6, we have a description of the class. In other words, each object that is an instance of the class company will be manipulated only through the given set of operators that constitute their interface. This will be further clarified in subsequent sections.

A class definition (minimally) includes the following:

  a. The name of the class.
  b. The external operations for manipulating the instances of the class. (These operators typically have a target object and a number of arguments.)
  c. The internal representation.
  d. The internal implementation of the interface.

We assume an implicit target object to which the operator applies. The target object is explained in more detail in Section 3.3.1.3. Intuitively it is the "recipient" of the message or operator. In other words, each invocation of an operator applies to one and only one instance of the class. That instance is the target. For this example it will be one of the companies: IBM or AT&T or DEC. Here are the descriptions of some of the operators of Company.

  1. Name: *Get Profit*
     Result: The company's profit for the current fiscal year.
  2. Name: *Get Subsidiaries*
     Result: Returns the set of all the subsidiaries of the target parent company.

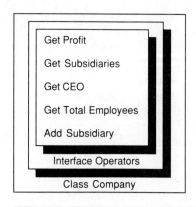

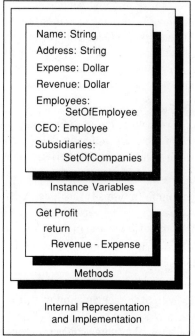

Figure 3.6 Company represented as a class.

3. Name: *Add Subsidiary*

Argument: An instance of Company that is to be made a new subsidiary of the target parent company.

Effect: Inserts the argument in the current set of subsidiaries of the target parent company.

Other elements of the class Company include:

4. *The internal representation:* Name, Address, Expense, Revenue, Employees, CEO, and so on.

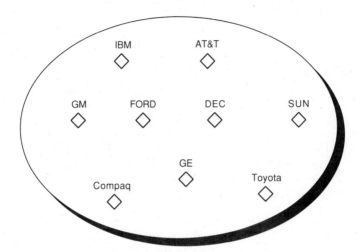

Figure 3.7 Some instances of Class Company.

5. *The internal implementation:* As we shall see in the next two sections, the operators are implemented by retrieving values and updating the variables of the internal representation (these are called *instance* variables as discussed in Section 3.3.1.1).

Thus, a class contains descriptions of object states (internal representation) as well as the code to implement the interface operators of the class. It is important to note that the values of the variables in the internal representation of the instances of the class are all different and pertain to individual objects. For example, IBM's internal representation consists of its particular Expense, Revenue, set of employees, CEO, subsidiaries, and so on. The aggregation of these values captures the state of the IBM instance of Company. Thus for each instance of a class, memory storage will be allocated to maintain the internal representation.

However, all the instances share the codes that implement the interface operators. Thus, there will be a single code base that implements Get Profit, Get Total Employees, Add Subsidiary, and all the other interface operators. As we said, these operators are invoked with a target object as argument. The object-oriented system knows how to apply the appropriate operations to the target objects, without violating their internal states. This is very similar to procedure calls in conventional programming languages.

3.3.1.1 Instance Variables

The internal representation of a class is captured in the instance variables. Thus for the previous example, all the variables that hold the state of objects that are instances of the given class are instance variables. As illustrated in Figure 3.6, each instance variable declaration is of the form

Name:	string,
Address:	string,
Expense :	Dollar,
Revenue :	Dollar,
Employees :	SetOfEmployees,
CEO :	Employee
Subsidiaries:	SetOfCompany

and so on.

The class name on the right hand side of the colon indicates that the instance variable will be an instance of that class. For example, for any instance of Company such as IBM or AT&T, Expense will be an instance of the class Dollar. Employees will be an instance of SetOfEmployees.

It is an error to assign any other type of object to these instance variables. *Type constraints* such as this are commonly used in many typed programming and database languages. In these languages, the types (classes) of the variables or record fields are explicitly declared and specified.

These type constraints enhance understandability and many times avoid run-time type errors. A type error occurs when, for example, an operator expects an argument to be an instance of a particular class C1 but is called with an argument that is an instance of a totally unrelated class C2. The type errors are detected at compile time. Examples of object-oriented languages that do extensive compile-time type checking include Trellis/Owl (Schaffert et al., 1986), and Eiffel (Meyer, 1988).

Another advantage of specifying the class of instance-variable objects, which is important to object-oriented database systems, is potential performance advantages in storage organization and optimization. Section 3.6 discusses this in more detail.

This example also illustrates the fact that the definition of instance variables can be either in terms of built-in classes such as integers and strings, or user defined classes such as Employee.

Not all object-oriented languages require the specification of a class name for the instance variables. There are "typeless" languages such as Smalltalk, APL, or LISP which do not specify types (classes) for their variables. In Smalltalk for example, the programmer cannot specify the class of the object named by an instance (or any other) variable. The same variable X, for instance, could be bound to the integer 5 and then subsequently to the string 'XY' within the same session or program.

Furthermore there could be several operators with the same name but pertaining to different classes. In other words, operators could be "overloaded." This notion of overloading is commonly used in conventional programming languages such as Pascal where, for instance, the same operator " + " is used to add both integers or floats.

With typeless object-oriented languages such as Smalltalk, the binding of an operator (selector) to a particular code (method) is made at run time, based on the class of the operator's argument(s). This notion of dynamic binding is discussed in more detail in Section 3.3.2.

3.3.1.2 *Object Creation*

Instances of a class are created through invoking a *New* operator on the class. Thus, the class may be thought of as a factory that contains the description of its output and responds to requests to fabricate its next product instance as depicted in Figure 3.8. New is a generic operator that could be redefined for each class. For example, we can define New for Company to accept the Name and Address of the company as arguments that initialize the corresponding instance variables. In other words, assume we are creating a Company instance for IBM, whose Address is, say, 111 Success Street, New York. We then just invoke

   IBM := New(Company, "IBM", "111 Success Street New York")

whose meaning can be explained in the following way. The class Company is asked to fabricate, initialize, and return an instance of itself—that is, the Company class. For the created object, the value of the instance variable Name will be a string object with value "IBM". The value of the instance variable Address will be a string object with value "111 Success Street New York". The other instance variables (e.g., Budget, Expenses, etc.) will not be initialized. The invocation of New will create and return this object. The variable IBM is assigned the return value of the newly created instance of Company and hence will serve as a *handle* to the object.

Other instance variables could be initialized or updated through operators such as

   Set-Revenues(IBM, $5,000,000,000)

which sets the Revenue of the IBM object to five billion dollars.

Note that we chose a particular syntax and strategy for creating an instance of a class and initializing some of its instance variables. Other languages have chosen different

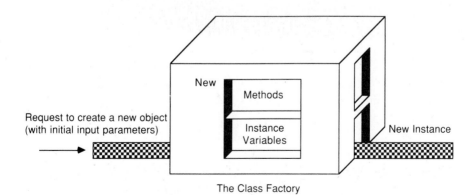

The Class Factory

Figure 3.8 An analogy between a class and a factory.

strategies for creating new objects and initializing instance variables. The following section discusses these and other issues regarding class operators in more detail. The main point here was that instance variables are initialized either at object-creation time through the New operator, or subsequently through calling special operators that manipulate or update the state of the instance variable.

3.3.1.3 Methods and Messages

A class also specifies the operators that define the behavior of its instances. Invoking an operation involves

1. The target object.
2. The name of the operator.
3. The arguments of the operator.
4. Calling the code that implements the operator, binding the parameters to the actual arguments of the invocation.

Object-oriented languages differ in their syntax of operator invocation (or sending messages to target objects).

Assume the variable GM represents General Motors in the Fortune 100 database, and GM is an instance of Company. In addition, assume Hughes is also an instance of Company, and we want to insert it as a subsidiary of GM. As previously mentioned, we have an operator AddSubsidiary to perform this.

In Smalltalk, adding (inserting) the subsidiary will take the form

    GM AddSubsidiary: Hughes

The corresponding operation in C + + would be

    GM.AddSubsidiary(Hughes)

and in Eiffel it would be

    AddSubsidiary(GM, Hughes)

In all these examples, the target object is GM, the name of the operator is AddSubsidiary, and the argument is Hughes.

Note that the New operator that was introduced in the previous section used the last format. In other words, the target was the class Company and its arguments were some initial values for instance variables of the newly created instance of Company. The observant reader will realize that there is some conceptual difference between the invocation of AddSubsidiary on GM and New on Company: the target object of the latter is a class, whereas the target object of the former is an instance. Thus, a class object was treated like an object in New. One can ask if Company is itself an instance of yet a higher level (meta) class. This treatment of classes, instances, and metaclasses has created some confusion and will be treated in more detail in Section 3.4.4. For the time being, we just indicate that Company is indeed an object on which we can invoke operators.

The jargon used to describe the operators and operator invocations differs from one object-oriented system to another. Below we discuss some of the terminology of perhaps the most influential object-oriented language, namely, Smalltalk. The Smalltalk terminology, though sometimes confusing, is permeating object orientation at large (Cox, 1984).

In Smalltalk, the procedure implementing an operator is called a *method*. To apply an operation to a target instance, one sends a message to the target object. The message includes (1) a selector, and (2) one or more arguments.

The selector of a message selects the appropriate method from all the methods associated with the target object. This is illustrated in Figure 3.9 for inserting the subsidiary Hughes in company GM.

Hence a selector is nothing but the name of a method. The corresponding method is "called," with the message's arguments binding the method's parameters. Of course, this is exactly what happens when a procedure is invoked in a conventional programming language! Perhaps one important difference is that this binding is done

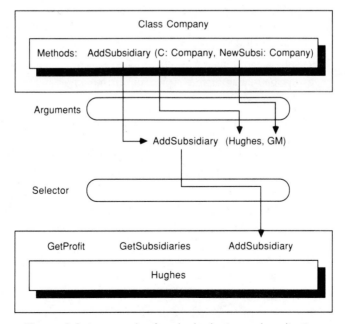

Figure 3.9 An example of method selection and application.

at run time, depending on the class of the target object. We shall return to this important property of dynamic binding in Section 3.3.2.

Assuming the set of subsidiaries is implemented through an array of (currently) TotalSubsid entries, the pseudocode for AddSubsidiary (using a Pascal-like syntax) is:

> AddSubsidiary(C: Company, NewSubsi: Company)
>   C.Subsidiaries[TotalSubsi] := NewSubsi
>   TotalSubsi := TotalSubsi + 1

where NewSubsi is the method's formal parameter and TotalSubsi is an instance variable storing the current cardinality of the set of subsidiaries. When

> AddSubsidiary(GM, Hughes)

is invoked NewSubsi is bound to the object Hughes. This is illustrated in Figure 3.9.

In the following sections we shall use the terminology of methods, messages, and selectors with a Pascal like syntax and pseudocode for some of our illustrative examples. As indicated in the previous example, the first parameter will indicate the target object.

3.3.2 Dynamic Binding

In promoting the advantages of the object-oriented style of programming, one of the most often cited characteristics is *dynamic binding* (also called *late binding*). In fact some would argue that we actually do not have an object-oriented system without this powerful capability.

Simply stated, dynamic binding means that the system will bind at runtime a selector to the particular method (procedure) that implements it, based upon the recipient object's class. This run-time binding capability is needed because

1. The same message or method name (i.e., selector) could be used by different classes (overloading).
2. A variable's object class might not be known till runtime (e.g., when the language is typeless and variables can be bound to objects of different types in the same program).

A prototypical example illustrating the advantages of dynamic binding is a print message applied to every element of a heterogeneous collection of objects. Assume we have a stack that can contain any kind of object and we are interested in printing every entry in the stack. Furthermore, assume a print method with particular implementation is associated with each class (hence all these print methods are different and totally unrelated). Assuming the stack is *St*, and is implemented as an array 1 to Top of objects, the pseudocode for printing every element of the stack is

> for i: = 1 to Top do Print(St[i])

Thus, each object St[i] would execute its appropriate print method, depending on the class to which it belongs. This is illustrated in Figure 3.10. The key point is that the object decides what piece of code to execute for the print message. Thus, unlike procedure names in more conventional programming languages, the selector *print* by itself does not identify a unique piece of code. The print message to a particular target object (which of course is an instance of a particular class) identifies the unique code that prints the target object.

If the language did not have a dynamic binding capability, it would have forced the user to have a large *case* statement and invoke the appropriate print routine, based on the selected object's type. Thus, each entry in the stack will be a pair

<object type (class)> <object>

and depending on the number of types, we will have a corresponding collection of print operators like PrintInteger, PrintString, PrintFloat, and so on. To print each element of the stack will involve checking the type of the stack and calling the appropriate routine. Hence, the pseudocode would be

```
for i := 1 to Top do
    case St[i].type
        Integer:        PrintInteger(St[i].Object)
        Float:          PrintChar(St[i].Object)
        String:         PrintString(St[i].Object)
        Boolean:        PrintBoolean(St[i].Object)
```

Note that if a new type X is added, the case statement has to be extended with PrintX, and the whole routine that prints all the elements of a stack has to be recompiled.

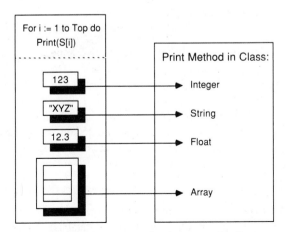

Figure 3.10 An example of dynamic binding.

In contrast, with dynamic binding the system could be extended with any number of new classes without ever affecting the method that prints all the elements of a stack, or any other previously defined method that uses generic selectors like print.

The advantage of this strategy is flexibility and extensibility. The main disadvantage is the performance penalty of the run-time binding and/or type checking that must be done to guarantee correctness. If the binding is performed through a search for each invocation of each method, dynamic binding could be expensive. Although accelerators such as hash tables or indexes could be used to enhance the performance penalty of dynamic binding, the cost could still be expensive when compared with compiled strategies (where the corresponding cost is just an address jump) of conventional languages such as Pascal.

3.3.3 Constraints

In Section 3.3, we indicated that in order to support abstract data, typing the operations associated with an abstract data type (an ADT) must be complete and correct. We also indicated that this notion, unlike information hiding or the class-object paradigm, is impossible to enforce.

The semantics of the "real" abstract data type, be it a Company, or an Employee or a data structure such as a Stack, exists only in the mind of its creator (the programmer). Therefore the completeness or correctness of the ADT is as good as the completeness or correctness of the code which captures the ADT's behavior. If the object-oriented programming language does not provide any constructs to indicate the "constraints" which assert the correctness or completeness of the ADT, then the full behavior of the ADT will not be captured in the code or the application programs.

In Section 2.7.3 we mentioned a similar problem for relational databases when we described Codd's Rule Ten. As far as databases are concerned Codd makes the specific point that integrity constraints must be stored in the DBMS data catalog, rather than encapsulated in particular application programs. Many recent DBMS languages such as SQL provide explicit language constructs to express these integrity constraints through "triggers" and other mechanisms such as foreign key constraints.

For intelligent databases, there are two approaches for providing language constructs to capture correctness or completeness. These constructs enable the programmer to express the constraints which reflect the semantics of the abstract data type.

> **1.** *Constraints on Objects and Object Fields (slots, instance variable, etc.).* With this approach, access and update constraint routines are executed when manipulating instances of the abstract data type. These constraint routines are incorporated in the definition of the class and associated either with the object instance as a whole or particular instance variables of the object.

This is similar to the notion of triggers which are executed when updating a record pertaining to a relation in relational database. For example, to capture the constraint that an employee's salary should not be greater than his/her manager's salary, a constraint will be associated with the employee's salary field such that every time the field is updated, the trigger is "fired" to go check the updated salary against the current salary of the manager.

Similarly, in the Intelligence/Compiler (Parsaye and Chignell, 1988) there is the notion of *attached predicates* which could be used to restrict access, evaluate missing information or enforce constraints on the slots (fields) of the frames in a semantic network. Attached predicates are described in more detail in Section 4.7.2.

2. *Pre- and Postconditions of Methods.* An alternative approach to using attached procedures is to associate preconditions and postconditions with the operations (methods) of the abstract data type, rather than with the objects or the instances. In other words, one could introduce certain constraints on the instance variables that must be satisfied before a particular method is executed (pre-condition) and other constraints that must be satisfied upon terminating the execution of the method (post-conditions).

This is the approach taken in Eiffel (Meyer, 1988) where, for example, to guarantee the semantics of a Stack one can introduce preconditions and postconditions for the Push and Pop operations (methods). A precondition for Push is the requirement that the stack instance must not be full. A precondition for Pop is the requirement that the stack instance must not be empty. Similarly a postcondition for Pop is the requirement that the stack instance is no longer empty and its total number of elements is increased by one.

To choose between constraint on objects and preconditions and postconditions on methods is mainly a matter of convenience and taste. The two approaches attempt to achieve the same affect, namely to help the programmer express the semantics of the abstract data type as directly as possible. As indicated earlier, there is no "magic" in constraints and conditions on either objects or operators: the completeness or correctness of the ADT is still as good as the completeness or correctness of the code which captures the ADT's behavior. It is up to the programmer to use these constructs to express the semantics of the ADT more explicitly.

■ **3.4 INHERITANCE HIERARCHIES**

The second powerful concept that characterizes object-oriented languages and systems is inheritance. Through inheritance we can build new classes on top of an existing less specialized hierarchy of classes, instead of redesigning everything from scratch. The new classes can *inherit* both the behavior (operations, methods, etc.) and the representation (instance variables) from existing classes.

For example, profit-making companies and nonprofit organizations have a lot in common. Both types of companies contain information storing the company name, company address, personnel, and so on. Nonprofit organizations have more specialized information such as government grants, supporting businesses, international nonprofit organizational liaisons, and so on. Similarly, profit-making companies have specializations such as nontaxable deductions.

Thus, to capture the common information and behavior of nonprofit and profit-making companies we can construct a generic class Company and allow two additional classes CommercialCompany and Non-ProfitOrganization to inherit from it. Every instance of CommercialCompany or Non-ProfitOrganization is also an instance of Company. This is illustrated in Figure 3.11, which demonstrates both the inheritance hierarchy and *set-inclusion*. Note that there are some instances of Company which are neither instances of CommercialCompany nor instances of Non-ProfitOrganization. For example, we

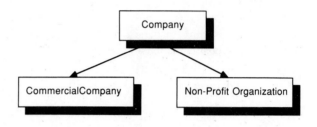

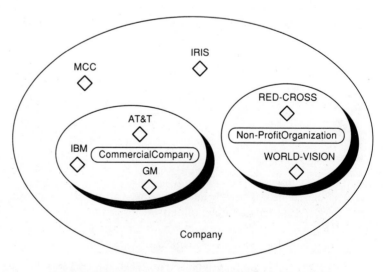

Figure 3.11 An inheritance hierarchy and a set inclusion.

can have a company that is owned by several other profit-making companies, without being a subsidiary of any one of them, without generating any profits, and without being a nonprofit organization. A typical example is the MCC research consortium, which is owned by about 20 American semiconductor and computer companies. MCC is a company that is neither a nonprofit organization nor a profit-making commercial company; its charter is to produce original results for its shareholder companies.

The classes CommercialCompany and Non-ProfitOrganization are called *subclasses* of Company. The class Company is a *superclass* of CommercialCompany and Non-ProfitOrganization. The subclass and superclass relations are transitive. This means if X is a subclass (superclass) of Y and Y is a subclass (superclass) of Z then X is also a subclass (superclass) of Z. For example, if SemiconductorFirm is a subclass of CommercialCompany, then by transitivity it is also a subclass of Company. This means it inherits behavior and representation from Company through CommercialCompany. Of course, in addition it inherits from CommercialCompany all the behavioral and representational aspects that are particular to CommercialCompany but that do not pertain to instances of Company in general (e.g., information and functions to evaluate the company's profit and due taxes on the profit).

As we can see from these examples, there are two main aspects of inheritance.

a. *Structural.* This means instances of a class such as Non-ProfitOrganization, which is a subclass of Company, will have values inherited from Company for instance variables such as Name, Address, and so on. Section 3.4.1 discusses this in more detail.

b. *Behavioral.* The class Company has methods such as AddSubsidiary, EvaluateBudget, and so on, which are inherited by its subclasses Non-ProfitOrganization and CommercialCompany. This means we can send a message with selector AddSubsidiary to an instance NPO of Non-ProfitOrganization and execute the method AddSubsidiary in Company with NPO as the target object. Section 3.4.2 discusses this in more detail.

From a modeling point of view, inheritance is a very natural and powerful way of organizing information. As indicated earlier, some of the most popular knowledge representation techniques in AI, namely, semantic networks and frames, make extensive use of *is-a* links which build inheritance hierarchies. Frames and inheritance are discussed further in Chapter 4. AI models have primarily emphasized structural inheritance. Object-oriented languages, on the other hand, emphasize behavioral inheritance.

3.4.1 Inheriting Instance Variables

In AI knowledge representation and most database data models, there is no encapsulation and hence the only type of inheritance that makes sense is structural inheritance.

The class of an object describes its structure through specifying the object's instance variables. Instances of a subclass must retain the same type of information as instances of their superclass.

One way to achieve this is to inherit the instance variables of the superclass directly and allow methods in the subclass to access and manipulate the instance variables of its superclass(es) without any constraints. This is the strategy in Smalltalk.

However, with encapsulated abstract data types where the instance variables are *hidden* from the *users* of the instances, it is not clear if a subclass should directly inherit and access the instance variables of its superclass.

In other words a class has two sorts of *clients*.

1. Those who just create instances of the class and manipulate those instances through the methods associated with the class—these are called *instantiating* clients.
2. The sub-classes of the class that inherit methods (behavior) and structure from the class—these are class *inheriting* clients.

Object-oriented languages have differed in the strategies for giving access and visibility to these two types of clients.

As far as instance variables are concerned, Smalltalk, for example, allows unrestricted access to the inheriting clients, but completely restricts instantiating clients. Going back to the previous example, assume the Subsidiaries instance variable of Company is implemented as an array of Company. Non-ProfitOrganization and Commercial-Company are subclasses of Company. Therefore, with the Smalltalk approach, any method defined in Non-ProfitOrganization or CommercialCompany can directly access or update this variable *as an array*. However, if a client has just created an instance C of Company, it can access or update the instance variable Subsidiaries only indirectly through messages with selectors AddSubsidiary or GetSubsidiaries, and so on, whose methods manipulate the Subsidiaries instance variable.

Some (e.g., Snyder, 1986) have correctly argued that making the instance variables visible to the subclasses violates both uniformity and encapsulation. Thus, when the implementation of the superclass is modified through modifying the instance variables, all the subclasses utilizing these instance variables have to be modified! For example, if the implementation of Subsidiaries is modified such that Subsidiaries is a "list of Company," then all the methods in subclasses of Company that directly access or update Subsidiaries have to be modified.

More specifically, the method EvaluateProfit in CommercialCompany traverses the Subsidiaries and adds all the profits of each company, thus evaluating an aggregate sum. With an array implementation, the profit will be accumulated through

```
EvaluateProfit(C: Company)
    TotalProfit := 0
        If TotalSubsi = O then return C.Revenue - C.Expenses
        otherwise
    for i: = 0 to TotalSubsi - 1 do
        TotalProfit := TotalProfit + EvaluateProfit(C.Subsidiaries[i])
    return TotalProfit
```

If a linked-list implementation is used, the sum will be accumulated through

```
EvaluateProfit(C: Company)
    TotalProfit := 0
    NextSubsi := C.Subsidiaries
    If NextSubsi = Nil then return C.Revenue - C.Expenses
    otherwise
        while NextSubsi <> Nil do
            TotalProfit := TotalProfit + EvaluateProfit(NextSubsi)
            NextSubsi := NextSubsi.Next
    return TotalProfit
```

where the Next field in the linked list of subsidiaries points to the record of the next subsidiary.

These two alternative implementations of Subsidiaries illustrate the fact that a method in the subclass CommercialCompany of Company has to be modified since an implementation in the parent (superclass) of an instance variable was modified. Thus *all* inheriting clients that utilize the modified instance variable have to be modified.

In CommonObjects (Snyder, 1985), on the other hand, a completely different approach is taken. Here the inheriting clients cannot directly access or manipulate the instance variables of their superclasses. In fact, instance variables in the inheritance hierarchy are independent from each other.

> if the type child inherits from a type parent, then each object of type child automatically includes as part of its representation the local state (instance variables) of an object of type parent. These inherited instance variables are distinct from instance variables defined by the type child and any instance variable inherited by child from other types regardless of the names of the instance variables.

Therefore, as illustrated in Figure 3.12 an object of type (class) Chevrolet that is a subtype of type Car, in turn a subtype of Vehicle will have instance variables pertaining to its state as a Vehicle, Car, and Chevrolet respectively. The states are stored in the instance variables of the corresponding classes but are totally unrelated. ENCORE (Zdonik and Wegener, 1986) uses a similar strategy. It is important to note that with this approach, methods of a subclass (subtype) cannot access the instance

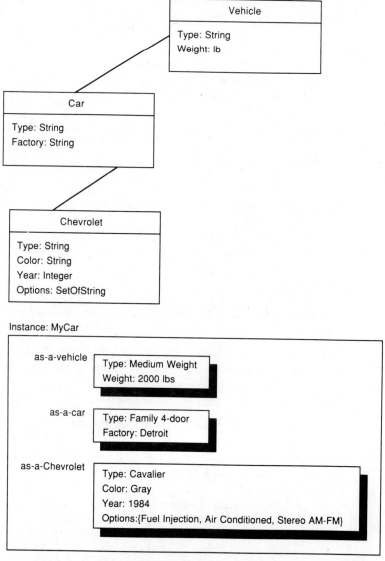

Figure 3.12 An inheritance hierarchy.

variables of the superclass directly: like instantiating clients, the instance variables of the superclass must be accessed and/or updated through the methods of the superclass.

The most general approach, which combines efficiency and flexibility, is to support the notions of *public*, *private*, and *subclass visible* and leave it to the implementation to specify the desired protection. A class can have two kinds of clients. These three options are defined as follows:

1. *Public*. If an instance variable or a method is declared to be private, then *any* client can directly access, manipulate, or invoke it.

2. *Private*. If an instance variable or a method is declared to be private, then *no* client can directly access, manipulate, or invoke it.

3. *Subclass Visible*. If an instance variable or a method is declared to be subclass visible, then it can be accessed, manipulated, or invoked directly only by inheriting clients (i.e., they are private as far as instantiating clients are concerned).

Both C++ and Trellis/Owl support the notions of public and private methods or instance variables. Trellis/Owl in addition supports the notion of subclass visible.

If these three options are supported, then the implementor can initially choose to be conservative and make most of the instance variables and some of the methods private. After some stability in the code base of some classes, the instance variables and methods can be made public or subtype visible, providing more efficient and direct manipulation by the instantiating and inheriting clients.

3.4.2 Inheriting Methods

As indicated earlier, a class defines both the structure and behavior of a collection of objects. The behavior is specified in the methods associated with the instances of the class. Methods are operations that can either retrieve or update the state of an object. Object states are stored in the instance variables.

In an inheritance hierarchy, a method defined for a class is inherited by its subclasses. Thus, the inherited methods are part of the interface manipulating the instances of the subclass.

For example, we can have the class Window with BorderedWindow and TextWindow as subclasses (Cox and Hunt, 1986). The methods such as MoveWindow, ResizeWindow, and RotateWindow can also be invoked on instances of TextWindow and BorderedWindow. In the TextWindow subclass, more specialized methods for editing and modifying the font, character size, and so on of the text strings in the window are defined. These methods are not defined on instances of Window that are not also instances of TextWindow (e.g., instances of BorderedWindow). BorderedWindow can have its own methods (Edit, Font, etc.) that are totally unrelated to the methods with the same selector names of, say, TextWindow. Thus, classes that are *siblings* (i.e., have the same parent or ancestor class) can have operators (methods) with the same name that are totally unrelated.

In addition, a subclass can override an inherited method. In other words, a method called M in class C can be overriden by a method also called M in a subclass C' of C. Thus, when a message with selector M is sent to an object O, the underlying system will bind M to the method with the same name in the most specialized class of O.

For example, in the hierarchy of company classes, with CommercialCompany and Non-ProfitOrganization as subclasses of Company, assume ForeignCommercial is a subclass of CommercialCompany. Due to different tax rules and other constraints the formulas that have to be applied to evaluate the profit of a foreign company are different from local or U.S. companies. Thus, there is another EvaluateProfit method of ForeignCommercial that overrides the method with the same name in CommercialCompany.

Sometimes it is useful to call within a method of the subclass an overridden method of the superclass. For example, in the implementation of EvaluateProfit for Foreign-Commercial, we might like to call EvaluateProfit as implemented in the class Com-mercialCompany. For simplicity assume the profit of a foreign company is evaluated as

<profit of company as a U.S. firm> − <foreign taxation>

where the first term is evaluated through EvaluateProfit of CommercialCompany. Then an obvious way to invoke this method is through quantifying its name with a class name. Thus, if the method is M and we desire to invoke its implementation in class C, we simply use the selector C.M.

Note that methods with the same name could appear in many places in a class hierarchy. A quantified method name will indicate the implementation that is either defined in the indicated class or is in the most immediate predecessor of the quantifying class name.

With this simple and intuitive strategy, the implementation of EvaluateProfit in For-eignCommercial will be

EvaluateProfit(FC: ForeignCommercial)
    return CommercialCompany.EvaluateProfit(FC) −
        ForeignTax(FC)

Of course, the only restriction needed to make this strategy work is to require class names to be unique, which is a very reasonable restriction.

3.4.3 Multiple Inheritance

In many situations it is very convenient to inherit from more than one class. For example, a commercial company that is both a foreign company and a semiconductor firm has properties (instance variables and methods) that pertain to its characteristics both as a foreign company and as a semiconductor firm.

With *multiple inheritance* we can combine several existing classes to produce con-glomerate classes that utilize each of their multiple superclasses in a variety of usages and functionalities.

As a simple example, consider a class hierarchy consisting of the superclass Person, with subclasses Student and Employee. A student who is also a worker has charac-

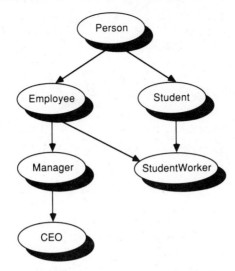

Figure 3.13 An example of multiple inheritance.

teristics pertaining to his or her nature as student and employee. If we allow multiple inheritance, then we can have a StudentWorker subclass of students and employees. This is illustrated in Figure 3.13.

An instance of StudentWorker would have the state and behavior of an employee and a student. If the inheritance scheme of the language allows the subclasses to manipulate the instance variables of their superclasses directly (as in Smalltalk), then with multiple inheritance the instance variables of a subclass will be a superset of the union of the instance variables of all its subclasses. For example, if employee's instance variables are

{name, age, salary, rank, department}

and student's instance variables are

{name, age, GPA, courses, advisor}

then StudentWorker's instance variables will contain

{name, age, salary, rank, department, GPA, courses, advisor}

Note that since *name* and *age* were both inherited from person (by employee and student) we do not have a problem. However, as we show in the example, StudentWorker should have one copy (instantiation—Snyder, 1986) of these instance variables. The *interface* or methods of the subclass is always a superset of the methods defined by all its superclasses (except overridden methods).

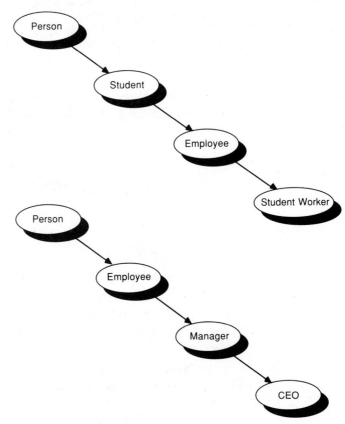

Figure 3.14 Alternate inheritance paths.

In inheriting instance variables or methods from more than one class, the most obvious question is what happens when there is a conflict. By "conflict" we mean different methods or instance variables by the same name are defined in a totally unrelated way by more than one superclass. For example, assume students and employees had a *bonus* method with totally different semantics and implementation. Which bonus method should apply to StudentWorker? Different languages and systems have pursued different solutions to this problem.

1. If totally unrelated instance variables or methods are inherited through the multiple-inheritance mechanism, then issue an error and/or require the subclass to redefine the conflicting method or instance variable. This is similar to the approach taken in Eiffel and Trellis/Owl.

2. Linearize the inheritance hierarchy and use single inheritance to avoid conflicts. Thus with this approach, the inheritance hierarchy of Figure 3.13 would be interpreted as Figure 3.14. Hence, StudentWorker would inherit bonus from

student, since student overrides the bonus of employee. This is the approach taken in Flavors (Moon, 1986) and CommonLoops (Bobrow et al., 1986).

There are other solutions for resolving conflicts with multiple inheritance. The key issue here is that although multiple inheritance is a powerful and useful tool, care should be taken in defining a consistent and intuitive semantics when multiple methods and instance variables (with possibly the same name and even argument types) pertaining to different classes are inherited by the same class.

Solution (1) is simpler to understand and enforce. Although it is somewhat restrictive, method and variable names that are conflicting can be quantified by their class names (see Section 3.4.2).

3.4.4 Metaclasses

In earlier sections we described objects as instances of classes. A class contains the description of its objects' structure—through the instance variables and behavior and through the methods pertaining to the instances of the class.

As illustrated in Figure 3.8, a class is like a factory that creates and initializes its instances. As we saw in Section 3.3.1.2, the method New was the selector of a message sent to a class. In fact, one can think of other methods and instance variables that are pertinent to classes as whole: Total number of instances for any class, AverageSalary for the class Employees, MaximumSize for the class Window, MinimumUsOwnership for ForeignCommercial operating in the United States, and so on.

Thus, classes behave like objects. They have states and one sends them messages like New, AverageSalary, and MaximumSize, which are implemented through methods associated with class. Are classes instances of other classes? And if yes, what is the class that describes them and where does the transitive closure end? Object-oriented languages have pursued conflicting and somewhat confusing solutions to this problem.

Let us first start with Smalltalk's approach. In Smalltalk, a class is an instance of the particular type of class called a *metaclass*. Thus, a metaclass is a class whose instances are also classes.

The dynamics between classes, metaclasses and "special" classes such as *Object class* and *Metaclass* is rather confusing in Smalltalk and hence we shall illustrate this concept with figures and examples.

In Figure 3.15 we have the class Object and some subclasses of Object such as Person, Window, and Vehicle. The class Object is the root of all classes and hence every class is a subclass of Object.

Using a set-inclusion notation, Figure 3.16 illustrates the class hierarchy by having instances for the classes. Each class in Smalltalk is an instance of another class associated with it; namely the class's metaclass. How is the class hierarchy reflected

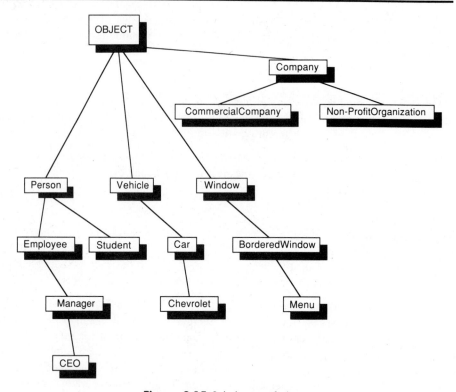

Figure 3.15 Subclasses of object.

on the metaclasses? Each class is the unique instance of its metaclass and the metaclass hierarchy is parallel to the class inheritance hierarchy! Figure 3.17 illustrates this for the class hierarchy rooted at Person.

Metaclasses in Smalltalk are not explicitly declared by the user. Instead, in the creation and definition of a class the user distinguishes between *class methods* and *class variables* (as opposed to instance methods and instance variables).

One can think of a class method as the instance method declared in the metaclass, and a class variable as the instance variable of the class (as an instance) also declared in the metaclass. The most typical class methods are instance creation and initialization methods. For example, *new* for Company could be defined to create and initialize instances of Company through specifying, say, their names:

Company new: IBM

The relationship between special classes *Object, Class, Metaclass* and their metaclasses is rather confusing. We briefly describe it here to demonstrate the complexity of this solution. Our intention is not to be complete but to make a point. The interested

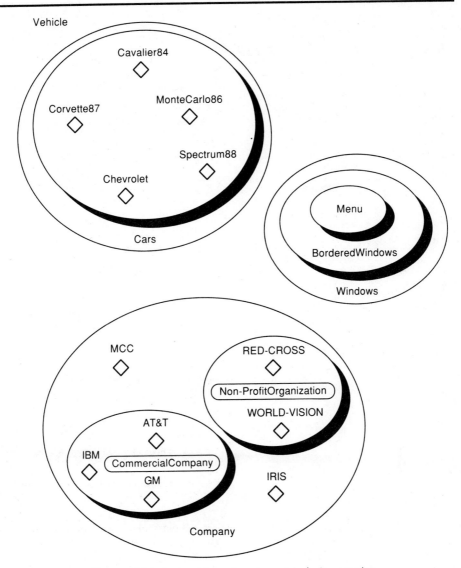

Figure 3.16 A class hierarchy using set-inclusion notation.

reader can consider Chapter 16 in (Goldberg and Robson, 1983). The metaclasses of the special classes will be italicized.

1. Object. Every object is an instance of Object and every class is a subclass of Object. The metaclass of object is *Object class*. *Object class* is a subclass of Class. However, *Object class* does not have a metaclass.

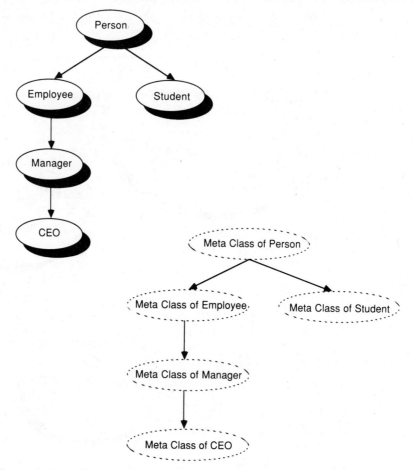

Figure 3.17 Parallelism of the metaclass hierarchy and the class inheritance hierarchy.

2. Class. Every metaclass is a subclass of Class. The metaclass *Class class* (of Class) is a subclass of *Object class* which, as we said earlier, is itself a subclass of Class! Thus, *Class class* is transitively a subclass of itself.
3. Metaclass. All metaclasses are instances of Metaclass. The metaclass of Metaclass is *Metaclass class* which is a subclass of Class.

To say that this meta-information is quite confusing is probably an understatement! In fact we have presented only a small portion of the rather involved interrelationships amongst the special classes of Smalltalk. It is not even clear that the uniformity in having everything an object is worthwhile, due to the confusion it creates for the users. The good news is that the users do not need to worry or deal with metaclasses directly. For most practical purposes, all the user needs is the declaration of the class, the instance variables, the (instance) methods as well as some class variables without worrying about the involved relationships between classes and metaclasses.

As indicated earlier, object-oriented languages have different approaches in handling the instance, class, and metaclass trichotomy. We presented the Smalltalk solution (so to speak) to illustrate the propagation of complexity in one popular object-oriented language, when for uniformity types (classes) are treated as objects.

A much simpler approach taken by Flavors (Moon, 1986) sacrifices uniformity for simplicity. Flavors is a dialect of LISP. A flavor in this language describes a type and every object is in fact an instance of a flavor. However, unlike Smalltalk, a flavor (which describes the structure and behavior of its instances) is not itself an instance of another flavor. With flavors inheritance (in fact multiple inheritance) is supported. But the definition of a flavor is strictly the definition of a type, very similar to type declarations in Pascal, C, or other conventional programming languages.

Finally, let us note that frames can be thought of as either classes with a single instance or as *classless* objects. Frames, like classes, inherit from one another. Frame inheritance is primarily structural inheritance. Frames inherit state (slot values) from one another. This is different from most object-oriented systems where classes inherit methods and instance variables from one another. In fact, we believe that in an intelligent database model these two sorts of inheritance must both be supported. Frames are discussed in more detail in Chapter 4. The different types of inheritance in intelligent databases are discussed in Chapter 7.

3.4.5 Prototype Systems and Delegation

Our description of inheritance would not be complete without a discussion of an entirely different approach to information sharing, namely, prototype systems and the use of delegation.

Unlike Object/Class/Instance systems discussed so far, in prototype systems there is no distinction between classes and instances. Note that this is very different from saying that classes are themselves instances of metaclasses, as in the object-oriented languages Smalltalk and Loops. In these systems, a class describes a collection of objects of similar structure and behavior. The only type of instance that can fabricate objects is a class (an instance of a metaclass).

An instance of a class that is not a metaclass cannot be used to share code or information. Examples of this more common type of instances include the person Joe, the dog Lassie, or a Chevrolet Cavalier model 1984 with California plate AZ 123.

Thus in the Smalltalk model, there are three types of objects and two types of instances: metaclasses, classes that are instances of metaclasses, and instances of classes that are not metaclasses. With prototype systems these distinctions are removed.

In a prototype system one first thinks of a particular prototypical object and then draws similarities and/or distinctions for objects that are like the prototype in some ways and different in others. Any object can become a prototype. The approach is to start with individual cases and then subsequently specialize or generalize. Lieberman (1986) elegantly describes the distinction between this approach and the object-oriented (set-oriented) approach.

> Prototype systems allow creating concepts first, then generalizing them by saying what aspects of the concept are allowed to vary. Set-oriented (object-oriented) systems require creating the abstraction description of the set (class) before individual instances can be installed as members.

In a sense, prototypes seem to be closer to the way we learn through association and specialization. For example, assume the first encounter of a child with a dog was a retriever called Lassie. Then the child subsequently encounters another dog named Poodle who is also brown, much cuter and smaller than Lassie, and whose main function is as a cuddly companion. Then we can think of Poodle delegating its common subparts or operations to Lassie, in the sense that these are already stored in the representation associated with Lassie as indicated in Figure 3.18. As far as its peculiar characteristics, Poodle either overrides Lassie's corresponding attributes, or introduces some new ones such as the name and experience of its hair stylist!

Lieberman has argued that delegation is more powerful than inheritance since it can easily be shown that inheritance can be modeled through delegation. However, Stein

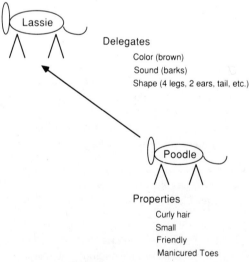

Figure 3.18 An example of delegation.

(1987) has shown that using classes to implement delegation (vs. instances) inheritance can also model delegation. More specifically, as we mentioned earlier, in many object-oriented systems classes are instances of metaclasses. However, unlike the instances, the classes have an inheritance hierarchy. Thus classes have class variables and class methods that are inherited from their superclasses. Since a class is-a superclass it should inherit not only the structure but also the value of its superclass variables in order to be consistent with the Axiom of Upward Compatibility.

> The Axiom of Upward Compatibility or Strict is-a Rule says that if A is-a B (i.e., A is a subclass of B or all A's are B's), then anything that is true of B must also be true of A, since a subclass is-a superclass, anything true of the superclass—like having a class attribute—must also be true of the subclass. Further, any changes to the superclass must be reflected immediately by the subclass: the subclass depends on the superclass.

In other words, the values of the class variables must be inherited. This is exactly what happens in delegation. Hence, the effect of delegation could be achieved through the class hierarchy.

Besides having a tradeoff in terms of space versus execution time (with prototype systems typically requiring less space but more time to bind methods or obtain attribute values), the choice between delegation and inheritance is a modeling or knowledge representation choice. Inheritance with set-oriented semantics supports direct sharing among object collections with similar structures. The method lookup is relatively fast. However, since instance variables have to be inherited for all subclass instances, they typically need more space. On the other hand, the main problem with delegation is the lack of direct representation of collection of objects that differ only in the values of their attributes. Another disadvantage of delegation is the number of messages in the method lookups.

■ 3.5 OBJECT IDENTITY

Another powerful object-oriented concept is *object identity* (Khoshafian and Copeland, 1986). An identity is a handle which distinguishes one entity from another. In a complete object-oriented system, each object will be given an identity that will be permanently associated with the object, immaterial of the object's *structural* or *state* transitions. In fact, for persistent objects the identity will be maintained across multiple program or transaction instantiations.

Let us explain this with a simple example. Each of us as a person undergoes structural or state transitions. We grow older. We graduate from several schools and then join the routine of a professional career. We acquire new attributes such as a spouse, children, or excess weight. We might change our name, or even our social security number. Yet, no matter how many additional attributes we acquire, modify, or drop, there is presumably something unique about each one of us that is permanently associated with us.

Object identity brings these characteristics of the real world to languages and computation. Without object identity, it will be awkward if not impossible to assign self-contained objects to attributes or instance variables. Also without object identity it will be impossible to make the same object a component of multiple objects.

To be sure, there are many ways to distinguish objects from one another. For example, most programming and database languages use variable names to distinguish objects. This mixes addressability and identity. Addressability is external to an object. Its purpose is to provide a way to access an object within a particular environment and is therefore environment dependent. Identity is internal to an object. Its purpose is to provide a way to represent the individuality of an object independently of how it is accessed. Address-based identity in programming languages is typically implemented through *pointers* (i.e., virtual addresses). An address-based identity mechanism compromises identity.

There are practical limitations to the use of variable names without some built-in representation of identity and operators to test and manipulate this representation at an abstract level. One problem is that a single object may be accessed in different ways and bound to different variables without having a way to find out if they refer to the same object (Saltzer, 1978).

For example, a foreign commercial company C manufacturing textiles and operating in India may be accessed as the subsidiary of a U.S. company C′. With these characteristics C is bound to the variable X. The same company C, which is bound to the variable Y, may be accessed as a company in India that has more than 5,000 employees and a budget greater than 1 million dollars. Assuming X and Y can only be bound to objects (i.e., not to pointers), to correlate such identical objects bound to different variables we need a different type of equality. In fact, object-oriented languages such as Smalltalk provide a simple identity test with the expression $X = = Y$, which is different from the equality test $X = Y$. The identity test checks whether two objects are the same. The equality test checks whether the contents of two objects are the same.

For example, assume a rectangle is specified through two points.

    UpperLeftHandSide: Point
    LowerRightHandSide: Point

Suppose we instantiate two points and use them to instantiate two rectangles. Then the two rectangles will have identical *contents* (and hence be equal) without being identical. Thus, for Rec1 and Rec2 instantiated as

    P1 := New(Point, 2,1)
    P2 := New(Point, 2,1)

Rec1 := New(Rectangle, P1, P2)
Rec2 := New(rectangle, P1, P2)
Rec1 = Rec2 is "True" whereas Rec1 = = Rec2 is "False."

Besides the test for identical objects, built-in support for identity requires other operators to manipulate identity as needed. Next we briefly describe some of these operators.

Coalescing or Merging—Two objects with separate identity may later be discovered to be the same (the murderer is the butler!) and therefore need to be merged. Codd (1979) has argued for a *coalescing* operator in RM/T (discussed in Chapter 2) that merges identity. This operator basically checks if all the corresponding instance variables of two objects are equal ('=') and if yes, it makes one object identical to the other, such that all references to either object are now to one and the same object. The semantics and support of this operation could be tricky and expensive. The simplest approach is to require the two objects to have the same type and be equal. Then all that we need is to ensure all the references to the old objects and their subcomponents now refer to the merged object and its subcomponents. However, it is possible to make merging more sophisticated and provide support for merging differently structured objects. This is a very useful concept in statistical databases called record-linking (Wrigley, 1973; Howe and Lindsay, 1981), where an attempt is made to merge information that was gathered by different sources and that contains different sorts of information about the same objects.

Copying Objects—Different copy operators are also needed to indicate the degree of copying vs. sharing. Smalltalk-80 provides a *shallow copy* operator and a *deep copy* operator in addition to simple assignment. For example, suppose the value of Y is a set. Assigning Y to X causes X to share the same set object as Y. Assigning a shallow copy of Y to X causes X to be a new set object with its own identity, whose elements are shared with those in Y. Assigning a deep copy of Y to X causes X to be a new set object with its own identity, whose elements are new objects with their own identity, but that have the same values as those of Y. Figure 3.19 illustrates shallow and deep copying of a set S with two elements: O1 and O2. O1 represents the employee John who is 31 years old and who earns \$30,000; O2 represents the employee Mary who is also 31 years old and who earns \$40,000. A shallow copy of S will produce a new set S′ whose content will be exactly the same as that of S. A deep copy of S will produce a new set S″ whose content consists of the objects O3 and O4. Although O3 (O4) and O1 (O2) contain the same information about John (Mary), they are two different objects (and hence not identical or '= ='). Hence S and S″ are not (shallow) equal.

3.5.1 Identity through Identifier Keys

Database systems use record identifier keys to distinguish objects. In the relational model an identifier key is some subset of the attributes of an object that is unique for all objects in the relation. For example, the first and last name of a person or the

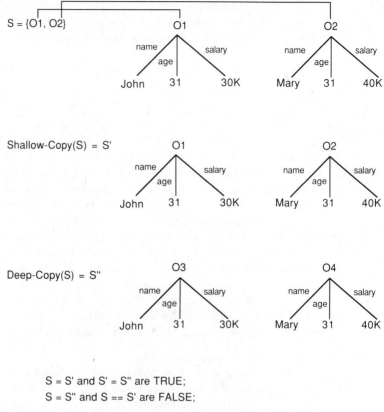

$$S = S' \text{ and } S' = S'' \text{ are TRUE;}$$
$$S = S'' \text{ and } S == S' \text{ are FALSE;}$$

Figure 3.19 Shallow and deep copying.

year and model of a car or account number in a bank. Using identifier keys as object identity confuses identity and data values (or object state). More specifically, there are three main problems with this approach:

1. *Modifying Identifier Keys.* One problem is that identifier keys cannot be allowed to change, even though they are user-defined descriptive data. For example, a department's name may be used as the identifier key for that department and replicated in employee objects to indicate where the employee works. But the department name may need to change under a company reorganization, causing a discontinuity in identity for the department as well as update problems in all objects that refer to it.

2. *Non-Uniformity.* A second problem is that the choice of which attribute(s) to use for an identifier key may need to change. For example, RCA may use employee numbers to identify employees, while General Electric may use Social Security numbers for the same purpose. A merger of these two companies would require

one of these keys to change, causing a discontinuity in identity for the employees of one of the companies.

3. *Unnatural Joins.* A third problem is that the use of identifier keys causes joins to be used in retrievals instead of path expressions, which are simpler, as in GEM (Zaniolo, 1983), FAD (Bancilhon et al., 1987), and OPAL (Maier and Stein, 1986). For example, suppose we have an employee relation Employee(EmpName, SS#, Salary, CompName) and a company relation Company (Name, Budget, Location, . . .), and the CompName attribute establishes a relationship between an employee and a company. Using identifier keys, Comp-Name would have as its value the identifier key of the company, for example, Name. A retrieval involving both tuples would require a join between the two tuples.

For example, in SQL to retrieve for all employees the employee name and the location the employee works in, we would use

    SELECT Employee.EmpName, Company.Location
    FROM Employee, Company
    WHERE Employee.CompName = Company.Name

The point here is that joins are *unnatural;* in most cases what the user really wants instead of the CompName is the actual company tuple. With normalization the user is restricted to a fixed collection of base types and is not allowed to assign and manipulate tuples, relations, or other complex object types of the attributes. Hence, normalization loses the semantic connectives amongst the objects in the database. In fact, relational languages such as SQL incorporate additional capabilities like foreign key constraints to recapture the lost semantics.

As we saw in Chapter 2, postrelational models allow a more direct and intuitive representation of object spaces. Consider the normalized representation of persons with spouses, education, and children as described in Figure 3.20*a*. If we allow relation-valued attributes, we can have a more compact representation for Education, which becomes a nested relation (Scheck and Scholl, 1986). This is illustrated in Figure 3.20*b*. However, note that the children are still represented separately, since each child pertains to both parents. Furthermore, the spouses refer to each other through foreign keys.

In the vast majority of cases the user wants to directly reference the Children, Spouse, and education of a person. The first normal form constraint of the relational models forces the programmer to normalize (flatten) everything. Non–first normal form models provide a partial solution. What is needed is the ability to share objects. The concept of *sharing* is somewhat confusing and has been used in different connotations by AI, object-oriented programming languages, and database communities.

In a database framework, sharing relates to synchronizing concurrent accesses to

Normalized:

Persons	Name	Age	Address	Spouse
	John	35	3131 Park St.	Mary
	Mary	32	3131 Park St.	John

Education	Person	Degree	University	Year
	John	M.Sc	UT-Austin	1981
	Mary	Ph.D	UW-Madison	1985
	John	M.Sc	USC	1979
	Mary	Ph.D	UW-Madison	1986

Children	Person	CName	CAge
	John	Tim	5
	Mary	Jane	3
	John	Tim	
	Mary	Jane	

Figure 3.20*a* Normalized representations of persons with spouses, education, and children.

objects to ensure the consistency of information stored in the database. The database is accessed and updated through transactions, where a transaction is a program that is either executed entirely or not executed at all (i.e., transactions are atomic). Serializability of transactions is required (Eswaran et al., 1976; Papadimitriou, 1979) and is typically achieved through locking. Shared locks on an object allow multiple readers to access it, whereas an exclusive lock grants access to only one user (writer). Objects that are accessed concurrently by multiple users (transactions) will henceforth be called *concurrently shared objects*.

In an object-oriented framework, sharing relates to the support and maintenance of the references of the shared object (Rentsch, 1982). A reference to an object implies (shared) ownership by all referencing objects. An object that becomes nonaccessible from any other object is *garbage* and should be removed from the object space

Non-First Normal Form

Persons	Name	Age	Address	Spouse	Education		
	John	35	3131 Park St.	Mary	Degree	University	Year
					M.Sc	UT-Austin	1981
					Ph.D	UW-Madison	1985
	Mary	32	3131 Park St.	John	Degree	University	Year
					M.Sc	USC	1979
					Ph.D	UW-Madison	1986

Children	Person	CName	CAge
	John	Tim	5
	Mary	Jane	3
	John	Tim	5
	Mary	Jane	3

Figure 3.20b Non-first normal form representation of persons with spouses, education, and children.

(Lieberman and Hewitt 1983, Ungar 1984). So unlike the database perspective, where the users of an object could be thought of as concurrently executing transactions, the users in the object-oriented world are themselves objects owning or referencing the same shared entity. Objects that are accessible (and hence shared) by other objects will be called *referentially shared objects*.

Object identity supports and enables the referential sharing of objects. The persons example with object identity is illustrated in Figure 3.20c. Thus, arbitrary graph-structured object spaces are easily represented.

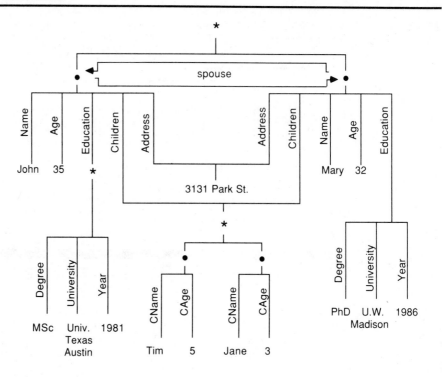

● = Tuple: Object with properties/attributes
★ = Set: Coffection of Objects

Figure 3.20c Hierarchical representation of persons with spouses, education, and children.

3.5.2 Preserving Identity through Object Modifications

Several researchers have argued for a temporal data model to support historical versions (e.g., Copeland, 1980; Clifford and Warren, 1983; Katz and Lehman, 1984; Copeland and Maier, 1984; Copeland and Khoshafian, 1987). The reason is that most real-world organizations deal with histories of objects, but they have little support from existing systems to help them in modeling and retrieving historical data. Strong support of identity is important for temporal data models, because a single retrieval may involve multiple historical versions of a single object. Such support requires the database system to provide a continuous and consistent notion of identity throughout the life of each object, independent of any descriptive data or structure that is user modifiable. This identity is the common thread that ties together these historical versions of an object.

▪ 3.6 OBJECT-ORIENTED DATABASES

Chapter 2 provided an extensive review of database data models. Earlier in this chapter we discussed how numerous object-oriented concepts and approaches have permeated the more recent data models. Figure 3.21a gives a summary of the history of the evolution of database data models, starting with the network and hierarchical models. The next dramatic step was the introduction of the relational model by Ted Codd. Database researchers soon realized the lack of semantics in the relational model and the evolution of database data models progressed along three somewhat independent lines: non–first normal form models, semantic and functional data models, and logic databases.

It took almost a decade for relational databases to become commercially available in products such as INGRES, ORACLE, and more recently DB2. Although some serious attempts, such as ADAPLEX, have been made to develop commercial products based on these paradigms, overall the postrelational models did not leave the research labs of industry or universities. However, perhaps through an eagerness to diversify in novel and emerging applications, both industry and research in databases took quick notice of the opportunities and potential of an object-oriented system with database capabilities (i.e., concurrency, persistence, access methods, querying, etc.).

With the introduction of GemStone, the first object-oriented database became commercially available in late 1986. The first object-oriented database workshop in Asilomar, during the summer of 1986, also demonstrated that an enthusiasm similar to the

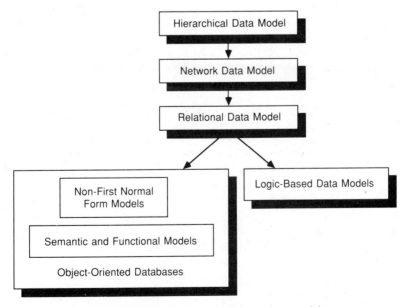

Figure 3.21a Evolution of database data models.

one in the object-oriented programming communities, was permeating the database community. The following years witnessed the development of several commercial object-oriented databases (Maier et al., 1986; Andrew and Harris, 1987; Jagannathan et al., 1988). Figure 3.21*b* demonstrates the evolution of commercial products based on the models of Figure 3.21 *a*.

Experts disagree as to what constitutes an object-oriented database. In fact, there is hardly any agreement in the constituency of an object-oriented system in general. Perhaps the most naive and obvious definition of an object-oriented database is the augmentation of an object-oriented system with database capabilities.

If we define these minimal database capabilities as

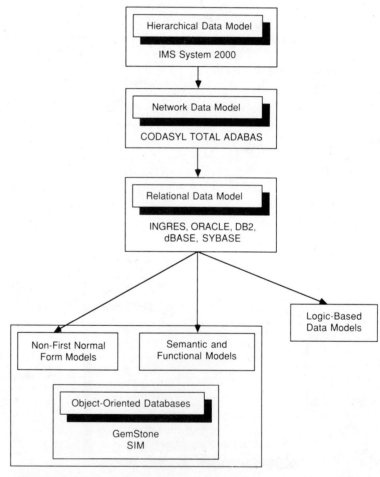

Figure 3.21*b* Evolution of commercial database management systems.

1. A high-level query language with query optimization capabilities in the underlying system.

2. Support of persistence and atomic transactions: concurrency control and recovery.

3. Support of complex object storage, indexes and access methods for fast and efficient retrieval.

Then we can define an object-oriented database as

Object-Oriented System + (1)–(3)

A less ambitious definition of an object-oriented database would be the capability of the database's conceptual model to represent and manipulate complex objects directly. Complex object support allows object properties (slots, attributes, instance variables, etc.) to be arbitrary objects themselves (rather than just an element of a base type). Diettrich (1986) characterized this as *structural* object orientation.

This type of structurally oriented characterization of object orientation has a lot of merit since a direct representation of, say, hierarchically or graph-structured objects is very natural and provides a semantically rich representation of an object space. Figure 3.21 demonstrates how the postrelational conceptual models are on a semantically "higher" level than the relational model, which imposes the first normal form (flat files). The rest of this chapter describes properties of object-oriented databases through a description of a commercial object-oriented database, GemStone.

3.6.1 GemStone

GemStone is an object-oriented database system that runs on minicomputers. The OPAL language that constitutes both the data definition and data manipulation (conceptual) database languages of GemStone is very similar to Smalltalk. In describing some of the features of OPAL, we shall be concentrating on its particular features as a *database* language.

As indicated earlier, a database management system must satisfy some basic features including querying, concurrent transactions, and fast associative retrieval capabilities. GemStone supports all these features. In fact, OPAL allows users to commit or abort their transactions, create indexes, and express queries.

3.6.1.1 Querying in OPAL

OPAL introduces a selection block (vs. "ordinary" blocks of Smalltalk) construct for special types of objects called *constrained Collections*. What are constrained Collections? Consider the OPAL class hierarchy initially provided to the user as described in Figure 3.22. Any instance of Collection is a collection of objects such as a set, a bag (which is a set with duplicates), or a dictionary.

A collection that is a set is quite similar to a table in a more conventional database query language such as SQL. However, one immediate distinction that comes to mind

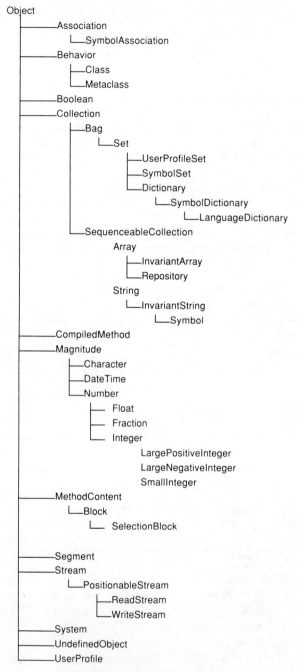

Figure 3.22 A hierarchy of concepts.

```
Object subclass: 'Employee'
instVarNames: #('name' 'age' 'address' 'company' 'salary')

  classVars: #()

  constraints: #[
                    #[#name, FirstLast],
                    #[#age, Integer],

                    #[#address, String],

                    #[#company, Company],

                    #[#salary, Dollar],
```

```
Set subclass: 'SetOfEmployees'
constraints: Employee
```

```
Object subclass: 'Company'
instVarNames: #('name' 'address' 'expense'
'revenue' 'employees' 'ceo' 'subsidiaries')

  classVars: #()

  constraints: #[        #[#name, String],
                         #[#address, String]
                         #[#expense, Dollar]
                         #[#revenue, Dollar]
                         #[#employees, SetOfEmployees]

                         #[#ceo, Employee]

                         #[#subsidiaries, SetOfCompany], ]
```

```
Set subclass: 'SetOfCompany'
constraints: Company
```

Figure 3.23 Constrained collections.

between a language such as SQL and a novel untyped language such as Smalltalk is that the former specifies a particular type for each of its columns (attributes) that corresponds to the instance variable of the elements of the collection in Smalltalk. In Smalltalk, corresponding instances variables can assume different types and the same instance variable can be updated to indicate a different type of object. For example, the age instance variable of a child can be set to the integer 1 and subsequently to the float 1.5.

SQL implementations make heavy use of the type constraints in storage organization, query optimization, and indexing. OPAL introduces constrained collections for similar reasons.

Let us illustrate this through a somewhat modified and extended example of Employees as described in Servio (1986). The constraints here restrict the types of the instance variables (which are completely unrestricted in Smalltalk). Thus 'Name' has to be an instance of the class FirstLast, 'Job' has to be an instance of the class String, and so on. These constraints must be observed for every instance of Employee. The constraint of SetOfEmployee indicates that every element of a set of employees (an instance of SetOfEmployee) must be an instance of Employee (Figure 3.23).

It is no secret that the run-time dynamic binding of messages to methods in languages such as Smalltalk is expensive. Motivated with this performance consideration, as well as a desire to provide querying capabilities, OPAL introduces *selection blocks*.

A selection block specifies a query that associatively filters the qualifying elements in a collection, very similar to a SELECT clause in SQL. Selection blocks are delimited by { and } and sent through select. For example, to obtain the subset of all employees in MyEmps (an instance of SetOfEmployees) who earn more than $60,000 the query is

richEmps := MyEmps select: {:anEmployee|anEmployee.salary > 60000}

Since a selection block vs. an ordinary block delimited by [and] is used, the underlying system will not use message passing. Instead the query will be evaluated procedurally, similar to query processing in, say, SQL.

The predicate in the selection block can be more complex and involve conjunctions. For example to retrieve the employees whose last name is Jones and whose job is secretary the query is

JonesSecretaries := MyEmps select:
{:anEmployee|(anEmployee.job = 'secretary') &
(anEmployee.name.last = 'ones')}

Notice how this illustrates a rather peculiar convention in accessing the instance variables of objects in the predicates; the instance variables are accessed directly through a dot notation! This *visibility* of instance variables clearly violates encapsulation. The motivation for allowing these paths is performance. The instances will be accessed directly (vs. indirectly through methods). Another usage is indexes, which are discussed next.

3.6.1.2 *Indexing in GemStone*

OPAL allows the specification of indexes explicitly on instance variables or paths to expedite associative retrievals. Without an index, the search in a selection block will traverse and consider every single element in the collection instance. Indexes restrict these exhaustive searches and hence drastically improve the performance.

Similar to other structurally object-oriented database systems such as FAD (Bancilhon et al., 1987), OPAL also supports the strong notion of object identity (see Section 3.5). Similar to Smalltalk and FAD, both the equality (=) and identical (= =) predicates are supported in OPAL.

Accordingly OPAL allows the creation of two types of indexes: identity indexes and equality indexes. Identity indexes are useful when the predicate in the selection block involves a = = on the indexed instance variable.

Equality indexes are useful in value-based comparisons such as = and > = . Equality indexes can be created only on base types such as booleans, numbers, strings, and so on. The following creates an equality index on the instance variable 'job' of MyEmps:

MyEmps CreateEqualityIndexOn: 'job'

An equality index on the last names of employees could be created through

MyEmps CreateEqualityIndexOn: 'name.last'

This latter index will be created on a path. As a "side effect" an identity index will be created on 'name'. In general, indexes on paths will create identity indexes on every instance variable in the path except the last instance variable, which could have an equality index as in this example.

An identity index is always automatically created on the elements of the constrained collection. Therefore, if the predicate in the selection block is

anEmp.name.last = 'Jones'

then

a. The equality index on last will be used to retrieve identities of name (e.g., surrogates of name — Khoshafian and Copeland, 1986) to retrieve the qualifying name objects.

b. The identity index on name will be used to retrieve identities on employees. Note that identity index on name associates identities of name with identities of employees, similar to the join index (Valduriez, 1987) concept used in the hierarchical storage scheme described elsewhere (Khoshafian, Franklin, and Carey, 1988) and (Valduriez et al., 1986).

c. The identity index on the employee collection instance will be used to retrieve the qualifying employees. These index traversals are illustrated in Figure 3.24.

Another important usage of identity indexes is in predicates involving = = . For example, if richDept indicates a particular department object, then

EmpsInrichDept := myEmps select: { :anEmp| :anEmp.dept = = richDept}

MyEmployees   createEqualityIndexOn   'name.last'

(i) Index 1: an equality index mapping last names to identities of name:

name.last	name Surrogate
Adams	S10
Copeland	S2
Jones	S1
Smith	S5

(ii) Index 2: an identity index mapping name identities to Employee identities

name Surrogate	Employee Surrogate
S1	eS12
S2	eS24
S5	eS3
S10	eS10

(iii) Index 0 : Maps Employee identities to Employee objects

Figure 3.24 Index traversals in an employee database. To obtain instance of employee in MyEmps with name.last = 'Jones'; traverse index 1 to obtain S1, using S1 traverse index 2 to obtain eS12, and use eS12 to traverse index 0 and obtain the object.

will retrieve all employees that are in that particular department. An identity index on the 'dept' instance variable will greatly accelerate the search.

3.6.1.3 *Transactions in GemStone*

A database management system must support persistence and atomic transactions on the persistent object space. GemStone is no exception. In fact, the OPAL language provides some primitives for committing and aborting transactions. The underlying system uses an optimistic concurrency-control algorithm based on a workspace model.

When a user logs in, he or she is given a new workspace and all updates to the database are done in this workspace, transparent to all other users. Therefore, only the user sees his or her updates, unless the user commits. Committing a transaction is achieved through sending a commit message to the system. In OPAL the syntax is

    System commitTransaction

The user might choose to continue the session after the commit. This will start a new transaction and create a new workspace. Alternatively the user might decide to undo all the updates to the database and abort the current transaction. This is achieved through the message

System abortTransaction

As before, if the user continues the session a new transaction will commence.

3.6.1.4 *Clustering in GemStone*

Through clustering it is possible to store (on disk) an object and its subobjects on the same storage extent such as a disk page, a track, or a cylinder. In more traditional record based databases in most cases clustering involves storing homogeneous records pertaining, say, to the same relation on the same disk page. Figure 3.25 gives an example of employee records stored on the same page. Since records are normalized or flat, special provisions have to be made in order to cluster *foreign* records such as address tuples in the same page. Most relational database implementations do not provide such capabilities.

Because of object identity, hierarchical and graph structured objects are very natural to express in OPAL. Thus, an employee's address, department, children, education, and so on could all become values of his or her instance variables as objects. Since these objects pertaining to an employee are typically accessed together with other atomic attributes such as age, name, or Social Security number of an employee, there would be considerable performance advantages if these objects were clustered with the employee. To this end, OPAL provides a number of primitives for clustering these objects together as close as possible. The OPAL command to indicate that an object may be clustered is

MyObject cluster

which acquires the next available disk page and assigns it to MyObject. Subsequent cluster messages will continue the clustering in the same extent. Thus, if the next clustering calls were

MyObject.x1 cluster MyObject.x2 cluster

Id	Name	Age	Address
S1	'John Jones'	25	'1312 Spring St.'
S2	'Jack Copeland'	31	'21 Broadway'
S5	'Mary Smith'	24	'1 First Street'
S10	'Don Adams'	44	'23 Lucky Blvd.'

Figure 3.25 Employee records stored on the same page.

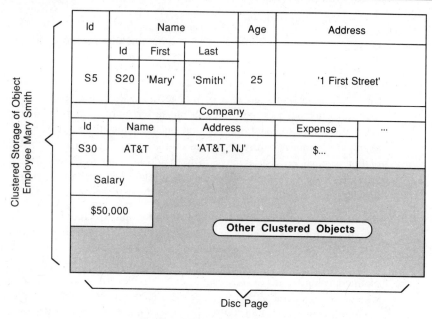

Figure 3.26 Clustered storage.

both x1 and x2 would have been clustered with MyObject. Thus, the order of clustering is entirely controlled by the user. In particular, the user might define methods to perform breadth-first, depth-first, or other types of clustering as he or she sees fit. One such method is given in Figure 3.26 for Employees. In fact OPAL has a built-in ClusterDepthFirst method, which performs (preorder) depth-first clustering of an object and all the objects reachable from it.

It should be pointed out that the cluster methods will basically ignore the clustering request if an object is already clustered. Remember that the object space in OPAL is a directed graph. Thus, objects are referentially shared. Hence, a different ancestor of an object could have already clustered the object. For example, if we have a JCPennyDepts constrained collection where each instance contains all the departments of a particular JCPenny store and all the department objects are clustered, then a ClusterDepthFirst or simply a cluster message from an employee object to its department will be ignored; the department is already clustered.

■ 3.7 APPLICATIONS OF OBJECT ORIENTATION

A natural domain of application for the object-oriented approach is in knowledge representation in AI and conceptual database modeling.

Several commercial expert-system shells provide an object-oriented approach in their knowledge representation. For example, the Intelligence/Compiler (Parsaye and

Chignell, 1988) supports frames, instances of frames, and inheritance of frames, thus supporting inheritance and complex object modeling.

Besides the obvious suitability of object orientation in knowledge representation in general, there are some specific areas that have come to be recognized as application domains of object orientation. The three main areas discussed here are discrete event simulation, design engineering, and software engineering.

3.7.1 Discrete-Event Simulation

In a very real sense, discrete-event simulation paved the way for object-oriented programming. The notion of a *process* in the language Simula laid the foundation for object-oriented programming. Similar to the more recent extensions of popular languages with object-oriented paradigms; more than two decades ago to facilitate the modeling and programming of simulation models, Simula was introduced as an extension to Algol. Simula introduced (Dahl and Nygaard, 1966) "Means of describing processes, generating processes dynamically, and referencing existing ones. . . . Means of making data local to processes accessible from other processes."

Thus, the notion of processes in Simula is very similar to the notion of objects; they are data carriers and execute actions. In fact, the original paper (Dahl and Nygaard, 1966) even introduced and used notions such as "classes" and "instances" in an event simulation context.

> The concept of an activity which is a class of processes described by the same declaration is distinguished from the concept of a 'process' which is one dynamic instance of an activity declaration.

The motivation of these extensions to Algol in Simula was discrete-event simulation; the processes correspond to instances of activities that, due to some local processing, could cause other processes to be activated.

Client-server simulation models as depicted in Figure 3.27 are well-suited to object-oriented solutions. Consider the automatic car-wash model as depicted in Figure 3.28. The driver pays to the cashier who activates the automatic washer. Subsequently the Brushers soap the car and pass it to the next process, namely, rinsing. The Rinser, after it terminates, passes the car to the Dryer.

Both servers (the cashier, Brushers, Rinser, Dryer, etc.) and clients (the cars) could be modeled as objects. The arrival of a car to be washed is an event that causes an interaction between the driver and cashier and a subsequent chain of events as the car passes through the automatic car wash. The internal state of the car (including the driver who parts with some money but is eventually satisfied with his clean car) changes as it is processed by the servers. Similarly, the state of the servers is modified when a service is performed (the station gets richer, soap is utilized by the brushers, etc.). The events in the automatic car-wash are messages that are sent from/to servers to/from clients.

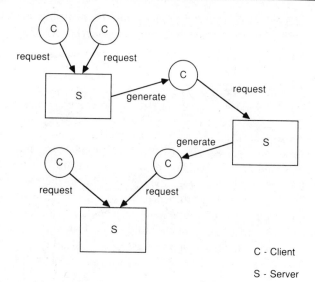

Figure 3.27 A client-server simulation model.

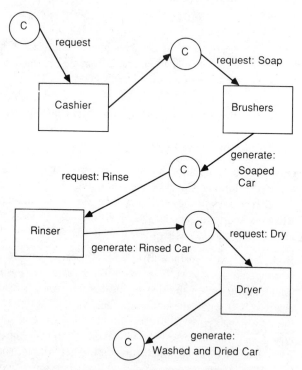

Figure 3.28 An automatic car-wash model.

Although this example is oversimplified, it illustrates the appropriateness of object-oriented programming in capturing client-server models, where events are messages and both servers and clients are objects with internal states and processing capabilities. However, our oversimplification ignores a very fundamental aspect of simulation, namely the temporal aspect and the consequent need of synchronization, since in the real world many events occur simultaneously.

It is curious to note that although the description of object-oriented languages includes notions with concurrent connotations such as *messages* and *active objects* processing these messages, the underlying execution model is typically sequential.

A case in point is Smalltalk-80, which introduces additional notions such as processes and semaphores to model concurrent tasks and communication primitives. However, having both objects and processes is confusing and problematic, as explained elegantly by Yokote and Tokoro (1987).

> Smalltalk-80 [Goldberg and Robson, 1983] is one of the typical object-oriented languages/systems. Message passing in Smalltalk-80 is defined to have the same semantics as procedure calls, and computation is done sequentially. . . . In order to describe a problem which contains concurrency, the notion of process is employed. A process is created by sending a fork message to a block context. However, this decision eventually imposed upon the programmer the cumbersome labor of modeling the problem in two different level modules: objects and processes. This impairs descriptivity and understandability. We claim that a programmer should just describe a problem in single level modules and that such modules be executed concurrently according to necessity.

Thus, several concurrent object-oriented languages have been proposed, including Hewitt's actor model (Hewitt, 1977), Lieberman's Act 1 (Lieberman, 1981), and Concurrent Smalltalk (Yokoto and Tokoro, 1987). Next we briefly discuss the main features of ABCL/1 (Shibayama and Yonezawa, 1987), which has been proposed and used for discrete-event simulation.

Objects in ABCL/1 execute concurrently. An object is either dormant, waiting, or active. Objects get activated upon receiving messages. When an object has processed all its messages it becomes dormant. When an object attempts to obtain a particular message that has not yet arrived it becomes waiting.

The temporal aspect is also incorporated in the message types. Thus, there are three types of messages: past, now, or future. With these and additional temporal capabilities (such as *time stamps, rollbacks,* and so on), ABCL/1 provides a uniform and powerful programming environment for discrete-event simulation. In conclusion, although encapsulation, and to a lesser extent inheritance, provide powerful modeling primitives, discrete-event simulation requires an additional concurrent execution model.

3.7.2 Design Engineering

The three main characteristics of object orientation provide powerful modeling tools for engineering applications. The objects in these domains are typically composites or aggregates (Katz, 1987) of components. The components pertain to the next level of detail in an engineering object's representation (Batory and Kim, 1985). The term *composite object* is commonly used to capture this layered abstraction model. In an object-oriented language an object's instance variables (properties, attributes, etc.) would store or reference the components of a composite object.

A composite object has an interface description that defines its behavior. Each of the components of a composite object can itself be a composite object with specific behavior.

Figure 3.29 describes a simplified representation of a Car, which consists of (composite of) an Engine and a Body. The Engine itself consists of (composite of) a steering system, a propulsion system, and a braking system. The Car at the top of the hierarchy corresponds to an encapsulated class. The decomposition of the internal representation (Engine and Body) will not be visible or relevant to the user. Instead the user will interface with the Car through the methods that capture the Car's behavior (ignition, acceleration etc.). Similarly the Car's Engine is an abstraction consisting of three components at a lower level of abstraction.

Through the development phases of a composite object there could be several versions, or alternatives, before a final release. These versions can have common subcomponents. We saw in Section 3.3 that object identity provides a most natural paradigm for maintaining the uniqueness of objects, independent of structure or content. Thus the object's identity could be used to maintain the link among all the various versions and alternatives of the same object. The support of referential sharing of objects

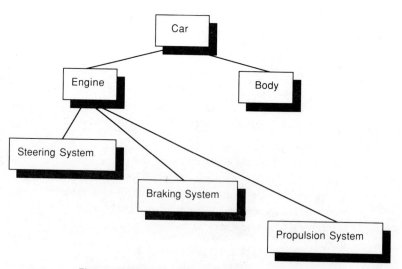

Figure 3.29 A simplified representation of a car.

(also through object identity) is also commonly utilized in design engineering since different abstractions or components of an object might share the same subcomponents.

As a simple example consider a robot and its arm as described in Figure 3.30a. Figure 3.30b shows two versions of the robot's arm. Version 1 shares with version 3 the rotational axis and the first translation axis. The robot's hand and the second translation axis are different. Both versions can have the same interfaces responding to the same commands to pick up an object, stretch the arm, rotate the hand, and so on. Also note that the robot's body shares the rotational axis as a common subpart with the arm.

Although in our examples we have simplified the representation of design engineering objects, the key point is that the object-oriented representation and abstraction paradigms closely and directly model complex, multiversion engineering objects.

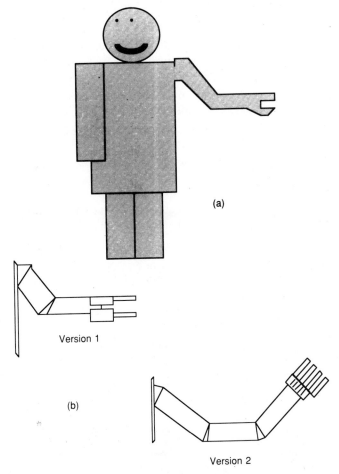

(a)

Version 1

(b)

Version 2

Figure 3.30 A robot and its arm.

3.7.3 Software Engineering

Another increasingly popular application of object orientation is software engineering of large and complex systems. Some of the goals of software engineering include the following:

a. *Modifiability.* The ability to modify a part of a computer system without unexpected side effects in other parts of the system.

b. *Maintainability.* The ability to readily make enhancements, adapt to new environments and correct problems.

c. *Understandability.* The ability to have systems that are understandable and reflect a clear design structure by having readable code.

d. *Portability.* The ability to have systems that can be readily transferred from one computer system or environment to another.

e. *Abstraction.* The ability to have both decomposition and composition in the system. Decomposition is the process of systematically breaking down a system into smaller parts. Conversely, composition involves grouping, abbreviating, simplifying, and summarizing to extract the essential properties of parts while omitting non-essential details.

f. *Information Hiding.* The ability to differentiate the what from the how. The what: information describes functionality. The how information includes implementation details such as data structures.

g. *Reusability.* The ability to reuse part or all of an existing code.

There is a lot of commonality among these goals. Furthermore, this list of goals is not exhaustive since it does not include other goals of software engineering such as traceability, localization, modularization, robust error handling, and so on. However, this list will be sufficient to illustrate the suitability of object-oriented methodology in meeting the goals of software engineering.

As discussed earlier, the main features of the object-oriented model are abstract data typing or encapsulation, identity, and inheritance. Encapsulation allows the collection of data structures representing object instances and their operations to be localized in *modules*. The separation of an object's interface (modules) from the internal representation, the *hiding* of the method's implementation, and the abstraction of types (hopefully) defined through a collection of complete operations capturing the behavior of abstract data types supports modifiability, maintainability, understandability, and portability.

Thus, method implementations could be modified without any effect on the rest of the system. This also greatly enhances portability. Since the whole system is represented as a collection of abstract data types where data types and operators are localized, it is easier to understand and maintain the system (Booch, 1986).

Meyer (1987) makes a strong case for reusability using an object-oriented design methodology and an object-oriented language such as Eiffel. The main approach is the construction of systems by reusing and combining existing software. The existing software consists of classes that could be combined and reused either through becoming clients of other classes or through inheritance. A class A is a client of class B if A contains an instance variable X whose value is constrained to be an instance of B.

For example, assume a class VMClass representing virtual machines contains the following instance variables whose values are bound to the indicated classes:

    Stack: StackClass
    CPU: CPUCLass
    Memory: MemoryCLass
    Accumulator: AcuClass . . .

Thus CMClass is a client of StackClass, CPUCLass, MemoryClass, and AcuClass. The MemoryClass is itself implemented as a subclass of ArrayClass. StackClass has a subclass FixedSizeStackClass that represents stacks which can grow up to a maximum fixed size. VMClass has several subclasses including RISC-VMClass, CISC-VMClass, and VectVMClass representing virtual machines with RISC architectures, CISC architectures and vector processing capabilities, respectively.

Using preexisting classes (code) as clients or through inheritance is a basic engineering approach. Since encapsulation allows the definition and construction of self-contained, independently modifiable classes, these class units could be used to construct new classes. Thus, existing classes are *massaged* and *specialized* to suit particular application domains, while maintaining or reusing the bulk of the existing code implementing the predefined classes. As Cox and Hunt (1986) pointed out, "what is truly revolutionary about object-oriented programming is that it helps programmers reuse existing code, just as silicon chips help circuit builders reuse the work of chip designers."

■ 3.8 SUMMARY

This chapter presented the key concepts of object orientation. It described the orthogonal notions of encapsulation, inheritance, and object identity, which characterize object-oriented systems and languages. Several existing object-oriented languages were discussed and compared. The characteristics of object-oriented databases were also discussed. Finally the chapter illustrated how the object-oriented style of programming may be applied to a number of application domains including discrete-event simulation, software engineering, and design engineering.

4

EXPERT SYSTEMS

Chapters 2 and 3 discussed databases and data models. Chapter 2 placed particular emphasis on the relational model. In Chapter 3, we focused on the object-oriented approach to database systems.

How can we extend these database models and systems so as to construct intelligent databases? The solution is to add extra knowledge representation and inferencing capability. The tools for knowledge representation and inferencing are provided within the context of expert systems. In this chapter, we introduce the essential elements of expert systems that will assist in making databases more intelligent. The two major elements of this assistance are

a. Expert systems provide higher level programming capabilities.

b. Expert systems provide a knowledge representation formalism.

It is, however, important to distinguish between these two elements. In our view, the first element will have major impact on the future of databases and programming systems in general. Consequently, in this book, we focus mostly on the use of expert systems as programming paradigms.

We begin with a general discussion of expert systems, then move on to the concept of *knowledge*. We then discuss inference and object-based knowledge representation. These concepts are then related to the database concepts introduced in Chapter 2 by showing how a relational database may be closely integrated with a reasoning system. We also show how objects and inheritance may be used as higher level structures in

161

dealing with relational databases. This provides a good deal of object orientation to relational databases.

In this chapter, the discussion of expert systems in the context of intelligent databases focuses on the integration of *deduction* and databases. Another important issue is *induction* which we will discuss in Chapter 7. Deduction is a process of drawing conclusions from a known set of axioms, while induction focuses on the discovery of unexpected results from a database.

In the following sections, we present a method of seamlessly integrating deduction, object-orientation and databases. The formalism adopted here follows that implemented in the Intelligence/Compiler system for combining SQL, object-orientation, and pattern matching rules.

We begin our discussion with an overview of expert systems concepts and follow this with discussions of rule-based inference and knowledge representation with frames and objects. We then show how these concepts may be uniformly merged with the database concepts introduced in the preceding chapters.

4.1.1   Introduction to Expert Systems

An expert system is generally defined as

> A computer program that relies on knowledge and reasoning to perform a difficult task usually performed only by a human expert. A human expert reasons and arrives at conclusions based on personal knowledge. In similar fashion, an expert system reasons and arrives at conclusions based on the knowledge it possesses.

However, although expert systems may be generally viewed as advisory systems, the underlying technology used in expert systems may itself be viewed as a more advanced programming technology that proves very useful in database applications. Thus not only do expert systems provide the machine reasoning capability that can make databases intelligent, but they may be viewed as higher level methods of database programming.

As shown in Figure 4.1, there are two components involved in developing expert systems.

a. New, higher level programming paradigms.
b. Methodologies for dealing with knowledge-intensive tasks.

Successful expert system applications require attention to both of these components. This is particularly the case in applying expert systems to the development of intelligent databases. There will be a need not only to represent the knowledge about a database in a form that can be used for deductive retrieval, but also a need to build a software interface between database management systems and expert systems.

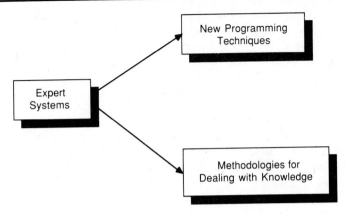

Figure 4.1 The two vectors of expert system development.

Thus there are two ways in which expert systems impact intelligent databases.

1. The higher level programming paradigms associated with expert systems are merged with database technology and are used for querying and programming.
2. The knowledge stored in the expert system is used for providing intelligent answers, making better decisions, optimization, and so on.

It is important to realize that in (1) we are not using the expertise of an expert at all—we simply use expert systems as higher level programming tools. This point is described in detail by Parsaye and Chignell (1988, Section 1.5).

In the remainder of this book we emphasize an approach to expert systems where they are seen primarily as high-level programming environments for information and knowledge-intensive tasks. Thus we use expert-systems technology as a general programming environment for putting intelligence into intelligent databases. In the rest of this chapter, we show how expert-system technologies and database technologies may be merged in this fashion.

4.1.2 The History and Evolution of Expert Systems

Expert systems arose from a research program that began with the development of the Dendral system in the 1960s (Lindsay et al., 1980), which dealt with the identification of chemical compounds from mass spectrometry data. The fundamental insight that was captured in expert systems was that much of expertise could generally be captured in terms of highly specific domain knowledge expressed in terms of "rules of thumb." This was in sharp contrast to earlier (domain independent) approaches in artificial intelligence that had stressed the importance of general approaches to problem solving.

Expert systems sprang into prominence with the success of the MYCIN and R1 expert systems and the development of expert system shells that simplified the process of building the knowledge bases and inference engines required by expert systems.

However, certain accidental features associated with the development of the first expert systems have tended to remain as part of much current thinking on expert systems. Perhaps the three most prominent features of early expert systems were their application to classificatory tasks such as medical diagnosis, their embodiment as a stand-alone "pseudoexpert" that offered consultative advice, and their limited availability on expensive LISP-based hardware and software platforms.

The embodiment of expert systems as stand-alone software environments has tended to slow their integration into other application environments such as databases. Consequently, it is not surprising that the relationship between expert systems, logic programming, and high-level programming was previously overlooked but is now well recognized (see Chapter 3 of Parsaye and Chignell, 1988). Once expert-system shells became easily available, there has been a natural, and justifiable, inclination to integrate expert systems and other programming or application environments. Movement towards intelligent databases represents perhaps the most important of these trends.

Traditionally, there have been several ways in which expert systems and databases have been related.

Accessing data in a database from an expert system—Here the database and the expert system are not integrated. This is typically done because the expert system needs data stored in the database.

Using an expert system for intelligent querying—Here the expert system is a front end for the database. This is typically done to augment the query power of the database with knowledge stored in the expert system. The expert system queries are translated to the database's own query system.

Using an expert system for management of data—Here the expert system is used as an adjunct to the database management system. This may be used for database optimization, and so on.

However, once a database and an expert system are closely integrated, the above may be much more easily achieved. In this case, the expert system itself may be viewed as an extension of the database query language. Thus, knowledge representation supercedes data representation.

4.1.3 Expert Systems as a New Programming Paradigm

One of the defining characteristics of expert systems is that they include a knowledge base, where knowledge is stored, and an inference engine, which implements procedures for reasoning with knowledge. This general architecture is analogous to the general distinction between data structures and control procedures that characterizes programming paradigms in general. When viewed in this way, expert systems can be seen to represent a new programming paradigm, but one whose lineage can be traced back to earlier programming paradigms. See Parsaye and Chignell (1988, Section 1.5) for a detailed discussion of this topic.

In expert systems, the data structures have become knowledge structures, generally consisting of frames and objects, while the control structure involves rules and the method of inference that is used to control the firing of rules. Once expert systems are viewed as programming paradigms, it becomes possible to examine correspondences between their data structuring methods and control procedures, and the equivalent components of database systems.

The storage, or data structuring, paradigm for most relational databases has been a relation, or table, while the control paradigm has generally been constructed as a programming language that typically corresponds to the Algol family of languages (e.g., C or Pascal). For instance, dBASE, one of the most widely used database systems, began by using a programming language as a control paradigm. As databases evolve, new control structures make programming them much easier. To the extent that expert systems represent the latest in an evolutionary family of programming paradigms, it makes sense to explore how the new control paradigms

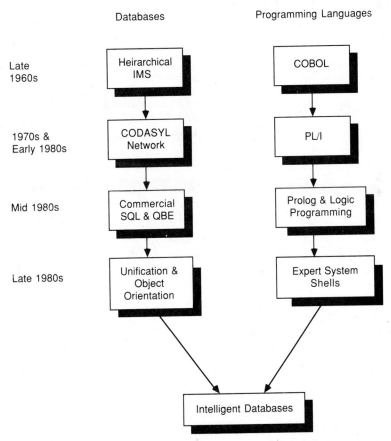

Figure 4.2 The parallel evolution of intelligent databases and programming languages.

used in expert systems may be applied in database development. Figure 4.2 shows the parallel development of database paradigms and programming languages.

4.1.4 Expert System Development

The expertise used in an expert system is a form of archival human knowledge. It is often embodied in a human expert. This *domain expert* typically provides the knowledge that will be used in the expert system. *Domain knowledge* is knowledge relating to the expert's domain, for example, knowledge of chemistry or medicine. Expert systems generally deal with a focused task with a rather narrow range of applicability and use highly specific knowledge for reasoning. In doing so, they are also able to explain their actions and lines of reasoning.

In advisory, or consulting, expert systems, the system must interact with a user who is performing a task. In order to be used and accepted, the expert system must perform a useful task reliably, be easy to use, and be maintained effectively. The knowledge used by the expert system is captured and encoded by the *expert system developer*. In some cases, the developer is a computer scientist who acts as a *knowledge engineer* — interviewing the expert, extracting the knowledge, and building the expert system. The task of building expert systems in this manner is known as *knowledge engineering*.

In intelligent databases, the conventional expert system must be modified to reflect the task of information management and retrieval. The knowledge representation and inferencing capabilities of the expert system then become modules within a much larger intelligent-database system (Figure 4.3).

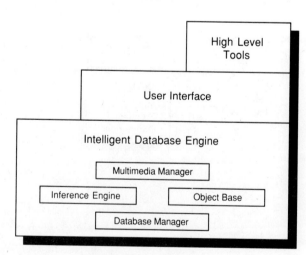

Figure 4.3 Knowledge representation and inference as modules within the intelligent database.

4.1.5   The Architecture of an Expert System

The *architecture* of expert systems is somewhat reminiscent of human cognitive structures and processes. The first part of human expertise is a long-term memory of facts, structures, and rules that represent expert knowledge about the domain of expertise. The analogous structure in an expert system is called the *knowledge base*. The second part of human expertise is a method of reasoning that can use the expert knowledge to solve problems. The part of an expert system that carries out the reasoning function is called the *inference engine*.

In this analogy the process of inference mimics thinking while knowledge is contained in the knowledge base. The difference between the knowledge base and the inference engine in an expert system also parallels the distinction between general-purpose reasoning and domain-specific knowledge that has been made in the field of artificial intelligence. In general, the domain knowledge is contained in the knowledge base. The general problem-solving knowledge is mostly built into the way the inference engine operates. Thus, the same inference engine can be used to reason with different knowledge bases.

In addition to the knowledge base and the inference engine, the expert-system environment includes a number of tools for helping the various people who build or use the expert system. When building the expert system, the developer uses expert-system building tools to acquire, encode, and debug knowledge within the knowledge base. Once the expert system has been developed, users utilize a variety of tools and interfaces to interact with the expert system. The expert system may be connected to real-time data and external databases, or it may be embedded in larger applications. In this book, we focus on the connection of expert systems to databases.

The *user-interface* of an expert system allows users to query the system, supply information, receive advice, and so on. The user interface aims to provide the same form of communication facilities provided by a human expert but often has much less capability for understanding natural language and general world knowledge. However, graphic user interfaces provide a form of human-machine communication that has no direct analog in human-human communication, as we show in the active database-querying model discussed in Chapter 7.

In the same way that human experts explain their recommendations or decisions, expert systems need to justify and explain their actions. The part of an expert system that provides explanations is called an *explanation facility*. The explanation facility not only satisfies a social need by helping an end-user feel more assured about the actions of the expert system but also serves a technical purpose by helping the developer follow through the operation of the expert system.

Figure 4.4 shows the basic structure of an expert system, which includes the user interface, a knowledge base, an inference engine, and methods for building and updating the knowledge base. Although most expert systems share the same overall architecture, the detailed architectures of specific systems vary across different knowledge domains.

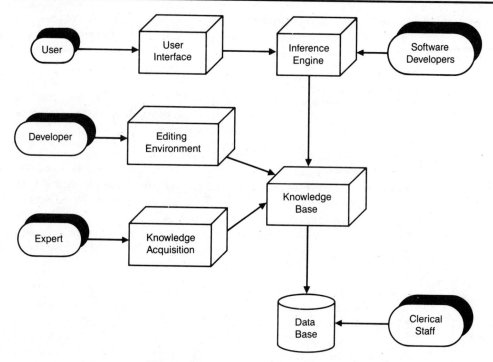

Figure 4.4 The expert system development team.

■ 4.2 KNOWLEDGE AND INFERENCE

Expert systems typically represent knowledge in terms of facts, rules, and frames. We introduce each of these methods for representing knowledge in the following sections. Our notation is based on "infix" predicate logic and uses underlining to signify predicates, as in

Columbia Pictures <u>is a subsidiary of</u> Coca-Cola Co.

Here "<u>is a subsidiary of</u>" is called a *predicate* or a verb, while "Columbia Pictures" and "Coca-Cola Co" are *arguments*. The format used in the statement above is referred to as *infix* notation, since the predicate (<u>is a subsidiary of</u>) is in the middle of its arguments (Columbia Pictures, and Coca-Cola Co., respectively). We shall signify *variables* in our notation by enclosing them in single quotation marks, as in:

'Subsidiary' <u>is a subsidiary of</u> Coca-Cola Co.

'Subsidiary' as used here, is an unbound variable. Through the process of pattern matching, this variable may be bound to a value such as "Columbia Pictures."

In predicate logic, a predicate, when combined with suitable arguments, is referred to as a *clause*. A fact may be represented in predicate logic as a clause with an associated truth value (e.g., true, false, or 75% sure). Rules, on the other hand, require the addition of the logical operators *and (conjunction), or (disjunction), not (negation),* and *implication.* We will use the words "and," "or," and "not" to represent conjunction, disjunction, and negation, respectively. Implication, which is the basis of rules, will be represented by the word "if." For a thorough discussion of predicate logic, see Parsaye and Chignell (1988, Chapter 3).

4.2.1 Facts and Rules

The first type of knowledge structure that we consider is a *fact*. The following are facts that make general statements:

> Plant 41 <u>is located</u> in Knoxville
>
> Folger's Coffee <u>is a subsidiary of</u> Proctor & Gamble
>
> Herman Zollinger <u>is president of</u> Smith Industries
>
> Carbon <u>is an</u> element

The first three facts are more transient than the fourth. Thus we may use facts to refer to either permanent or temporary knowledge.

Another basic knowledge structure often used by experts is a *rule. Production rules* were championed as a means of representing knowledge in a form that could be used for inference by Newell and Simon (1972). In this approach knowledge was represented as a series of *If-Then* rules based on propositional logic. Rules are a straightforward method of representing expertise, and they are frequently used to represent knowledge in expert systems.

The following are some simple rules:

> If
>> The salt intake <u>is</u> high
> Then
>> Blood pressure <u>is</u> high;
>
> If
>> A hazard <u>is</u> present
> Then
>> Injury or death <u>may occur</u>;

When combined with the facts, rules can be used to arrive at *conclusions*, which are new facts. For instance, one (possibly inaccurate) rule might be that the conclusion

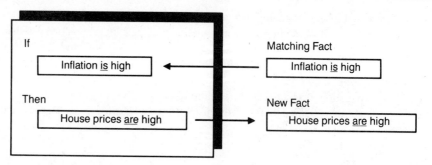

Figure 4.5 A simple knowledge system consisting of one fact and one rule.

House prices <u>are</u> high

is true, if the fact

Inflation <u>is</u> high

is true. Figure 4.5 shows the information used in drawing this conclusion. All that is needed in this case is one fact and one rule. Figure 4.6 shows how the fact and the rule are combined to give the conclusion.

Facts may be added to the database using a special predicate called *assert*. Similarly, facts may then be removed from the database using the *retract* predicate. For instance,

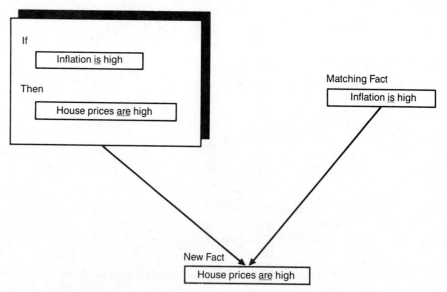

Figure 4.6 Deducing a conclusion based on the knowledge in Figure 4.5.

<u>assert</u> Sugar level <u>is</u> high

followed by

<u>retract</u> Sugar level <u>is</u> high

will leave the factbase unchanged.

An implication of the form "If A Then B," for example

>   If
>   rain <u>is present</u>
>   Then
>   clouds <u>are present</u>;

means that whenever A is true, B is also true. Note that if A is false, B may still be true.

Implications may be written forward, as in

>   If
>   A
>   Then
>   B;

or backwards, as in

>   B
>   If
>   A;

We will use the semicolon to signify the end of a rule.

An implication (rule) may even have a degree of confidence (or confidence factor, CF) attached to it. For example:

>   CF = 25
>   rain <u>is present</u>
>   If
>   clouds <u>are present</u>;

indicating a 25% confidence in the truth of this rule. Thus we have three forms of rules:

>   *forward rule*
>   If
>   rain <u>is present</u>

Then
    clouds <u>are present</u>;

backward rule

    clouds <u>are present</u>
If
    rain <u>is present</u>;

inexact rule

    CF = 25
        rain <u>is present</u>;
    If
        clouds <u>are present</u>

Note that the first two rules above are true 100% of the time whereas the third rule is only partially true.

4.2.2   Inference

The process of combining facts and rules to deduce new facts is referred to as *inference*. It is often useful to view inference in terms of a *tree of possibilities*. This provides a diagrammatic way of representing the structure of knowledge and helps in visualizing inference as a dynamic process.

Rules consist of premises and conclusions. We can construct inference trees whose *nodes* are the clauses used in rules and whose *branches* are arrows connecting the clauses. When clauses are joined by an AND connective, we have an "AND node"; whenever clauses are joined with the OR connective, we have an "OR node." The branching in such trees reflects the structure of a set of rules. Such trees are also called *AND/OR* trees.

Inference trees often provide good intuition about the structure of the rules. We can visualize the process of inference as a movement (traversal) along the branches of the inference tree. To traverse an AND node, we must traverse all of the nodes below it; that is, we have to prove every clause in the AND node. To traverse an OR node, it is sufficient to traverse just one of the nodes below, that is, to prove just one of the OR conditions.

The root of the tree is the *top-level goal* to be proved. To prove the goal, we have to traverse part of the tree by traversing the AND and OR nodes as described above. The parts of the tree that we traverse to prove the goal form a *path* along the nodes called a *proof path*. The proof path itself is a subtree below the top-level goal.

Different methods of inference traverse the tree in *different orders*, although they may produce the same proof tree. In *backward chaining inference*, we start at the root of the tree and follow the branches toward the leaves until we find facts in the factbase. In *forward chaining inference*, we start from the leaves and work our way toward the root until we find a chain of branches that leads to the top-level goal. Consider the two rules

If
    X
and
    Y
Then
     Z;

If
    Z
or
    V
Then
     W;

These rules are diagrammatically shown in Figure 4.7. In this figure, each rule is represented as a conclusion with the relevant premises nested beneath the conclusion. We have also indicated the type of links that connect the nodes. ANDs are represented by links with arcs. ORs are represented as links without connecting arcs. The rules are linked by the clause Z, which is a conclusion in the first rule and a premise in the second rule.

Suppose that we are to prove the goal W. Even with the simple inference tree shown in Figure 4.7, we have a choice as to how to control the inference process. One method is to take the goal and see what is needed to prove it true. To prove the goal W, for instance, we need to prove Z OR V, and in order to prove Z, we then need to prove clauses X AND Y. This strategy is referred to as backward chaining inference.

Another strategy is to see what facts are present and then draw whatever conclusions are possible, continuing until one of the conclusions turns out to be the goal or until

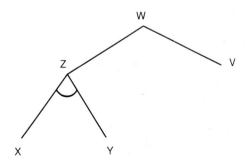

Figure 4.7 An inference tree.

no more new facts are available. Thus when facts X and Y are present, this inference method deduces Z. Once Z is known, the goal W is recognized as being true.

4.2.3   Backward Chaining Inference

In backward chaining inference, the system is provided with a specific clause called a *goal* to prove. To prove a goal, backward chaining inference begins with and focuses on the *conclusions* of rules. Backward chaining inference proves two-valued goals (true or false) by matching them with the factbase and conclusions of backward rules. For instance, suppose that we had the facts

> Broker-A <u>suggests</u> Silver
> Broker-A <u>suggests</u> Gold
> Broker-B <u>suggests</u> Silver
> Silver <u>is</u> overpriced
> Gold <u>is</u> undervalued

and the two rules

> *Rule 1:*
>   Investor <u>invests in</u> 'X'
> If
>   Broker-A <u>suggests</u> 'X'
> and
>   Broker-B <u>suggests</u> 'X'
> and
>   not 'X' <u>is</u> overpriced;
>
> *Rule 2:*
>   Investor <u>invests in</u> 'X'
> If
>   Broker-A <u>suggests</u> 'X'
> and
>   'X' <u>is</u> undervalued;

Let us trace what a backward chaining inference engine does to prove the goal *Investor invests in Gold*.

First it checks to see whether *Investor invests in Gold* can be concluded based on the facts and rules in our miniature knowledge base. The fact to be deduced is not initially in the factbase. A backward chaining inference engine therefore tries to find a rule whose conclusion matches *Investor invests in Gold;* during this effort it finds the first rule, binding 'X' to Gold. It tries to prove the premise of this rule. The premise has now become

> Broker-A <u>suggests</u> Gold and
> Broker-B <u>suggests</u> Gold and
> not Gold <u>is</u> overpriced;

The inference engine tries to prove each clause in the premise as a goal. The goal *Broker-A <u>suggests</u>* Gold is in the factbase and is true. The goal *Broker-B <u>suggests</u> Gold* does not match the factbase or the conclusion of any rule. We therefore fail to prove the premise of the first rule.

The inference engine now tries to match with the second rule and succeeds by binding 'X' to Gold. It tries to prove the premise of this rule. The premise has now become:

> Broker-A <u>suggests</u> Gold and
> Gold <u>is</u> undervalued;

Both of the clauses in the premise are found in the factbase, so the rule is proved and we succeed.

Now, if we had tried to prove a goal with an unbound variable, for example, *Investor invests in 'Y'*, what would the inference engine do? First, it tries to match *Investor invests in 'Y'* with the factbase; no match is possible. It tries to find a matching rule and matches with the first rule, binding 'X' to 'Y'. The premise now becomes

> Broker-A <u>suggests</u> 'Y' and
> Broker-B <u>suggests</u> 'Y' and
> not 'Y' <u>is</u> overpriced;

We try to prove each clause in the premise as a goal. The goal *Broker-A <u>suggests</u> 'Y'* matches the factbase, binding 'Y' to Silver. The premise now becomes

> Broker-A <u>suggests</u> Silver and
> Broker-B <u>suggests</u> Silver and
> not Silver <u>is</u> overpriced;

The goal *Broker-B <u>suggests</u> Silver* exists in the factbase and is true. The inference engine then tries to prove the goal *not Silver <u>is</u> overpriced*, and to do so, it tries to find the truth value for *Silver <u>is</u> overpriced*. This clause exists in the factbase and succeeds by returning a truth value of true; therefore, *not Silver <u>is</u> overpriced* fails and returns a truth value of false.

This means that the inference engine needs to go back and try alternative bindings. The process of going back to get a new binding or checking whether a goal can be proven another way is called *backtracking*.

We go back and undo the binding of 'Y' to Silver and try to prove *Broker-A suggests* 'Y' again. This time, the next fact in the factbase matches, binding 'Y' to Gold. The inference engine again tries to prove *Broker-B suggests Gold* and fails.

We go back again and undo the binding of 'Y' to Gold and try to prove *Broker-A suggests* 'Y' again. This time, no new facts match the goal. The inference engine therefore fails to prove the premise of the first rule.

We now try to match the top-level goal *Investor invests in* 'X' with the second rule and succeed by binding 'X' to 'Y'. We try to prove the premise of this rule. The premise has now become

> Broker-A suggests 'Y' and
> 'Y' is undervalued;

We try to prove each clause in the premise as a goal. The goal *Broker-A suggests* 'Y' matches the factbase, binding 'Y' to Gold. Both clauses in the premise may now be found in the factbase, so the rule is proved and we succeed with the binding 'Y' = Gold.

When a clause fails in the premise of a rule during backward chaining, *backtracking* takes place. Backtracking is the process of going back over clauses in a rule premise to find other ways of proving them. The process of backtracking is equivalent to backing up to a previous node in the inference tree and trying a new path.

For instance, consider the facts

> Broker-A suggests Oil
> Broker-A suggests Gold
> Broker-A suggests Silver
> Broker-B suggests Silver
> Broker-B suggests Bonds

and the rule:

> Investor considers 'X'
> If
> Broker-A suggests 'X'
> and
> Broker-B suggests 'X';

In trying to prove the goal *Investor considers* 'A', we first try to prove *Broker-A suggests* 'Y'. We match *Broker-A suggests* 'Y' with the factbase and first get a binding 'Y' = Oil.

When we fail to prove *Broker-B suggests Oil*, we backtrack to the previous clause, that is, *Broker-A suggests* 'Y'. We get another binding, that is, 'Y' = Gold. Again, when we fail to prove *Broker-B suggests Gold*, we backtrack to the previous clause, that is, *Broker-A suggests 'Y'*. We then get another binding, 'Y' = Silver. This time we succeed in proving *Broker-B suggests Silver*.

Thus the basic idea behind backtracking is

> If a clause in the premise of a rule fails, go back to the previous clause (if any) and try to prove it in a new way, for example, by getting a new binding or by matching with the conclusion of a new rule.

Backtracking may thus be used to find new solutions for goals.

4.2.4 Forward Chaining Inference

In some senses, forward chaining is the opposite of backward chaining since it focuses on the premises of rules rather than their conclusions. If the clauses in the premise of a forward rule are proved, the conclusion of the rule is added to the factbase.

Forward rules can be grouped into *rule sets*. A rule set is simply a partitioned set of rules. Consider the facts

Broker-A suggests Gold
Broker-A suggests Silver
Broker-A suggests Real Estate
Broker-B suggests Silver
Broker-B suggests Real Estate

and the rule-set Set-1; defined as follows:

Rule 1:
    If
        Broker-A suggests 'X'
    and
        Broker-B suggests 'X'
    Then
        Investor invests in 'X';

Rule 2:
    If
        'X' invests in 'Y'
    Then
        'X' owns 'Y';

The following behavior might be observed when a forward chaining inference engine deals with this rule set. The first rule is tried first. We try to match the premise of this rule with the factbase. The first fact in the factbase; that is, *Broker-A suggests Gold* matches this rule, binding 'X' to Gold. We then try to prove the next goal in the premise of the same rule; that is, *Broker-B suggests Gold*. *Broker-B suggests Gold* does not match a fact in the factbase.

In forward chaining, a rule can be applied or invoked only if *all* the clauses in its premise can be shown to match facts in the factbase. So the inference engine will continue searching for a match. Before considering the second rule, we find that there is a match for the first rule once we choose an appropriate binding for the variable 'X'. The two matching facts are

Broker-A suggests Silver
Broker-B suggests Silver

When we try the goal *Broker-A suggests 'X'* in the first rule, we match the first of the two facts shown above, binding 'X' to Silver. Next we find a match for the second clause in the premise, that is, *Broker-B suggests Silver*. Note that the binding of 'X' in the first clause of the premise has to match the binding of 'X' in the second clause of the premise, as it does when these two facts are used. Thus the two facts match successfully with the premise of the first rule. We now add the conclusion of the first rule to the factbase; that is, we add the clause *Investor invests in Silver* to the factbase.

The inference engine will now try the second rule, whose premise is matched by the fact that has just been generated by the application of the first rule. Application of the second rule then produces the conclusion *Investor owns Silver*. Since there are no more rules in the rulebase, we return to the first rule again. We begin pattern matching with the factbase and look for a binding different from that used in the previous application of the rule. This search for new bindings in a forward chaining rule interpreter is analogous to the strategy of the backward chainer when it backtracks. In both cases, a search for new information is occurring.

In the second application of rule one, *Broker-A suggests Real Estate* matches the first clause in the rule premise, and after 'X' has been bound to *Real Estate*, the second clause of the premise is matched by *Broker-B suggests Real Estate*. The conclusion clause *Investor invests in Real Estate* is then added to the factbase. When we try the second rule again; the clause *Investor owns Real Estate* is added to the factbase.

Now, when we go back to the first rule, no new matches for *'X' suggests 'Y'* may be found. We therefore fail to prove the first rule again. The same applies to the second rule, since its premise can not have any new matches either. The forward chaining process thus stops.

In this example, the forward chainer had no specific *hypothesis* to prove. We could have also invoked the same rule set with a hypothesis to stop forward chaining as soon as a matching fact is proved.

In this forward chaining example, we applied each rule in the rule set in turn; that is, we proved *all* the rules before going back to the first rule. There are, however, other forward chaining strategies, which differ in terms of deciding which rule to fire next when more than one rule applies. This type of decision process is referred to as conflict resolution and differences in conflict resolution strategy may lead to significantly different system behaviors.

Conflict resolution can be better understood if we view forward chaining as a three-step cycle.

1. *Match.* Match all the rules against the factbase and determine the successful matches.
2. *Resolve Conflicts.* If more than one rule matches the factbase, choose either one, some, or all the matching rules based on a conflict resolution strategy.
3. *Act.* Add the conclusion(s) of the selected rule(s) to the factbase.

Various conflict resolution strategies have been defined for forward chaining systems. Some strategies are

Do One. Choose the first rule that matches the factbase.

Do All. Apply all the matching rules in one batch, that is, add all new facts at once.

Do in Sequence. Apply the matching rules one by one in sequence so that a new fact proved by a rule can be used to establish the premises of rules further down the sequence.

Do the Most Specific. If there are two matching rules and the premise of one rule is a specific case of the premise of the other (e.g., the premise of one rule includes the premise of the other), this strategy favors the more specific rule.

Do the Most Recent. If there are two matching rules, select the one that matched a fact that has more recently been added to the factbase. This strategy, of course, requires the management of time-tags in the factbase.

Naturally the question "what is the best conflict resolution strategy?" comes to mind. However, the answer is most often dependent on the application. While the method of matching and applying rules is relatively fixed, there is considerable flexibility in conflict resolution and there may not be one best strategy for handling conflict resolution.

4.2.5 Inexact Inference

In some situations we need to be able to reason about uncertain information. In such cases we can no longer state that rules and facts are certainly true or certainly false. Instead, a multivalued form of logic is used and the resulting form of inference is referred to as *inexact inference*. The presence of inexactness does not change the nature of inference, but it does change the way in which truth values are calculated and propagated.

Inexact inference finds confidence factors (CF's) for goals by matching them with the factbase and conclusions of other rules. In backward chaining, we look for *some* method of success; that is, if a goal can be proved with one rule, we stop the backward chaining process without attempting any other rules. However, in inexact reasoning, we try *all matching rules* for a goal and combine the CF's obtained from them.

Inexact inference thus aims to determine the truth for a goal. The premises of inexact rules include clauses whose truth value is a number between 0 and 100. Such clauses may indeed be two-valued clauses which have either 0 or 100 as truth values. Thus exact and inexact inference may be integrated.

A variety of methods for estimating uncertainties of individual events and theories for calculating the uncertainties of compound or complex events exist. In this section, we begin by outlining a standard model of inexact reasoning. We then show how inexact reasoning can be extended to a version of semiexact reasoning that augments inexact inference methods by allowing the combination of exact and inexact inference during reasoning. Semiexact inference is the process of combining exact (i.e., two-valued) and inexact inference. Semiexact inference relies on the use of inexact inference to find the best value for use within exact inference.

There are a large number of mathematical theories that deal with inexactness in expert systems. However, each of these theories must at some point consider what actually happens when inexact values are used in an expert system. There are two basic steps in dealing with inexactness.

    a. Determining the uncertainty of a basic set of events.
    b. Combining the values obtained in step (a) to arrive at the uncertainty of compound or complex events.

For step (a), experts provide some inexact rules to describe the nature of their decision making and then supply inexact values for events referred to in these rules. The formulas of step (b) are then used to combine these values to produce eventual results for the system. Almost always, the system will not exhibit the desired results the first time it is tested. But what happens now? We have three choices.

    1. Change the values supplied in step (a) above.
    2. Change some rules in the system.
    3. Change the theory used in step (b) above.

After an inexact inference engine has been implemented, option 3 is rarely considered. Thus, in correcting the performance of an expert system that deals with uncertainty, one typically adjusts the earlier estimates of uncertainty or changes the rules used by the system. This process usually continues over time as the expert system is being developed and turns into a feedback process in which the original estimates and rules provided by the expert are repeatedly modified. Naturally, the sensitivity of the system to different rules and uncertainty values makes it extremely difficult to establish the supremacy of one mathematical theory of uncertain reasoning to another with respect to a particular application domain. In a good system the user is allowed to dynamically modify the criteria involved in (b) above, as required by the situation.

In some sense, the practical strategic issues involved in a theory of inexact reasoning resemble those in the design of a programming language. Each theory of inexactness provides a paradigm for inexact programming. If the paradigm is not well suited to the task, we shall struggle to express our concepts just as we may struggle if we attempt to express rule-based concepts with FORTRAN Do-Loops, or if we try to do matrix inversion in a forward chaining rule-based language such as OPS-5.

However, regardless of which theory of inexactness is used in a particular situation, we still need methods for selecting among alternative bindings of uncertain truth values. Probabilities, fuzzy logic, and certainty theory are some of the many definitions for dealing with inexactness. For inexact knowledge, a truth value is either 100 (definitely true), 0 (definitely false), or an integer between 0 and 100, such as 80 (meaning 80% sure). A special inexact truth value unknown may be used to reflect the fact that we have no idea about a truth value.

The term *confidence factor* (CF for short) will be used here to refer to truth values. The truth value for "5 > 3" is 100, while the truth value for "2 > 3" is 0. The truth value for John goes to school may be 100, while the truth value for John likes wine may be 70.

Let A and B be clauses. To perform inexact reasoning using backward chaining inference, we need to define four basic formulas for

> CF(not A)
> CF(A and B)
> CF(A or B)
> Combine(A, B)

The formula for *Combine* is needed to calculate the combined certainty when two or more rules support a hypothesis (Parsaye and Chignell, 1988, Section 6.5.1). A number of different methods have been suggested for defining these formulas, for instance, the following definitions are based on fuzzy logic and certainty theory:

> CF(not A) = 100 - CF(A)
> CF(A and B) = minimum[CF(A), CF(B)]
> CF(A or B) = maximum[CF(A), CF(B)]
> Combine(A, B) = CF(A) + CF(B) - [CF(A) * CF(B) / 100]

Although certainty factors represent inexactness, in some applications, we may wish to reflect the fact that we are totally uncertain about a fact. The special truth value *unknown* may be used when we have no idea about the truth value of an inexact fact.

Thus, an inexact truth value may be any number between 0 and 100, or the value may be *unknown*.

In general, the value unknown will propagate indeterminacy. For instance, if CF(A) = 60 and CF(B) = unknown, then

CF(not A) = unknown
CF(A and B) = unknown
CF(A or B) = unknown
Combine(A, B) = CF(A)

However, if CF(C) = 100, and CF(D) = 0, we have

CF(D and B) = 0
CF(C or B) = 100

since regardless of the value of B, CF(D and B) will be 0 and CF(C or B) will be 100. The truth value unknown combines with other inexact truth values as follows:

(unknown and X) = (X and unknown) = unknown if X > 0
(unknown and 0) = (0 and unknown) = 0

(unknown or X) = (X or unknown) = unknown if X < 100
(unknown or 100) = (100 and unknown) = 100

Combine(X, unknown) = Combine(unknown, X) = X

Thus, combining a truth value with an unknown value has no effect on the truth value. The reason for forcing all other operations involving unknowns to become unknowns is that we cannot predict how the results are to be interpreted. For instance, given

CF= 100
    A
If
    B
or
    C;

If CF(B) = 70 and CF(C) = unknown, it may, at first glance, seem reasonable to interpret CF(A) as 70 since we can in all cases be "at least" 70% sure about A, regardless of C. However, what we may really be looking for may involve the negation of A, for example,

CF= 100
    D
If
    not A ;

In this case, interpreting D as 30% true may lead to confusion, since C may be 90, resulting in 10% confidence in D.

To perform inexact inference, as in backward chaining, we provide an inference engine with a specific clause called a goal. However, rather than simply succeeding or failing, inexact goals will have a certainty factor, which is a number in the range 0 to 100. Inexact inference finds confidence factors, or CF's, for goals by matching them with the factbase and conclusion of other rules.

We may thus extend the concept of two-valued rule to the concept of an inexact rule. In either forward or backward rules, the certainty factor of the conclusion is based solely on the certainty factor of the premise; that is, the conclusion is true if the premise is true. Inexact rules, however, also allow for the concept of rule certainty.

The certainty factor for the conclusion of a single inexact rule is based on both the rule certainty and the certainty factor of the premise. The certainty factor (confidence) factor, for the conclusion is thus calculated by

$$CF(\text{conclusion}) = CF(\text{premise}) * \text{rule-certainty} / 100$$

In backward chaining, we look for some method of success; that is, if a goal can be proved with one rule, we stop the backward chaining process without attempting any other rules. In inexact reasoning, however, we may try all matching rules for a goal and combine the certainty factors obtained from them. Thus the purpose of inexact reasoning in an expert system application is to come up with the most likely conclusion or explanation on the basis of the available facts.

Inexact inference finds confidence factors (CF's) for goals by matching them with the factbase and conclusions of other rules. In backward chaining, we look for some method of success; that is, if a goal can be proved with one rule, we stop the backward chaining process without attempting any other rules. However, in inexact reasoning, we try all matching rules for a goal and combine the CF's obtained from them.

We can extend the range of possible inference methods by allowing the combination of exact and inexact inference during reasoning. Semiexact inference is the process of combining exact (i.e., two-valued) and inexact inference. Semiexact inference relies on the use of inexact inference to find the best value for use within exact inference. For a full discussion of inexact and semi-exact reasoning see Parsaye and Chignell (1988, Chapter 7).

■ 4.3 OBJECTS AND FRAMES

Frames (Minsky, 1975) represent a way to combine declarations and procedures within a knowledge representation environment. The fundamental organizing principle underlying frame systems is the packaging of knowledge. Frames provide a method of combining declarations and procedures within a single knowledge representation environment.

Frames incorporate a number of functions that make them useful in systems that represent knowledge and carry out influence on the basis of that knowledge. Each frame is characterized by

A frame name, for example, John Smith.

A parent for the frame, for example, Person.

A number of *slots*, which can take on *values*, for example, Age with value 24.

Most of the concepts involved in frames are very similar to concepts involved in object-oriented programming, as discussed in Chapter 3. The mapping between frames and objects is illustrated in Figure 4.8.

Concepts such as inheritance have been widely used in both frame-based and object-based systems. In many cases, the underlying concepts of frame-based and object-oriented systems are so closely related that the choice of using the term *frame* or *object* is sometimes more a matter of style rather than content.

Most of the expert systems–related literature (e.g., Parsaye and Chignell, 1988) uses the term frame rather than object, while the database literature generally uses the term object. Since this is a database-oriented book, we also use the term object here, as we did throughout Chapter 3. However, most of the ideas expressed for objects here may easily be rephrased in terms of frames.

In order to represent knowledge in a machine, it must be possible to define objective versions of knowledge for each domain of interest. Thus expert systems must deal with knowledge that has been structured and codified in a form that can be used for reasoning. This is in contrast to most computer programs that work with data. Thus,

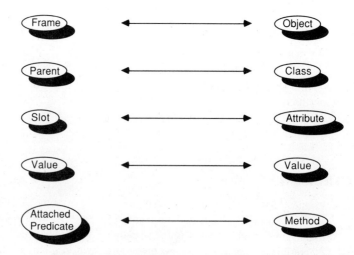

Figure 4.8 The mapping between objects and frames.

in expert systems, *knowledge structures* are used to store knowledge and reason with it, just as data structures are used to store and deal with data.

The major issues in knowledge representation can be illustrated using a framelike representation of objects. Like semantic networks, object representation (and frame) systems rely on two fundamental units.

1. *Nodes* represent concepts, or events.
2. *Links* represent relations between nodes.

Graphically, nodes are drawn as boxes, ovals, or circles. Links (also called *arcs*) are drawn as arrows connecting the nodes, as in Figure 4.9. In addition to organizing knowledge in inheritance hierarchies, objects can also be linked to rules, allowing predicates to be activated when knowledge is stored and retrieved.

We can apply objects to a variety of types of knowledge such as general information about people. The information may be about people's age, sex, telephone, address, etc. Objects can be used to create a general template describing information about a person and to store the description of each person in a separate object. For example, we may construct an object

Object: Person
Parent: Thing
Attribute: Social Security Number
Attribute: Age
Attribute: Sex

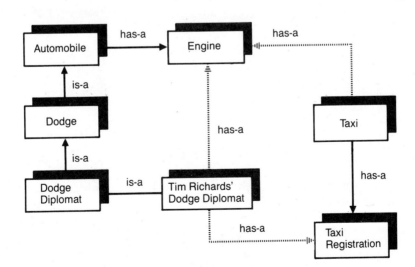

Figure 4.9 A semantic network.

> Attribute: Address
> Attribute: Telephone:

We may then define each specific person as a child of the object above, for example,

> Object: Philip Anderson
> Parent: Person
> Attribute: Social Security Number Value: 123 45 678
> Attribute: Age
> Attribute: Sex
> Attribute: Address
> Attribute: Telephone   Value: 321 7654

The concept *person* refers to a vast number of instances of actual people. Similarly, the concept *hazard* refers to a number of types of hazard. We can organize concepts into taxonomic classes by using objects in a number of applications.

4.3.1 Storing and Retrieving Knowledge in Objects

Information that we may need to store in a knowledge representation system includes

> The value of a particular property.
> The category to which the object belongs.

We can extend our notation for objects to define *object terms* which have the general form:

> (attribute-name of object-reference)

where *attribute-name* is the name of an attribute and *object-reference* is either the name of an object or another object term. The keyword *"of"* is used to separate the attribute-name from the object-reference. In the notation used here object terms are enclosed within parentheses. We may, for instance, write:

> (teacher of Paul)
> ('X' of 'Paul')
> (age of 'X')

This notation is roughly equivalent to the way in which object references are handled in natural language, where the general form *('X' of 'Y')* is frequently used to describe the attribute of an object. For instance, we often request information about a person's telephone number with a statement such as

> Please give me the telephone number of Philip Anderson.

The object term *(Attribute of Object)* is assigned the value of the attribute *Attribute* in the object *Object*. For instance, consider the following objects:

Object: Peter Anderson
Parent: Student
Attribute: Teacher
Attribute: Telephone Value: 123 7654

Object: Simon Richards
Parent: Staff
Attribute: Position   Value: Teacher
Attribute: Department   Value: Mathematics
Attribute: Office   Value: 321E
Attribute: Telephone   Value: 627 3758

The object term (Teacher of Peter Anderson) will have the value Simon Richards, while the object term (Telephone of Peter Anderson) will have the value 123 7654.

Object terms can be used to implement the functions of description and organization in knowledge representation. The term

(Telephone of Peter Anderson)

describes one of the attributes of Peter Anderson, namely, his telephone number. We can also use object terms to refer to other object terms as in

(Telephone of (Teacher of Peter Anderson))
(Department of (Teacher of Peter Anderson)).

Objects as defined here implement full-object identity (discussed earlier in Chapter 3). We can use object terms of this sort to retrieve information during reasoning. Retrieval is only one aspect of the problem in working with objects. We also need methods for storing the information that is later retrieved. How do we express the storage of information in natural language? One way of specifying information is as follows:

The telephone number is 555 1212

The use of the word *"is"* generally indicates storage or communication of information, but we could instead use the following:

Is the telephone number 555 1212?

In this case the word *is* asks a question that compares the stored value of the telephone number to another number.

In using objects, there is a clear distinction between the processes of *assignment* (storage) and *comparison* (testing). The two predicates

$$= \text{(equality)}$$
$$:= \text{(assignment)}$$

are distinct and have different meanings. Thus the clause

(Telephone of Peter Anderson) = 123 7654

will succeed, since it is equivalent to the evaluation of

123 7654 = 123 7654

However,

(Telephone of Peter Anderson) = 888 7654

will fail, since it is equivalent to

123 7654 = 888 7654

However, if we use the assignment predicate, the clause

(Telephone of Peter Anderson) := 888 7654

succeeds and *changes* the telephone number of Peter Anderson. The object now becomes

Object: Peter Anderson
Parent: Student
Attribute: Teacher
Attribute: Telephone   Value: 888 7654

Assignment is thus the process of adding or modifying a description within an object, while comparison is the process of comparing the value of an attribute in an object's description with a particular value.

4.3.2 Attached Predicates

Attached predicates monitor the storage and retrieval of information in an object system. Rules may be attached to the attributes of objects using attached predicates. Thus attached predicates allow us to invoke rules from within objects without difficulty.

Attached predicates extend conventional data structuring paradigms by providing *active structures*. In this object-based structuring paradigm, data are no longer passive.

In accessing data, or knowledge, rules may be automatically fired, output may be sent to the screen or other devices, and so on.

The object *Address*, for instance, may have an attached predicate that suggests that if the value of the attribute *State* is California, the zip code must begin with the number 9. This type of rule can be used to maintain the integrity of the knowledge, so that names of states are always consistent with the zip codes. Because each particular address (e.g., Tony Higgins' address) is an instance of the general structure Address, we would need to assert this rule only once and inherit it for any particular address.

Attached predicates provide the concept of *trigger*, that is, an action that automatically takes place under certain circumstances. Attached predicates modify the basic structure of objects. Thus, in addition to attributes and their values, there may be separate information referring to attached predicates. We show the effect of attached predicates in objects in Figure 4.10.

Attached predicates can also assist in making inferences about knowledge that we do not have exact information on. Attached if-needed predicates are invoked when the value of an attribute is retrieved. Attached predicates may also be used to monitor storage, for instance, attached if-added predicates are invoked when values are assigned to attributes.

Many different object representation systems can be defined within the general framework described here. In one such system, if-needed predicates act as gatekeepers during the retrieval process. Whenever the value of a attribute is to be retrieved in a statement of the form

'X' := (attribute-name of Object-reference)

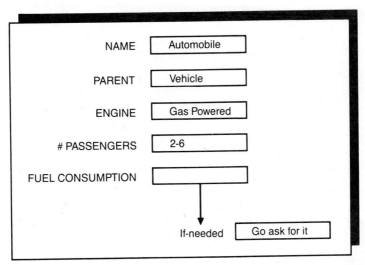

Figure 4.10 An object containing an attached procedure.

the if-needed predicate attached to *attribute-name* is invoked and must be proved successfully before the assignment takes place. Similarly, when a value is to be stored in an attribute with a statement of the form

(attribute-name of Object-reference) : = 'Y'

the if-added predicate attached to *attribute-name* is invoked and must be proved successfully before the assignment takes place. Attached predicates can provide a powerful style of programming. For instance, an attached if-needed predicate may be used for monitoring the behavior of an expert system and may be used as a debugging tool. Whenever the value of an attribute is read, the predicate may write a message to the screen.

4.3.3 Inheritance

Inheritance is a powerful way of retrieving information. It allows us to get the same information from a variety of sources, even though it has been stored in only one location. When combined with the use of attached predicates, inheritance provides a new programming paradigm that has a number of benefits. Inheritance allows the system to retrieve information that is shared among different members of a category or class of objects within a hierarchy. For instance, we may know that most automobiles have four wheels, but we don't want to explicitly store that information for each separate instance of an automobile that we have in our knowledge base. Instead, we can express this information as a property of automobiles in general. Thus we store the fact that automobiles have four wheels as a property connected to the automobile category node. If we need the number of wheels for a particular instance of an automobile, we retrieve it by using *inheritance* from the parent category of automobiles.

Inheritance is based on the concept that objects or concepts tend to form groups and that members within a group tend to share common properties. By using inheritance we can organize our knowledge in a way that allows the inference of information that is not directly available.

Inheritance in knowledge representation allows for the sharing of information among a set of elements with uniform structure. Objects are organized into a hierarchy or network, with each element at a lower level *inheriting* the properties of the elements at a higher level.

Since objects realize the concept of inheritance, each object must have at least one *parent*. An object *inherits* the properties of its parents. An object may have more than one parent. In this way, we have an *inheritance* network. We say that an object is a *child* of its parent and is a *descendant* of all objects from which its parent inherits in the inheritance network. Inheritance allows us to define an attribute once in some object and have that attribute shared by all the descendants of that object. This means that each object will inherit all the attributes of its ancestors, since its parents will inherit the attributes of their parents, and so on. For instance, consider the following objects:

Object: Person
Parent: Thing
Attribute: Age   Value:
Attribute: Sex   Value:

Object: Man
Parent: Person
Attribute: Sex   Value: Male

Object: Woman
Parent: Person
Attribute: Sex   Value: Female

Object: Tony Higgins
Parent: Man

In this example, the object Tony Higgins does not include the explicit attributes Age and Sex. The object would inherit the information about Tony Higgins' sex from the ancestor parent object Man. Thus, an object may inherit the values, if any, of inherited attributes. This means that the assignment

$$'X' := (Sex\ of\ Tony\ Higgins)$$

will assign the value Male to 'X'; that is, the object Tony Higgins inherits the value Male from its parent Man. Thus, although the attribute Sex is not explicitly defined within the object Tony Higgins, this attribute is implicitly present within the object by inheritance from Man. The object Man also implicitly includes an attribute Age. The object Tony Higgins inherits the attribute Age from its ancestor Person, but it inherits no value for Age. If either Sex or Age had any attached predicates, these predicates would have also been inherited by Tony Higgins.

The process of inheritance usually begins with a direct examination of the appropriate object. If the information is not stored there, one goes to the parent (superordinate) object and checks whether the information is stored there. Then, if the information is still not found, the same process is repeated with the parent of this current object, and so on; until either the information is found, or we reach the top of the hierarchy.

Hierarchies are easy to search for information in, but most real-world knowledge is not strictly nested and a hierarchy can only approximate the true structure of a knowledge domain. Thus we often need to allow each object to have more than one parent. The inheritance of properties from multiple parents is called *multiple inheritance*. Figure 4.11 shows an example of multiple inheritance.

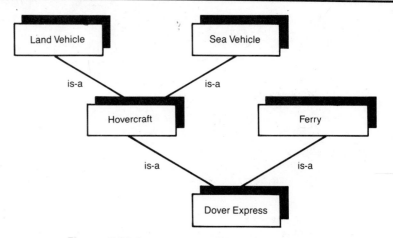

Figure 4.11 Representation of multiple inheritance.

With multiple inheritance, each object may have more than one parent. This means that an object may inherit attributes, values, and attached predicates from multiple parents. Multiple inheritance raises fundamental questions about the circumstances under which a concept may inherit information from more general concepts. Consider the example of the substance mercury. Its function will depend on the application being considered. It can be used in the process of gold refining, in the construction of thermometers, and so on. The ability to carry out multiple inheritance places more responsibility on the designer of an object representation system to ensure that the information retrieved will be consistent with the current application or context of the system.

■ 4.4 AN INTUITIVE MODEL OF KNOWLEDGE

It is often difficult to see how to formulate specific knowledge or expertise in terms of the representation schemes described in the previous section. In this section we briefly explore an intuitive model of knowledge that can guide people who are attempting to represent the knowledge associated with a particular domain.

In representing knowledge one must be able to discuss knowledge at multiple levels and describe, relate, and organize a set of elementary concepts or *objects*. Determining the right level at which to describe objects has a major impact on knowledge representation. In some knowledge domains, the right level at which to define objects is often fairly obvious and can be recognized by the conceptual objects used by experts in performing reasoning. In other knowledge domains, however, many different sets of objects may be used. In modeling transportation within a city, for instance, the objects may be particular vehicles such as buses, cars, and trucks, along with intersections, times of day, and related concepts. Viewing the same city from the perspective of crime prevention or health maintenance might lead to a very different set of objects being defined.

Once we have settled on a set of objects to use for knowledge representation, it is necessary to define them and their interactions. These definitions are based on the elementary components of knowledge.

Naming
Describing
Organizing
Relating
Constraining

These components of knowledge are generally present within many knowledge representation systems. However, each knowledge representation method deals with these components in its own way.

These components have intuitive analogs in the parts of speech used in natural language. The function of *naming* is usually performed by *proper nouns*, which can be signified by capitalizing the first letter or the name. For instance, we may name a chemical compound such as "acetone" or a component in a computer such as the "hard disk."

The function of *describing* is performed by *adjectives*, such as happy, blue, and tall. Adjectives generally modify nouns, which makes sense since they are describing objects. For instance, we may say that a patient is old or that a chemical substance is hazardous. In formal notation we may use *values*, as well as adjectives, for describing an object. For instance, we may say that the age of the patient is 67 or that a microcomputer uses a Motorola microprocessor chip.

The function of *relating* is performed by *transitive verbs* and special *nouns* that describe relationships. From a knowledge representation perspective we can distinguish between different relationships expressed by verbs, for example,

Action—electricity <u>flows through</u> the wire
Structural description—the pipe <u>is connected to</u> the valve
Relation—Coca Cola <u>is-parent-company-of</u> Columbia Pictures

The function of *organizing* objects is handled in a variety of ways including *categorization* and *possession*, for example:

municipal bond <u>is-a</u> bond

which indicates that one object is an instance of a general class of objects or automobile <u>has-a</u> engine type

which indicates that an object possesses some attribute type.

Constraints are generally handled by *conditions* that define what descriptions of objects or patterns of relationships between objects are admissible. An example of a constraint is

Any person whose age is less than 17 should not watch an R-rated movie unless accompanied by an adult.

We may describe this constraint as a rule.

> If
> (age of 'X') < 17
> and
> not 'X' <u>accompanied by adult</u>
> and
> 'Movie' <u>has</u> R-Rating
> and
> 'Age' = (age of 'X')
> and
> 'X' < 17
> Then
> 'X' <u>should not watch</u> 'Movie' ;

We now consider these basic components of knowledge in more detail.

4.4.1 Components of Knowledge

In packaging and representing knowledge, frames (objects) provide five major functions. These five major functions are

1. *Naming*. A unique *name* is assigned to each object.
2. *Describing*. The body of an object is composed of a number of *attributes* that have values. These attributes describe the properties of the object or link different objects together.
3. *Organizing*. Each object (except the top-level object in a hierarchy) has one or more *parents*, providing an *inheritance* mechanism.
4. *Relating*. The values of object attributes may be other objects. Objects may thus be related by having one object as the *value* of an attribute in another object. Objects may also be related to *rules*.
5. *Constraining*. Each attribute in an object may have attached *predicates*, which are invoked whenever the attribute is read or modified. Attached predicates include an *if-needed* predicate that is activated when information is retrieved and an *if-added* predicate that is activated when information is stored.

Frames and objects provide a firm foundation for knowledge representation and inference. The object name provides a label, the attributes provide a mechanism for describing properties and relations, and organization of objects can be achieved by defining parent-child relations. Relations may also be defined with attributes or with rules. The resulting knowledge base can then be constrained by using attached predicates to control the processes of storing and retrieving information.

The basic structure of an object consists of

> The name of the object.
>
> The parents of the object.
>
> The attributes (if any) of the object and their values.
>
> The attached predicates (if any) for each attribute.

The components of an object attribute are

> *Attribute Name.* Each attribute should have a unique *name* within the Object. However, attribute names are local to objects. Hence two distinct objects may have the same attribute name.
>
> *Attribute Value.* Each attribute should have a *value* field, as well as a name. The value field in an attribute may be empty when the attribute is first defined and may later be assigned and read.

In the object "IBM" for instance, we might have the attribute "founder" with the value Thomas Watson. The situation where an attribute has been defined, but no value for it is yet available, is like knowing that something must have a property, because of the type of object that it is, without knowing what the value of the property is. Thus we know, for instance, that a company must have a founder, even if we do not know who that founder is.

> *If-Needed Predicate.* Each attribute may have an *if-needed* predicate. If an attribute has an if-needed predicate, then before the value of the attribute can be read and obtained, the if-needed predicate must be successfully proven.

If-needed predicates are frequently used to enhance the flexibility of retrieval. For instance, when the value of an attribute is not available directly, we might be able to consult a table of expected values on the basis of other information that we know about the object. Thus, if we do not know the age of a person, but the birthdate is known, an if-needed predicate can calculate the desired information by subtracting the current date from the birthdate.

> *If-Added Predicate.* Each attribute may have an *if-added* predicate. If an attribute has an if-added predicate, before the value of the attribute is assigned a value, or the value is changed, the if-added predicate must be successfully proved.

If-added predicates can be used to screen erroneous values before they are added to attributes. For instance, an if-added predicate might accept a number as the age of a person only if it is less than 125 and greater than 0.

Figure 4.12 shows the general template for an object, including attributes and their values. Figure 4.13 provides a pictorial representation of an object showing how if-needed and if-added predicates function as filters in storage and retrieval.

A) Written Form:

Object: The name of the object

Parent: The parent of the object

...

Parent: Another parent for the object

Attribute: The name of the first attribute   Value: v1 (or empty)

Attribute: The name of the second attribute   Value: v2 (or empty)

...

Attribute: The name of the nth attribute   Value: vn (or empty)

B) Pictorial Form:

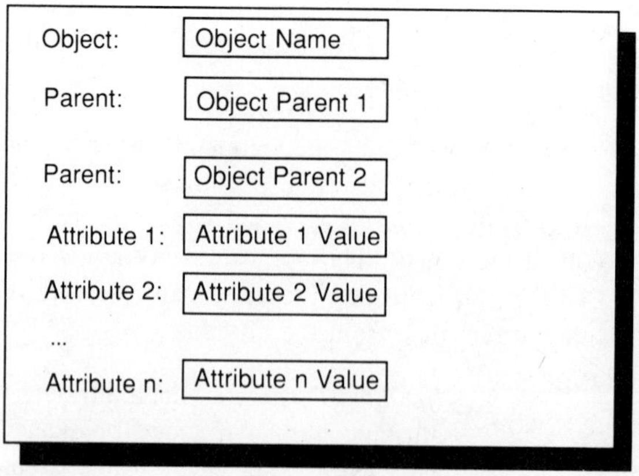

Object:	Object Name
Parent:	Object Parent 1
Parent:	Object Parent 2
Attribute 1:	Attribute 1 Value
Attribute 2:	Attribute 2 Value
...	
Attribute n:	Attribute n Value

Figure 4.12 The general template for an object.

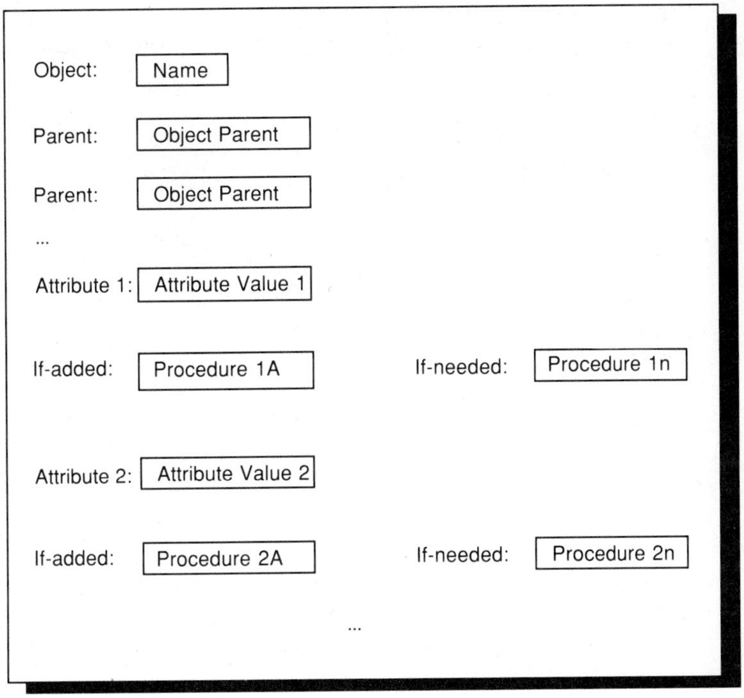

Object: [Name]

Parent: [Object Parent]

Parent: [Object Parent]

...

Attribute 1: [Attribute Value 1]

If-added: [Procedure 1A]   If-needed: [Procedure 1n]

Attribute 2: [Attribute Value 2]

If-added: [Procedure 2A]   If-needed: [Procedure 2n]

...

Figure 4.13 A pictorial representation of an object with attached predicates.

4.4.2 Naming, Describing, and Organizing

We typically denote objects by name. For instance, "General Motors" is the name of a company, "acetone" is the name of a substance, and so on. The names that we assign should be unique so that we do not become confused as to whom or what we are talking about.

We should also be able to describe the important properties that an object has in representing the knowledge about the object. There are a huge number of properties that potentially describe most objects. A complex object such as a person will have a wide range of properties such as physical features, experience, age, occupation, and skills. In describing people, we could focus on aspects of their personality, their appearance, their past experience, and so on. The properties that should be described depend on the application we are dealing with. A medical diagnostic system will focus on physical properties and symptoms, whereas a personnel selection system might focus on qualifications and employment history.

Although the basic process of description is very straightforward, it can lead to different forms of expression in different knowledge representation methods. In logic, for instance, description is handled by predicates and arguments. Thus we could describe someone's age in logic as

John has-age 24

In an object system, however, the same description would be made by placing the value of the age in the corresponding attribute of the Object that described John.

(age of John) : = 24

Here the notation:

('Slot' of 'Object')

is used to signify which object and which slot of that object are being referred to. The ":=" operator is used to indicate the assignment of the value 24 to the age slot of the John object.

In addition to methods for describing objects and their relations, there should be methods for organizing objects into conceptual categories. One way of organizing objects is to describe some objects as instances of more general objects. Thus an automobile is a type of vehicle.

The analogy of the parent and the child is often used to capture the essential features of the relationship between a general concept and a specific instance of that concept. Thus "vehicle" is a parent concept of automobile that is, in turn, a parent concept of "1987 Ford." Repeated nesting of concepts and subconcepts produces a hierarchy. In an *inheritance hierarchy*, the values of slots in lower-level concepts may then be inherited from the categories that they belong to, if need be.

4.4.3 Relating and Constraining

After we have named, described, and organized objects, we need to *relate* them. Part of the skill in describing relationships between objects is in choosing the right level of analysis and deciding whether to include particular entities in a relationship. The number of entities involved in a relationship may thus depend on the level of analysis and the depth of the knowledge used.

Relations represent a gray area where knowledge representation shades into inference. Some types of relation, such as family relations, can be naturally expressed in terms of the organization of knowledge. Other types of relation are best expressed as procedures involving inference.

Relationships act as links that connect objects. For instance:

Family relationships such as parent and grandparent relate objects that are individuals.

A hazardous relationship produced by the combination of a dangerous substance with an inappropriate container relates the attribute of one type of object (chemical substance) with another type of object (container).

The relationships between salt intake, blood pressure, and heart disease involve at least three conceptual objects, and potentially many more.

Different knowledge representation systems express relationships in different ways. In logic, relationships are expressed with clauses and rules, while in objects, relationships are expressed in terms of either attribute values or inheritance.

Constraints govern the properties of objects. They are used to limit ranges of values, relationships, and organizational structures. For instance, a constraint can be used to express the fact that the property of an object can take on only a certain range of values, as in the case in the age or height of a person, where the range does not exceed a certain value. Constraints can also be used to determine one property based on other properties. Thus an employee's telephone number may be constrained by the place of work, while the city of an address may be constrained by its zip code.

Constraints can be used to check the validity of knowledge, infer information that is not directly available, and regulate access to information. The rules of the road are examples of constraints that govern the behavior of motorists, while the laws of the land are examples of constraints that govern behavior in general.

Constraints can be designed to protect the integrity of a knowledge base. Consider a system for managing patients in a medical practice. Relevant portions of the patients' records might include their names, age, weight, medical information, and so on. There are a variety of constraints that one can impose on the patient records, such as

> *Check for duplication*—No two patients may have identical names and addresses.

> *Check age*—No patient may have a birthdate indicating that the patient is older than 125 or that the age is negative.

> *Check gender*—A patient whose gender is male cannot be pregnant.

Constraining is particularly important in intelligent database applications where it is necessary to implement integrity constraints and control the quality of data over time.

4.4.4 Blackboards

In general, there are a number of sources of knowledge that are relevant for any given topic or problem. Blackboard approaches allow the knowledge of multiple sources to be represented in a single representation system.

The blackboard model was developed for the HEARSAY-II speech understanding system (Erman, Hayes-Roth, Lesser, and Reddy, 1980), and the idea behind the blackboard model may be described as follows:

> We have a group of human experts, each of whom is highly qualified in a specific field. We are trying to coordinate the knowledge of these experts to solve a difficult problem. As it turns out, the experts will not directly speak to each other, but in order to help solve the problem will agree to interact with a *coordinator* or *scheduler* and to read from and write on a *blackboard*.

> We gather the experts in a room with a large blackboard and write the initial statement of the problem on the blackboard. The experts read the problem statement

and begin to think. As each expert comes up with an interesting hypothesis or an important idea, he writes it on the blackboard for everyone to see. This helps the other experts in their thinking, and provides them with important clues based on knowledge outside their own domain. Eventually, one of the experts solves the problem and writes the final solution on the blackboard.

When this model is used in an expert-system context, we call each participating expert a *knowledge source*. A knowledge source need not be a human expert, but may be a knowledge base devoted to performing a specific task. The blackboard then becomes a way of sharing hypotheses and information among the knowledge sources.

This model of problem solving was used in HEARSAY-II, an early speaker-dependent speech-understanding system that attempted to generate a coherent interpretation of spoken sentences drawn from a 1000-word vocabulary. The system had twelve knowledge sources. Each knowledge source carried out a different task. This allowed the use of diverse types of knowledge, such as phonetic knowledge and grammatical knowledge. For instance, PREDICT hypothesized all words that might syntactically precede or follow a given phrase, and so on. Each knowledge source functioned as a rule-based system. More recent blackboard environments include HEARSAY-III (Erman, London, and Fickas, 1981), AGE (Nii, 1980), and BB1 (Hayes-Roth, 1984, 1985).

From a general perspective, the blackboard model aims to address three distinct problems that appear as the size of a knowledge base grows.

1. The system becomes harder to understand, since there are many rules, facts, and so on.
2. Different types of knowledge and different knowledge representation and inference methods need to be integrated.
3. Response time begins to deteriorate as the amount of required computation increases.

The blackboard model deals with these issues by separating knowledge into modular knowledge sources that use different knowledge representation and inference methods and that may reside on separate computers. A blackboard architecture is thus made up of three basic components.

1. A global database (the *blackboard*).
2. Independent knowledge *sources* that have access to the blackboard.
3. A *scheduler* to control knowledge source activity.

The knowledge sources are independent and influence each other by responding to and modifying information on the blackboard. Blackboards are distinguished more as an architecture for distributed problem solving than as a distinct method of knowledge representation. In fact, a number of different knowledge representation methods can be used for each knowledge source without disturbing the overall blackboard structure, providing that any information on the blackboard can be read and used by the knowledge sources that need it.

Thus the blackboard model provides three distinct advantages.

    a. It can be used to organize knowledge in a modular way.

    b. It can easily integrate different knowledge representation methods.

    c. It may be executed in a distributed computing environment for greater efficiency.

Although a blackboard system may be implemented on a single computer, the blackboard model is ideally suited for distributed problem solving. Each knowledge source can be implemented as a knowledge-base on a separate processor to work independently on a component of a problem. Of course, one must ensure that only one knowledge source at a time writes on the blackboard. But this is not a major issue compared to the problem of *coordinated thinking*, which appears if we do not have a truly distributed (or multiple processor) implementation of a blackboard.

■ 4.5 INTEGRATING EXPERT SYSTEMS WITH DATABASES

The integration of the expert system with conventional software and links to the outside world is a key issue in intelligent database development. Intelligent databases as described in this book will require an advanced development environment that includes hypertext, knowledge engineering, text management, and database management facilities.

The integration of expert systems and database systems within the framework of intelligent databases is particularly appealing because the user can directly manipulate the semantics of the database in a straightforward fashion, in contrast to approaches where the semantics are "hard-wired" into the data model. This removes the need to predefine complex semantic constructs within the basic language of the database. The following capabilities represent a partial list of potential capabilities of an expert database system:

• Sophisticated queries can be expressed, such as transitive-closure queries and recursive queries.

• Customized front ends can be developed, such as a natural language interface, or even sophisticated front ends where the system can give a partial answer to a query that would have failed otherwise or can come up with a reasonable answer instead of simply returning no data.

• Expert rules dealing with data can be programmed in the same environment, without using any external expert system tool. Ordinary database applications (such as data entry, report generation, and application generation) and intelligent processing of data can be mixed together.

- Integrity constraints of databases can be expressed and enforced naturally in a nonprocedural way; concurrent access to the same database from different expert-system applications can be readily performed.

Most of the early connection schemes between an expert system and a relational database management system made use of a very loose integration technique for retrieval that typically involved spawning of SQL queries on the fly (dynamic SQL) and passing data through import/export facilities of the two systems. This tended to result in very poor performance because of the number of SQL calls made to the database system and the number of files generated by both systems.

Tight coupling of database systems and expert systems within an intelligent database environment requires much more than a simple I/O link between an expert system and a database system. It requires an integration of systems and behavior at each of the following levels:

- At the language level, in terms of logical syntax of the overall system and in terms of the underlying architecture for implementing this syntax
- At the program-development environment level, in terms of developing applications using both knowledge base techniques and database techniques
- At the user environment level, so that the user only has to interact with one system that has both sets of capabilities
- At the concurrency control and recovery levels, which incorporate support for both database and knowledge base activities

Due to the different retrieval schemes between a DBMS and an expert system shell (set-at-a-time retrieval versus tuple-at-a-time retrieval), the inference engine of the expert database system must be allowed to access the database at the lower level directly without bypassing the multiuser concurrency control and recovery primitives. The solution of transferring the entire set of tuples of a retrieval request into the expert system workspace is computationally expensive in terms of both space and time. The reason is that the inference engine typically only needs to have the first valid answer until it needs to backtrack, after which other answers may be sought.

Close integration between expert systems and databases requires a new implementation of cursors on the database side. Cursors are a good way of stepping through a table one tuple at a time as needed. These cursors provide the necessary data to the inference engine. Since the inference engine typically generates a large number of cursors in the course of unification (in recursive queries for example), there should be an efficient way of spawning a cursor (sometimes taking advantage of a similar cursor already in existence), stepping through a cursor, and cancelling a cursor when the inference engine does not need any extra solutions.

Integration of the development environments of the database system and expert system shell requires extending the paradigm of both subsystems. Typical expert system development facilities such as customized editing, error checking, and rule tracing ought to be extended to take into account the database interaction. Traditional modules such as data entry or report generation in database systems must also be modified to accommodate the interaction with an expert system. An explanation mechanism for the reasoning process of the knowledge-based system should be incorporated into database activities such as report and application generation.

In a multiuser environment, concurrent accesses to the same knowledge base must also be controlled. If there is a shared knowledge base, there could be concurrency conflicts very similar to those in database systems. These conflicts arise when trying to assert or retract a fact or a rule used by another concurrent transaction. Recovery mechanisms for expert systems should provide conventional database systems services such as undoing changes made by aborted queries and protecting the database and knowledge base from hardware failure.

4.5.1 Relational Objects and Relational Predicates

In this section we demonstrate how expert system shells may be closely integrated with relational databases using relational predicates and objects. The method and notation described in this section are implemented in the Intelligence/Compiler expert system shell (IntelligenceWare, 1988a).

The integration relies on two interchangeable models for representing database relations within a knowledge base.

1. The predicate model.
2. The object model.

The two models are fully interchangeable and may be freely mixed. For example, you may define a relation with objects and retrieve it with predicates, and vice versa. This provides a great deal of flexibility. For instance, at one point you may add a record to a database with an assert predicate, then retrieve it with an object reference of the type (Attribute of Object), or vice versa.

The predicate model represents relations within a *virtual* (disk-based) factbase. Data are added using the *assert* predicate, removed with the *retract* predicate, and retrieved with standard predicate matching from within the expert system shell.

One issue that drives the relationship between predicates and relations is referred to as the *independence assumption* (Parsaye, 1983a). This assumption states that there is generally an inverse relationship between the number of facts and the number of rules used in describing a procedure. That is, if a procedure (predicate) has a large number of facts in its definition, it will have relatively few rules defining it, and vice versa.

In the object model, relations are represented as *instances* of objects. Data are added and removed through special predicates and retrieved and modified through standard object access. The object model has the advantages of more powerful querying and easier handling of records with large numbers of fields.

From a programming language designer's point of view, objects and logic are simply a natural extension and evolution from existing databases. In fact, objects and logical inference may be viewed as a method of adding higher level structuring and control to relational databases.

The integration of objects, predicates, and relations is achieved by using tables to represent all three structures. As we saw earlier in Section 2.4.2.3, a relational database consists of a set of tables. Each table consists of columns (also referred to as attributes or fields) and rows of data records. A row in a table represents a relationship among a set of attributes. The definition of a table's fields and domains is called the database schema. The particular table shown above, and many others of the same type, are called database instances. For most purposes, the schema of a database is all a database designer may be concerned with from a logical point of view. The concept of a relation scheme is thus somewhat analogous to an Object template with attributes.

4.5.2 Defining Schemas

Each relational database needs to have a *schema*. In the predicate model, the user defines relations by defining a series of special predicates, most likely as facts. The first predicate is the *relational* predicate:

> relational Employees

This identifies the predicate Employees as a relational predicate. Of course, we can define a schema for this relation with the SQL data definition method. However, here we also illustrate how schemas may be defined logically with assertions.

To set up the schema for the relation, the following predicates are defined:

> ID, Integer, 1 is-a-field Employee
> Last Name, String, 20 is-a-field Employee
> First Name, String, 20 is-a-field Employee
> Age, Integer, 1 is-a-field Employee
> Salary, Integer, 1 is-a-field Employee
> Department, Integer, 1 is-a-field Employee

These facts define the fields, types, and array sizes of the relation Employee.

In the object model, relations are defined by a series of special objects, each having "Relation" as one of its parents. The following example illustrates how the same relation can be defined using objects:

> Object: Employee
> Parent: Person

Parent: Relation
Attribute: ID Value: Integer, 1
Attribute: Last Name Value: String, 20
Attribute: First Name Value: String, 20
Attribute: Age Value: Integer, 1
Attribute: Salary Value: Long, 1
Attribute: Department Value: Integer, 1

Note that only explicitly named attributes are interpreted as fields. Inherited attributes are not interpreted as fields, although they may be accessed by inheritance.

In addition to predefined types such as characters, integers, reals, and strings, field types may also be the name of another relation, thus allowing a record to have a *direct link*, (i.e., pointer) to another record.

4.5.2.1 Defining Indices

Indices are defined with predicates in a two-step procedure.

a. Create an index with the: Index-name *is-an-index* Relation predicate.

b. List the fields to which the index refers with the: Index-name *has-index-field* Field predicate.

This two step procedure provides necessary flexibility in creating multifield indices. For instance, consider the following definition:

Name Index <u>is-an-index</u> Employee
Name Index <u>has-index-field</u> Last Name
Name Index <u>has-index-field</u> First Name

The first fact here creates an index called *Name Index* for the *Employee* relation. This index currently has no fields. The second and third assertions then indicate that fields *Last Name* and *First Name* are part of this index. This creates a single index whose key consists of two fields.

During retrieval or in performing the relational operations, the database will use all indices available to it as indicated by the index definitions created using the predicates *is-an-index* and *has-index-field*.

4.5.3 Dynamic Schema Modifications and Transactions

Once a record schema has been defined, new record schemas can be added and new indices created. Record schemas and indices can also be removed. Schemas and indices are added and removed if the file is opened with an appropriate predicate that we will refer to here as the <u>open-update-relations</u> predicate.

Record schemas and indices may also be dynamically added and removed by updating the factbase and/or objectbase schema and then proving an update-schema predicate that reads the factbase/objectbase schema information and modifies the schema accordingly.

All modifications to relations are considered temporary. They should not become a part of the relation file until explicitly commanded. In this way the integrity of the relation file is maintained. Modifications can be grouped into *transactions* that are guaranteed to be performed as a single unit. This guards against a portion of the modifications succeeding and a portion failing, thereby leaving the file in an inconsistent state.

Transactions are completed with a predicate such as <u>commit-relations</u> that makes all modifications to the relationbase permanent. This predicate then affects every relation and all schema modifications. Conversely, a predicate such as <u>abort-relations</u> throws away all modifications to the relationbase since the last time the <u>commit-relations</u> predicate was used.

4.5.4 Adding and Removing Data

In the predicate model, records are dynamically added with the <u>assert</u> predicate and removed with the <u>retract</u> predicate. These predicates perform a relational assertion (or retraction) if the asserted or retracted predicate is a relational predicate.

In the object model, adding a record is done as follows:

1. Fill in the attributes of a child of the relation object with values, for example with

   (Attribute1 of Child) := Value-1.

2. Prove the predicate

   <u>add-instance</u> Relation, Instance

   for the child above.

For example, if one creates a child of Employee with

   <u>new-Object</u> New Emp, Employee

then one may write

   (ID of New Emp) := "7494" and
   (First Name of New Emp) := "John" and
   (Last Name of New Emp) := "Smith" and
   (Age of New Emp) := "26" and
   (Salary of New Emp) := "25000" and
   (Department of New Emp) := "14" and
   <u>add-instance</u> Employee, New Emp

The last goal will add this record to the database. Proving add-instance again will add another record.

The object model supports record removal with the predicate delete-instances, as shown in the example.

> delete-instances
> *from* Employee,
> *where* Department = 14, Age < 65

This predicate removes from the *Employee* relation all records whose Age field is less than 65 and whose *Department* field is equal to 14. If no matches are found, the predicate fails.

4.5.5 Retrieving Data

We introduced in Chapter 2 the relational algebra as a method for operating on relations. The relational algebra also provides a concise language for representing queries to databases. However, database system products require query languages that may be easily used and interfaced to programs. The language SQL (Structured Query Language), is the most widely used relational query language.

As discussed in Chapter 2, SQL expressions are made up of three clauses: *select, from,* and *where*. A query in SQL has the form

> *select* Attribute$_1$, Attribute$_2$, . . . , Attribute$_n$
> *from* Relation$_1$, Relation$_2$, . . . , Relation$_m$
> *where* Predicate

In this notation, the list of attributes may be replaced with a star (∗) to select all attributes of all relations appearing in the *from* clause.

The result of an SQL query is a relation. SQL acts as follows:

a. It forms the product of the relations named in the *from* clause.
b. It performs a relational selection using the *where* clause predicate.
c. It projects the result onto the attributes of the *select* (in the SQL sense) clause.

SQL can thus be viewed as an outgrowth of the relational algebra. Consider the table shown in Figure 4.14. To find those customers in Beverly Hills owing more than $5000, we pose the following SQL query:

> *Select* Name
> *from* Cust-account
> *where* City = "BevHls" and
> amount > 5000

Cust-Address

Name	Cust #	Street	City	Amount Owed
Hughes	1712	Sepulveda	Culver	70,000
Aamco	2487	Washington	Venice	100,000
MGM	1464	La Brea	Hollywd	89,000
Gucci	3577	Rodeo	Bev Hls	72,000
SAG	2667	Stone Cnyn	Bev Hls	56,000

Figure 4.14 A modified customer database.

It is possible to combine SQL statements into fairly complex queries. SQL statements may also be embedded in programming languages for general-purpose computation. In the remainder of this section, we show how SQL statements may be embedded as standard retrieval operations within an expert system shell.

In the predicate model, retrieving data from a relation is very easy. One simply uses the relation name as the predicate. Pattern matching is then performed exactly as it is normally performed in factbase searches. Any constants and bound variables are matched to a record. Any unbound variables are then bound to the corresponding fields of the record. For instance:

Employee 7494, 'Last Name', 'First Name'

searches the "Employee" relation for the value 7494 in the *ID* field. When a match is found, 'Last Name' is bound to the *Last Name* field and 'First Name' is bound to the *First Name* field. If no match is found in the relation base (i.e., there are no employees whose number is 7494), the rulebase is searched and any matching rules are fired. In the system described here, relational predicates generally use backtracking to find new matches until there are no more.

To retrieve data using the object model, we may use a predicate such as get-instance that incorporates an SQL-like syntax for retrieving information. Consider the following example:

get-instance 'Record ID',
select First Name, Last Name,
from Employee,
where Department = 14, Age > 18

In this example, the *get-instance* predicate selects from the "Employee" relation all employees older than 18 who are in department 14, and it binds 'Record ID' to a string that uniquely identifies the first one. Upon backtracking, 'Record ID' is bound to the identifier of the next matching record. If there are no more matches, the predicate then fails.

The predicate *get-instance* may be defined so that criteria listed in the *where* clause are ANDed together. Under such a definition, the record must satisfy all criteria listed in the clause in order to qualify for selection. However, criteria that have the same field name are ORed together, meaning that only one must be satisfied. These properties are illustrated in the following example:

> get-instance 'Record ID',
> *select* First Name, Last Name,
> *from* Employee,
> *where* Last Name = Jones, Last Name = Smith, Age > = 18

In this case, get-instance selects all employees 18 years or older who are named "Jones" or "Smith."

If the *select* clause is omitted, all fields are selected. If the *where* clause is omitted, all records will be qualified. The *from* clause is required. Once the record ID is obtained from the get-instance predicate, data can be retrieved from the record by standard object-attribute access. Thus, in the notation defined here:

> 'C' : = (Salary of 'Record ID') and
> 'A' : = (Age of 'Record ID')

Records may be similarly updated, as in

> (Salary of 'Record ID') : = "25000"

These changes are effected immediately, but will not be made permanent until the commit-relations or close-relations predicate is fired. Naturally, this is a very important feature, since the update may later be invalidated if backtracking is required.

It is also possible to link records of a relation just as one can link standard objects. For example, with objects one may create a link as follows:

> (Boss of John) : = Jim

This creates a direct link from the "Boss" attribute of the object named "John" to the object named "Jim." In the same way, links can be created to relational objects by using the *Record Identifier* instead of an object name.

The record-id predicate facilitates getting the record identifier of a record, as in

> get-identity 'X'

This predicate binds 'X' to the record identifier of the last record added or asserted, or to the last record retrieved with a relational predicate or <u>get-instance</u>.

The following example illustrates the process of linking Jim to John's boss field:

> <u>assert</u> <u>Employee</u> 1112, Johnson, Jim, 120000, 14 and
> <u>get-identity</u> 'Boss ID' and
> <u>assert</u> <u>Employee</u> 1113, Smith, John, 60000, 14, 'Boss ID'

Direct links are then accessed just as in objects. First we must get John's record identifier either by using the object model, as in

> <u>get-instance</u> 'Record ID',
> *select* Last Name, First Name,
> *from* Employee,
> *where* Last Name = Smith, First Name = John

Or, by using the predicate method

> <u>Employee</u> 'X', Smith, John and
> <u>get-identity</u> 'Record ID'

Once we have the record identifier, we may use it as if it were an Object name to show information about John's boss.

> 'Boss L' := (Last Name of (Boss of 'Record ID')) and
> 'Boss F' := (First Name of (Boss of 'Record ID')) and
> 'Boss Sal' := (Salary of (Boss of 'Record ID')) . . .

■ 4.6 USING THE INTEGRATED EXPERT DATABASE SYSTEM

Within an integrated framework for intelligent databases, rules extend relational databases by providing virtual tables, and objects may extend relational databases by providing virtual attributes and virtual values.

Predicate logic views the world in terms of *clauses* which include *predicates* and *arguments*. A predicate is a verb or concept that relates its arguments. For example, "John is the father of Mary" can be represented in logic as

> John <u>is the father</u> of Mary

where *is the father of* is the verb of this sentence and *John* and *Mary* are the arguments. A *clause schema* consists of a predicate name and an integer, indicating the number of arguments of the predicate.

Each argument in a clause may be a constant or a variable. Two clauses have the same *predicate schema* if they have the same predicate name and the same number of arguments.

A rule consists of two parts: the premise and the conclusion. For example, the rule "A *is the grandfather of* B if A *is the father of* X and X *is the father of* B" can be specified in logic as

> 'A' is the grandfather of 'B'
> If
> 'A' is the father of 'X' and
> 'X' is the father of 'B';

Thus each predicate schema in logic maps to a *relation*. This suggests that pattern matching with logic is a natural way of extending relations and providing users with a higher level of expressive power.

Similarly a clause such as

> Employee 'Number', 'Name', 'Salary', 'DeptNo'

is used to represent the employee schema. Inference is done by firing rules. This can be done either forward or backward. For instance:

> highly-paid-employee 'Name'
> If
> Employee 'Number', 'Name', 'Salary', 'DeptNo'
> and
> 'Salary' > 60000;

Thus the matching of the fact Employee 'Number', 'Name', 'Salary', 'DeptNo' with a logical factbase is actually equivalent to the operation of accessing a record from the database.

An object-oriented system views the world in terms of objects. Each object is a conceptual entity that is associated with a set of *attributes*. Each attribute in an object may have a *value*. We call the definition of a database object an *object schema*. An *instance* of an object is a record of values corresponding to the attributes in the object.

An object that has "Relation" as its first parent is viewed as a database object. The instances of this object are then viewed as database entries. For example, the Employee relation above can be defined as

> Object: Employee
> Parent: Relation
> Parent: Person
> Key: EmpNumber
> Attribute: Name
> Attribute: Salary
> Attribute: DeptNo

and an instance of "Employee" could be

Instance: 1101
Parent: Employee
Attribute: Name   Value: David Smith
Attribute: Salary   Value: 36000
Attribute: DeptNo   Value: 109

A logical language provides a set of predicates to access object instances. For example, to get the list of employees who earn more than 60000 one can write

highly-paid-employee 'X'
If
    'Emp' is-a Employee, Name = 'X'
and
    (Salary of 'Emp') > 60000 ;

The predicate *is-a* will return an instance of an object schema. It includes the object name, followed by one (or more) keys. During rule execution, the backtracking mechanism will go through the database record by record to return the next instance for the object schema. Thus, the object system may be fully integrated with the logic system.

Again, each object schema maps to a relation, suggesting that relations are a suitable method of integrating objects, logic, and databases. The integration of rules and logic with SQL provides a knowledge management system. There are three basic elements to the integration.

1. *Logic with embedded SQL statements*

SQL may be embedded in the logical host language of rules. The user can use SQL statements to access the database while the SQL user can use the inference, control, and inexact reasoning system provided by the inference engine to analyze and evaluate the database.

The following "backtrackable" rule illustrates the embedding of SQL in logical rules:

highly-paid-employee 'Employee', 'Dept'
If

    select NAME, DEPTNO
    from EMPLOYEE
    where SALARY > 60000;

Here the variables 'Employee' and 'Dept' are mapped to the attributes appearing in the SELECT portion of the SQL statement. In effect, the SQL statement builds a "logical schema" for the predicate calling it. The SQL statement thus creates a temporary relation (factbase) storing the query result. In this case, the result of this query is a list of employee names and departments whose salary is greater than 60000. This will only be executed once when the highly-paid-employee predicate is invoked. Every time the system backtracks to this predicate, the backtracking mechanism is able to tell it where to backtrack.

2. *SQL with objects*

Here SQL is used with inheritance in the object-based or object-oriented manner. Two ways in which objects and SQL statements interact are

a. Inheritance—where attributes are obtained from parents.

b. Tuple-valued items—where statements of the form SELECT (A of B) appear within SQL statements.

To illustrate (a) above consider the relations:

Employee = (EmpNumber, Name, Salary, DeptNo)
Engineer = (EmpNumber, Specialty)

and the objects

Object: Employee
Parent: Relation
Attribute: EmpNumber
Attribute: Name
Attribute: Salary
Attribute: Department

Object: Engineer
Parent: Employee
Attribute: Specialty

In this latter example the Engineer object schema inherits the attribute definitions Name, Salary, and Department from its parent object schema Employee. For instance we can say

```
.
.
.

SELECT Name
FROM Engineer
WHERE Specialty = Electrical

.
.
.
```

The object mechanism will then retrieve this information from the Employee database. With the inheritance property, each relation can inherit attributes from its parent relations. This provides an elegant way of implementing the type hierarchy. A mapping between objects and relations easily provides the inheritance features of the object-oriented paradigm.

To illustrate point (b) above consider:

> Object: Department
> Parent: Thing
> Attribute: Manager

Now we can say

> *Select* (Manager of Department), Name, Salary
> *from* Employee
> *where* Salary > 60000

3. *SQL with logical predicates*

Logical predicates may be included in *where* conditions in SQL statements. This allows users to specify more complex selection criteria using predicates. The following gives an example of using a predicate to quantify the *where* condition:

> *select* NAME
> *from* EMPLOYEE
> *where* suitable for promotion EMPLOYEE.NAME;
>
> suitable-for-promotion 'Name'
> If
> Employee 'Number', 'Name', 'Salary', 'DeptNo'
> and
> 'Salary' < 60000

The SQL processor should be intelligent enough to deal with predicates within the SQL statement. Each of these predicates is treated as a Boolean function call that returns TRUE or FALSE. The predicate returns TRUE if it succeeds and FALSE otherwise.

We can illustrate this integration by showing how each of the integrating strategies may be used with a shared example. Consider how the COMPANY database can be viewed in each of the three ways.

a. In relational form:

> Employee = (EmpNumber, Name, Salary, DeptNo)
> Department = (DeptNo, Function, Manager)

b. With objects:

> Object: Employee
> Parent: Relation
> Key: EmpNumber

Attribute: Name
Attribute: Salary
Attribute: DeptNo

Object: Department
Parent: Relation
Key: DeptNo
Attribute: Function
Attribute: Manager

c. With logical predicates:

Employee EmpNumber, Name, Salary, DeptNo
Department DeptNo, Function, Manager

Similarly, an instance of the Employee can be also be represented in three different ways: With a table (Figure 4.15); with an object instance, as in

Instance: 1101
Parent: Employee
Attribute: Name   Value: David Smith
Attribute: Salary   Value: 36000
Attribute: DeptNo   Value: 109

and with logic, as in

Employee 1101, David Smith, 36000, 109

Thus a database has three styles of representation, namely: object-based, predicate-based, and relation-based. The relation-based representation is the conventional way of representing the database contents and provides the bridge to conventional database systems such as dBASE[tm], ORACLE[tm], RBASE[tm], and so on.

Employee	Soc. Sec. No.	Department
Small	999-20-1154	Accounting
Martin	467-75-3322	Marketing
....		

Figure 4.15 Employee instances represented within a table.

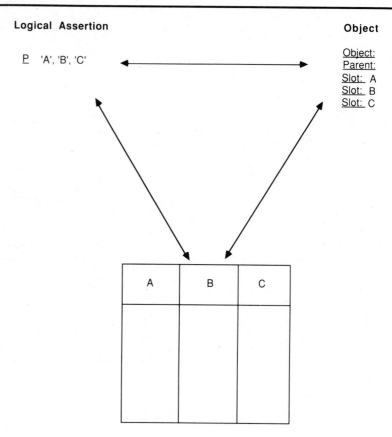

Figure 4.16 The relationship between logic, frames, and relational databases.

Relational Databases	Objects	Logic
Schema	Object	Clause Schema
Attribute	Attribute	Argument
Value	Value	Value
Record	Instance	Fact

Figure 4.17 The mapping of terms between tables, predicates, and objects.

Users can access the database in several ways: object-related predicates, facts, and SQL statements. For example, to know who earns more than $60,000 annual salary in the company, a query can be expressed in any of the following ways.

a. Object-based predicate:

highly-paid-employee 'Employee'
If
  'Emp' <u>is-a</u> Employee, Name = 'Employee' and
  (Salary of 'Emp') > 60000;

b. Logic-based predicate:

highly-paid-employee 'Employee'
If
  Employee 'EmpNo', 'Employee', 'Salary', 'Dept'
and
  'Salary' > 60000;

c. SQL predicate:

highly-paid-employee 'Employee'
If
  select NAME
  from EMPLOYEE
  where SALARY > 60000;

We thus have a three-way mapping (Figure 4.16) between tables, predicates, and objects. Figure 4.17 shows the mapping of terms between these structures. Thus relational databases, objects, and logic may be uniformly integrated in a framework for intelligent databases that supports the combined use of rules, relations, and objects.

■ 4.7 DYNAMIC DATA MANAGEMENT WITH OBJECTS

In this section we illustrate some of the ways in which an object system may facilitate the operation of a database. We focus in particular on the use of attached procedures to carry out tasks such as integrity maintenance and dynamic data management.

4.7.1 Integrity Maintenance with Attached Procedures

One way to use attached predicates is as guardians for information retrieval and storage. In this mode the predicates restrict the information that may be retrieved from an attribute or stored in an attribute.

As an example of this type of application of an if-needed predicate, one may restrict access to parts of the data in an object by defining a password predicate. Consider the following objects:

<u>Object</u>: Employee
<u>Parent</u>: Person
<u>Attribute</u>: Employee Number   <u>Value</u>:
<u>Attribute</u>: Salary   <u>Value</u>:
<u>If-Needed</u>: <u>check password</u> hidden3

<u>Object</u>: Tony Higgins
<u>Parent</u>: Employee
<u>Attribute</u>: Employee Number   <u>Value</u>: 1925364
<u>Attribute</u>: Salary   <u>Value</u>: 50000

Here the if-needed predicate <u>check password</u> is attached to the attribute Salary in the object Employee and will be inherited by the object Tony Higgins. When the value of Tony Higgins' Salary is to be read or obtained through an assignment operation of the form

    'X' : = (Salary of Tony Higgins)

the attached if-needed predicate will be proved as a goal. The following backward rule may then be called by this predicate:

    <u>check password</u> 'X'
If
    <u>write</u> Please Enter Password and
    <u>read</u> 'Y' and
    'X' = 'Y' and
    <u>write</u> Thank you ;

When invoked, the attached predicate matches 'X' to hidden3 and tries to prove the premise of the rule. The user is prompted for a password value, and the result is compared with hidden3. If this test succeeds, the attached predicate succeeds and the salary of Tony Higgins will be retrieved. However, if the test fails, the retrieval operation will also fail.

We can also use <u>check password</u> as an if-added predicate to protect the attribute Salary from changing without a password of higher-level authority. For instance

<u>Object</u>: Employee
<u>Parent</u>: Person
<u>Attribute</u>: Employee Number   <u>Value</u>:
<u>Attribute</u>: Salary   <u>Value</u>:
<u>If-Needed</u>: <u>check password</u> hidden3
<u>If-Added</u>: <u>check password</u> mystery4

Object: Tony Higgins
Parent: Employee
Attribute: Employee Number   Value: 1925364
Attribute: Salary   Value: 50000

In this case, if the value of Tony Higgins' Salary is to be changed through an assignment operation of the form

(Salary of Tony Higgins) : = 60000

the attached if-added predicate will be proved as a goal. Thus, to obtain the salary, we need to know the password hidden3; however, to change the salary, we need to use the password mystery4. Similarly, If-added predicates may also be used to safeguard information storage.

4.7.2 Dynamic Data Management with Attached Predicates

Another mode for using attached predicates is for dynamic information retrieval and storage. In this mode, one may either directly calculate the value of an attribute on the basis of other information or dynamically determine the possible range of values for an attribute. This facility is particularly useful in intelligent databases where some of the information may change relatively quickly, and it is necessary to update it continuously. Consider a database that presents the latest stock prices as part of an information system for stock market investment analysts. Using an attached predicate, the latest stock prices could be fed to the user as they become available. However, if the value of a particular stock is not queried, the system does not have to maintain its latest value in the database. This type of feature would be especially attractive where some information is available externally on a pay-per-use basis. Attached predicates could then be used to display the information and carry out associated accounting operations.

Other uses of attached predicates allow values of missing information to be inferred. For instance, the price-to-earnings ratio of a stock could be calculated on the basis of other information, or an if-needed predicate might calculate a person's age by retrieving the current date and the birth date of the person and subtracting the birth date from the current data to obtain the age. Consider the following objects:

Object: Employee
Parent: Person
Attribute: Employee Number   Value:
Attribute: Year of Birth   Value:
Attribute: Age   Value:
If-Needed: calculate age Age, Year of Birth

Object: Tony Higgins
Parent: Employee

Attribute: Employee Number   Value: 1925364
Attribute: Year of Birth   Value: 1959
Attribute: Age   Value:

The attached predicate calculate age may be defined as a backward rule. For instance:

     calculate age 'Age', 'Year'
If
     current year 'Date'
and
     'Age' := 'Date' − 'Year' ;

Here current year is again a predicate that retrieves the current year from the factbase. In this way the value of the attribute Age is always dynamically determined. There is no need to update this attribute as time changes. This facility may be used in a myriad of applications, such as simulations and strategic analysis.

If-needed predicates may also be used to dynamically determine a range of admissible values for an object attribute during inference. When a user is interacting with an expert system, situations often arise when data needs to be supplied by the user. However, all data values supplied by the user may not be valid, or the user may be unaware of the range of possible answers. The user thus needs to be informed of the acceptable set of possibilities for the value of an attribute during inference.

Of course, in some situations, these values may be *predetermined* and displayed to the user when the need arises. However, in many cases, the admissible values are dependent on a number of factors and need to be determined *during* inference. In such cases, attached predicates are very useful since they can invoke rules that *dynamically* determine a set of acceptable values from which the user may select.

For instance, consider a financial expert system that makes investment recommendations to a user. After obtaining some basic data such as age, amount of desired investment, and current tax bracket, the system begins to interact with the user. During the interaction, the user may need to make some decisions or suggestions; for example, the user may have to suggest a certain type of investment. Not all investments may be applicable to the user, however, and there is little point in showing the user a long and potentially distracting list of investments, many of which are not relevant.

What is needed here is a facility for dynamically determining the suitable investments for an investor and then asking for a choice. For instance, consider

Object: Investor
Parent: Person
Attribute: Tax Bracket   Value:
Attribute: Amount
Attribute: Risk

Attribute: Length
Attribute: Main Investment Type   Value:
If-Needed: get choice Investor, Main Investment Type

Object: Steven Porter
Parent: Investor
Attribute: Tax Bracket   Value: 30
Attribute: Amount
Attribute: Risk
Attribute: Length
Attribute: Main Investment Type

In this example, after Steven Porter has supplied his current tax bracket, amount of investment, and so on, we need to show him a set of possible investment types (stocks, bonds, etc.) to choose from. His choice will then be placed in the attribute *Main Investment Type*.

However, the choices to be displayed will depend on the answers Steven Porter has provided to the earlier questions, as well as other facts such as the amount of sodium he consumes and the current prime interest rate. For instance, there is no point in displaying the choice real estate to someone interested in a very short-term investment and who wishes to invest a small amount of capital. Consequently, investment choices should be *dynamically determined during a consultation based on a set of rules* and will tend to differ among investors. Attached predicates thus allow us to have dynamic menus whose contents are not fixed before the execution of the program begins, but are dynamically adjusted with a set of rules.

■ 4.8 SUMMARY

Expert systems not only provide a way of archiving expertise and making it available when it is needed, but provide higher level language constructs that are useful for database programming. These constructs include backward and forward rules, attached predicates, knowledge representation, and relational predicates. Expert database systems seem to offer a way of combining the best features of database systems and expert systems.

There are two main components to the task of linking expert and database systems. The first task is to provide an appropriate programming environment. We have shown how this can be done by emphasizing the role of an expert system shell as a high-level programming environment and by linking relations as expressed in the facts and rules of expert systems to the relations expressed in relational databases. The second task involves the development of common data models. Here, the knowledge base of an expert system can be used to extend the semantics of the database model. The secret to this semantic elaboration of databases is to recognize that both databases and expert systems refer to objects and their interrelations. Thus our solution to the problem of integrating expert systems and databases relies on the development of object representation as a common framework that allows us to map database semantics into the representational methods of expert systems, and vice versa.

In the following chapters we will use facts, rules, objects, and inference engines as basic tools for knowledge representation and inference. We shall find these basic components of expert systems to be very useful in constructing computational models of conventional databases, hypertext systems, and in building the more advanced systems for text interpretation and retrieval that intelligent databases require.

5

HYPERMEDIA

■ 5.1 INTRODUCTION

As we discussed in Chapter 1, the world today is approaching, if it has not already exceeded, the point of information overload. This is not to say that information isn't still being used effectively, but that the effective use of information today is just a small fraction of what it could potentially be given the appropriate storage and retrieval mechanisms.

One of the barriers to the exploitation of information is a failure to identify interconnectivities that allow us to recognize links and similarities between pieces of information that are normally stored in separate locations. Just as the invasion of England in A.D. 1066 by the Normans lives on today in the influence of medieval French on the language that this book is written in, so too information is linked in a rich network of cause and effect relationships. We lose much of this richness when we decompose information into isolated records, files, and so on.

Hypertext is a tool for building and using associative structures. A normal document is linear, and one tends to read it from beginning to end. In contrast, reading hypertext is open-ended and one can jump from idea to idea depending on one's interests. The nearest thing to a hypertext document that most people are familiar with is a thesaurus. A thesaurus has no single beginning or end. Each time the thesaurus is consulted, it is entered at a different location based on the word used to initiate the search. Hypertext can be thought of as an enriched thesaurus where, instead of links between words, links between documents and text fragments are available.

We will focus on the functionality of hypermedia in the following sections. We assume an underlying object-oriented formalism for implementing the hypermedia.

Although this strategy may appear obvious, existing hypermedia systems are only weakly object-oriented. The intermedia system, for instance, is largely based on a relational database formalism, while the HyperCard system contains some, but by no means all, of the features of an object-oriented environment.

In this chapter we define hypertext and hypermedia and describe current hypertext development systems. We then show how hypermedia acts as an extremely general form of knowledge representation environment, and we build a semiformal specification of hypermedia. We evaluate some of the strengths and weaknesses of hypermedia and we also discuss a variety of hypermedia applications.

5.1.1 Hypertext: A Definition

The human mind seems to be inherently associative in nature. There are many sources of evidence for this associativity, ranging from the richly interconnected structure of the brain itself to the patterns of associative memory and thinking that are frequently observed in human behavior.

The associative nature of the human mind has been observed in many contexts and has been formalized in network models of human memory (Collins and Loftus, 1975; Eich, 1982; Murdock, 1982; Anderson, 1983). This associative structure of the mind is very different from the linear way in which books and information are generally organized. A book, as a linear arrangement, represents a single path through a topic. In contrast, there are many possible paths through associative structures.

Hypertext can be simply defined as the creation and representation of links between discrete pieces of data. When this data can be graphics or sound, as well as text or numbers, the resulting structure is referred to as hypermedia. Conceptually, the notion of hypertext is closely related to the idea of semantic networks, with text and data being represented in nodes. As is the case with semantic networks, there are potentially many meanings that may be assigned to the links between nodes, but we will focus here on a stripped-down version of hypertext that encompasses a few of the major types of links that are the most relevant to the development of active databases.

Hypertext is simultaneously a method for storing and retrieving data. Hypertext incorporates the notion of linking pieces of information, allowing users to navigate through a network of chunks of information. Information is provided both by what is stored in each node and in the way that information nodes are linked to each other. For our purposes, hypertext can be thought of as a database system with unrestricted links among records and files. Figure 5.1 shows an example of a hypertext network relating to the U.S. Constitution.

Hypertext by itself is not a form of artificial intelligence (Oren, 1987). This is because AI and hypertext serve different purposes. Hypertext uses machines to augment human cognition by providing a dynamic storage medium for information, whereas AI strives to represent human knowledge and physical reality in a form that permits sophisticated machine reasoning. However, as we show later, hypertext and AI form a potent combination in the development of intelligent databases.

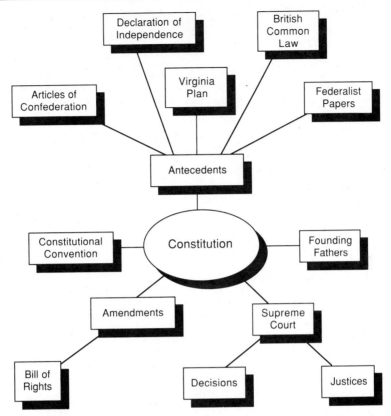

Figure 5.1 A hypertext network relating to the U.S. Constitution.

5.1.2 Why Hypertext?

The concept of hypertext was originally greeted with a certain amount of skepticism. The unstructured nature of hypertext seemed to create great difficulties in retrieving specific information from the massive libraries of hypertext that were being proposed. As we see later in this chapter, there was a great deal of validity to these objections, but much of their force can be removed by modifying the role of hypertext and adding a small amount of structure to the original definition.

The proponents of hypertext use terms such as *freedom* and *access* rather than the traditional information science evaluative criteria of precision and recall. The standard method of structuring databases is to create links from individual documents to index terms. There are relatively few links per document, and there is no straightforward way to browse the database. Even in full text retrieval, words and phrases are used as de facto index terms by the user. Thus conventional full-text retrieval allows users to create their own indexes without changing the structure of retrieval access. Hypertext, on the other hand, allows one to browse within the document space. In addition to links between documents and index terms, one can also create links within the set of documents. Thus with hypertext, users can smoothly move from one document to another along a particular chain or path of ideas.

It is interesting to note that these two styles of information retrieval (i.e., conventional indexes and full-text versus hypertext) have their analogies in the process of retrieval from human memory. In cued retrieval, a person is given a clue or a tag (indexed query) and is asked to provide the information specified by that query. Examples of retrieval cues are

> the capital city of Australia
> customers with good credit
> the date and time of the next departmental meeting

Cued retrieval is built around the idea of a question or query. In contrast, associative retrieval returns information that is similar to the starting information, rather than an explicit answer to a question or query.

Explorations of associative memory appear to form the basis of much of human thinking and conceptualization. The theoretical properties of associative memories have been studied for a number of years (e.g., Kohonen, 1977) and have been used, for instance, to develop computer tools for face recognition, handwritten character recognition, and for pattern recognition in general.

Once we understand the essential difference between hypertext and conventional text retrieval, we see that the question of which system is better is actually inappropriate. Hypertext provides a different type of service, that is, associative instead of cued (queried) retrieval. However, hypertext may supplement conventional methods of information retrieval by allowing users to discover retrieval cues (i.e., formulate queries), which can then be used for information retrieval.

There are a number of ways in which the existence and use of hypertext may be justified. We focus here on two of them.

1. Hypertext corresponds to the associative way in which people think.
2. Hypertext is a flexible knowledge structuring principle that can be used to implement and embed other knowledge structures.

Many people are familiar with the associative nature of thought from their own experiences. We can also demonstrate the existence of associative thought using a technique originally developed as a psychoanalytic tool. The method of free association is used by some psychotherapists to take advantage of naturally occurring associative mechanisms.

The associative structure of the mind can be observed by asking persons to free associate when they are in a relaxed state. One might begin with the word "summer," leading to a sequence of associations such as the following:

summer–swimming–sea–fish–dinner–plate–cutlery–silver–ring–wedding–white–snow . . .

Needless to say, such associative structures can be highly idiosyncratic, but this is precisely why they have been used to provide clues about personality and motivation. Freud, who is generally regarded as the founder of psychoanalysis, believed that the method of free association gave the analyst a chance to observe the inner workings of the mind because the unstructured nature of the task tended to prevent the internal censors from operating on the material being generated by the subconscious.

Regardless of the psychological status of free associations and the precise mechanisms with which they are generated, we can observe considerable variation both within and among people in terms of the associative output that is produced. For instance, we might go back to these same persons a few days later and again ask them to free associate on the word "summer." On this occasion we might obtain a response such as the following:

summer–sun–star–astronomy–telescope–Galileo–Pisa–Pizza–cheese–Swiss–Pope–Rome–Italy . . .

Each reader might, in turn, develop entirely different associative sequences to this stimulus word, even though we have a similar conception of what the word "summer" means and we share much of the same cultural and educational background.

Why should text be linear, when the mind clearly is not? There are two main ways to answer this question.

1. Writing and text output is dominated by the left hemisphere of the brain, which tends to think linearly.
2. Past technologies of writing and text production did not permit nonlinear text to any great degree.

The specialization that apparently occurs between the two hemispheres of the brain has been described by a number of authors (e.g., Bradshaw and Nettleton, 1983). Although the details of this specialization remain controversial, there is evidence to suggest that language production and linear thought are both controlled by the left hemisphere in the majority of right-handed individuals. We might expect this joint control of text production and proclivity towards linear thought in the left hemisphere to tend to produce linear text output.

The tendency of the left hemisphere to produce linear text has been matched by technologies of text production and cataloging that could only cope with linear structures. Books are essentially linear, and libraries continue to use linear cataloging schemes. It is interesting to speculate on the relative contribution that brain mechanisms and text production technologies have made to the overwhelming linearity of text. Hypertext proponents are guessing, in effect, that linearity is largely a result of the way that text was produced in the past, rather than an inherent property of human text processing, and that people will be able to switch to nonlinear methods of text processing if given the chance.

■ 5.2 THE HISTORY OF THE HYPERTEXT CONCEPT

As long ago as 1945, Vannevar Bush proposed a nonlinear structuring of text that would correspond to the associative nature of the human mind. In 1965, Ted Nelson christened such nonlinear text hypertext and began the task of implementing hypertext on computers.

The idea of nonlinear text is an appealing one and has been used by many people when they try to put their ideas onto 3 × 5 index cards and then make references from one card to the next. In fact, this intuitive and pervasive model forms the concrete metaphor used as the basis of the HyperCard system described in Section 5.3.1. In the following sections we describe some of the early approaches to hypertext.

5.2.1 The Memex

Bush (1945) first described the concept of hypertext, although he did not use the term "hypertext" in describing the concept. He described a machine, which he referred to as a memex, that could be used to browse and make notes in a voluminous online text and graphics system. The memex contained a large library of documents in addition to personal items such as notes, photographs, and sketches. The memex was to have several screens and a facility for establishing a labeled link between any two points (nodes) in the library.

In Bush's view, the essential feature of the memex was its ability to link pairs of items in a way that transcended existing methods of indexing, which he characterized as follows:

> Our ineptitude in getting at the record is largely caused by the artificiality of systems of indexing. When data of any sort are placed in storage, they are filed alphabetically or numerically, and information is found (when it is) by tracing it down from subclass to subclass. It can be in only one place, unless duplicates are used; one has to have rules as to which path will locate it, and the rules are cumbersome. Having found one item, moreover, one has to emerge from the system and re-enter on a new path.

The memex was expected to overcome these problems by a method of associative indexing where "any item may be caused at will to select immediately and automatically another." Items would be linked together in pairs, and successions of linked items would form trails. As Bush put it, "It is exactly as though the physical items had been gathered together from widely separated sources and bound together to form a new book. It is more than this, for any item can be joined into numerous trails."

These trails would then become literary constructs in their own right, so that one could pass on a particularly useful trail onto someone else who would then incorporate it into their memex structure. Bush even foresaw the development of a new profession of trailblazers who would establish useful trails through the enormous mass of the common record.

At the time of its conception the memex could not be built, although Bush speculated on how microfiche and technologies of the 1940s could be adapted to the task of constructing a memex. Today, however, we recognize that hypertext and the modern computer can be used to implement much of the functionality of Bush's memex.

5.2.2 NLS

Engelbart (1963) was influenced by the memex idea while working at the Stanford Research Institute. He saw computer technology as representing a new stage in human evolution.

> In this stage, the symbols with which the human represents the concepts he is manipulating can be arranged before his eyes, moved, stored, recalled, operated upon according to extremely complex rules—all in very rapid response to a minimum amount of information supplied by the human, by means of special cooperative technological devices. In the limit of what we might now imagine, this could be a computer, with which individuals could communicate rapidly and easily, coupled to a three-dimensional color display with which extremely sophisticated images could be constructed . . .

These ideas eventually resulted in a system called NLS (oN Line System) described by Engelbart and English (1968). NLS was an experimental tool designed to meet the needs of a research group by

> placing in computer store all of our specifications, plans, designs, programs, documentation, reports, memos, bibliography and reference notes, etc., and doing all our scratch work, planning, designing, debugging, etc., and a good deal of our intercommunication, via the consoles.

NLS was an early hypertext system consisting of files that were organized into segments of 3000 words or less that could be linked both hierarchically and nonhierarchically. NLS consisted of

- a database of nonlinear text view filters that selected information from this database
- views that structured the display of this information for visual presentation

NLS has since evolved into a hypertext system known as Augment, and Engelbart continues to advocate the development of systems that augment human capabilities

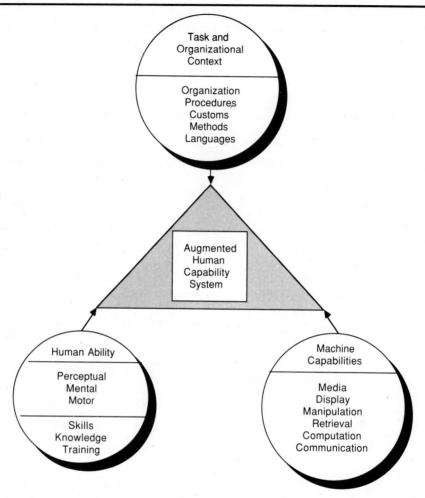

Figure 5.2 A schematic representation of a system that augments human capabilities with computational capabilities.

(Engelbart and Hooper, 1988). Figure 5.2 shows a schematic representation of Engelbart's goal of such a system of human capabilities augmented with computational capabilities.

5.2.3 The Xanadu Project

Nelson's (1965) version of the hypertext concept was more expansive in some senses than that of Engelbart, emphasizing the creation of a unified literary environment on a global scale. It was Nelson who actually coined the term *hypertext*. The Xanadu project got its name from the "magic place of literary memory" mentioned in the poem "Kubla Khan" by Samuel Taylor Coleridge. The long-term goal of the Xanadu project

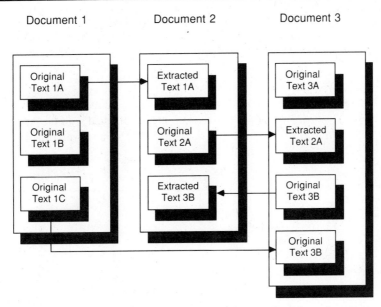

Document 1   Document 2   Document 3

Figure 5.3 The basic ideas behind "xanalogical storage" show how documents may be constructed as composites or as originals and included material.

at that time was to place the world's literary resources online and to use hypertext to link them in a way that facilitates their use.

According to Nelson (e.g., 1988, p. 225), Project Xanadu began in 1960 as a term project for a graduate course he was then taking at Harvard. Nelson referred to the structuring methods used in the project as *xanalogical storage*. One of the basic ideas behind xanalogical storage is illustrated in Figure 5.3 (after Nelson, 1988, Figure 1). Here portions of original documents are "mixed and matched" to create new composite documents. These composite documents then consist of a composite of material that is native to the document (not imported from elsewhere) and material that has been extracted from other documents. Much of the work in the Xanadu project has been concerned with efficient methods for this task of storing segments of text that are shared by different documents.

In 1988 the Xanadu project was taken over by Autodesk, a large software development company. Thus the ideas of Project Xanadu, which have been largely experimental in the past, may become part of a commercial system that will have a much larger impact on information management technology.

■ 5.3 HYPERTEXT SYSTEMS

Since the middle of the 1980s, there has been an explosion in interest in hypertext, along with the development of a large number of hypertext systems. Although these systems are based on the same general notion of associative structuring of text, graphics, and so on, they differ markedly in terms of their implementation. We now consider some of the most prominent hypertext systems as of this writing.

5.3.1 HyperCard

Since its introduction, HyperCard has become the most widely used hypertext system. This is hardly surprising, since it is now bundled with the Apple Macintosh computer and is available to existing users for $49. Almost every Macintosh user is either using or is considering using HyperCard.

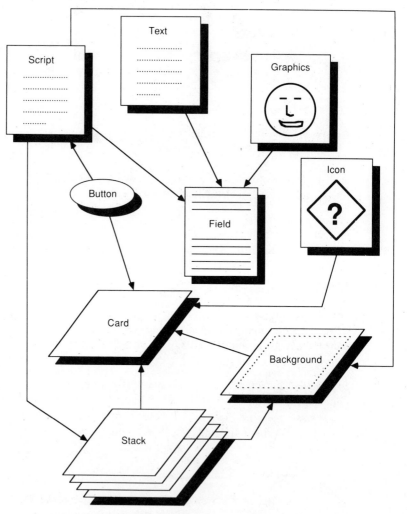

Figure 5.4 The conceptual structure of the HyperCard environment.

The introduction of HyperCard in 1987 completely changed the scale of hypertext development. Initially, hypertext developed in research labs such as Xerox Parc (Palo Alto Research Center) and the Institute for Research on Information Systems (IRIS) at Brown University. When HyperCard was introduced, for instance, the NoteCards system had an installed user base of about 100 users (Trigg, personal communication). A few months later, however, there were thousands of HyperCard users, and the development of HyperCard stacks was proceeding at an almost frightening rate.

HyperCard was developed by Bill Atkinson. It has a number of attractive features, including the integration of MacPaint-like tools into the HyperCard environment. This makes it easy to design cards that contain sophisticated graphics, along with text fields.

HyperCard also contains the HyperTalk language. This is more of a traditional programming language than it is a hypertext authoring language, although it has a syntax that is easy to use. The HyperTalk language is used to write scripts that are attached to the buttons that appear on the cards within a HyperCard stack. The conceptual structure of the HyperCard environment is illustrated in Figure 5.4, with HyperTalk scripts being linked to various HyperCard elements such as buttons, fields, and stacks. One button on a card might have the script shown in Figure 5.5. In this simple example, the script tells the system to move to the next card. Thus when the user clicks on the button icon (a forward arrow, say), the system displays the next card in the stack. Similarly, one can define a back arrow button that will have a script that directs the system to the previous card in the stack, as shown in Figure 5.6.

HyperTalk is an extremely easy language to use and as a result, a lot of simple applications are being developed in HyperCard by "nonprogrammers." HyperCard is particularly useful as an interface design tool (Chignell and Hancock, 1988), and it encourages a style of programming where the interface is designed first and then the desired computations and functionality are added through links, buttons, and the procedures executed by button scripts.

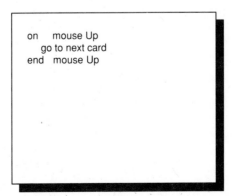

```
on    mouse Up
      go to next card
end   mouse Up
```

Figure 5.5 A simple HyperCard script that tells the system to move to the next card.

Figure 5.6 A HyperCard script that tells the system to go back to the previous card.

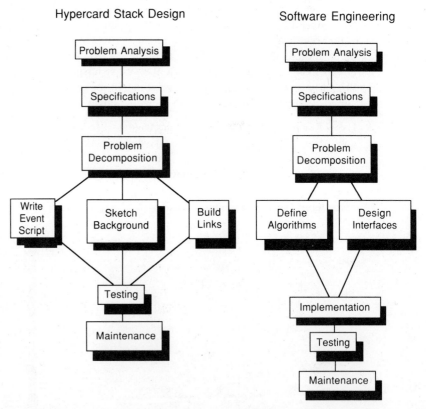

Figure 5.7 The similarity between HyperCard stack design and general software engineering. Iterative loops in the process have been omitted for the sake of clarity.

Extensive experience with HyperCard and the HyperTalk language suggests that the process of building HyperCard stacks is both similar to, and different from, conventional software design. The similarity is stressed in Figure 5.7, where there are clear analogies between the steps used in HyperCard stack design and those generally used in software engineering. The team nature of stackware design is emphasized in Figure 5.8. This figure shows the variety of skills that are needed in hypermedia design, necessarily making it a team process that involves graphics design, interface design, information acquisition, and so on, in addition to programming per se.

Although it is not a fully-functioned object-oriented programming environment, HyperCard embodies many of the features of an object-oriented programming language. Five important components of object-oriented programming are

1. objects
2. methods
3. messages
4. classes
5. inheritance

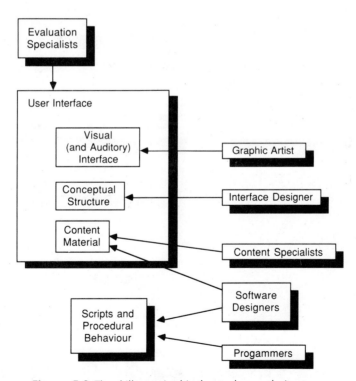

Figure 5.8 The skills required in the stackware design team.

These components are present to some degree in the HyperTalk language. The five types of object in HyperTalk are stacks, backgrounds, cards, buttons, and fields. Each of these objects can send and receive messages. Each object may be associated with a script, which contains a method (referred to as a handler in the HyperTalk jargon).

HyperCard is integrated very closely to the characteristics of the Macintosh microcomputer. As a result, it is event-driven and stacks act as main-event loops that wait for events to which they must respond. In general, events lead to system messages being sent to objects which then react according to the handlers contained in their scripts. In addition to having these event handlers, objects in HyperTalk also have properties that typically represent characteristic behaviors. Thus a button may have an associated sound that is played whenever it is pressed.

The concepts of class and inheritance are not so obvious in HyperTalk. Messages pass through a hierarchy of entities (see Figure 5.9), but the major features of this hierarchy are system, rather than user, defined.

HyperCard also has five levels of user involvement, as shown in Figure 5.10. This

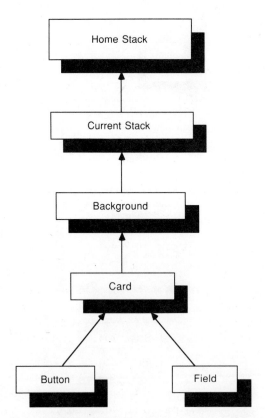

Figure 5.9 The hierarchy of entities in HyperCard.

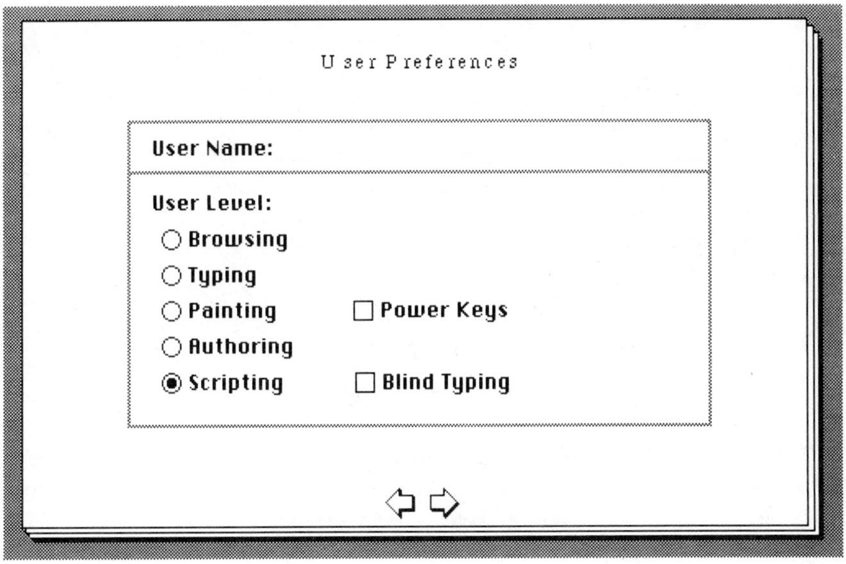

Figure 5.10 The HyperCard user preferences card showing the five levels of user involvement.

allows different types of users to use HyperCard for different reasons. At the browsing level, users have read-only access to the information in a stack, that is, they can look but not touch. In order to make changes to the text they need to move up at least one level. At the typing level, for instance, users can enter and edit text in card fields, but they cannot change the structure of the stack itself or its graphic appearance. At the painting level, graphic objects can be added to stacks or cards using the MacPaint-like tools that are built into HyperCard. At this level, users can make major changes to the appearance of the stack, but they cannot change its basic functionality.

Authoring access allows users to modify the general structure of the stack, including backgrounds, fields, and buttons, but scripting access is required to have complete control over a HyperCard stack.

5.3.2 NoteCards

Although sometimes referred to as an "information structuring system," NoteCards is also a hypertext environment developed in the Intelligent Systems Lab at Xerox PARC (Halasz, Moran, and Trigg, 1987). NoteCards has good browsing tools, including a hierarchical system for organizing complex NoteCards networks.

Its designers view NoteCards as an idea processing environment (Halasz, Moran, and Trigg, 1987) that distinguishes it from systems such as Intermedia that focus on education. Its general goal is similar to that of Augment (Engelbart, 1984a, b), but it is structurally different from Augment in that it is network-based rather than outline-based.

The basic NoteCards construct is a semantic network made up of a set of NoteCards interconnected by typed links. NoteCards provides a set of tools for organizing, displaying, and managing this network, as well as methods and protocols for creating programs to manage the network.

NoteCards consists of four basic entities.

1. NoteCards
2. links
3. browsers
4. FileBoxes

A notecard is an electronic analogy of a 3×5 index card. Each notecard has a title and may contain material that can be edited, such as text or graphics. Different types of notecards are defined in an inheritance hierarchy of card types. The current editor in NoteCards depends on the type of card that is active. Thus a text card will activate a text editor, and a sketch card will activate a sketch editor. Multiple cards can be displayed simultaneously in separate and resizeable windows.

Links connect individual notecards into networks of related cards. Each link is a directed connection between a source card and a destination card. Links are "typed" by a user-chosen label that specifies the nature of the relationship being represented. A link from one card to another appears as a link icon within a source card (c.f., buttons on a HyperCard). A link can be traversed by clicking on the link icon. This causes a window with the link's destination card to be opened.

A browser is a notecard that contains a structural diagram of a network of notecards. In the NoteCards system, browsers are generally viewed as tools that support editing. Users can edit the underlying structure of the network by operating on the nodes and edges as represented in the browser. Users can also experiment by making temporary changes to the browser and then testing them before deciding to convert them into permanent alterations.

FileBoxes help users manage large networks of NoteCards. FileBoxes can be used to build hierarchical category structures which provide efficient storage and retrieval of cards independently of their network interconnections. Thus, FileBoxes provide a hierarchical view on portions of the network.

Major features of the NoteCards hypertext system have been summarized as follows (Marshall, 1987, p. 255):

> The central construct in the NoteCards system is a semantic network that consists of electronic notecards as the nodes connected by typed links. Each notecard contains an arbitrary amount of information embodied in text, graphics, images, or some other editable substance. Each link designates a specific relationship between two notecards; the relationship may be either user or system defined. The system provides two specialized types of cards, browsers and fileboxes to

help manage networks of cards and links. A browser contains a structural map of a network of cards; it may be system-generated or user-created. Browsers are both a presentation tool and editing mechanism. Fileboxes can be used to cluster and organize collections of notecards, yielding a hierarchical filing structure managed by the system. NoteCards also includes a set of protocols and functions for creating new types of cards and manipulating the information in the network. This applications-oriented extensibility plays an important role in preserving and formalizing a representation so it may be applied in other situations.

NoteCards incorporates a number of information management ideas that may be useful in developing intelligent databases. Like most hypertext systems it provides a uniform method of accessing and managing information. The storage and retrieval of graphics is handled in the same way that text is handled, through manipulations of cards and links. NoteCards also provides, through the browsing tools, a navigational interface for viewing not only the information in the network, but also the structure of that information. The third useful feature is the way in which NoteCards combines the flexibility of a network with the organizing efficiency of hierarchies.

5.3.3 Guide

Guide was the first hypertext system available for the Macintosh (Owl International, 1986). It was originally conceived as a tool for building electronic documents and began as a research project at the University of Kent at Canterbury in 1982 (Brown, 1987). Although not a full-functioned word processor itself, it provides a very flexible way of building electronic documents with a variety of cross-referencing and annotation. Electronic versions of documents created in Guide can be exported as MacWrite files and wordprocessed into more traditional hard-copy versions.

The Guide system is generally more text-oriented than HyperCard and NoteCards. It was developed in England and ported from a Unix environment to the Macintosh. Guide uses a number of different types of links.

1. *Replacement links* cause the text in the current window to be replaced by text that is the destination of the link. The existence of a link within the text is indicated by a change in the appearance of the cursor as it passes over the link. Users may also change the appearance of the text (using boldface, italics, etc.) to enhance the recognition of different types of link.

2. *Note links* display the destination text in a pop-up window.

3. *Reference links* bring up a new window with the destination text. These links allow the user to move among related topics in different documents or different parts of the same document.

4. *Inquiry links* are like replacement links except that they are mutually exclusive so that only one of the replacements for an inquiry can be displayed on the screen at a single time. If you click one button in the inquiry, the other disappears. An example of an inquiry in Guide is shown in Figure 5.11.

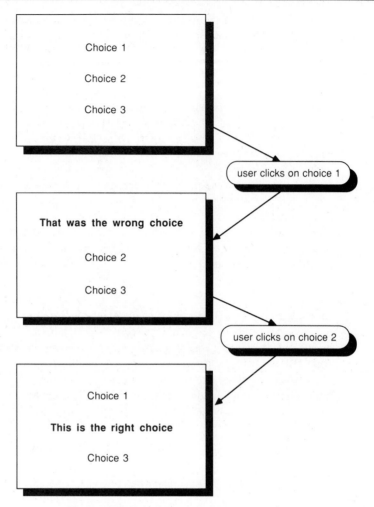

Figure 5.11 An example of a Guide-like inquiry.

5.3.4 Other Systems

Some of the forerunners of the evolving hypermedia systems are shown in Figure 5.12. Hypertext systems are being developed at a rapid rate. As a result it is difficult to compare and contrast the features of current systems or to predict the types of system that may be available in the future.

Although HyperCard, NoteCards, and Guide are influential hypertext systems, there are a fairly large number of alternative systems; we briefly review some of the most well known in this section.

Intermedia is a hypermedia system developed at Brown University for university research and teaching. The Institute for Research in Information and Scholarship at

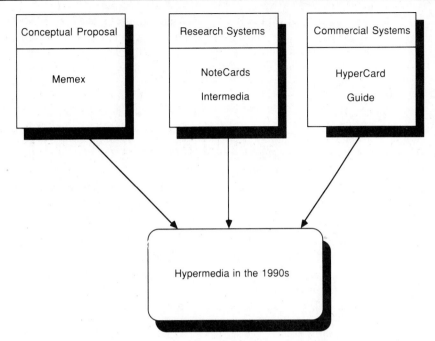

Figure 5.12 The development of hypermedia systems.

Brown University has been carrying out hypertext research for over 20 years. The first system developed at Brown was the Hypertext Editing System in 1968. It was used to produce documentation on the Apollo Space Program. Intermedia is a current hypertext tool developed at Brown. It is both an author's tool and a reader's tool. Creating new materials, making links, and following links are all integrated into a single environment. However, Intermedia is not readily available as a commercial product and has seen little use outside of Brown University, where it was developed.

The Intermedia system is built on the 4.2 BSD UNIX operating system and runs on IBM RT/PC and Sun workstations. Newer versions also run on the Macintosh II. Intermedia includes five applications: a text editor, a graphics editor, a scanned-image viewer, a three-dimensional object viewer, and a timeline editor.

One interesting feature of Intermedia is the use of webs, which define specific perspectives on hypertext (cf. views in relational databases). Opening a web in intermedia causes a particular set of links to be imposed on a set of documents while that web is opened. Webs can be used by users to impose their own views on a shared document set. Intermedia also uses visual representations of the link structure (global maps) as roadmaps for the hypertext. Like NoteCards, the Intermedia system is not widely distributed, although it has had a major impact on the development of hypermedia systems.

Produced by Lotus, Agenda is not marketed as a hypertext product. Most links in

Agenda are not explicitly built as links, but are derived from field values according to where the user types information on the screen, or by keywords. Agenda integrates hypertext and facilities such as relational data management. Agenda's "conditions and actions" language also functions as a type of hypertext language that can manipulate data and structures.

A hypertext system that has not generated much publicity, but which contains interesting features, is the Neptune system developed by Tektronix. The front end of Neptune is a Smalltalk-based user interface, while the back end is a generic hypertext model called the Hypertext Abstract Machine (HAM). Like most hypertext systems, HAM provides operations for creating, modifying, and accessing nodes and links. It also maintains a complete version history of each node in the hyperdocument and provides rapid access to any version of a hyperdocument. Many of the features of HAM are particularly useful for distributed databases. It provides distributed access over a computer network, a complex network versioning scheme, and transaction-based crash recovery. Neptune also has extensive browsing capabilities.

A major feature of Neptune is that predicates may be used to query the values of attributes within nodes. This provides the machine reasoning capability integrated within a flexibly structured database that is the hallmark of intelligent databases.

■ 5.4 KNOWLEDGE REPRESENTATION WITHIN HYPERTEXT

Due to the way in which it has evolved, and the emphasis that has been placed on its unstructured nature, hypertext has generally been regarded as an informal way of providing information that can be browsed. One of our goals in this chapter is to show that this is a rather limited view. Hypertext is in fact an extremely flexible knowledge representation environment that is analogous in many ways to semantic networks. Like semantic networks, hypertext also consists of nodes (objects) and links. Different types of knowledge representation formalism can be implemented in hypertext by structuring and defining the basic types of nodes and links in different ways. We will now define a set of node and link types that will be most useful in using hypertext to build intelligent databases.

5.4.1 Node Types

Basic hypertext systems allow the user to create text fragments as nodes. These nodes are objects, in the sense discussed in Chapter 3, although this point has generally been missed in earlier discussions of hypermedia. However, the chief function (method) of these node objects is generally to display information.

Hypermedia systems are more flexible than traditional information structuring methods in that they allow information in a variety of forms (media) to be attached to nodes. Thus, a node in hypermedia may consist of a sound, or picture, as well as text. Nodes in hypertext (hypermedia) will generally include buttons that provide links (send messages) to other nodes. However, as we saw in the case of HyperCard, buttons may also have scripts (methods) attached to them, so that a powerful programming capability can be embedded within a hypertext representation. We now consider a basic set of node types.

1. *Text nodes.* These consist of text fragments. The text itself may (a) be a document or define the object represented by the node; or (b) represent base-level information, such as that provided in a document. Text may be thought of as information that has not been predigested into a knowledge representation formalism. Instead, it is designed to be read, and the reader extracts the knowledge from the text. Thus text is not appropriate input for an inferencing system other than the human.

2. *Picture nodes.* Pictures may be embedded within text nodes, or they may be nodes in their own right. A picture and text may be mutually documenting, as when one uses a painting to illustrate a biography of Leonardo da Vinci, or when one pursues biographic details of the artist after viewing a picture. Pictures with zoom links (see Section 5.4.2.1) can be examined in greater detail, as often occurs in technical manuals when a part is exploded into several pieces. Like text, pictures represent uninterpreted information, rather than knowledge.

3. *Sound nodes.* Like pictures, sounds may be embedded within text or exist as nodes in their own right. Sounds may generally be treated in similar fashion to pictures, although they are less likely to be zoomed. Sounds, too, represent uninterpreted information that does not correspond to any of the five components of knowledge discussed in Chapter 4.

4. *Mixed-media nodes.* These nodes contain some combination of text, pictures, and sounds. In many cases, the same information may be represented in a combination of linked nodes or as a single mixed-media node. Factors such as the size of screen, the ease of traversing links in the hypermedia system, aesthetic considerations, and the memory and attentional capabilities of the user will influence the decision about when to split the information up among more than one node.

5. *Buttoned text* or mixed-media. We make a distinction here between buttons and links. A link connects a pair of nodes, whereas a button executes a procedure. Buttoned nodes can be used to get things done. These nodes allow hypermedia to act as a high-level program or database interface. Complex hypermedia will generally use buttoned mixed media nodes as they provide maximum flexibility. The other four types of informational nodes listed are restricted versions of this more general node type.

These first five node or object types represent information, rather than interpreted knowledge. They are designed to be read, viewed, and heard. They cannot be used by an expert system, for instance, until they have been represented in terms of the five components of knowledge using a standard knowledge representation language. It seems natural to express each of these node types as a separate class within an object-oriented representation of the hypermedia network.

We can also define organizational and inferential nodes.

6. *Indexed text.* Indexed text nodes contain index links that point to index nodes (see following). Indexing is a method of describing nodes.

7. *Index nodes.* These nodes consist of a single index term. They will generally contain links that point to a definition of the concept represented by the index term, links that point to related terms or synonyms (thesaurus links), links that correspond to corresponding columns in relational tables, and links that point back to the indexed text nodes that reference them.

8. *Object nodes.* These nodes describe objects. They consist of slots, inheritance links, and attached procedures. As in the case of relational tables, the object system would typically not be implemented in hypertext, but individual objects would be incorporated as nodes in the hypertext and these nodes would be linked to an object system existing outside the hypertext. Object nodes and is-a links (described in Section 5.4.4.2) can be used to represent organizing knowledge.

9. *Rule nodes.* These nodes list rules and may point to combinations of objects that satisfy the rules, justifications for the use of the rule, explanations of when the rule applies, and so on.

These nodes may also be described as classes and will generally satisfy our requirements for intelligent database development, although a number of other node types could conceivably be defined.

5.4.2 Link Types

The variety of nodes that can be defined in hypertext make it an extremely flexible knowledge representation tool. This flexibility is further enhanced by providing a variety of link types. Links define the structure of hypermedia and provide the capability for browsing and exploring the nodes. There are many different types of links that can be defined, one of which is navigational links. As with node types we can also construct links that are inferential or organizational in nature. We will focus on these three types of link in our model of hypertext, although we recognize that a number of other types of link could no doubt be formulated.

5.4.2.1 *Navigation Links*

We consider here four main types of navigational link. The intuitive meaning of these links can be grasped by analogy to the operation of a video camera. Links as navigational entities correspond to changing perspectives on a display in roughly the same way that the operation of a video camera changes the appearance of a visual scene. One might start by simply moving the camera back and forth (move to link). One might then zoom in on a particular portion of the scene (zoom link) and then pan back out to the larger picture (pan link). Finally, one can use different filters to highlight different aspects of the scene, and in hypertext one can use view links to make links conditional on particular sets of contextual constraints. Thus, our four types of navigational link are

1. *Move to links*. These links simply move to a related node. They allow one to move around or navigate through hypertext.

2. *Zoom links*. These links expand the current node into a more detailed account of the information. The effect is similar to moving from an abstract to a complete view of the document in text, or to zooming to a magnified view of a small part of the complete picture, much as one might move from a map of an entire city to a map of the downtown area enlarged to fit the same page area as the city map.

3. *Pan links*. These links return to a higher level view of the hypertext (these links are particularly useful in browsing facilities). Pan links are normally the inverse of zoom links so that every zoom link will have a corresponding pan link and vice versa. Thus these links may also be referred to as zoom-out links.

4. *View links*. The availability or activation of these links is conditional upon the stated interests or purposes of the user. They may also be used for security purposes. View links are hidden unless they are of interest or a particular user has access or has been cleared to use them. As an example, there may be a view link between mercury and planet nodes that is active for astronomers but suppressed for environmental chemists and meteorologists. Under some conditions, view restrictions could be disabled so that hidden links were seen. Views provide the fundamental mechanism for customizing hypertext to the needs and interests of different users. They also help prevent hypertext from becoming unnecessarily complex with users being bombarded by information that is not relevant to their needs.

These view links are of course similar to the webs used in the Intermedia system. An Intermedia web is analogous to a set of view links that are constrained in the same way.

5.4.2.2 *Organizational and Inferential Links*

A second class of hypermedia link types deals with the organization of nodes and the linkage of hypermedia to more general machine reasoning and programming capabilities. We focus here on five organizational and inferential link types.

5. *Index links*. These links move the user from an indexed node to the corresponding index entry for that node. The index can then be used to enter the relational database or to find documents that share a particular index term. Indexing hypertext is a good way of controlling the proliferation of links between nodes.

6. *Is-a links.* These links are similar to those used in semantic networks and object systems to indicate membership of a category. Is-a links permit nodes to be organized.

7. *Has-a links.* These links are used to describe the properties of nodes. They will generally be used by objects, although they can also be used to implement objectlike capabilities within hypertext.

8. *Implication links.* These links are used to connect facts in inference trees. They are generally equivalent to rules that are being, or have been, fired. The use of implication links will generally be confined to inferential hypertext (see Section 5.6.4)

9. *Execute links (buttons).* The final link type that we consider here is the execute link or button. This link type allows hypermedia to be a high-level programming interface. Buttons cause actions to be carried out, typically, the execution of some code.

In the HyperCard implementation, execute links correspond to buttons with HyperTalk scripts attached to them. These scripts may then include hooks into more conventional programming languages such as C or Pascal.

5.4.3   An Illustration of the Hypertext Model

We will make this characterization of hypertext more concrete by showing how these node and link types map into the development of hypermedia. We shall try to keep the discussion generic, but it is almost impossible not to be influenced by the features of specific hypertext systems. Our presentation of hypertext here is loosely based on the NoteCards and HyperCard systems. Thus the basic nodes are organized as cards and stacks. However, we shall see that while the cards and stacks define an initial (linear) ordering of the information, the functionality of the hypermedia is created when we add a variety of nonlinear link types.

We illustrate the fundamental features of our representation with a hypertext representation of the U.S. Constitution. In this illustrative system, the text of the Constitution is written on a series of cards, which serve as basic informational nodes in the system. These nodes are generally buttoned text and mixed media.

These cards form a linear stack representing the order of the text in the Articles of the Constitution, the Bill of Rights, and the Amendments. Other stacks contain biographical information about Founding Fathers and Supreme Court justices. Relevant Supreme Court decisions are stored on another set of cards that also act as a linear sequence of nodes. The basic buttons on each card in these stacks will be directional, allowing users to move forwards or backwards in the sequence.

Once the nodes have been defined in linear sequence, nonlinear linking can begin. Thus cards within the Court decisions stack can be linked to the cards within the Constitution stack that they refer to. However, there are other stacks that may be of related interest. We may have a stack of newspaper or magazine articles referring to issues raised by a particular portion of the text of the Constitution (e.g., the 14th Amendment). This online database of relevant material then forms a stack of citations.

Furthermore, this stack of citations may be indexed using a hierarchy of terms that are themselves represented as a set of cards (menus). This leads to a further complication where we find the clean distinctions among node types as previously defined breaking down. These citation nodes are informational nodes, but they are also indexed with index buttons that allow users to jump from the citation stack back to the information stack where the index terms are described and stored.

The information stacks will generally contain background information about the index terms referred to in the citations or even in the text of the Constitution itself. This information, consisting of documentation and definitions for the terms, is combined into this additional stack of cards. Figure 5.13 shows a sample definition card that explains (describes) the term *equal protection*.

The index terms may also be linked into an is-a hierarchy, thereby simplifying the task of searching for relevant index terms when looking for information or citations. This can be done by creating separate cards (nodes or menus) for each level of the hierarchy. Index terms at each level are then represented as buttons (links) on the card.

The final link type that we illustrate in this example is the execute link. We create a button (link) that stores selected information in a file. In this system, we represent this

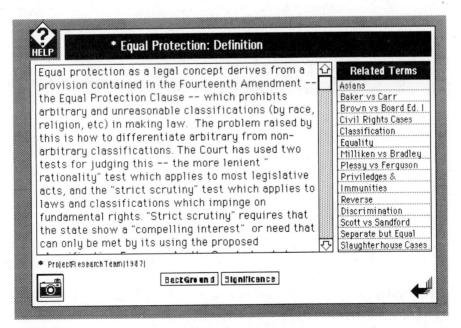

Figure 5.13 A screen showing a definition of equal protection within the Jefferson Notebook.

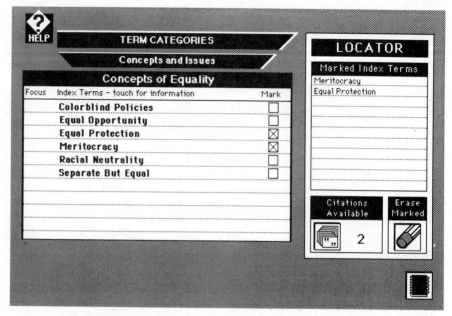

Figure 5.14 A portion of the Jefferson Notebook index hierarchy.

link using a camera icon (as shown in the lower left corner of Figure 5.13). Another execute link is used to search for documents that contain selected index terms and add them to the citation stack. Figure 5.14 shows the operation of this link. The current node of the index hierarchy is "concepts of equality" and meritocracy and the following five terms represent more specialized terms. Marking the corresponding box with an X instructs the execute link to add that term to the search query and rebuild the citation stack. In Figure 5.14, the citations are shown as a "stack of cards" icon immediately to the left of the number 2 on the screen. The user may then see which citations have been retrieved by the current query by clicking on that icon.

■ 5.5 A MODEL OF HYPERTEXT

We require a model of hypertext that will formalize the process of building hypertext applications. Experience has shown that without such a model the development of hypertext applications becomes unmanageable as networks of nodes and links grow on an ad hoc and unstructured basis. We begin the development of the model by drawing an analogy between hypertext and semantic networks.

5.5.1 Hypertext and Semantic Networks

Hypertext is a knowledge representation tool in its own right. Structurally, hypertext is equivalent to a semantic network where nodes can be expanded into a variety of text and graphics forms. As with semantic networks, the two major constructs that define a hypertext structure are nodes and links. We can distinguish different hypertext systems according to the types of nodes and links that they permit. As is also the case with semantic networks, the richness of the hypertext concept and the many ways in which it may be implemented creates a barrier for standardization. Thus there are many potential models of hypertext, and each of the research and development groups working in the general area of hypertext has a somewhat different model of what hypertext really is and how it should be implemented.

Elsewhere, we have outlined a model of knowledge that is particularly useful in understanding the processes of knowledge acquisition and knowledge representation (Parsaye and Chignell, 1988, Chapters 4, 5, and 9; Chignell and Parsaye, 1989). This model is also useful in understanding the storage and retrieval of knowledge in hypertext and the use of that knowledge in inference. The main features of this intuitive model of knowledge were introduced in Section 4.2.6. We will now assess which of the node and link types discussed in the previous section are necessary for a practical model of hypertext. While there are many other potentially useful models of hypertext, we have constructed ours with particular reference to database applications.

5.5.2 The Proposed Model

We begin by considering the tasks that our hypermedia documents should be capable of performing. These include

> knowledge representation
>
> linkage to inference systems
>
> information retrieval
>
> browsing

We consider each of these functions in turn in the following sections.

5.5.2.1 *Knowledge Representation*

We can break the task of knowledge representation down into at least four subtasks that handle the first four components of knowledge discussed in Section 4.4 and elsewhere (Parsaye and Chignell, 1988). The fifth component of knowledge (constraints) is not well understood and may be handled through external rules that operate on the hypermedia. The subtasks are

1. Representing text and graphics.
2. Representing concepts.
3. Representing organizational structures.
4. Representing relations between concepts.

The representation of text and graphics is straightforward and typically consists of screens of information sometimes segmented into various fields and windows. Concepts within hypermedia may generally be handled as objects embedded within the overall system. An object hierarchy, like any other object, may be linked as a hypermedia node, but there will be special rules governing processes such as inheritance within the subregion defined as the object hierarchy.

In addition to object hierarchies, organization may be applied to hypermedia nodes in general. Our model here is to use a type of Cartesian parallelism where each hypermedia node may have multiple representations within different organizational structures. We will focus on five types of organizational structure.

a. A conventional hypermedia network. Here the nodes are linked associatively in an unconstrained fashion.

b. A linear path. Here a collection of nodes are linked into a single linear structure (just like the chapters of a book). A single node may exist in a number of different paths.

c. A hierarchy. Here the nodes are linked in a hierarchy defined by a particular context. Thus, a person may simultaneously be defined in terms of the hierarchy of terrestrial organisms or in terms of the organizational hierarchy of a corporation.

d. An indexed table. Here the nodes are linked as columns in a relational table. Each node may appear in more than one table and the tables themselves are linked to a relational database with the full power of the relational algebra.

e. A rule. Here nodes are linked to the rules that "mention" them. Thus, a rule that defines a relationship between four objects may be linked to each of the

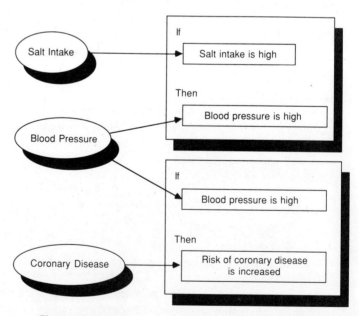

Figure 5.15 An example of using rules to organize nodes.

corresponding nodes, with the type of the link specifying the particular usage of the rule by which the object is being referred to. An example of this method of using a rule to organize nodes is shown in Figure 5.15.

The key to maintaining this multiplicity of organization structures for each node is to link the multiple representations of each node. Once this is done, the user may switch from one type of organizational structure to another with ease, as shown in Figure 5.16. In this example the user is dealing with the 14th Amendment to the U.S. Constitution. The amendment exists as part of a linear path (the full-text of the Constitution), and it also exists as part of a hierarchy of topics relating to the U.S. Constitution. Finally, the figure shows the 14th Amendment embedded as part of a hypermedia network. The user begins by following the linear path defined by the text of the Constitution. When the 14th Amendment is reached the user switches to the hypermedia representation and explores the related concept of due process. The user then returns to the 14th Amendment and now switches to the hierarchical structure. Each of the three representational structures proves useful for different tasks. Linear paths are useful for following a line of reasoning or reading a prepared argument or sequential text. Hypermedia networks provide a browsing capability. Hierarchical structures allow the user to explore categorical relationships and provide the indexing structure that is generally needed in information retrieval tasks.

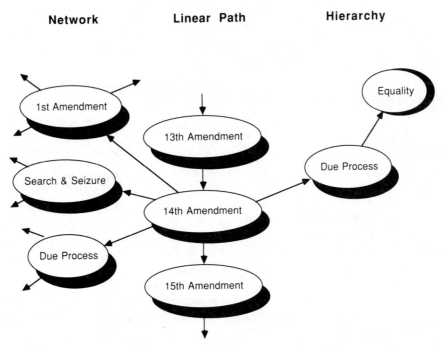

Figure 5.16 Different types of organizational structuring of the 14th Amendment.

5.5.2.2 Linkage to Inference Systems

Relations between concepts will generally be handled by specially labeled links. In a semantically rich hypermedia system, the meaning of these links will be defined by predicates. We see a great deal of opportunity in using logic programming to augment the capability of hypermedia and the definition of embedded link predicates. In the same way that facts in a logic program may be defined explicitly or deduced by rules, links may be defined explicitly (authored) or created at run time through the operation of a reasoning system.

As an example of a link that may be defined explicitly or created through inference at run time, consider a financial information system designed to help investment analysts and advisors. In viewing information about a particular company, a link may be made to each subsidiary of that company. However, in some contexts users may not need to know about subsidiaries and showing this link may be unnecessary. Thus an inferential system might show users links only if it can be inferred that those links are relevant to the current information search context.

Another use for integrated hypermedia and inference is to provide a visual representation for knowledge bases. Semantic networks illustrate how objects can be represented as nodes and predicates as links between nodes. Rules can then be represented as links (predicates) between nodes (classes of objects) that are conditional upon other rules or facts being true, and facts as links between specific objects. Figure 5.17 shows how a small knowledge base can be illustrated within a hypertext network. In principle, there is a one-to-one mapping between a knowledge base of facts and rules, and equivalent network representations, and thus it is possible to compile knowledge bases into hypertext. This promises to facilitate greatly the processes of browsing and debugging knowledge-based systems.

One of the features of the evolving relationship between hypermedia and inference is that it expands the functionality of rules. Rules may be used to (a) define links, (b) implement predicate attachments on links, (c) filter links, (d) execute actions, and (e) discover links in text.

5.5.2.3 Information Retrieval

The linkage of hypermedia nodes to corresponding hierarchical representations provides a powerful form of indexing. Conventional information retrieval capability can then be achieved by having selection operators that allow users to identify terms within the hierarchical structures that should be added to an information retrieval query. Thus, like inferencing, information retrieval is a separate process that may be linked to the hypermedia representation. Our solution here is to achieve inferencing in hypermedia through the link predicates while providing an information retrieval capability by attaching a retrieval engine to the hierarchical index. Thus our hypermedia model does not replace conventional information retrieval but incorporates it within a broader model of information access and utilization.

An alternative solution is to implement a hypertext capability within an expert system

Rules 1A and 1B

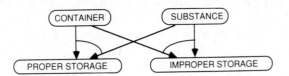

Rule 2

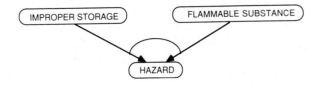

Hypertext

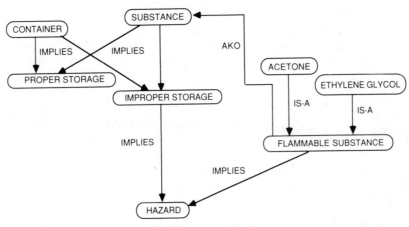

Figure 5.17 A small knowledge base embedded within a hypertext network.

shell. This latter approach seeks to implement hypertext as a special type of inference where display text and information are side effects. This is an alternative to the approach described earlier where inference is formulated as a special type of hypertext.

5.5.2.4 *Browsing*

The ability to browse is generally regarded as one of the strongest reasons for using hypermedia. Browsing is implemented through the is-related-to link type. Browsing can be further facilitated through the attachment of maps and browsing tools.

Browsing through hypertext is a delicate process that is constrained on the one hand by the need to have flexible access to information and on the other by the need to avoid disorientation. In general, the more paths that the user is permitted to explore, the more likely it is that the user will eventually get "lost."

Thus, our model consists of a basic set of node and link types that permit multiple and interlinked representations of knowledge within hypermedia. This model is then supplemented with ancillary tools and processes to provide the capabilities of browsing, knowledge representation, inferencing, and information retrieval that are critical to the performance of an intelligent database.

5.5.3 Extending the Model

The proposed model provides a preliminary structuring of hypermedia aimed at implementing the tasks of browsing, inferencing, and information retrieval within intelligent databases. In complex hypermedia, multiple types of retrieval engine may be used. One problematic feature of the hypermedia model, however, is how to handle the variety of contexts and perspectives with which one may view information.

Contexts may be used to provide perspectives or partitions in hypertext (Delisle and Schwartz, 1987). A single object can have multiple instances in different contexts, and an object may be described by a global identifier (which identifies all instances of that object in all contexts) and a local identifier (which identifies the instance of an object in a given context). Thus, the solution to the issue of contexts is again that of using multiple representations of the concept or object. Thus, contexts will generally be handled as different regions within hierarchical structures. Consider the term *mercury*. It represents a planet and a chemical element, along with other uses such as brand names for cars and boat engines. In these cases, the same word is being used to represent different concepts. We handle this by specializing the naming to prevent such ambiguity. Thus we might name the corresponding nodes

> Mercury (the planet)
> Mercury (the chemical element)
> Mercury (the make of car)
> Mercury (the make of boat engine)

Within the same concept usage, however, we may still have different contexts. Consider mercury (the element). We can view mercury from the perspective of its chemical structure or in terms of its uses in areas such as smelting gold or in thermometers. We may handle these different contexts by defining mercury (the element) as a hierarchical node. This node might look something like Figure 5.18. This hierarchical node may then be linked to hypermedia networks, linear paths, or to hierarchical or other structures. We can even define a new structure called the periodic table of elements and then link mercury (the element) to this as well.

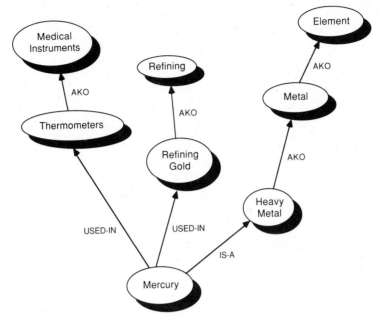

Figure 5.18 Representation of "Mercury" as a hierarchical node with multiple parents.

5.5.4 Alternative Models

We have attempted to define a model of hypertext that is sufficiently broad to encompass the major features that will be needed in intelligent databases. We now briefly consider alternative proposals that have been made.

Hammwohner and Thiel (1987) outline an alternative view of hypertext that adopts the strategy of imposing constraints with *activist software*. They assume a model of hypertext where users browse a set of *text units*. These text units represent interpretations of the meanings, or concepts, of the underlying text. Three types of text unit are considered.

1. Simple semantic structures.
2. Sentences with linear surface structure.
3. Graphic primitives.

These text units may be browsed in two ways. In undirected browsing, the user investigates text units in arbitrary order, whereas in directed browsing, navigation between text units can only occur across meaningful links. Hammwohner and Thiel only concern themselves with directed browsing. The term *directed browsing* appears to be equivalent to the term *structured browsing* used by Marchionini and Shneiderman (1988).

Knowledge representation and parsing can be used to capture the contents of text units. Simple semantic structures are represented as relational tables or objects. More complex semantic structures are parsed in terms of an object system using a semantic parser (a set of word experts). The interpretation of text units results in a hypertext model that contains

1. A network of tangled hierarchies.
2. Fragments of world knowledge located as nodes in the network.
3. Factual information represented as filled slots within objects.

The advantage of building semantic representations of text is that it allows the user to interact with the knowledge directly and then refer back to the text or text fragments that cover particular concepts. The network structure of knowledge that is produced also provides a new type of browse facility that may enhance the memorization of text contents and meaning (e.g., Danserau and Holley, 1982).

Hammwohner and Thiel (1987) regard links as a type of relation. They distinguish three types of relation.

1. Continuations between adjacent text units in text.
2. Semantic relations.
3. Pragmatic relations. Pragmatic relations reflect the situational context of the dialog between user and hypertext system and can be defined on an "as needed" basis. Some types of relation that may prove generally useful include

   a. Informational smoothing. This is the use of relations that overcome apparent inconsistencies.
   b. Concept references. Concept references allow users to explore the usage of a concept in different documents or nodes (e.g., this concept appears in this text fragment).
   c. Analogy and similarity. In instructional settings, these nodes can act to compare and contrast concepts, thereby sharpening and clarifying their definitions in the minds of users.
   d. Details. These relations act like replacement buttons in Guide, moving down a level of detail. These relations are particularly useful in text processing.
   e. Generalization. These relations are the obverse of detail relations in that they are used to guide the user up an abstraction hierarchy that is embedded in hypermedia.
   f. Implication. These relations were defined earlier in Section 5.4.2. We see a generally close resemblance between this relational model of hypertext and the definitions of nodes and link types proposed in Section 5.4.

In this second model, two types of hypertext relation are distinguished, namely, semantic relations and pragmatic relations. Semantic relations are represented as relations between objects. Objects are used to interpret and process text. A number of definitions are then proposed to represent types of relation that can occur between objects. Examples of these definitions include

1. Complement. Information in one object is confirmed and completed by information in a second one.
2. Disjunction. Both objects are needed to obtain complete information on a concept.
3. Conflict. The objects contain inconsistent information.
4. Coincidence. Similar properties are defined for distinct objects.

This type of formalism is reminiscent of the work done in developing complex knowledge representation languages. It's interesting, but the languages themselves become difficult to use.

Perhaps the most interesting aspect of this second approach to the formalization of hypermedia is the treatment of pragmatic relations. These relations between text units reflect the situational context in which the dialog between the user and the hypertext system takes place. Two relevant criteria in the formation of pragmatic relations are

a. The amount of detail the text units contain.
b. The specificity of the user's wishes.

In applying this second model of hypermedia and text understanding, Hammwohner and Thiel suggest the following:

> If the user's interests are highly specific then the system behaves like an encyclopedia where terms are selected from a subject index.
> If queries and interests are general or unknown, the system encourages high level browsing.

A third approach to hypermedia models has been suggested by Garg (1987). The fundamental components of this model consist of predicates, attributes, objects, and their instantiations. Each of these constructs can be dealt with by the node and link types described above. Originally the model was defined in set-theoretic terms, but we will paraphrase it in our own terminology.

Relations are described as predicates, much as we have treated them elsewhere in this chapter. Attributes, or descriptions of objects, are also similar to our own treatment. The novel feature of Garg's model is that he distinguishes between primitive objects and information objects. Information objects are constructed out of combinations of primitive objects which serve as concept primitives. In strongly defined hypertext, all information objects have their primitive objects defined. In a system where the software actively imposes constraints, information nodes are required to be chosen from a preexisting pool of primitive objects and a new node cannot be created unless a primitive node of the same category is first defined. Garg (1987, pp. 381-382) gives the example of defining a square as an information object (i.e., a square is a figure that is a rectangle with all sides of the rectangle being equal and that has a particular graphical representation). Information objects of this type can then be described using a formal language such as that defined by Shasha (1985).

In this third model, aggregating objects allows them to be collectively referenced by an identifier. An aggregate object closely resembles the notion of tuples in relational databases. Thus we can define projections, joins, selections, and other relational operations on aggregations.

Another form of aggregation involves the creation of hierarchies. This can be viewed as a process of categorization, where the parents of a node represent higher level categories that it belongs to. In generalization or categorization, a collection of objects is referenced by a generic object (prototype, or exemplar) which captures the essential similarity between the objects in the collection. Object hierarchies (c.f. Section 3.4) represent examples of generalization where object instances inherit the characteristics of higher level objects.

Hypertext nodes can be aggregated by referring to collections of nodes by a common name. This can be implemented in terms of embedded hierarchies, categories, or neighborhoods within a larger hypertext representation. This aggregation then becomes a new abstract entity within the hypertext (c.f., Smith and Smith, 1977). This allows multiple levels of abstraction to be defined within hypermedia. One may define a network of generic objects and then a separate neighborhood for each object. Users can then pan and zoom between the different levels of abstraction.

■ 5.6 HYPERMEDIA DESIGN

In the absence of formal models of hypermedia, it is hardly surprising that there are no models of how to carry out the process of hypermedia design. At present most hypermedia developers work with the concept of what "looks and feels good." We can split the hypermedia design issues into those that are unique to hypermedia and those that are shared with software design in general. One issue that is pervasive throughout software development of all types is that of revision control.

Needless to say, the editing of complex hypermedia structures and aggregated information objects becomes a serious problem in large hypertext systems. We can develop a Revision Control System (RCS, Tichy, 1982) that stores changes to information rather than creating multiple copies and that allows for the merging of two revisions that represent different modifications of the same original file. Revision control in hypertext may be implemented by defining special operators for adding and deleting text to a node. Ancestral links between different versions of a document or text fragment can be traced by defining some nodes as revisions of other nodes. Date stamping allows the sequencing of these revisions to be maintained. Merge operations can be used to combine redundant nodes that contain equivalent information.

5.6.1 Hypermedia and CD-ROM

Other design issues arise not only because of the nature of the hypermedia concept, but also because of the characteristics of the mass storage devices used to store hypermedia.

The Apple Learning Disk, distributed by Apple in 1988, represented a multifaceted CD-ROM demonstration of hypermedia. This follows the earlier availability of Grolier's Academic American Encyclopedia on CD-ROM, which included a hypertext capability.

At first glance, CD-ROM would appear to be an inappropriate medium for hypermedia because of its static nature. However, as Oren (1987, pp. 291–306) has pointed out, hypermedia and CD-ROMs can work well together when a suitable hypermedia architecture is adopted.

CD-ROM is a read-only storage medium with a large capacity (typically about 550 megabytes). Once hypermedia is stored on CD-ROM, it cannot be removed or altered (except by recording a new version of the hypermedia on a different CD-ROM).

The implementation of hypermedia on CD-ROM and other read-only storage media removes the problem of updating hypermedia by preventing the possibility of updating. However, although the basic structure of the document cannot be changed in read-only media, it may still be possible to add new nodes and make annotations.

The distinction between static and dynamic hypermedia is fundamental. Whereas dynamic hypermedia is a tool for creative tasks such as cooperative writing and online publishing, static hypermedia is a fixed medium that transmits information without feedback from the reader to the author (see Figure 5.19 for a schematic representation of the difference between static and dynamic hypermedia).

5.6.2 Hypermedia Design Guidelines

Large hypermedia projects require a design team that includes a mixture of expertise, ranging from text authoring and selection, to information structuring, indexing, and graphic arts. Managing and coordinating this team can be a daunting problem. One approach is top-down hypermedia design. This consists of an approach to hypermedia design that includes graphic design in the earliest stages of the design process, along with rapid prototyping of nodes, node-link structures, and visual metaphors. In this design approach, the interface and hypermedia structure are built first, and then ancillary processes, such as inference engines, general programming capabilities, and relational or object-oriented databases are attached to the basic structure.

Other advice on hypermedia design has focused on how to recover the desirable features of print within hypermedia (Oren, 1987). For instance, "bookmarks and fingers are used by humans to replace the cognitive task of remembering page numbers and the physical task of looking them up again. The electronic equivalent of a finger in the book is a browser which remembers the previous position when following a link."

Static Hypermedia

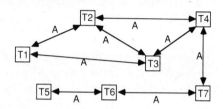

Dynamic Hypermedia

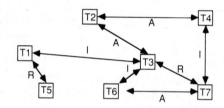

A - indicates explicit authoring of link.

I - indicates inferencial construction of link.

R - indicates reader-dependent selection of link.

T - indicates an information fragment

Figure 5.19 A schematic representation of the difference between static and dynamic hypermedia.

Hypertext "bookmarks" can be created by creating links to a document that are generated at the user's request and stored with some associated comment or picture. This corresponds to the glossary feature available in some word processors. Other features of the print medium are the ability to highlight (by underlining or making bold), to write annotations in the margin of a book, and to stick temporary notes onto pages. Writing in the hypermedia "book" itself is a thorny issue, since one person's notes may not be useful to another person, and it is difficult to know how the different personalized versions of hypermedia should be controlled. However, annotations may be linked as separate files or nodes. In this case, we could have a *personal annotation* link which includes the name of the author of the annotation.

Another desirable feature of books is that they have a uniform appearance ranging from the uniformity of paper they are written on to consistency of page formatting, font selection, and placement of tables and figures. This is a major benefit that we tend to take for granted until we compare a well-presented book with a draft of a graduate student dissertation, for example. Thus, books have a limited number of data types that they present to the user. A good hypermedia system will also have only a fraction of the many data types that are possible. Limiting data types will also simplify the installation of hypermedia applications on different systems. In the early stages of Project Jefferson, for instance, one particularly irritating bug that was found on some systems, but not others, was determined to have been caused by the availability of certain fonts on some systems, but not others.

Books also encourage a form of browsing where things "catch the eye." What may seem like irrelevant information to the screen designer can thus be highly functional. One is faced with a dilemma.

> Do you design the screen so that the user is forced to focus on a particular concept?
> or
> Do you place less relevant information on the periphery of the screen in case it catches the eye and possibly leads to a fortuitous chain of associations?

The *Whole Earth Catalog,* for instance, uses pictures to draw attention to documents. Oren (1987, p. 295) suggests the use of a feature where pictures are linked in a list and users may start flipping through these pictures at any point in the list. The user could stop this "slide show" at any point in the list and examine the related document.

One of the major design decisions for a hypermedia developer will be the threshold of relevance required for associative links. At one extreme, nodes may be linked associatively only if they are directly related or equivalent. At the other extreme, documents may be linked almost randomly. It is even conceivable to develop settings where the user controls the number and strength of associations that are seen. Thus in this type of application, the user might ask to see no more than ten links per node, with these links ranging from high to moderate associative strength.

Another feature of books that is lost in hypertext is the concept of distance, knowing how far one has gone and how much further there is to go. As most readers will have experienced, however, distance in pages is not the same thing as distance in reading time. A short, but difficult, chapter in a book may take much longer to read than a longer chapter that contains more familiar material that is skimmed. In browsing, there is generally no way of knowing how much of a particular database has already been seen or even how to get to the topics that have not yet been seen. Thus capabilities should be designed into extensive hypermedia applications so that users may ask the system to (Oren, 1987, pp. 295–296)

> Show me something new
> Show me a new path to something I've seen before
> Let's review the paths I have taken to this node
> Put me back in the context of last Tuesday
> Tour this section using link types I most frequently choose

Other design issues relate to the provision of cues to the user about where they are in the hypermedia. We consider some of these issues in our discussion of browsing tools below.

5.6.3 Hypermedia Utilization

Once we have adequate models of hypermedia and design guidelines for how applications should be developed, we need to consider how the hypermedia will be utilized. Like many software applications, hypermedia systems will generally require a certain amount of training and they will be targeted at different types of users who may use the hypermedia in different ways for different purposes.

Information filtering in hypertext corresponds to the process of making queries and retrieving information in databases and conventional information retrieval systems. One form of filtering in hypertext is equivalent to views in databases or to pruning a search tree, a metaphor that is borrowed from artificial intelligence terminology. Indexing is a major form of information filtering. It allows database-like functionality to be imported into hypertext. Links may be indexed as well as nodes. Hypermedia-based information retrieval systems should filter information to suit the needs of the user. The task of filtering information in hypertext is similar to defining views in a database or using a query language to retrieve information from a database. The success of query languages in database applications strongly suggests the need for some type of querying mechanism in hypertext.

It is often useful to view the structure of a document rather than its contents, as in the use of outlines and tables of contents. One of the major contributions of hypertext is the way that it merges information presentation with information structuring.

Primitive hypertext corresponds to the basic structure of hypertext and the authoring tools that can be used in constructing hypertext applications. Application hypertext refers to the information contained in the hypertext. This raises interesting authorship and ownership issues that have been discussed elsewhere. We can distinguish between the authorship and ownership of primitive hypertext and the authorship and ownership of application hypertext.

■ 5.7 EVALUATION OF CURRENT HYPERTEXT SYSTEMS

Hypertext systems are evolving so rapidly that it is difficult to make specific evaluations of existing systems since they are likely to be obsolete in a few months or years. Instead, we will focus on the general features of hypertext and will assess the strengths and features that are intrinsic to the basic concept of hypertext. We will avoid peripheral features of particular software implementations that are likely to change as new products and versions of products are developed.

5.7.1 Strengths

The strengths of hypertext arise from its flexibility in storing and retrieving knowledge. Any piece of information, whether it be text, graphics, sound, or numerical data can be linked to any other piece of information. This flexibility makes it possible to construct a "seamless information environment" (Yankelovich, Haan, and Meyrowitz, 1988).

Hypertext is an extremely powerful information management tool because one is able to represent knowledge, browse, carry out structured searches, and make inferences, all within the same environment.

In discussing the strengths of hypertext, we will focus on two of the most important properties of hypertext; associative structuring and the exploratory type of information retrieval that it permits.

5.7.1.1 *Associative Structuring*

As we discussed earlier, people are used to dealing with information in a linear fashion. Consider two text documents (Figure 5.20). To extract the information from the documents, one has to read them. One usually reads them in the order in which they are written (linearly), but one can put them side by side and browse from one to the other. This tends to be a difficult process, and there are no pointers in the text to guide the reader from a point made in one piece of text to a related point made in a different document. We can build an associative structure by constructing pointers that make the relations between points made in the two documents explicit. These pointers may refer to points made within the same document or they may link points made across different documents. We can now represent the document as a network of points, as shown in Figure 5.21. We are not losing anything in doing this, since we still have the original documents in linear text form, and correspondences between portions of the original documents and fragments of the network representation may be identified, as shown in Figure 5.22. Thus, the original documents can themselves become nodes in the network, which includes various points made in addition to the text of the documents. One can then add pictures to illustrate the points made, the authors of the documents, and so on. Similarly, one can also add nodes that may present sounds, graphics, or numerical data.

The features of hypertext that implement this powerful associative structuring capability are

1. A network of nodes, as previously described.
2. A set of links that create relations between nodes.
3. Authoring tools that allow users to build links and nodes out of new material, or existing text, graphics, and so on.
4. Windowing facilities that allow one to view one or more nodes, plus special windows (browsers) that allow users to view portions of the network. These latter windows allow users to view the associative structure of hypertext.

Document 1	Document 2
Recent recognition of the importance of writing and critical thinking skills, both within and beyond the scope of the university, has focused attention on the role of the research paper in the composition course. However attempts to teach the research paper, for the most part, have been unsuccessful. What is needed is a new model for the research paper which can be incorporated into the composition course. At USC we have developed such a model in the Project Jefferson interface. In this paper we discuss our experience in using the Project Jefferson model to author hypermedia based curricular tools and discuss issues in authoring hypermedia structures based on that experience. We report the results of structured interviews carried out with the personnel who were responsible for authoring the hypertext and index for Project Jefferson. We also interpret features of the authoring process in terms of their impact on the resulting compatibility between software structures and student cognitive structures. The version of the Project Jefferson prototype interface used in this research is an adaptation of Hypercard to teach freshman students how to do research within the framework of a writing assignment. It is a self-contained research tool which assists in the development of skill s to do research in the real world. Its overall conceptual metaphor is that of an electronic notebook with which students can gain access to a paper assignment on the US Constitution; read a dictionary or encyclopedia for background information on Constitutional issues, and download key ideas to their electronic notebook; search a database of bibliographic information, taking notes if need be, or simply downloading citations; and finally dumping all this information into a text file as the raw materials of a research paper.	Hypertext can be simply defined as the creation and representation of links between discrete pieces of data When this data can be graphics, or sound, as well as text or numbers, the resulting structure is referred to as hypermedia. The strengths of hypermedia arise from its flexibility in storing and retrieving knowledge. Any piece of information, whether it be text, graphics, sound, numerical data, etc., can be linked to any other piece of information. In many ways, the problems of hypermedia stem from the very flexibility that is its chief advantage and justification. It is difficult to maintain a sense of where things are in a relatively unstructured network of information. While the associative nature of hypermedia increases the availability of large amounts of diverse information, this very diversity makes it easy for information and users to get lost. Hypermedia exacerbates the problem of getting "lost in information space" by providing a complex associative structure that can be traversed, but not fully visualized. Information gets lost because it becomes difficult to organize and tag effectively while users get lost as they lose sense of where they are in the hypermedia. Getting lost or disoriented occurs when one doesn't know where one is. Solutions to the problem of disorientation in hypermedia appear to fall into two general classes. First, one can create maps or browsers that allows users to determine where they are in terms of the overall network, or regions thereof. Second, one can create tags, markers or milestones which represent familiar locations, much as a lighthouse signals location in the middle of a foggy night. This paper reports basic research on the identification of landmarks in a hypermedia application.

Figure 5.20 Side by side representation of two text fragments.

5.7.1.2   Exploration

Although the advantages to be gained in the exploration of hypertext are awaited with great anticipation, the jury is still out when it comes to passing a final judgment on the exploratory value of using hypertext. The fact is people have had little experience in using large hypertext systems, so there is a dearth of firm data to back up the current expectations and promises.

We will mention one of the few research studies on the use of hypertext that is available as of this writing. It was carried out using the Hyperties system and briefly described by Marchionini and Shneiderman (1988).

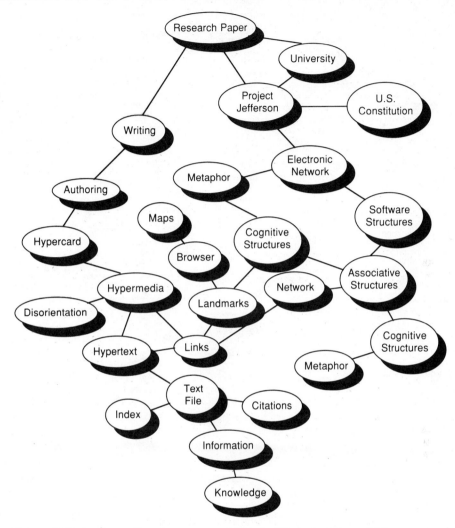

Figure 5.21 Representation of concepts embedded within text of Figure 5.20 as a network of points.

Hyperties (Hypertext based on the Interactive Encyclopedia System) uses what Shneiderman refers to as an embedded-menus approach that corresponds to the replacement buttons in Guide, for instance. Boldfaced words within text represent links to further information about a topic. The two hypertext systems studied by Marchionini and Shneiderman were structured browsing systems designed for casual users. They could not be modified by users, and the goal of the researchers was to focus on the user and system components of information seeking.

In one study, two versions of Hyperties were compared, one that used embedded menus and another that used an index to search for specific facts. However, aside

Recent recognition of the importance of writing and critical thinking skills, both within and beyond the scope of the university, has focused attention on the role of the research paper in the composition course. However attempts to teach the research paper for the most part, have been unsuccessful. What is needed is a new model for the research paper which can be incorporated into the composition course. At USC we have developed such a model in the Project Jefferson interface. In this paper we discuss our experience in using the Project Jefferson model to author hypermedia based curricular tools and discuss issues in authoring hypermedia structures based on that experience. We report the results of structured interviews carried out with the personnel who were responsible for authoring the hypertext and index for Project Jefferson. We also interpret features of the authoring process in terms of their impact on the resulting compatibility between software structures and student cognitive structures, as observed in two related studies

Hypertext can be simply defined as the creation and representation of links between discrete pieces of data. When this data can be graphics, or sound, as well as text or numbers, the resulting structure is referred to as hypermedia. The strengths of hypermedia arise from its flexibility in storing and retrieving knowledge. Any piece of information, whether it be text, graphics, sound, numerical data, etc., can be linked to any other piece of information. In many ways, the problems of hypermedia stem from the very flexibility that is its chief advantage and justification. It is difficult to maintain a sense of where things are in a relatively unstructured network of information. While the associative nature of hypermedia increases the availability of large amounts of diverse information, this very diversity makes it easy for information and users to get lost. Hypermedia exacerbates the problem of getting "lost in information space" by providing a complex associative structure that can be traversed, but not fully visualized. Information gets lost because it becomes difficult to organize and tag effectively, while users get lost as they lose sense of where they are in the hypermedia.

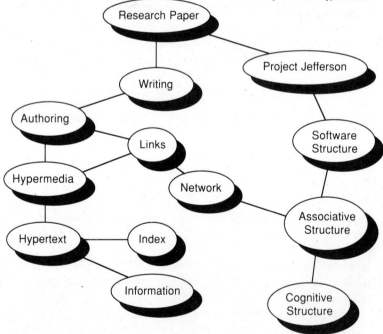

Figure 5.22 Linking the hypermedia network to the corresponding concepts embedded in the text.

from this difference, both systems contained the same information. All the tasks that were given to the subjects in the study could be accomplished with either search strategy, but index users located facts more quickly than embedded menu users. The differences in performance between the groups decreased as they gained more experience with the system. In a different study, Shneiderman (1987) found advantages for embedded menus over explicit menus in terms of both speed of fact retrieval and subjective preference. Yet another study Marchionini (in press) used the full-text of Grolier's Academic American Encyclopedia on CD-ROM. The hypertext version of this encyclopedia consisted of 60 megabytes of text and 50 megabytes of indexes containing pointers to each occurrence of every word in the encyclopedia. The search software for this system provides rapid access to all occurrences of any word or phrase entered by the user, along with the ability to enter queries as Boolean strings. Marchionini examined the information-seeking strategies used by elementary school students. These students used the system successfully in spite of having difficulty in building Boolean search queries. It appeared that the hypertext features of the search system compensated for some of the difficulties that the children had with more formal search methods.

Thus the initial results on structured browsing in hypertext appear promising. It is likely that there will be an explosion of research on hypertext in the next few years and by the early 1990s we should have a good idea of the advantages of hypertext exploration. It should be remembered, however, that exploration is a task or orientation in its own right and that it would be foolish to use exploratory forms of retrieval to answer straightforward questions. We can illustrate this point with the example of what people do when they have to recall a telephone number. When the option is available, they find it preferable to look the number up directly in an indexed directory. It is only when this type of strategy fails that they resort to an exploratory strategy. Thus exploration in hypertext should be seen as a supplement to, rather than a replacement for, traditional methods of database management and information retrieval.

5.7.2 Problems

In many ways, the problems of hypertext stem from the very flexibility that is its chief advantage and justification. It is difficult to maintain a sense of where things are in a relatively unstructured network of information. Thus there may be some benefit to adding indexing features to the basic hypertext concept. We explore this concept further when we consider how hypertext may be linked to relational databases.

At present, there are three major problems that confront hypertext developers and users. These are disorientation, the lack of firm training policies, and the lack of standards. We expect that each of these problems will be minimized by the early 1990s, but they will have a great impact on the way that hypertext is used and absorbed into information management systems of the future.

5.7.2.1 *Disorientation*

Although the associative nature of hypertext increases the availability of large amounts of diverse information, this very diversity makes it easy for information and users to get lost. Hypertext exacerbates the problem of getting "lost in information space" by providing a complex associative structure that can be traversed, but not fully visualized. Information gets lost because it becomes difficult to organize and tag effectively, while users get lost as they lose sense of where they are in the hypertext.

Getting lost or disoriented occurs when one doesn't know where one is. Hypertext is roughly akin to a semantic network connecting pieces of information in arbitrary ways to form an associative structure. The problem of disorientation in hypertext has yet to be solved, but it may help to represent hypertext as a real-world object that can be mapped and browsed.

Solutions to the problem of disorientation in hypertext appear to fall into two general classes. First, one can create maps or browsers that allows users to determine where they are in terms of the overall network, or regions thereof. Second, one can create tags, markers, or milestones that represent familiar locations, much as a lighthouse signals location in the middle of a foggy night.

Spatial memory aids are promising ways for improving navigation through hypertext. In classical times, the method of loci was used as a memory aid. Simply put, this technique involves associating the items to be remembered with different physical objects or positions in a very familiar location such as a temple or house. This technique improves recall by associating unfamiliar items with familiar items.

5.7.2.2 Training

The novelty of hypertext as a software environment raises training problems, most of which stem from the need to adapt users to nonlinear media. Proponents of hypertext claim that it is more "natural" in some senses, but this does not seem to be borne out by the performance of people using hypertext for the first time. The study by Marchionini and Shneiderman (1987), for instance, indicated that even in a structured browsing environment, users initially performed better using conventional search via an index.

We can draw an analogy here with the use of typewriters. The standard QWERTY keyboard was originally designed to slow down maximum typing speed so that collisions between mechanical keys in the typewriters of the nineteenth century did not occur. Since that time, a number of more natural and efficient keyboard layouts have been suggested, but the QWERTY layout continues to predominate. The major reason for this inertia appears to be the unwillingness to replace existing typewriters and learn new skills. This example shows that natural methods do not remove the need for training. In fact, they represent more of a training challenge, since it may be difficult to train an apparently natural behavior. It may be that hypertext is like riding a bike, where one has to learn largely through experience, but at present we cannot be sure and adequate training methods have yet to be developed. It is possible that the development and use of hypertext may be significantly retarded if adequate training is not provided to prospective users.

It is somewhat ironic that training should be an issue in hypertext development since training is one application area where hypertext promises to be particularly useful.

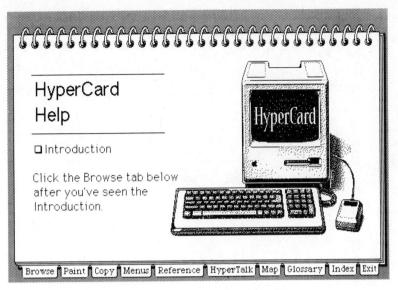

Figure 5.23 The opening HyperCard help screen.

The online help system for the Symbolix workstation, for instance, is a good example of the use of hypertext as an online help and training tool (Walker, 1987).

The online help available from HyperCard is another example of how hypertext may itself be used as a training medium. In this case, hypertext itself is used as a tool in training the user to use a hypertext development system. Figures 5.23 to 5.25 show three screens from the HyperCard help stacks that illustrate this point, with links to related information being indicated as tabs at the bottom of a card, as menu boxes within a card, and as boxes in a tree representation, respectively.

5.7.2.3 Standards

Early hypertext systems have generally been developed by research groups and have then migrated into commercial products. Two apparent exceptions are the NoteCards system developed as a research tool by Xerox and the HyperCard system whose development was sponsored by Apple. Yet even here there appears to be little doubt that at least part of the inspiration for the HyperCard system came from the earlier NoteCards system. In general, however, different hypertext products have developed fairly autonomously, and this has resulted in a wide variety of approaches to the implementation of hypertext.

As one views and works with different hypertext products it is sometimes difficult to see how they are all representations of the hypertext concept. At the very least, there are significant differences in the details. As the hypertext technology matures, there will inevitably be a search for standards, in spite of the natural tendency for companies to emphasize the differences between their products and those of their

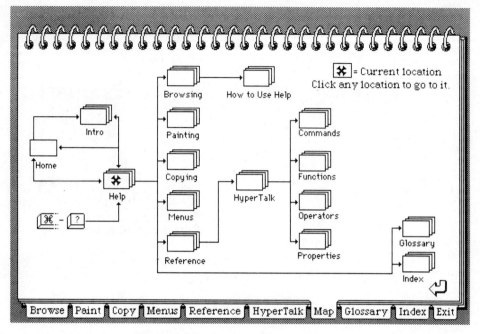

Figure 5.24 The HyperCard help system map.

competitors. The development of relational databases provides a good example of how the use of standard methods for representing and operating on data has enhanced the general technology of database management.

There is as yet no standardized model of hypertext. There is general enthusiasm over the idea of replacing linear methods of storing and retrieving information with nonlinear and associative methods, but there are many ways in which such replacement could occur. The hypertext systems on the market today vary considerably in the associative structuring methods that they employ, and no doubt many other structuring principles are also possible, waiting to be described and implemented in software.

We anticipate a general movement towards the development of standards in hypertext in the future. At present, it appears that the two concepts that all hypertext systems share are nodes and links, although these concepts may be referred to by different names in different systems.

Since the basic components of hypertext are the nodes and the links, potential hypertext standards represent methods for constraining the ways in which nodes and links can be defined and used. In current hypertext systems, there is a great deal of variation in the freedom with which the system permits the user to define new types of node and link. In some systems the user has a great deal of freedom, while in others the software plays an active role in maintaining the integrity of the hypertext.

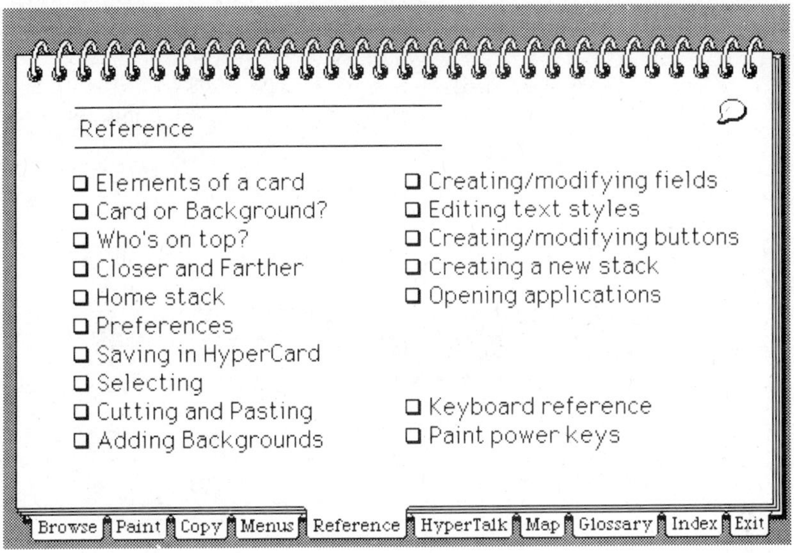

Figure 5.25 The HyperCard help system reference menu.

5.7.3 Browsing Media and Maps

Browsing is a major capability provided by the flexible structuring of knowledge and information in hypertext. However, browsing is a double-edged sword because the same flexibility of structure which allows browsing to be carried out also allows one to get lost fairly easily.

Hypertext can generally be browsed in a number of ways, including

    a. By following links and moving from one card to another via these links.

    b. By searching the network for a particular string, keyword, or attribute value. This is of course a primitive querying facility that may be enhanced using relational queries in extended models of hypertext.

    c. By navigating through a visual representation of the hypertext network such as a map or tree.

The existence of a map or tree that indicates where one is in the hypertext becomes more and more necessary as the hypertext becomes more complex both in terms of the number of nodes and the density of links. We shall now describe a few of the tools that can be used to assist the process of browsing in hypertext.

5.7.3.1 The NoteCards Browser

The NoteCards browser is an integral part of the NoteCards hypertext system described in Section 5.3.2. This browser is a notecard that contains a structural diagram of a network of notecards. An example of a browser notecard is shown in Figure 5.26. In this browsing system, each box represents a notecard (whose title is shown inside that box). The links between boxes in the browser represent corresponding links between notecards in the hypertext. The visual appearance of the link in the browser indicates the type of link between the two notecards that it connects.

Since NoteCards has a multiple windowing capability, the user can view the browser continuously, while exploring the hypertext and reading notecards. The browser can

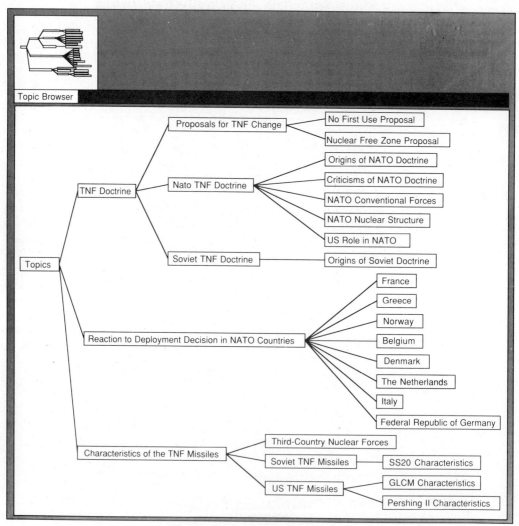

Figure 5.26 A NoteCards browser.

also be used to move around the network so that by traversing a link on the browser one can retrieve the corresponding notecard.

The notecard browser also facilitates the process of editing the hypertext. Users can edit the underlying structure of the hypertext by carrying out operations on the nodes and edges in the browser. Users can also try out different network organizations by modifying the browser notecard without making corresponding changes to the underlying notecards and their links.

5.7.3.2   The Fisheye Lens Model

The fisheye lens model (e.g., Furnas, 1986) is built on the observation that humans often represent their own neighborhood in great detail, yet only indicate major landmarks for more distant regions. The most celebrated example of a fisheye lens model is probably the "New Yorker's View of the United States" (The poster by Steinberg has been simplified and redrawn as a Los Angeleno's view in Figure 5.27).

Computer programs, databases, maps, and many other complex entities are generally viewed through windows that may be as small as the 24 x 80 character window of a traditional video display. Typically, these windows into massive structures provide few facilities for navigating round the larger structure and finding out about "where I am." This leads to the problem of disorientation that was discussed in Section 5.5.2.1.

Furnas has pointed out that

> While this representation is certainly a distorted view of the U.S., it is a manageable abbreviation in which the most important features of the New Yorker's world are preserved. The view allows the New Yorker to answer local questions like, 'Where is the closest mail box?', but also more global questions like 'To ski in the Rocky Mountains, does it make more sense to connect through LA or Chicago?'

Ideally, fisheye representations provide both local and global detail about where one is in the larger structure. This is particularly useful in hypertext browsing where one simultaneously needs to know about where one is in the overall structure and about what concepts and information are related to the information currently being examined.

While the fisheye concept is easy to understand, it is not obvious how it should be implemented in interfaces. In some senses, the NoteCards browser described in the previous section embodies the fisheye lens principle since it can simultaneously show the global information in the browser notecard, while representing local information in terms of regular notecards. However, in this case there is no smooth transition between the local and global information such as one gets with the New Yorker's view of New Jersey. Instead, there is a discontinuous jump from the local view of a notecard to the global view represented in the browser.

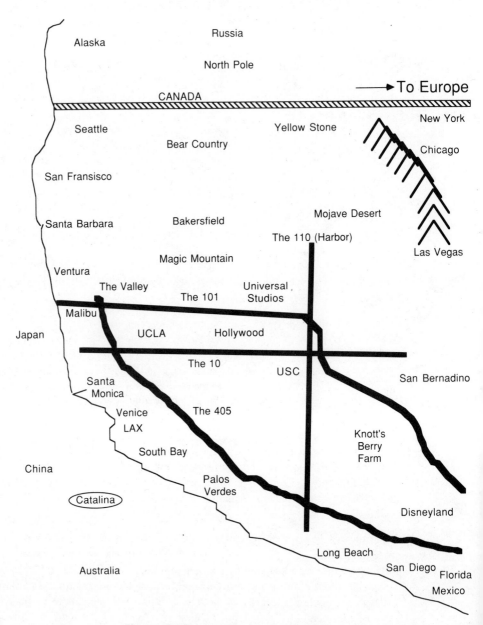

Figure 5.27 A Los Angeleno's view of the world.

Attempts have been made to formalize the fisheye lens model by using a *Degree of Interest* (DOI) function to determine whether or not a particular point or node should be shown in the current fisheye lens view (Furnas, 1986, p. 170). One method is to divide DOI into two components, one representing the a priori interest (API) of a node, the other representing the distance—$D(x,y)$ of that node *(y)* from the current viewpoint *(x)*.

In using fisheye views to reduce disorientation in hypertext, one suggestion is to designate certain nodes in the hypertext as landmarks, because of their familiarity, memorability, or salience. These landmarks would act like the familiar landmarks in a city, giving users a chance to orient themselves around objects that have known locations. We shall outline a version of such a landmark model in the next section.

Given a set of landmarks, one could then provide a fisheye view of these landmarks where a map is constructed that includes a number of the landmarks that are close to the current location and relatively few of the distant landmarks. This type of browsing tool assumes of course that there is a spatial representation of the network that allows these distances to be calculated. One informal measure of distance between two objects in a hypertext network is of course the minimum number of links that must be traversed in getting from one object to the other across the network.

5.7.3.3 Landmark Views

Browsing through hypermedia is a delicate process that is constrained on the one hand by the need to have flexible access to information and on the other by the need to avoid disorientation. In general, the more paths that the user is permitted to explore, the more likely it is that the user will eventually get lost. The landmark model is a modification of the fisheye view approach to browsing that designates certain nodes in the hypermedia as landmarks, because of their familiarity, memorability, or salience. These landmarks act like the familiar landmarks in a city, giving users a chance to orient themselves around objects that have known locations. One may then provide views of these landmarks where users have a chance to view landmarks that are at different sets of conceptual distances from the current location.

The process of using landmark views is illustrated in Figure 5.28. First, the user is provided a button that allows him to move to a new node. When this button is pressed a pop-up window appears with different view options. The user then selects the landmark view. The system then provides a choice of distances from which to view landmarks. For instance, the user in Figure 5.28 is given a choice of viewing landmarks that are in the far distance, middle distance, or close by. The user, in this example, selects the close landmarks and is shown a list of these landmarks.

Valdez, Chignell, and Glenn (1988) carried out a study to investigate how landmarks may be recognized in a hypermedia network. They focused on the following set of 30 terms (used in the Project Jefferson computer-based instructional system at the University of Southern California).

1 =	Concepts and Issues	2 =	Equality
3 =	Race Prejudice	4 =	Meritocracy
5 =	Affirmative Action	6 =	Organizations
7 =	Political Institutions	8 =	NOW
9 =	Judiciary	10 =	Universities
11 =	People	12 =	Justices
13 =	Allan Bakke	14 =	William Douglas
15 =	Blacks	16 =	Discrimination
17 =	Types of Compensation	18 =	Religious Prejudice
19 =	Equal Opportunity	20 =	Preferential Treatment
21 =	Social Institutions	22 =	Educational Institutions
23 =	NAACP	24 =	Legislature
25 =	Grade Schools	26 =	Students
27 =	Minorities	28 =	Marco DeFunis
29 =	Sandra Day O'Connor	30 =	Hispanics

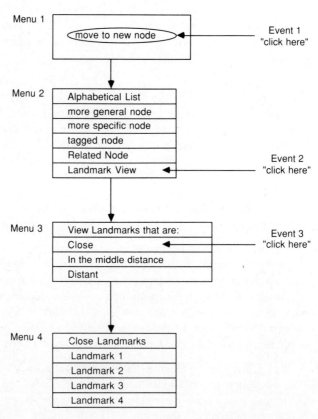

Figure 5.28 Using a landmark view by clicking on successive menus.

They hypothesized that landmarks are remembered better in the same way that category exemplars are generally more representative (Rosch and Mervis, 1975) and representative items tend to be more easily recalled (Kahneman, Slovic, and Tversky, 1982). They also expected that landmarks should tend to represent either basic level or high-level categories, given the special nature of such categories (Rosch, Mervis, Gray, Johnson, and Boyes-Braem, 1976). Finally, they anticipated that landmarks would tend to be connected to more objects than non-landmarks in the same way that major hubs serve as landmarks in airline systems.

The connectedness of each term was calculated in two ways. First-order connectivity for a term was defined to be the number of terms that were directly related (linked) to it. Second-order connectivity was calculated as the number of terms that can be reached from a particular term via two relational links. Thus, if A were related to B, and B were related to C, then there would be a second-order connection between A and C. In practice, one may calculate second-order connectivity by taking all the terms that are linked to the current term and summing the first-order connectivities for each of them.

After deriving theoretical predictions of landmark quality based on measures such as memorability and connectivity, Valdez et al. then ran an experiment to see whether these predictions were reasonable. They sought to determine the landmark quality of terms empirically, using the assumption that one generally uses landmarks to construct paths through spatial structures. Intuitively, we use landmarks all the time in giving directions to strangers in a city or neighborhood. Thus one might say "the administration building is right behind Tommy Trojan," or "go down Pico Boulevard until you see the bowling alley and then turn right." Thus landmarks are useful in defining paths and we can use this fact to develop an operational measure to assess the landmark quality of a term directly. We can ask people to think about getting from point A to point B and then judge whether point C is on the path between A and B. On average, C should be more likely to be selected as being on the path if it is more of a landmark. This led Valdez et al. to design a new experimental procedure where pairs of points are displayed and a participant is asked to judge whether or not a third point lies on a path between the first two points.

An operational measure of landmark quality was generated as the number of times that an item appeared as a landmark in a path. Data was aggregated over the subjects in the experiment and an empirical measure of landmark quality was thus obtained. As might be expected, first- and second-order connectivity were highly correlated ($r = .923$), but second-order connectivity had the highest correlation with the empirically derived landmark quality ($r = .616$), of the predictors considered by Valdez et al.

With this empirically observed relationship between connectivity and landmark quality, we can then derive a simple way of constructing landmark views based on a network of terms used to index a set of documents. The following algorithm is not intended to be conclusive, but it provides an interesting and potentially useful method for constructing landmark views.

1. Obtain a set of documents indexed by the terms of interest.
2. For each possible pair of index terms, calculate the number of times that they co-occur in the index of the same document. This number will be referred to as the *distance* between the two terms in the pair in step 5 below.
3. Convert this matrix of co-occurrences to a link matrix using an appropriate threshold, as shown in Figure 5.29.
4. Calculate the second-order connectivity for each term and interpret this as the measure of *landmark quality* referred to in step 5.
5. Group the terms according to their distance from each node. Construct a landmark view for each node by allowing a user to select a distance (e.g., close) and display the terms that are connected at that distance, ordered according to the amount of landmark quality that they possess.

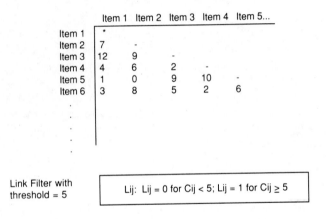

Figure 5.29 Converting a matrix of co-occurrences to a link matrix.

In normal human commerce, a place where paths cross often becomes a landmark. Thus it is not surprising that connectivity appears to be a good predictor of landmark quality. We expect that good software interfaces should have crossroads built into them that correspond to cognitive landmarks. Even in the Jefferson prototype interface, where no attempt was made to deliberately construct landmarks, de facto landmarks appear to exist, such as "affirmative action" and "discrimination." Further studies are needed to determine whether landmarks and crossroads generally exist in hypermedia applications or whether or not the cognitive compatibility of interfaces may be significantly enhanced by adding, or encouraging the development of, landmarks.

The notion of landmarks as discussed here is presumably related to many other intellectual concepts including categories and icon symbols. Once landmarks have been identified it should then be possible to attach visual semantics to them that enhance their interpretability and usefulness.

5.7.4 Converting Text to Hypertext

The task of converting text into hypertext is taking on increasing importance as mass-storage capabilities improve and hypertext becomes more popular. Needless to say, there are billions of pages of linear text in the world, and many people are concerned with the problem of converting these vast textual resources into the form of hypertext.

Text conversion is a challenging problem that requires careful analysis of the original document in order to determine its content and structure. Sections of the text are tagged as instances of particular concepts and then linked to other text fragments that share a related concept. In many cases, though, determining the content and structure of a document may be problematic even for human experts, especially when the document was created decades or centuries ago and one cannot be sure of the author's original intent. The need to develop faster ways of converting text to hypertext will provide a great stimulus to the development of text processing methods.

We illustrate the problems associated with converting text to hypertext with the example of a project whose goal is to create a hypertext version of the Oxford English Dictionary (Raymond and Tompa, 1987).

The Oxford English Dictionary (OED) is the largest dictionary of written English and is the standard reference for disputes relating to the meaning and spelling of the "Queen's English." It was produced over a thirty-four-year period, ending in 1928, after almost thirty years of preliminary effort in planning and collecting material. In its standard form, the OED consists of 12 books containing 42.51 million words in 252,259 entries, and 1.86 million quotations. Additional material and changes have appeared as a supplement to the OED since 1958. The OED has a remarkable range of entry sizes, from just a few words to extended commentaries of several thousand words.

The OED is particularly attractive for hypertext conversion because it has already been segmented into entries and it is natural to think of each entry as a potential node in the hypertext. As a browsing tool, the OED would form a wonderful intellectual resource. Users typically browse and query the OED as part of a larger task. The abilities to cut and paste fragments of OED text into other documents, annotate text fragments, and sort and filter extracted quotations are all tools whose integration could be facilitated by having hypertext as a simple and consistent interface.

■ 5.8 HYPERTEXT APPLICATIONS

What can hypermedia do? Although the idea of hypertext has been around for a while, it is only very recently that practical systems have been available for building and using hypertext. As a result, no one is yet sure what uses will ultimately be found for hypertext and hypermedia systems. At present, however, hypermedia shows a great deal of promise in a number of areas such as text authoring, online information retrieval, online help for software systems, computer-based instruction, and even computer-aided software engineering (CASE).

5.8.1 Text Processing and Authoring

One of the most fruitful early uses of hypertext is in the area of text processing and authoring. The Guide system, for instance, seems to be particularly well suited to the task of word processing. The freeze capability in Guide allows one to move easily between writing and editing text and linking that text into an associative structure.

As well as being a tool for the individual author, hypertext may also enhance cooperative writing among multiple authors (Trigg, 1983). One of the appealing features of cooperative writing in hypertext is that one doesn't have to commit oneself to a particular linear sequence of ideas when writing. Ideas can grow and evolve naturally over time while a consensus builds on how they should be linked. Our own experience in authoring suggests that most disputes over material concerns its organization and primacy rather than the basic content. Cooperative authors will usually agree on which areas of expertise each of them covers so that disputes over content are usually deferred to the recognized expert in that area. However, ordering of topics lies outside traditional domain expertise and there is a great deal more scope for argument. Hypertext preempts many of these arguments by allowing a variety of orders to be constructed and tested.

5.8.2 Hypertext and Databases

Trends in the development of databases have generally followed two paths.

1. Increased power in indexing information and describing relations between different pieces of information.
2. Increased power in expressing complex queries.

In general, as more powerful ways of describing information and data were developed, correspondingly powerful ways of querying that information were made possible.

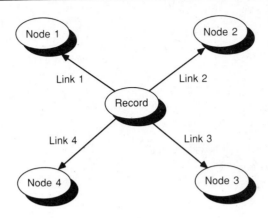

Name	Link 1	Link 2	Link 3	Link 4
Record	Node 1	Node 2	Node 3	Node 4

Figure 5.30 Representation of hypertext nodes and links in a relational database.

Hypertext will have a momentous impact on databases, but only if ways are found to harness its inherent flexibility so that there is sufficient structure available to build meaningful queries. This will require a fairly radical departure from the approach that has permeated much of the discussion about hypertext, which has emphasized the "freedom" that hypertext provides and the ability to browse. Hypertext database applications will require the capability to carry out structured searches.

However, the problem of linking conventional databases to hypertext has not received much attention as of this writing. Consider how the abstract structure of a generic hypertext node compares with a record in a relational database (Figure 5.30). In hypertext terms, the database record consists of text that is linked to columns in a relational table. A link to a particular column in the table is present if the corresponding index term describes the content of the document, the link is absent otherwise. This is a very constrained structure, since there are no links possible between documents. However, what the relational description does provide is an analysis of the document into a set of index terms. This functionality can be simulated in hypertext by creating index terms as nodes. Figure 5.31 shows how a relational table might look in a hypertext representation. The emulation of relational databases in hypertext is somewhat messy. Although hypertext representations of relations provide a good conceptual way of understanding the structuring principles involved, in implementing the relational data model we are much better off relying on the conventional methods of building relational databases.

The implementation of a relational database functionality within hypertext required

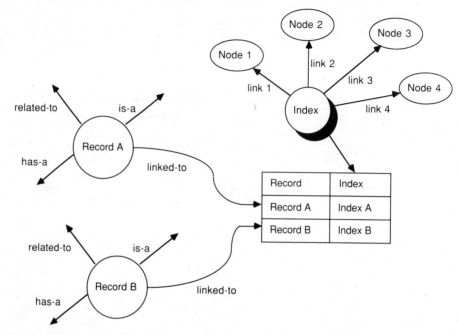

Figure 5.31 An illustration of how a relational table might look in a hypertext representation.

the use of index nodes and index links. We now utilize the set of node and link types defined in Section 5.4. We can then use hypertext as a high-level database machine and knowledge representation tool.

5.8.3   Information Retrieval

Hypertext offers several features that may prove useful, if not revolutionary, for information retrieval.

Documents that are linked in a hypertext network can be directly browsed, rather than indirectly through the index. This distinction is illustrated in Figure 5.32 where we see that the searcher can directly move from one document to another in hypertext whereas one can only link to documents via the index terms in the traditional structure. Direct browsing of documents represents a new form of information retrieval that may suit many users much better than traditional methods based on obtaining citations. The major advantage of document browsing is that one gets to see the information in the document immediately, and once one has tracked down a concept in one document, it can lead one to related concepts in other documents. Contrast this with conventional information retrieval where concepts are not linked except through some type of Boolean search string. Here one has to go through a multistep process in order to view the relevant information.

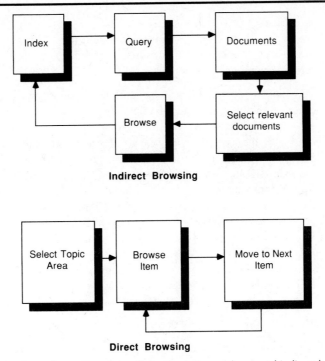

Figure 5.32 An illustration of the distinction between direct and indirect browsing.

1. Construct a query that represents a search concept of interest (this may be fairly difficult).
2. View the citations and abstracts of the documents retrieved to determine which documents are relevant.
3. Read the documents to get the information. In some cases this is done online, in others a hard copy of the document must be obtained.
4. If you now want to move to a related concept, you have to reformulate the query accordingly, starting at step 1.

5.8.3.1 *Hypertext and Query Formulation*

Hypertext also shows a great deal of promise as a query formulation aid. Intermediaries typically spend a large amount of time translating the language and terminology of the user into the language and terminology of the database. Thesauri are frequently used to move between different patterns of word usage. Hypertext can be used to create sophisticated online thesauri where words are linked to their definitions, to synonyms and related terms, and so on. Thus, users can browse hypertext and then select terms for subsequent queries. This approach ensures that the user understands the meanings of the terms and uses them in a way that the system also understands. Thus, query formulation will be greatly assisted as the hypertext allows the vocabularies of the user and the system to converge prior to carrying out search.

5.8.4   Expert Hypertext

Given the flexibility of hypertext, it should not be surprising that hypertext may be used as a vehicle for documenting, explaining and enhancing expert systems. We refer to such hypertext applications as expert hypertext.

The capability for implementing inference within hypertext may have a major influence on the development of intelligent databases. As with objects and relational indexes, we expect that the rule base and inference engine will independently exist outside of the hypertext. However, rules and facts may also be defined as hypertext nodes. The advantage of the hypertext representation is that it allows one to explore the meaning and relations between rules. We can, for instance, attach justifications for the construction and use of a particular rule to its corresponding hypertext node, thereby providing a powerful documentation and explanation capability. More speculatively, perhaps, it is possible to envision facts as hypertext nodes. Rules would then establish links between facts. This inferential form of hypertext would then function as an inference network or tree (see Parsaye and Chignell, 1988, Chapters 2 and 7). This inferential hypertext would be constructed during a reasoning process. The use of inferential hypertext may allow new forms of tracing and debugging facilities to be developed for expert systems and logic programs.

The hypertext model may be extended to expert system applications and expert hypertext.

In a traditional Hypertext system links are "explicit," that is

A <u>is linked to</u> B

C <u>is linked to</u> D

In other words, hypertext has "hardwired" links that are fixed prior to use. As hypertext is linked to databases and expert systems, however, new possibilities arise for creating links on the basis of deduction. Successful deduction of hypertext links is useful because of the time-consuming nature of the task of authoring hypertext links. There is a strong analogy between the need to automate knowledge acquisition in knowledge engineering (Parsaye and Chignell, 1988, chapter 9) and the need to deduce hypertext links automatically.

In a deductive Hypertext system, the links may be implicit and may be obtained by rules.

'A' <u>is linked to</u> 'B'

If

'A' <u>has property</u> 'Z'

and

'B' <u>has property</u> 'W'

and . . .

Further, the links may be inexact, that is

> CF = 40
> 'A' <u>is linked to</u> mathematical physics
>
> If
>
> 'A' <u>has property</u> scientific
>
> and
>
> 'A' <u>has property</u> mathematical
>
> and . . .

The user may set levels of minimal acceptance for the links to be shown, thereby controlling the strength and number of associative links in the hypertext. We can further enhance the process of hypertext authoring by using machine learning to derive the rules that create hypertext links. Thus, the rules may be automatically "learnt" from large databases.

Automated hypertext creation using intelligent databases, machine learning, and deduction would then be followed by an editing and tuning process. One method for doing this would be an adaptive learning procedure where links are weighted according to the number of times they are used. Underutilized links could then be screened for possible deletion by human experts. Facilities could also be provided for users to tag apparently nonsensical links. These could then be filtered by the hypertext editors. There appears to be a great deal of promise in using neural networks to implement adaptive learning within hypermedia, but this is a topic that lies outside the scope of this book.

■ 5.9 A HYPERTEXT CASE STUDY

The use of hypertext is best illustrated by example. To the extent that each example is unique, however, no one example can capture all the aspects of hypertext which is by its nature extremely flexible. Thus we will describe a project that illustrates different aspects of what hypertext can do. Project Jefferson is being carried out at the University of Southern California and is aimed at allowing freshman college students to carry out online information searches as part of their course assignments.

5.9.1 Project Jefferson

In this section we discuss how the Jefferson interface hypertext was constructed and give examples of its use, including screen dumps from a session carried out by freshman students at USC who are using the software in their courses. One of the features of the project is its use of hypertext to organize the background information and index terms so that they can be browsed prior to and even during online searches.

Project Jefferson has two major goals: (1) to develop an effective model of computer-based instruction that includes the use of research tools and a standard interface that can act as the front end for courseware across a variety of different disciplines, and (2) to develop a researcher's notebook that will permit easy access to online information. We see these goals as fairly closely related and grounded in the need to bring the information age into the college campus and vice versa. Although it is often pointed out that we are living in an information age in which independent individualized learning is possible through electronic access to information, one doesn't see much evidence of this in the typical college undergraduate program. Simply having laboratories full of computing equipment does not suffice as evidence, since these laboratories are typically used outside classtime for word processing, and the basic lecturing style of instruction remains as it has been for centuries. Thus, the first goal of Project Jefferson was to design computer-based instructional software appropriate for the information age.

This major goal was approached from a number of perspectives. From an educational perspective, the Freshman Writing Program at USC wanted to develop a tool that would teach students to learn how to learn by using information technologies, not just how to do research to survive the last paper assignment. Meanwhile, the Library was engaged in designing a new Teaching Library, and wanted to learn how people use online services in order to design them better. From the perspective of engineering design, Project Jefferson was an experiment with a hypertext environment in which different kinds of software could be summoned, and different kinds of information accessed, all within a consistent and individualized interface.

The overall goal of Project Jefferson was to develop a model of research and instruction that could be learned within the writing program and subsequently transferred to more advanced courses in the undergraduate curriculum. This model of research and instruction is being developed through a notebook metaphor.

A major specification for the software was that the interface should embody a consistent model that assisted naive users (e.g., freshman writing students) in performing what would otherwise have been a difficult task. It was also felt that this model should correspond to a familiar metaphor that would accelerate the adaptation of naive users to the interface.

The Project Jefferson interface prototype that we will describe here was designed to assist freshman students in writing assignments about topics relating to the U.S. Constitution. It was demonstrated at the EDUCOM conference in Los Angeles in fall, 1987 and was used by a number of freshman writing students at the University of Southern California in the fall and spring of 1987-1988. The prototype described here has since been superceded by a later version *(The Jefferson Notebook)* that is sold through Kinko's Academic Courseware Exchange.

The Constitution is a complex topic that is difficult for freshmen to master without appropriate assistance. Initially, it was felt that the Constitution could be modeled using a set of topics such as the following example:

The infringement of *civil liberty* of *agent* by *group* in *situation*

A domain expert participated in a series of interviews aimed at building a conceptual representation of the Constitution. The outcome of these interviews was a simple template for analyzing Constitutional issues. This template (model) was based on the assumption that the best way to understand the Constitution is to examine the way in which specific cases are analyzed and interpreted. Each controversy or case can be analyzed with this template into the basic Constitutional values that are involved, along with the evidence and arguments that support each side. A query can then be expressed by filling in each of the windows in the template (Kinnell and Chignell, 1987). The concrete model of a court case was used to assist the students in recognizing the structure of the model. Filling in the template (i.e., instantiating the model for a particular query) involved answering questions such as the following:

Who is the judge?
What event created the current controversy (court case)?
What were the background circumstances leading to the conflict?
Who are the two sides in the cases?
What action does the defense want to take?
What alternative is proposed by the prosecution?
What is the "real" motivation of the defense?
What is the "real" motivation of the prosecution?

The effectiveness of the preliminary model was tested within a classroom setting. Two classes of students within the freshman writing program (about 40 students in all) were given an assignment on a constitutional controversy. It concerned a report of human-rights violations in a "friendly" third world country, and the dilemma of the newspaper editor who had to weigh first amendment issues against those of national security, and so on. After the students had worked on the assignment for two or three weeks they were given a written description of the courtroom model (the generic template discussed above), along with a 30-minute lecture on how to make an analysis using the template (using a different example based on the controversy over whether creationism should be taught alongside evolution in high schools). They were then asked to fill in a questionnaire for the human-rights violation controversy that they had studied in their assignment. Sixteen sets of responses were obtained from each class.

The questionnaire consisted of 22 questions. On average, less than half the questions were answered correctly. Seventy-five percent of the students got between four and eight of the 22 questions correct. Thus informal evaluation of the courtroom model of Constitutional issues showed that typical freshman students had serious problems in using it. Students come in with prior models (which may be incorrect, fuzzy, or just plain different) that differed from the "true" model, which reflected the way that documents are indexed in the database. This example illustrates the importance of finding an appropriate conceptual model of the retrieval interface for users who do not have good a priori knowledge about databases and information retrieval.

Thus our empirical analysis of the adequacy of the metaphor of the court case demonstrated that it would not be appropriate for this application. After a considerable amount of trial and error, the student notebook was chosen as the predominant metaphor for the interface (Figure 5.33). The notebook has the advantage of being a general metaphor that is familiar to students and that can be applied across a variety of instructional settings. The notebook metaphor also allows one to use dividers to separate out the different modules of a topic in a natural way. For instance, in the prototype interface described here, the notebook was divided into five major sections. These are

1. Focus Questions
2. Assignment
3. My Own Ideas
4. Background Information
5. Citation

The focus questions and assignment sections were based on the way that the freshman writing instructors typically introduced assignments to their classes. The Citation section reflected the online database interface that had been the initial motivation for the project. The remaining two sections really arose out of the methods and orientations used in the project. The organization of the five sections of the notebook

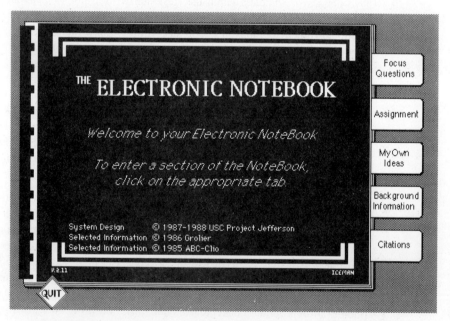

Figure 5.33 The opening screen of the Project Jefferson prototype software.

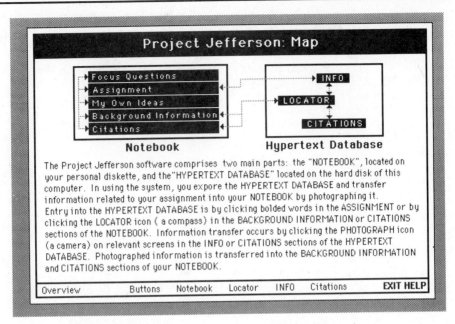

Figure 5.34 A map of the Project Jefferson prototype software.

is illustrated in the map of the interface shown in Figure 5.34. This screen is part of the current online help system. Figure 5.34 also shows that the notebook is linked to a hypertext database that is in turn linked to the locator (an online retrieval interface).

Hypertext (hypermedia) frees knowledge from the constraints of the fixed page and linear or hierarchical relationships. Consequently, hypertext is an extremely flexible way to represent knowledge. It may be used as a browsing tool, an authoring tool, or for a number of other tasks that are as yet only dimly understood. Specific hypertext networks also embody a great deal of flexibility; an expert user and a novice may be able to use the same piece of hypertext, albeit in different ways. The expert may trace a number of different paths, comparing and contrasting the use of different concepts in the hypertext, while novices may move more or less randomly through the hypertext from concept to concept noting interesting information as they encounter it. In the Jefferson interface, the hypertext exists as a space that lurks behind the functionality of the electronic notebook. For instance, if the student clicks on the term *equal protection* which is boldfaced in the assignment (as shown in Figure 5.35), he or she is then taken to the hypertext, entering at the point where the concept of equal protection is described (as shown earlier in Figure 5.13).

One might think of this domain as being like a road map. The individual terms— Equal Protection, Reverse Discrimination, Allan Bakke, Supreme Court, Affirmative Action, etc.—are like cities on the surface of that map. For each term, all of the information available is organized into one or more of six broad types: Overview,

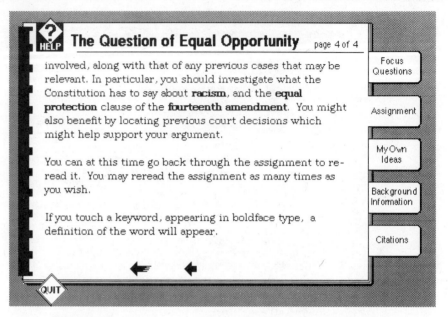

Figure 5.35 Hypertext links (in bold) embedded within an assignment.

Definition, Biography, Background, Significance, Full-Text. For each term one of the available types is made prominent and designated as the focused type: for abstractions, this may be Definition; for people, Biography; for events, acts, and situated abstractions, Overview; for parts of the Constitution, Full-Text. In terms of our metaphor of the map, we may think of this focused type for a given term as the center of that city, and the other types as suburbs adjoined to it. When students access information on a term they go first to the focused type for that term—to the downtown area. From there, they may get to other types of information on that given term (that is, explore the surrounding areas) by clicking on the buttons like *Background* or *Significance* that appear at the bottom of the card (as shown earlier in Figure 5.13).

Since there are never more than five other information cards for a given term (and typically fewer), by far the richest dimensions in this hypertext space are the relations between terms—the links between the various "cities." By clicking on terms in the Related Terms Box the student enters a rich network of pre-established relations between terms that can be freely browsed. Although this hypertext space is a closed system, there is a symmetry condition (requiring that if term A is linked to B then B is generally linked to A) and a minimum condition (requiring that a given term be linked to at least three others) that ensures that there are no deadends as the student moves from one "city" to another.

As the students browse they can click on the camera icon (described earlier as an execute link) to "take pictures of"—that is, save—information that is found, with the substantive content going to the background information part of the notebook and the source of that content going to the citations part of the notebook. At any point students can click on the return arrow in the lower right portion of the card and go back to exactly where they entered the hypertext space—in this case at a particular page of the Assignment. In this way the hypertext environment allows students to adjust their requests for information to their level of knowledge and interest, to boldly follow their own search path without being cut-off, becoming lost, or losing track of the larger task that each is working on.

On leaving the Assignment section of the notebook the student can click on the "My Ideas" section of the notebook. This section provides a word processor to take notes, jot down ideas, or perhaps later in the process, sketch an outline. Alternatively, the student could skip this section and focus on the content and citation information that was saved to the notebook as the student browsed and took pictures in the hypertext network. These can be accessed by clicking on the appropriate notebook tab.

Another major part of the functionality of the Jefferson software was a retrieval interface that allowed users to carry out searches on a database without any previous search experience, nor the assistance of a search intermediary. For a description of the retrieval functionality of the Jefferson Notebook refer to Chignell and Lacy (1988).

■ 5.10 SUMMARY

In many ways hypertext and hypermedia require different ways of thinking about tasks such as writing text and searching for information. The proponents of hypermedia claim that it is more "natural," and that its associative and nonlinear nature corresponds to the way the human mind works. These claims have generally focused on the use of hypermedia as a browsing medium and an interface for knowledge. The projects described in the previous section illustrated this type of hypermedia use.

Although it is generally overlooked, hypermedia is also an extremely flexible knowledge representation method, and we explored this issue in Section 5.4. We showed how relational databases, objects, facts, and rules could all be regarded as special cases of a general form of hypermedia. Thus hypermedia provides a uniform environment for expressing many different kinds of knowledge including uninterpreted information such as sounds, full-text, graphics, and pictures. We will expand on this knowledge representation capability of hypertext in Chapter 7 when we consider how to use hypertext in the development of intelligent databases.

Hypermedia is also being considered as a tool in the development of intelligent software systems. Intelligent hypertext systems assist in the performance of information handling tasks. This concept can be extended to include expert system reasoning in the expert hypertext concept.

In the evolving technology of intelligent databases that is presented in this book, hypermedia is used as a user interface to the powerful information management capability available in an intelligent database. We will show how hypermedia may be used in this fashion in our discussion of the intelligent database user interface in Chapter 7.

6

TEXT MANAGEMENT AND RETRIEVAL

■ 6.1 INTRODUCTION

The retrieval of information embedded within text is a fundamental problem for individuals and for society. For individuals, there is the problem of remembering where certain information may have to be recalled during the performance of a task. For society, there is a massive amount of information that has to be stored and retrieved when needed. Thus information may be thought of as a resource that should be available for general use, but that has to be distilled out of the text within which it is embedded.

In Chapters 2 and 3 we considered data models and object-oriented databases. These chapters focused on databases that have already been represented or interpreted in terms of a data model. In this chapter we focus on text databases where such data models are sketchy or absent. For historical reasons, the literature on text management has used the term "frames" rather than "objects." Consequently, we will also use the term "frame" in this chapter, recognizing its approximate interchangeability with "object." We review traditional information science methods for retrieving information from text databases, and we then outline techniques of text interpretation and management that supplement the traditional methods. We conclude by considering how text databases may be integrated into intelligent database applications.

■ 6.2 INFORMATION RETRIEVAL

Information retrieval is concerned with the representation, storage, organization, and accessing of information items (Salton and McGill, 1983). The advent of computers

293

and the development of inexpensive and efficient high-speed storage devices has led to a marked imbalance in information science. Current capabilities for storing information far exceed the amount of information that can be organized and retrieved efficiently. Put simply, the problem is that we have vast amounts of information to which accurate and speedy access is becoming ever more difficult (van Rijsbergen, 1979). Methods are needed for representing, organizing and accessing information that can match information storage capabilities.

The need for information retrieval capabilities should be obvious. Lack of appropriate information is typically a severe handicap. Consider the case of someone who has to drive to an unfamiliar location without a map or set of directions. In this case there is inadequate information and the journey becomes a set of wrong turns and requests for information from sources encountered during the trip. Since information is a resource whose absence is often costly, we assign value to it and build systems that make it available at the right place at the right time and in the right form.

The problem of information retrieval, the storage and retrieval of information, is central to almost all activities. In this section we focus on the methods of information retrieval that have been developed for dealing with very large textual databases with millions of documents and document representatives (i.e., abstracts or citations standing in place of the original document). These online retrieval systems have generally been considered to be in the domain of information science and there has been relatively little integration of these textual online retrieval systems with conventional databases. Part of this separation between databases and online retrieval systems may stem from the different types of data (i.e., text documents versus records) that are stored in the two systems. Other aspects of the separation, for example, the development of completely different querying methods, appear to be unnecessary. We will begin by reviewing the properties and techniques of online retrieval systems. Then in Chapter 7 we consider methods for integrating databases and online retrieval systems within a uniform model of information retrieval.

6.2.1 Developments in Information Technology

We generally think of the development of information technology as unidirectional, where methods continuously advance and improve. In some cases, however, new technologies may have unwanted side effects, which may be apparent only after a certain amount of time has passed. Consider the invention and use of paper. After its invention, paper continued to be quite expensive, even though it permitted the relatively cheap printing of large numbers of books. Then in the 19th century, methods were available for making paper in vast quantities out of wood pulp. For the past 150 years most books have been made out of this paper, but the paper has also had a high acid content. Currently there is a crisis in libraries where many of the books written in the last 150 years are deteriorating rapidly due to the effects of the high acidity in the paper out of which they were made. Only recently are attempts being made to reduce the acidity of paper on a large scale.

The key concepts of information representation and retrieval were developed in the paper environment. Although cave walls, clay tablets, animal hides, and so on could be used to represent information, it was relatively cheap paper and printing that made information something that could be mass-produced. Along with the mass production of information came the need to organize it. Cataloging systems were developed so that documents could be referred to indirectly. This allowed documents to be retrieved more efficiently. The catalog itself then became a source of information.

Technologies such as microfiche simplified the storage of large amounts of information. Information could be stored in a very compact form and then reproduced on paper when needed. Microfiche offered convenience and increased storage capacity, but it did not allow direct processing of information, which became a possibility with the development of the computer and the availability of online storage of information. It may be argued that the widespread use of microfiche has been a mixed blessing because it has slowed down the construction and use of online information retrieval systems. In the 1980s many libraries continue to use microfiche as a major storage medium. As optical character readers and cheap mass storage proliferate, the continued use of microfiche may act as a retarding influence on the pace at which these newer technologies are generally adopted.

The impact of electronic media on information retrieval is almost incalculable. First, it opens up capabilities for representing and organizing information. Second, it permits a great deal of information processing, including that provided by database management systems and query languages. Third, it will provide the ability to perform machine reasoning, once the problems of symbolic programming and knowledge representation have been solved (Parsaye and Chignell, 1988, Chapter 1). However, until recently, the technologies of information retrieval and machine reasoning have been largely dissociated. This has meant that there have been few cases where expert systems could directly utilize the information in large databases. Instead, knowledge bases were handcrafted for specific expert system applications. Thus the fourth effect of electronic media, the ability to integrate information retrieval and machine reasoning, has yet to be fully realized.

6.2.2 The Nature of Information Retrieval

The basic model of information retrieval is very simple. Information is stored, and later, when it is needed, it is retrieved. For instance, a customer may buy a product on credit. At the time of purchase, the name and address of the customer are added to the accounts database along with details of the purchase. Then, when the bill falls due, the database is searched for the name and address of the customer so that an invoice may be sent. However, this kind of simple example ignores the complexities that arise in defining actual information retrieval systems. How, precisely, is the information pertaining to the customer and the purchase to be defined and stored? We need a language for describing (indexing) the information so that it can be tagged for later retrieval.

Current online retrieval systems typically consist of a large database of stored document surrogates. Words and phrases that describe each document's contents (index terms) are selected either from a controlled vocabulary of standard terms, or freely from the document's title and abstract. The index terms serve as descriptors of, or pointers to, the document they represent. The information need of a user is represented as a query. In the current paradigm, the query is essentially phrased in the form "what documents do you have that conform to the following set of constraints?" The constraints are input as a search query that consists of a series of terms (keywords) combined in a structured query language often based on Boolean logic. The proper use of logical operators enables selective intersection, union, and exclusion operations on sets of documents whose index terms *match* the combination of keywords entered.

We can summarize the current information retrieval paradigm as being a *matching* process where the relevance of documents is judged according to the *similarity* between the keyword index entries of each document and the search query (Figure 6.1).

The way in which information is stored and indexed is determined by the methods of retrieval that are going to be used. In our customer example, we may need to identify customers by their last name, by the size of their account, or by some other criterion required in a particular task. In this case each customer record will need to be indexed according to the last names, account sizes, and so on of the customers.

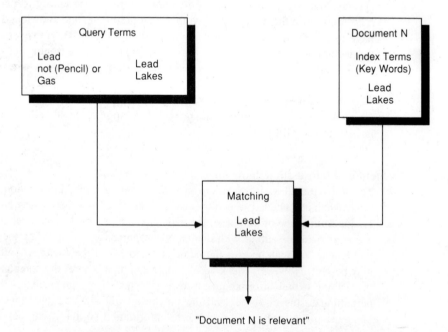

Figure 6.1 A schematic representation of the "matching" paradigm of information retrieval.

It would appear that the type of relational database discussed in Chapter 2 would be sufficient for storing this type of information. However, the problem of information retrieval is not directly analogous to that of database systems because information retrieval systems deal with text rather than records. Thus the indexers of a 50-page paper, for instance, must find some way of representing the information and ideas embedded in the document. Needless, to say, this can be a difficult and controversial task. We will illustrate this point with an anecdote.

One of the authors visited a major database producer to discuss the indexing process. He met with several of their indexers and brought with him a selection of document abstracts from one of that company's databases. The abstracts were each around 100 words in length. The indexers were asked to assign index terms to each abstract. This was not an unfamiliar task for these indexers, since this company routinely assigned index terms on the basis of abstracts that had previously been written. It was found that no two indexers could agree on a set of index terms for any of the documents and spirited discussions (arguments) quickly broke out among the indexers. These discussions arose because the indexers could not agree on the meaning of the text, could not agree on the way that index terms should be assigned to a particular concept represented in the text, or some combination of these two disagreements.

Bismarck once made a remark to the effect that people should not observe the process of how laws or sausages are made. Perhaps we should now add indexing to this prescription. Even in cases where we have observed indexers at work in database companies where a strict, controlled vocabulary is used, there is still a surprising amount of disagreement between indexers about how index terms should be assigned to specific documents. Needless to say, this inconsistency in indexing will be propagated into uncertainty over how a particular concept or information need can be expressed as a query as users attempt to find information in the inconsistently indexed database. Thus, information retrieval in text databases is currently a far more uncertain process than is data retrieval in other types of database.

6.2.3   A Definition of Information Retrieval

Although information is a familiar concept, it can be defined in a number of different ways depending on one's perspective. The communication engineer, for instance, defines information according to the statistical properties of signals. One way of measuring the amount of information that one has received is the amount of surprise that one experiences after hearing the information (Attneave, 1957). Thus being told what one expects or already knows is not very informative compared with being told something totally unexpected.

Defining information in terms of the "amount of surprise" one experiences when receiving a message may seem odd to some, but information turns out to be a concept that is generally taken for granted and that is difficult to define in simple terms. In one edition of Webster's dictionary, for instance, information is defined as "the act or result of informing," while to inform is either to "communicate facts to; tell" or "instruct." The verb communicate is then defined as to "convey, impart," while to instruct is defined as "give directions to; order; command." It is interesting that this 1972 edition of a dictionary makes this distinction between what would now be called declarative and procedural information, but as those familiar with dictionary definitions would realize, we could chase the trail of words for a long time without getting too much closer to the central concept of what information is. Thus, for our purposes, we will loosely define information as the extent to which one's knowledge is enhanced upon receiving the information. Notice that this is a relative, rather than absolute, definition that depends on the prior knowledge of the person receiving the information. The relativity of information should not be surprising in view of the fact that it is almost impossible to define information in the abstract.

Consider the case of a database containing geographical facts. One of the entries in this database might state that

Paris is the capital city of France

Now there may be a new fact:

Paris is located in France

Does this second fact provide information? Obviously, it depends on one's concept of information. The fact that Paris is the capital city of France logically entails that Paris is located in France, yet if we do not want to, or cannot, draw this inference, then the second fact does provide additional information. Thus information is relative to the current knowledge of the recipient and the ability of that recipient to construct the logical entailments of information as they are needed.

For the purposes of this chapter we will define information in two related ways.

1. Information is a resource that is needed to perform tasks. It will generally consist in the form of text and data expressed as facts and rules, but it may also be expressed in other forms such as pictures and sound.
2. The amount of information in a signal or communication is dependent on the observer and will correspond to the difference between what the observer knew after hearing the information and what he knew before.

We have chosen to focus on two aspects of information in our definition because information is not a passive concept. Information is a resource that is used in enhancing productivity and making decisions. Consequently, we are interested both in what information is and what it can be used for. One of the criteria for an intelligent database is that relevant information be provided to users. The ability to define this useful, or relevant, information will be important in telling people what they need to know rather than overwhelming them with general information, much of which is not useful to them.

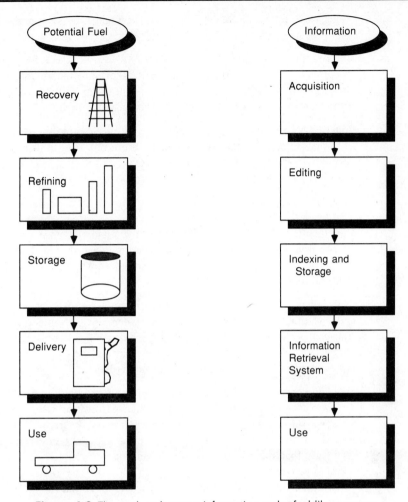

Figure 6.2 The analogy between information and a fuel-like resource.

Like any other resource, information has to be stored and made available when it is needed. We can draw an analogy between information and fuel in a vehicle (Figure 6.2). Vehicles need fuel to run. This fuel has to be stored, and then made available when it is needed. In cars, for instance, the fuel is gas, and the storage mechanism consists of underground tanks at a gas station. The retrieval mechanism consists of pumps which raise the fuel out of the tanks and delivers them to the car's internal storage tank through a hose and nozzle. Unlike information, however, fuel is a fairly homogeneous resource and does not require much organization. Two organizational issues that do arise, though, are the separation of different types of fuel (e.g., high and low octane) and the maintenance of satisfactory ratios of fuel to water in the underground tanks. Once the fuel is placed in the car, it must then be processed in some way. Internal combustion allows the fuel to be converted into energy which is then transformed into a form of propulsion.

Information as a resource also has to be stored, organized and retrieved. In the same way that internal combustion processed the fuel, information may have to be processed so that it is useful in a particular task. One form of processing corresponds to the operation of the relational algebra in database applications.

Queries are requests to process information in a certain way. The task of processing information in text databases is generally referred to as information retrieval, and the systems that carry out information retrieval are referred to as information, or online, retrieval systems.

The term *information retrieval* was coined in 1950 (cited in Foskett, 1963) and can be defined as searching and retrieval of information from storage according to specification by subject. At that time, the major advance provided by information retrieval was seen as the organizing function that it provided where libraries were no longer just storehouses of books, but also places where the information was cataloged and indexed.

Specialists in information retrieval (information scientists) have generally viewed their role as that of informing users about where the information is: "An information retrieval system does not inform (i.e., change the knowledge of) the user on the subject of his inquiry. It merely informs him on the existence (or nonexistence) and whereabouts of documents relating to this request." (Lancaster, 1968, p.1)

We can characterize this model of information retrieval as one where the goal is not to provide information directly, but rather to provide information about where the relevant information can be found. In a relational database, this would be somewhat analogous to telling a person where to find a relevant record without telling him what is inside that record. Alternative models of knowledge-based information retrieval seek to provide the user with the information directly rather than just with citations or with the documents within which it is expected that the information will reside.

The processes involved in the traditional model of information retrieval are represented schematically in Figure 6.3 (after Lancaster, 1968, p. 4). Two types of people are associated with the IR system. The information staff act as indexers and searchers, in storing and retrieving the information. In contrast, the system users input requests to the file.

The need to have indexers and searchers makes the development and use of information retrieval systems extremely labor-intensive. It also creates the potential for a number of communication problems to arise due to incompatibilities between the languages and terminologies used respectively by indexers, searchers, and users.

6.2.4 Indexing

An information retrieval system may be viewed as a memory where items are stored and then tagged for later retrieval. Retrieval of the items (documents) is initiated by

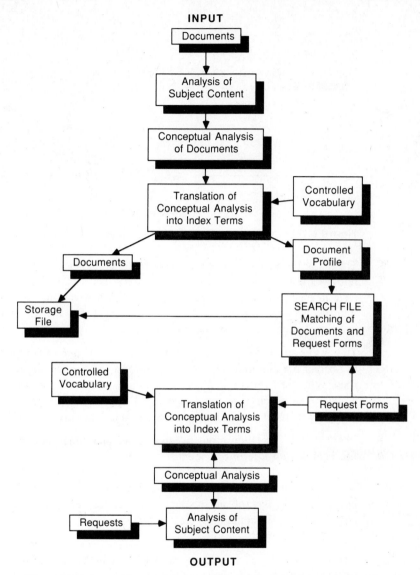

Figure 6.3 Process involved in the traditional model of information retrieval.

requests (queries) that specify the properties that the relevant (desired) items have. Ideally, the properties specified in the query will match the way that documents have been tagged (indexed) in the memory (database). Figure 6.4 (after Salton and McGill, Fig. 1.5, p.11) shows how these components of information retrieval systems are related. A distinction is generally made between author indexes, where the documents are indexed according to their author, and subject indexes where documents can be retrieved according to their subject matter.

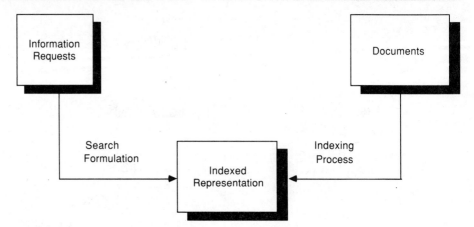

Figure 6.4 Relationships between the major components of an information retrieval system.

The major technical challenge in any retrieval process is to formulate a query that will retrieve the relevant documents. The success that a particular retrieval process will have in meeting this challenge will depend on the way that documents are indexed (the adequacy of the indexing and index language), and the way that the relevance of individual documents is assigned on the basis of a query.

The process of indexing creates an indexed file structure of the type discussed earlier in Chapter 2. In information science, indexed files are generally referred to as inverted files. When searching for information using an inverted file, the index is examined to determine which items satisfy the search request. Searching through the index will generally be much faster than searching through the original documents.

There is a close relationship between inverted and direct file structures. The inverted file begins with a term and identifies all the documents that are indexed with that term. In contrast, the direct files provide the index terms that are associated with each document. Thus inverted and direct files are just two different ways of examining the relationship between documents and index terms. The relationship between inverted and direct file structures is indicated in Figure 6.5 (after Salton and McGill, Fig. 1.12, p.20).

In the traditional model, indexing is seen as a classification process where documents are labeled according to the subjects that they cover or touch upon. This type of index is similar to the one seen in the back of most books, except that it is constructed out of a controlled vocabulary of terms that are chosen to cover the space of possible concepts without including overlapping terms and synonyms. The vocabulary is "controlled" since new terms are only added if they represent new concepts. Otherwise they are referred to the corresponding controlled vocabulary term.

The Dewey decimal system, published in 1876, was the first modern classification system. Other subject-based classification systems include the Universal Decimal Classification, the Library of Congress Classification, and Bliss' Bibliographic

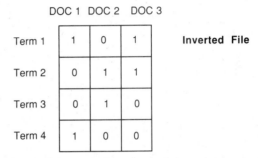

Figure 6.5 The relationship between inverted and direct files.

Classification. Some attempts have been made to develop script-like classification systems. For instance, Mills (1963) recommended putting index terms in the form of an ordered list of elements.

> Whole Thing – Kind – Part – Material – Properties – Processes – Operations – Agents

Using this approach, a document that discussed "stretch forming of welded stainless-steel pressure vessels" might produce the index entry

> Pressure Vessels, Welded, Stainless Steel, Stretch Forming

The central issue of indexing is always "can documents be retrieved effectively on the basis of their index entries?" A document that discusses "stretch forming of welded stainless-steel pressure vessels" should be retrieved both by queries on that specific topic and by more general queries such as "Stainless-steel welded pressure vessels."

6.2.4.1 *Manual Indexing*

The process of indexing documents may be carried out manually or automatically. Manual indexing is generally seen as being a difficult task and as a result database companies frequently apply rules to assist indexers and to enforce indexing consistency. In Chemical Abstracts Services, for instance, a "three or more rule" has been used in indexing chemical compounds. What this rule says is that if an article mentions three or more members of the same chemical family, then the name of that family is used in the index, rather than the original names of the substances. For instance, if an article mentioned mercury, cadmium, and lead, the term *heavy metals* would be used in the index since these three terms are all members of the family of elements that are generally referred to as heavy metals.

In general, there are a number of components of the manual indexing task, including

1. Choosing an authority list for names of relevant concepts.
2. Using rules to construct the names of complex subjects.
3. Scanning a document to determine which concepts (subjects) are referred to.
4. Using a variety of rules (some official, others unofficial) to control the use of the authority list in assigning index terms. These generally are used to reduce ambiguity and enforce consistency among indexers.

The model of indexing discussed above uses a precoordinated controlled-vocabulary indexing language. This means that the indexer has to rely on the existing controlled vocabulary and the rules that govern the assignment of index terms in particular contexts. These rules may be so specific that the indexer has to use the phrase "coal, production" rather than the alternate "production, coal."

It should be clear that manual indexing is an extremely difficult task. Not only must indexers read and comprehend many documents, but they must also remember the controlled vocabulary and the rules for assigning controlled vocabulary terms. Methods of assisting the manual indexer include hierarchical dictionaries and a variety of cross referencing systems and thesauri.

In principle, manual indexing can lead to detailed index entries that reflect the contents of the indexed documents. In practice, manual indexing is difficult, and the results can be disappointing, with the promise of strictly controlled indexing languages being only partially met. With extremely large databases, it is almost impossible to maintain complete consistency among different indexers. Even the same indexer may show inconsistent indexing practices over the course of time.

These considerations have led to the development of postcoordinated indexing terms where concepts are coordinated or linked together on the basis of their co-occurrence. Postcoordinated terms are sometimes used in automated indexing.

6.2.4.2 Automated Indexing

In view of the difficulties that can arise in manual indexing, it seems natural to consider how the labor-intensive manual indexing task might be automated in some way. Automated indexing is often based on statistical analysis of the words and phrases used in the text of documents. One method of automated indexing follows this statistical approach using the following steps:

1. Calculate the frequency of each unique term for each document in the database. The frequency of term k in document i is then denoted as

    $FREQ_{ik}$

2. Determine the total frequency of each word across all the documents in the database, that is

    $TOTFREQ_k$

3. Arrange the words in descending order according to their frequency in the database. Remove the high-frequency words.

4. Remove the low-frequency words. This removes terms that occur so infrequently that their absence from the index is unlikely to affect retrieval performance.

5. Use the remaining medium-frequency words as index terms for the database.

This basic method of automated indexing may be extended in a number of ways (Salton and McGill, 1983, chapter 3). Some of the methods involve cleaning up the set of terms to remove plurals and other words that have the same stem and differ only in the suffix. More complex methods examine the statistical co-occurrence of words and remove those that appear to be synonymous or overlapping. Automated methods of indexing can be combined with manual methods to form interactive methods of indexing. We shall consider methods of interactive indexing in the sections on text management later. Having discussed storage and indexing, we now turn to the other side of the information retrieval task—retrieval and search.

6.2.5 The Search Intermediary

Specialized expertise is usually required to understand the indexing policies employed in databases and to formulate search queries in the language of the database. Since most end users do not have this expertise, they require the aid of a search intermediary in carrying out a search. Librarians are typically the intermediaries between information providers and information seekers. They identify sources of information, selectively acquire some and develop systems for getting at the rest, organize materials and produce location tools, and assist users with the minor and major questions of their information needs.

The role of intermediary is most obvious at the library reference desk. There the user is taught and assisted with the library collection and the tools that fill reference rooms. Some of these tools have changed to electronic form—notably the online information services—as online databases and optical storage techniques such as CD-ROM become readily available. The use of online retrieval systems has removed the user further from direct access to needed information, increasing the importance of the intermediary role. With print tools, users always had the choice of circumventing the reference librarian and going directly to the source. Few occasional users can directly search an online database, however, because of the expertise required and the costs associated with inefficient and unsuccessful searches. Many users are forced to turn to an intermediary who takes charge of the process.

Most current systems are made for information retrieval specialists who are paid to know which database to search, how to develop a search strategy, and how to conduct the search. In the ideal situation, the client is an expert in his or her field, with a working knowledge of the pertinent information resources. The intermediary should have at least a working knowledge of the client's general field. In many cases though, the intermediary may not have a good working knowledge of the relevant search topic, particularly if it is highly technical or specialized. The process of query negotiation bridges the gap between the user's and the intermediary's understanding of the topic and is designed to transform the perceived information need into search commands that will be recognized by the database management system.

The major goal of the search intermediary is to choose the appropriate research tools (e.g., offline or online information, if online, which specific databases?) and to turn the user's information needs into concrete search terms. This initially requires gauging the user's expertise and the scope of the information need. The latter part of the task requires the skills of a translator, one who is less than intimately familiar with the language of the speaker and who is dependent upon a thesaurus to map the terminology of the user onto that of the database.

The role of the intermediary is multifaceted, as shown in Figure 6.6. The intermediary stands as an intelligent third entity between the user and the online retrieval system. In the terminology of information theory there are two communication channels in operation during an online search. The first communication channel is used by the end user and search intermediary in formulating search queries. The second channel is used by the search intermediary in interacting with the online database. Faulty communication in either of these channels will result in poor retrieval performance.

The demands of online text retrieval require that users and intermediaries be jointly knowledgeable about the processes of retrieving information as well as being knowledgeable about the content of the information itself.

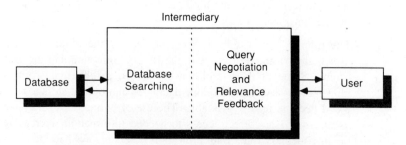

Figure 6.6 The role of the online search intermediary.

In order to conduct an effective bibliographic search, at least five broad classes of knowledge are necessary.

1. Procedural expertise in the use of computer systems is needed in order to initiate and sustain an effective pattern of communication with the retrieval system. In addition, a higher-level component of procedural expertise involves the user's developing an internal representation of user-system interaction, permitting successful prediction of system behavior under a variety of conditions. Ideally, an online retrieval system should require a minimum of procedural expertise since this is not directly relevant to the actual content of the retrieval task.

2. Domain knowledge, consisting of knowledge about the concepts, relationships among concepts, and terminology in the database domain is necessary. For example, knowledge of the database domain of environmental pollution encompasses such concepts as pollutants, affected organisms, geographic locations, methods for removal, media, and the effects of particular pollutants.

3. Strategies for query formulation, both general and database-specific, represent a substantial body of essential expertise. A vital component of the skilled searcher's expertise lies in a facility for combining logical operators with keywords. Indeed, expert searchers may demonstrate considerable skill in using such operators.

4. Knowledge of database-specific construction and indexing policies is also needed, and may have implications for deciding which search strategy is most promising in the context of the particular database.

5. Higher level search decisions appear to be a major part of search expertise. Hawkins and Wagers (1982) delineate four approaches to search, selection of the best method being contingent upon such aspects as the breadth of the initial search topic. Tradeoffs must be carefully weighed. For instance, the building block approach involves the formulation and execution of a separate search for each concept, with the results of each subsearch combined to yield a final document set. This logically constrained approach does not lend itself well to the exploration of unanticipated interesting paths (e.g., browsing). The best general search strategy frequently depends on characteristics of the particular database, such as indexing policies.

Although the search intermediary is an essential part of the current information retrieval paradigm, there are a number of problems associated with working through an intermediary.

1. The role of the intermediary is labor intensive and costly. As information retrieval technologies mature, the cost of the intermediary's services will become a larger proportion of the total cost of information retrieval.

2. Many who wish to conduct bibliographic searches have access to information retrieval systems via remote terminals, yet do not have ready access to skilled intermediaries.

3. Knowledgeable though they are, human search intermediaries cannot be expected to have complete knowledge of all domains contained within the available databases. Furthermore, simply due to uncertainty and ambiguity in the use of language, critical nuances of end-users' topics can be lost or distorted during interaction with the intermediary.

4. There is a trend toward full text databases without much indexing. Subject experts may be better able to search this less structured information than search intermediaries.

Aside from these objective reasons, users are motivated to interact directly with online retrieval systems because they like the feeling of direct access (no need to make appointments and work through an intermediary) and they like to have a feeling of control and direct involvement. Although some institutions subsidize the cost of online retrieval, cost is a factor for most users when choosing whether or not to use intermediaries. For instance, some systems are cheaper to use at night when intermediaries generally aren't available and this leads to dilemmas where the user trades off cheaper connect time at night against more efficient searching in the day.

The need for search intermediaries, in spite of the problems associated with mediated information retrieval, is indicative of inappropriate software interfaces for online retrieval. Consider the following query in the area of environmental pollution:

WASTE(W) (TREATMENT OR REMOVAL) AND
(PRECIPITATION OR PPTN) AND
(METHYLMERCURY OR CADMIUM)

This example demonstrates several problems with the use of Boolean search strings which is the predominant method of expressing online search queries at present. First, the user must anticipate the various synonyms and abbreviations that may have been used. For PRECIPITATION, this list might include PRECIPITATE, PPTN, and PPTG. Second, the user must be aware that a specific character string may have more than one meaning. Even in the limited domain of environmental pollution PRECIPITATION refers both to airborne water such as rain or snow and to a waste removal process. Third, in some databases such as the *Chemical Abstracts*, documents are indexed at only the most specific level. Therefore, users interested in a broader topic such as heavy metals must enter this term along with all terms naming specific heavy metals. Otherwise they will only retrieve documents specifically indexed under HEAVY METALS and not, for instance, those that are indexed under CADMIUM. These problems are compounded by the need to identify concepts in the form of Boolean statements.

There is consistent evidence that the formation and comprehension of logical expressions exceeds normal human information processing limitations for the population at large (Landauer et al., 1982; Wason and Johnson-Laird, 1972). Selection and placement of appropriate logical operators has been found to be difficult even for expert searchers (Oldroyd and Schroder, 1982). Effects of order and scope of activation of logical expressions, and use of negation have proven especially troublesome in the context of online retrieval systems. These findings indicate that effective unmediated online search should either provide user assistance in the construction of search queries, or else make the process transparent to the user. Thus there are compelling reasons to develop knowledge-based information retrieval systems that do not require the translation of concepts into Boolean logic. However, almost all large online databases currently require queries based on Boolean logic, and this situation is likely to persist for some time.

In summary, three main types of knowledge constitute search intermediary expertise, namely, Boolean search strategies, domain knowledge (of general chemistry), and database knowledge (including knowledge about search commands and the way in which the database is indexed). Review of the literature suggests that database knowledge may be the major factor in search efficiency. It is obvious that domain knowledge is important also, but as a means of organizing the database knowledge rather than knowledge which has to be learned for its own sake. There are many things that a search intermediary could know about chemistry, for instance, but only knowledge which assists in accessing information within the database will be effective in improving search performance.

6.2.6 Query Formulation

Information retrieval is at some point a process where the information needs of the user are compared with the information that is available. This has led to the matching paradigm of information retrieval (Bates 1986) where the information need is represented as a query, and the potential information (i.e. documents) is represented as a collection of index terms which can be matched against the query. Those documents whose index representations most closely match the query are then assumed to be relevant and their citations are passed to the user. The matching process can either be deterministic or else based on some metric of distance or similarity (e.g., Salton and McGill, 1983, chapter 4).

In deterministic matching, a Boolean search string is typically constructed and documents are retrieved only if they match precisely the constraints expressed in the query. Thus, if the query is expressed as:

> recycling and water pollution

then only articles which refer to both these terms will be retrieved. On the other hand, if the query had been expressed as:

> recycling or water pollution

then the same set of articles would be retrieved, plus those articles which mentioned one of the two terms but not the other. If the user wanted articles that refer to either recycling or water pollution, but not to both terms (an exclusive or), then the query could be expressed as:

recycling and not water pollution or water pollution and not recycling

or perhaps more clearly:

(recycling or water pollution) and not (recycling and water pollution)

This brief example illustrates the use of the three main Boolean operators—and, or, not. It turns out that most people find it difficult to express concepts in terms of strings of words and Boolean operators (e.g., Borgman, 1986). For instance, people often confuse the meaning of the operator OR with AND, treating AND as if it were an inclusive OR. Thus a major part of the expertise of search intermediaries has involved the careful construction of Boolean queries to represent specific search concepts.

A second approach to the matching paradigm is to develop representations of the query and document space that allow measures of similarity to be calculated between queries and documents. This allows documents to be sorted according to their similarity or relevance to the query. The advantage of this approach is that it allows sophisticated methods of relevance feedback to be used (see Section 5.2.5). However, the widespread adoptance of similarity-based matching is hampered by disagreements over how similarity measures should be constructed and how large databases should be indexed so that similarity matching is even possible. In spite of these difficulties, query formulation and evaluation based on similarity matching is intuitively appealing because of the large role that concepts of similarity appear to play in human concept formation and memory (e.g., Gregson, 1975).

The second paradigm of query formulation and evaluation involves exploration instead of matching (Belkin and Vickery, 1985). In this paradigm the user explores the information more directly and picks out what seems to be appropriate. This paradigm is becoming more popular as hypertext systems proliferate. Ideally, the matching and exploration paradigms of information retrieval can be combined within intelligent databases to allow both browsing and the utilization of structured queries. The difference between these two paradigms is characterized in Figure 6.7.

There is also a third paradigm of information retrieval that has so far been tested only on small experimental databases. This third paradigm is generally referred to as conceptual retrieval (Kolodner, 1983; Chignell, 1984). Here the user expresses the information need as a concept rather than as a collection of keywords connected by logical operators. Thus conceptual retrieval is a type of sophisticated matching paradigm. Examples of conceptual queries are:

Give me documents about the poisoning of fish in Lake Erie

Give me articles about meetings between Mrs. Vance and Mrs. Begin during the Camp David peace negotiations

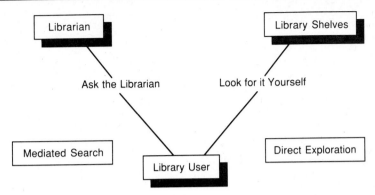

Figure 6.7 Two paradigms for information retrieval.

In conceptual retrieval, the system tends to retrieve documents on the basis of inferences about concepts that they may contain even if these concepts are not explicitly indexed in the form of the original query. Thus conceptual retrieval represents a major step in the direction toward question answering systems (Lehnert, 1979) and the retrieval of information per se rather than of documents that contain information. We see conceptual retrieval as an evolving technology that will also merge with intelligent databases.

6.2.7 Relevance Feedback

Information retrieval was originally conceived of as a batch process where one submitted a query, reviewed the results obtained with that query, and then constructed a new query. Since the process of constructing queries is fairly difficult, it makes sense to consider how the old query can be refined based on the judged relevance of the documents obtained with it. This idea is the basis of relevance feedback. Relevance feedback is based on a scoring algorithm where the weights associated with terms that appear in relevant documents are increased, while terms that appear more often in irrelevant documents are either removed from the query or have their importance weights reduced.

Thus relevance feedback involves an iterative search process where search queries are progressively refined based on feedback from the database. We shall now outline two forms of relevance feedback, one simple, the other more complex. A simple form of relevance feedback is to examine the documents obtained through a query, choose those that are relevant based on the titles and/or abstracts, and then add the index terms that are associated with the relevant documents to the search query, removing those terms that do not generally appear in the relevant documents. However, this informal relevance feedback method places a great burden on the user or intermediary as they try to assess the effectiveness of individual index terms manually.

A more complex, but easier to use, alternative is to develop an automated relevance feedback system, such as that used in the SMART system (cited in Salton and McGill, 1983, chapter 4). The operation of this relevance feedback system is illustrated in

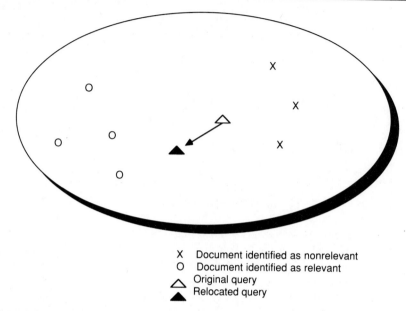

X   Document identified as nonrelevant
O   Document identified as relevant
△   Original query
▲   Relocated query

Figure 6.8 An illustration of using relevance feedback to relocate the query within the document space.

Figures 6.8 and 6.9. In this system the relevance of each term in the query is assigned a weight which is adjusted according to the judged relevance of the documents retrieved using the query. This adjustment is made using equation 1 (shown in Figure 6.9). In this expression, an updated query is specified as the vector sum of the old query plus the weighted difference between the average of the relevant items and the average of the nonrelevant terms. Alpha, beta, and gamma are constants that are determined empirically so as to produce satisfactory relevance feedback performance. Q is the original query vector. DOC(i) represents the vector of term weights for a particular document. The term weights for each document are assigned according to the weight, or importance of each term in the document. This obviously requires an additional step in the indexing process since most indexing only considers the presence or absence of terms in documents, not their relative importance as used in the document. Furthermore, the vector DOC(i) represents all the terms in the database, whether or not they appear in the documents currently retrieved.

The assignment of documents into the relevant or nonrelevant categories is made by the user. The effect of the second term on the right-hand side of equation 1 is to add terms to the set of relevant terms or increase the weights of terms already judged to be relevant, while the effect of the third term is to remove terms from the list of relevant terms or at least reduce their weight. Experience suggests (Salton and McGill, pp. 143–144) that the information contained in the relevant documents is more valuable for query reformulation purposes than the terms which originate in the nonrelevant terms. Thus Salton and McGill suggest that gamma be assigned a smaller weight than beta in equation 1.

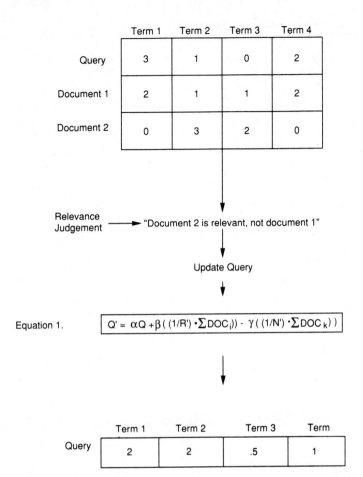

	Term 1	Term 2	Term 3	Term 4
Query	3	1	0	2
Document 1	2	1	1	2
Document 2	0	3	2	0

Relevance Judgement $\longrightarrow$ "Document 2 is relevant, not document 1"

Update Query

Equation 1.
$$Q' = \alpha Q + \beta\left(\left(1/R'\right)\cdot\sum DOC_j\right)) - \gamma\left(\left(1/N'\right)\cdot\sum DOC_k\right))$$

	Term 1	Term 2	Term 3	Term
Query	2	2	.5	1

Figure 6.9 The relevance feedback process for a retrieval system where queries are expressed as weighted terms. The subscript i in equation 1 denotes the R' documents judged to be relevant while the subscript k denotes the N' documents judged to be nonrelevant.

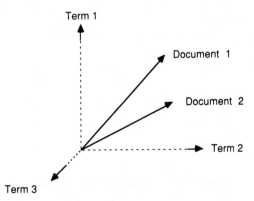

Figure 6.10 Vector space representation of documents showing three dimensions (one for each of 3 terms).

In the SMART system, documents are represented as vectors in a space defined by the weights of the terms assigned to them as illustrated in Figure 6.10 (after Salton and McGill, Fig. 4-2). The effect of relevance feedback is illustrated in Figure 6.11. Figure 6.11 shows a two-dimensional space corresponding to only two terms. In practice, the document space has high dimensionality which is not easily represented on the printed page. In the SMART system, the query is a vector (or position) in the space. The relevance of documents is then judged according to their distance from the query vector. The process of relevance feedback in this model corresponds to shifting the query vector so that it is closer to the centroid of the cluster defined by the relevant document vectors, as illustrated in Figure 6.11.

The SMART system for online information retrieval and query reformulation is intriguing, but it has yet to achieve widespread use. Part of this may stem from the additional indexing effort that it requires. Other problems arise from the need

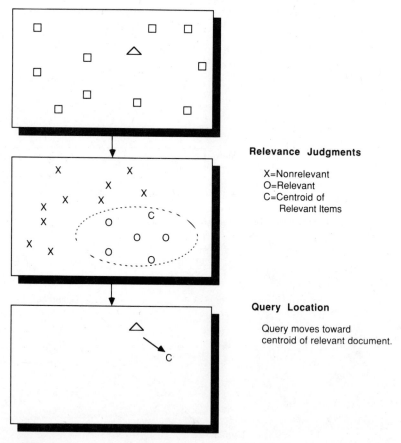

Relevance Judgments

X=Nonrelevant
O=Relevant
C=Centroid of
    Relevant Items

Query Location

Query moves toward
centroid of relevant document.

Figure 6.11 Moving the query towards the relevant documents. The amount of movement depends on the values of α, β, and γ used in equation 1 (Figure 6.9).

to perform a large number of numeric computations during each search. This has probably deterred owners of large databases from experimenting with the system.

■ 6.3 EVALUATING RETRIEVAL PERFORMANCE

In conventional systems, the onus for intelligent behavior is on the search intermediary. Even human experts, though, may not provide adequate retrieval performance as the information in the database increases in size and complexity. The inability of humans to remember and retain in working memory large amounts of information is well known (e.g., Miller, 1956; Peterson & Peterson, 1959). This is a severe constraint on a search intermediary who must monitor the progress of the search, while updating her model of the user's information need (demands on working memory) and remembering the command language and terminology of the database (long-term memory requirement). Research on expert decision making in experimental psychology has also shown that experts are inconsistent in the application of their knowledge and are often outperformed by simple (but consistent) models of their behavior (Dawes, 1979). The highly structured nature of current information retrieval systems, in contrast, demands more, rather than less, consistency from the search intermediary.

Factors which may affect search performance include

> the setting
> the user
> the request
> the database
> the search system
> the search process
> the searcher
> the search outcome

The effect of expertise on search performance has been evaluated using several objective measures. Fenichel (1980) reviewed a number of these studies and concluded that beginning subjects performed surprisingly well in comparison to experts. Howard (1982) compared the search performance of subjects at five distinguishable levels of experience using two search problems (one straightforward and one difficult problem). Her results showed very little difference (on a simple search task) in the search performance of moderately and very experienced searchers. The experts did, however, show marked superiority in the more difficult problem.

Traditionally, retrieval performance has been assessed using two measures, namely recall and precision. These measures are typically based on subjective judgments of relevance made by users as they inspect document citations and abstracts. We add a third evaluation criterion here which is somewhat more demanding, (i.e., utilization).

Utilization can be thought of as the number of documents obtained in the search that were actually used by the user.

Recall and precision may be defined as follows:

> Recall - the proportion of relevant documents in the database that were actually retrieved

> Precision - the proportion of documents that were relevant within the set that was retrieved

Study of the literature on online searching suggested that expert search intermediaries do not always perform significantly better than moderately experienced searchers. Recall for searchers in general seemed particularly poor, with only about a quarter of the relevant documents being retrieved on average. As an example of this, one of the authors carried out two searches with an expert searcher interacting with an expert user at Chemical Abstracts Services to determine the level of performance that can be expected under optimal conditions. Search 1 was a time-consuming search which required a lot of knowledge about CAS Online (including how to conduct substructure searches) and the chemistry of sugars. The results, as assessed by the user (a post-doctoral research chemist), were disappointing. Estimated precision for the search was 11% and estimated recall was 10%. Search 2 was a fast and relatively simple search which produced much better results (27% precision and 80% recall). These results raise questions about the role of expertise in searching. Analysis of the search protocols showed that the search expert used a considerable amount of knowledge about the database and the way that substances are represented within the database. The first search was largely unsuccessful because the searcher did not pursue a major component of the search (biosynthesis) which she felt to be outside her area of expertise. These results suggested that database knowledge was extremely important in difficult searches, but that any one expert would have detailed knowledge about only a small portion of the contents of the database. They pointed out a need for exhaustive knowledge of the contents of the database in order to achieve good retrieval performance.

6.3.1   Recall

As mentioned earlier, recall is the ratio between the number of relevant documents that were retrieved by the user and the number of relevant documents that actually exist in the database. Recall (and precision) will vary between 0 and 1 when expressed as a fraction, but it is more usually presented as a percentage. If there were 100 relevant documents in the database and we retrieved 35 documents that were deemed to be relevant, then the measured recall would be 35 percent, for instance.

Recall is more difficult to estimate than precision because the total number of documents relevant to a particular search (and available in the database) is usually unknown. In assessing recall, an alternative to exhaustive enumeration of documents within the database is to use the union of outputs method (Howard, 1982), where one counts all the unique relevant references retrieved by the searchers. This method will grossly underestimate the true number of relevant documents in many cases. In the studies that Fenichel (1980) reviewed, recall varied between 41 and 61% whilst precision varied between 17 and 81%. Wanger, McDonald, and Berger (1980) calculated average recall and precision on the basis of 535 searches and obtained average values of 23% and 67% respectively. These estimates of recall and precision in online searching can be considered as upper bounds on the true values and it seems fair to conclude that there is room for improvement in the performance of search intermediaries.

6.3.2 Precision

The precision of a search is defined as the ratio (percentage) between the number of relevant documents that were retrieved and the total number of documents (relevant or irrelevant) that were retrieved. Say that we had retrieved 70 documents in our search of which 50 (as indicated above) were judged to be relevant. In that case we would have obtained 35 percent precision.

Precision is important in an intelligent database because users do not want to be distracted by irrelevant information. As far as possible, the system should be able to narrow down information and selection choices to what is relevant, given the skills, background, and experience of the user and the nature of the task that is being performed. For text databases, methods for increasing precision have generally included using more specific index terms (such as "lead" instead of "heavy metals") and combining index terms into more specific concepts using the operator AND. The use of the operator NOT to rule out unwanted information has also been recommended elsewhere, but in practice it is often difficult to frame a search query using NOT in such a way that it rules out irrelevant information without removing relevant information as well.

We may distinguish between methods that increase precision during browsing and methods that increase precision during structured search. In browsing, increasing precision generally involves filtering the associative links that emanate from each information node according to the current context. In searching, precision involves modifying the algorithm for calculating the relevance of information nodes or documents. This distinction between precision in browsing and precision in searching is illustrated in Figure 6.12.

6.3.3 Utilization

Recall and precision are useful measures of retrieval effectiveness, but they don't directly address the bottom line, i.e., what did the user get out of the search? After all, a supposedly relevant document is no good to the user if he makes no use of it. Thus utilization measures of retrieval effectiveness look at the combination of retrieval system and user, since it is up to users to make use of the information once it has been provided to them by the information retrieval system.

Utilization can be defined in a number of different ways such as

Precision in Browsing

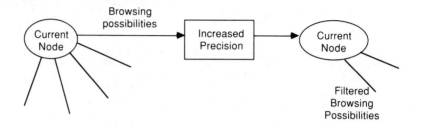

Precision in Searching

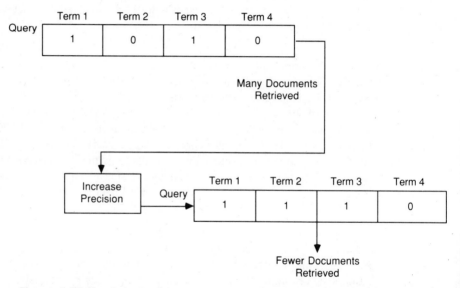

Figure 6.12 The distinction between precision in browsing and precision in searching.

How many documents were read?

How many documents were later cited in papers and reports?

How many documents were filed in hard copy version?

If asked, how many of the documents obtained in the search could the user remember seeing after a gap of one week, one month, etc?

The effectiveness of retrieval systems is a controversial topic. Our own experience has been that both precision and recall fall well short of perfection (100 percent) with measures of recall generally being lower than corresponding measures of precision for most searches. We expect that measures of utilization will be even lower.

■ 6.4 TEXT MANAGEMENT

While conventional information retrieval systems have received a great deal of attention and use, they are likely to benefit from a knowledge-based approach, like many other complex software systems. Ideally, an information retrieval system should function as knowledge expert and search intermediary in addition to carrying out the storage and retrieval of information. Such a system would be knowledge-based, drawing on domain-specific knowledge (e.g., about environmental chemistry) and on knowledge about search strategies such as using one relevant document to identify the index terms which can be used to find other relevant documents (pearl growing). In this section we consider some techniques of knowledge-based retrieval that utilize text interpretation and management.

6.4.1 Text Management vs. Information Retrieval

Information retrieval as currently practiced is an interaction between an active human and a passive database. The database has the information, but to get it, the user has to ask the right questions. As a result, information retrieval is a complex communication process. Figure 6.6 showed a schematic representation of this process. There are two communication channels, one between the user and the intermediary, and the other between the intermediary and the database. Each of these two communication channels has two associated directions of information flow. The four combinations of channel and direction of information flow represent four tasks, each of which is critical for good retrieval performance. The first two of these tasks constitute question negotiation.

1. The intermediary should understand the query.
2. The intermediary should ask the user intelligent questions which can lead to refinement of the initial query.

The third and fourth tasks are concerned with accessing information from the database on the basis of the query.

3. The intermediary translates the query into search commands in the language of the online search system.
4. The overall retrieval system should ensure that the intermediary receives good responses to the search query and understands those responses.

In conventional systems, the fourth task is largely ignored, since the output of the search query is a set of documents that is completely determined by the form of the search query. In a more flexible system for text management and retrieval, however, this task becomes critically important, as the database (assuming that it has intelligence) may pass back to the intermediary a variety of information relating to the availability of various types of knowledge, rather than simply listing the citations of documents that may be relevant. The database may also modify the query based on the knowledge actually available in the database. Thus, in a text management system much of the distinction between intermediary and database breaks down, and there is a migration of intelligence from the intermediary toward knowledge structures in the database.

The tendency for previous research in information science has been toward developing data structures that improve information accessibility, provided that the searcher utilizes a highly constrained vocabulary correctly. Improved performance is obtained by simplifying the task, using controlled vocabularies, well-defined query languages, and explicit organization (by categories) of the terms in the vocabulary (Thompson, 1971). Another approach is to increase the accessibility of database information by using a relational database formalism (discussed in Chapter 2). Relational databases provide a consistent data representation as well as powerful operators for accessing information. A third approach emphasizes flexibility in the processing of search terms. Clustering of the database records (Salton & McGill, 1983) combined with techniques such as relevance feedback allows flexible responses to the user's input query, but this approach is not yet feasible with large databases because of the nonlinear (accelerating) relationship between number of objects and clustering time (e.g., Everitt, 1974). The ideal approach may be to allow natural language queries while allowing constraints existing in the database to develop an unambiguous interpretation of the natural language input (Kolodner, 1983; Dyer, 1983; DeJong, 1979). Once again, however, processing time increases disproportionately with depth of understanding, and approximate natural language understanding has been demonstrated only in restricted contexts.

6.4.2 The Role of Knowledge

Cognitive psychology and artificial intelligence both stress the central role of knowledge in expertise. In some senses, developing systems for text retrieval should be made easier by the large amounts of information in databases. The challenge for the knowledge engineer is that of determining how to transform that information into usable knowledge. The information in current databases consists of facts about documents (e.g., keywords) which are relatively unstructured. Structure (organization) is required to transform the information into knowledge (Tou, 1980). The advantage provided by the extensive amount of information in a database is counterbalanced by the complexity and variety of that information.

In a large database such as CAS Online, for instance, there are well over 10 million document representatives, many of which cover highly technical topics. In order to constrain the problem, we might focus on a manageable subportion of the database, environmental chemistry. Even with this constraint, the knowledge required to understand a topic such as environmental chemistry to the degree of understanding of a retrieval expert is considerable. Necessary technical knowledge includes the interaction of pollutants with environmental media, the formation of pollutants in industrial processes, and the chemistry of polluting substances. The representation of substance information is a particularly difficult problem. Substances are the backbone of chemistry and they also create special problems for information retrieval. There is no single widely accepted classification of chemical compounds. One compound might be seen as an alkaloid or an amide, depending on the context, while another might be both a polymer and an ether. Here again, however, we can use local context to constrain ambiguity. The set of pollutants is smaller and more easily classified than the set of substances. In a global context, the term 'mercury' might refer to a planet, a useful component of thermometers, barometers and amalgams, or a toxic pollutant. In the context of environmental chemistry, though, any mention of mercury is likely to refer to its role as a pollutant.

6.4.3 Concept Indexing in Text Management

Much of the work on database systems (e.g., Ullmann, 1982) and in artificial intelligence (e.g., Brachman, 1977, 1979) emphasizes the importance of representing knowledge in a form that is compatible with intelligent behavior. It is not the language in which the knowledge is stored that is of concern (such as predicate calculus, production rules, frames and conceptual dependencies), but rather the operations that can be carried out on the knowledge structures.

In the case of CAS Online, the document representatives contain information which has already been processed by expert indexers. Figure 6.13 shows how a document is represented within that database. An abstract, keywords, and index terms are available, as well as the bibliographic information. The index terms are of particular interest. They consist of a controlled vocabulary term (such as Candida albicans) plus an associated uncontrolled text modification. The index terms represent propositional statements about the knowledge contained in a document. The first index term in Figure 6.13, for instance, can be translated as:

> germ-tube formation induction in Candida albicans by immobilized acetylglucosamine.

This knowledge will be accessible directly if it can be parsed into appropriate data structures. In the case of the CAS Online index terms, there is sufficient syntactic consistency for a pattern-matching parsing process (Winograd, 1983) to work. The index terms can be translated into frames within a relational database. These frames represent a convenient compromise between keyword and natural language understanding approaches, constraining the knowledge representation so that useful knowledge is accessible, but at a reasonable processing cost.

The creation of a relational database will not of itself guarantee the accessibility of knowledge/information. Some means of translating the user's query into a form that is recognizable by the database is required. This translation requires an appropriate reorganization of the knowledge within the relational database. This reorganization should be capable of conveying relationships between, and classifications of, the terms in the relational database. The formation of a hierarchy is a useful way of achieving the desired reorganization.

CAS ONLINE®

SEARCH RESULTS - P314020D 10 NOV 83 12:12:18 PAGE 7

ANSWER 4

AN CA98(25):212685a

TI Candida albicans germ-tube formation with immobilized GlcNAc

AU Shepherd, Maxwell G.; Sullivan, Patrick A.

CS Sch. Dent., Univ. Otago

LO Dunedin, N. Z.

SO FEMS Microbiol. Lett., 17(1-2-3), 167-70

SC 10-3 (Microbial Biochemistry)

DT J

CO FMLED7

IS 0378-1097

PY 1983

LA Eng

AB Whereas glucose was ineffective, *N*-acetylglucosamine (GlcNAc) stimulated germ-tube formation by *C. albicans*. Similarly, agarose-GlcNAc induced germ-tube formation in high yields when the cells were provided with an exogenous C source. An examn. of the agarose-GlcNAc before and after germ-tube formation showed that the covalently bound GlcNAc was not removed during incubation of the cells. 2-Deoxyglucose (dGlc) at 10 mM did not affect the growth rate of yeast cultures in minimal media with either glucose or GlcNAc as C source at 28 or 37°. Low concns. (50 μM), however, completely inhibited germ-tube formation. Incubation of yeast cells at 28° for 2 h with GlcNAc induced the uptake system and enzymes for GlcNAc metab. A subsequent temp. shift from 28 to 32° produced germ tubes after 3 h. The addn. of dGlc to the 28° phase of the incubation abolished germ-tube formation, but dGlc added only to the 37° phase had no effect on morphogenesis.

KW acetylglucosamine germ tube formation Candida; development Candida morphogenesis

IT Candida albicans
(germ-tube formation induction in, by immobilized acetylglucosamine)

IT Microorganism development
(morphogenesis, of *Candida albicans*, germ-tube formation induction by immobilized acetylglucosamine in relation to)

IT 9012-36-6
(acetylglucosamine immobilized on, germ-tube formation stimulation by, in *Candida albicans*)

IT 154-17-6
(germ-tube formation stimulation by acetylglucosamine inhibition by, in *Candida albicans*)

IT 7512-17-6
(germ-tube formation stimulation by immobilized, in *Candida albicans*)

****

Figure 6.13 An indexed document, as represented in CAS ONLINE.

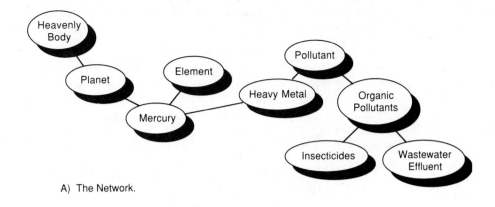

A) The Network.

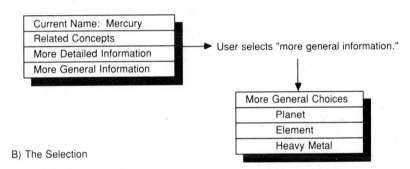

B) The Selection

Figure 6.14 A method for switching between hierarchical perspectives.

The use of hierarchies in this way might seem restrictive, and it may be effectively argued that many concepts will actually appear in a number of different hierarchies, depending on the organization perspective. Thus a hovercraft, for instance, may appear as an element in one hierarchy of land vehicles, and then appear in a completely different context in respective hierarchies of amphibious craft, air-cushioned devices, sea vehicles, and so on. The solution to this problem is to recognize that one does not have to rely on a single hierarchical organization, and that many different hierarchical organizations may be overlaid on top of a complex network structure such as the type of hypermedia document that was considered in Chapter 5. Figure 6.14 illustrates one method for switching between hierarchical perspectives. Here the user has reached a node that is embedded within a number of different hierarchies. The user is given the choice of moving to related concepts, exploring more detailed versions of the current concept, or moving to more general versions of the concept (i.e. moving higher up the hierarchy). If the user chooses to move to a more general concept, the selections of the menu indicate the different parents available in the different hierarchical organizations that the current concept (node) is embedded in.

6.4.3.1 Concept Indexing with Frame Hierarchies

A concept hierarchy can be constructed in a number of ways. One method is to ask a set of subject experts to sort the collection of terms into a hierarchy directly. The terms themselves may generally be obtained from standard reference sources. The hierarchy can then be updated and expanded interactively with the assistance of the human experts. Statistical techniques and machine learning methods may also be used to form or update the hierarchy.

The previous paragraphs described methods of automated indexing where the vocabulary of index terms was constructed based on statistical frequencies and co-occurrences of words in the database. An alternative method is to decide beforehand what the key concepts are and then find ways of recognizing them in text. This is a difficult problem in text analysis, but it is not equivalent to the well known complexity of natural language understanding since the system is only looking for clues in the text to indicate the presence of general concepts, that is, a detailed interpretation of the meaning of the text is not required.

This type of concept indexing requires a representation of the knowledge domain much as is typically seen in an expert system. Thus many of the concepts that would be of use in indexing a database on environmental pollution, for instance, may also belong in the knowledge base of an expert system dealing with the domain of environmental pollution.

Ideally, the knowledge base of the indexer should represent knowledge in a form which is as complete, rich, and readily-searched as that of the human domain expert. In turn, the indexed concepts should be represented in a form that allows easy access during querying. One form of representation which meets this requirement is the frame hierarchy. To illustrate, consider the partial concept hierarchies shown in Figure 6.15.

Each node of the hierarchy is a particular instance of the concept which labels the entire structure. Each subordinate node is a more specific instance, and each super-ordinate node a more general instance. By implementing each node as a frame, properties of each instance can be stored locally with that instance, and can also be propagated down the hierarchy to the successors. Most importantly, critical semantic relationships among instances are preserved, and can be used to structure search.

Frames contain slots that can be filled with specific instances or data. In general, one of these slots (attributes) will point to a superordinate category (frame) to which the current frame belongs, while other slots will point to subordinate frames which are specialized instances of the current frame. These special slots (known variously as isa or ako - "a kind of," instance, parent, and child slots) allow one to define categories and subcategories of frames within a frame hierarchy. In addition, some attached procedures will act as relations, specifying how the attributes (slots) of one frame will be affected by the values of slots in one or more other frames (objects).

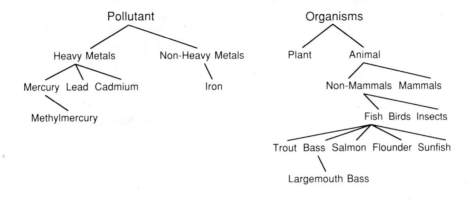

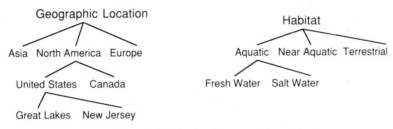

Figure 6.15 Partial concept hierarchies.

In Figure 6.15, heavy metals is a subordinate of the *pollutant* frame. An attached procedure in this example could assess the toxicity of a particular compound based on the heavy metals it contains and the solubility of the compound.

If we use the following syntactic structure for frames:

```
'Frame Name'
    'slot1'    'filler1'
    'slot2'    'filler2'
    . . .
    'slotn'    'fillern'
```

then the frame representation of a document in environmental pollution might look like

```
Document N
        Pollutant:   Cadmium
        Location:    Great Lakes
        Organism:    Large-mouthed Bass
```

In addition to the filler containing the value of a slot, there may be separate information referring to attached procedures. The alternative pieces of information that can be placed within the slot of a frame are usually referred to as facets. Another facet may contain an if-added procedure. Such a procedure would contain the name of a rule telling the system what to do if information has been added to a slot. Activating the mercury concept frame, for instance, may *trigger* a rule which checks that the term "mercury" is in fact referring to a heavy metal in the context of environmental pollution.

We may now utilize the inheritance property of the hierarchy where the objects tend to form groups where members within the group tend to share common properties. In environmental pollution, for instance, we know that cadmium is a type of heavy metal, which in turn is a type of metal. Thus we expect cadmium to retain all the basic properties of metals and heavy metals, but with further restrictions. We can make assumptions about some of the characteristics that cadmium has based on our knowledge about heavy metals in general. Thus, if we don't have any information to the contrary we might assume that cadmium is a toxic substance since heavy metals in general are toxic. This type of assumption is made possible by using *inherited* information.

The combination of frames, attached procedures, and inheritance allows one to develop a flexible strategy for building a concept-based indexing system. The chief advantage of frames is that they are a sufficiently flexible data structure so as to meet a variety of demands. One way of expressing necessary properties that a frame must possess to be an instance of a concept is to create an attached procedure which polices the requirement. Thus we might mandate that non-aquatic birds should not be considered as target organisms when retrieving information about the topic of water pollution. This requirement can be policed by attaching appropriate procedures which check the validity of each new instance.

The preservation of semantic relationships within frames eliminates some of the difficulties that arise in the course of interacting with traditional online retrieval systems. For instance, instead of having to recall all species of fish to increase recall, a knowledge-based system using concept hierarchies can use semantic relationships between concepts to infer that the user is interested not only in fish, but in all species of fish as well, and add documents discussing them to the active list.

Other information besides properties of particular instances can be stored in each frame within the hierarchy. Each node is an index term. Synonyms may also be stored locally at each hierarchy node. For example the term "quicksilver" could activate the <u>MERCURY</u> node in the pollutant hierarchy in Figure 6.15. This property can help to resolve the problem of synonymy where the same concept can be expressed using a number of different words or phrases.

6.4.3.2 *Interactive Concept Indexing*

One of the arguments against concept indexing in text management is that it is too laborious to be carried out for more than a few documents. Handcrafted concept indexes exacerbate the difficulty of the indexing task that is already labor-intensive and expensive. Current methods of natural language and discourse understanding do not yet permit fully automated and reliable concept indexing. Thus the best solution

	Manual Indexing	Interactive Indexing	Automated Indexing
Human	1. Read Documents 2. Assign Terms	3. Assist with "difficult" Indexing 4. Monitor and Edit Indexing	No Human Tasks
Machine	No Machine Tasks	1. Parse Document 2. Assign Terms	1. Parse Document 2. Assign Terms

Figure 6.16 The three approaches to indexing.

may be an interactive form of concept indexing that balances the need for efficiency with the need for human supervision of the text analysis and concept indexing process.

Typically, automatic indexing will be more consistent than manual indexing, but complex and context-sensitive concepts will be handled better by human indexers. Thus, interactive indexing represents a compromise (Figure 6.16) which is faster and more efficient than manual indexing while being more flexible and context sensitive than automated indexing. Given the state of current technology it seems reasonable to provide the best of both types of indexing in an interactive indexing environment. We outline below two methods of interactive indexing that have been used with some success.

Figure 6.13 shows a typical indexed document in the CAS Online database. The last five entries prefaced by the letters "IT" are known as index terms. Chignell (1984) developed a method for converting these index terms into concept frames for a very limited context (874 documents on environmental pollution). The basic method used is summarized in Figure 6.17. First the relevant index term was identified (step 1). Then, using syntactic analysis, the index term was parsed into one of a set of generic templates (step 2). The concepts in each of the slots in the templates were then recognized and a corresponding frame representation was built for the document (steps 3 and 4). The method worked quite well, but it required assistance from a human expert from time to time in the re-indexing process. Nevertheless, the method was capable of re-indexing 874 documents in terms of concept frames in just a few hours.

More recently, interactive indexing has been used at the National Library of Medicine, based on a frame representation of document concepts (Humphrey, 1987). The Indexing Aid System is a system for interactive knowledge-based indexing of the medical literature developed by the National Library of Medicine. The capabilities of the system include inheritance, enforcement of restrictions and other functions that are implemented by procedural attachments, implemented as part of a frame system.

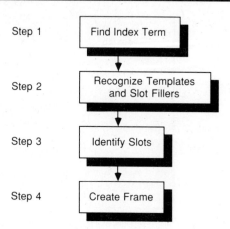

Figure 6.17 A method for converting index terms to concept frames within a limited context.

The prototype Indexing Aid System operates by prompting the indexer for indexing terms which fall into general categories such as *Disease Process* and *Procedure*. The system works by guiding indexers through a network of categories and relations in the medical domain. The eventual goals of the project are to produce, for each document in the database, a set of knowledge-based document-specific frames known as indexing frames which are linked as instances to a knowledge base of frames representing general domain knowledge. Humphrey (1987) described the techniques used by the system in more detail, but the essential point to note here is that the type of interactive indexing that should eventually be possible with the Indexing Aid System produces the same type of concept (frame based) indexing that is required by knowledge-based information retrieval systems.

Projects such as the two described above give us confidence that knowledge-based search intermediaries are viable for small databases of a few thousand documents or less. But what about huge databases which reside on mainframe computers? The solution may be to make a clear distinction between large global text databases and smaller subsets of those databases that are processed locally. Thus conventional retrieval methods may be used to identify a set (neighborhood) of a few thousand possibly relevant documents. Then, instead of using standard relevance feedback techniques to refine the query and increase precision, the group of documents is passed to a text management system which then builds a concept index for that domain. This conceptually indexed neighborhood of documents may then be maintained and updated for future use.

In general, we can distinguish between four different modes of interactive indexing depending on the type of relationship that exists between the human and machine indexers

1. Human indexer cleans up the result of automated indexing.
2. Machine cleans up the work of the human indexer.
3. Machine becomes a help tool and advisor for the human indexer.
4. Human becomes an advisor, teacher, and technical consultant for the machine indexer.

The system described in Section 6.4.4 is an example of the first type of relationship, where the human indexer cleans up the result of an automated indexing process. The system developed at the National Library of Medicine falls into the third category where the machine acts as a help tool for the human indexer.

6.4.4 Text Interpretation

In this section we describe a relatively simple system for interpreting text as a frame system representation of index terms linked to a relational database. There are a number of basic principles which motivate the development of this system.

1. The information within a text database should be translated into usable knowledge. This may be partially achieved by converting document representatives into a relational database.
2. Capitalize on structure within the database to allow syntactic parsing of the information. (This syntactic parsing enables the system to extract knowledge from the database as well as from human experts.)
3. Hierarchical organization of knowledge constrains the combinatorial explosion of search possibilities within a database. This is an important issue since search through a relational database becomes difficult when there is a poor match between the vocabulary of the user and the vocabulary of the relational database (unless one restricts the vocabulary of the user).
4. Keyword phrases can be used as triggers for accessing a well-organized knowledge structure.
5. A text analysis and interpretation system should be able to learn from its interactions with users.

At present, text management systems are necessarily domain-dependent since they rely on contextual constraints to interpret queries. The text interpretation system described below is used here to illustrate some of the issues that arise in building knowledge based retrieval systems. The system was originally implemented as a frame system using a frame representation language (FRL, Roberts & Goldstein, 1977) operating within a LISP environment (ELISP) on a DEC20 host and resulted from research carried out at Ohio State University with the support of Chemical Abstracts Services.

The success of a text interpretation system depends largely on the power of its data structures and associated operators to store and utilize knowledge. Four major types of

A.   (Water pollution by heavy metals from abandoned mines, fish and invertebrates in relation to, of rivers Cain and Mawdach and Wen in Wales)

B.   (Mercury Cadmium Lead)

Figure 6.18 Lists representing (a) document information, and (b) heavy metals.

data structure that may be used are lists, frames, relational databases, and hierarchies. A list is a collection of ordered terms, which may themselves be lists or individual terms (referred to as atoms in the LISP programming language). Examples of lists are shown in Figure 6.18. The first list represents some of the information in a document (all the examples discussed here are taken from Volume 99 of the Chemical Abstracts). The second list contains a set of heavy metals.

In the example shown in Figure 6.19, the information in the first list of Figure 6.18 has been categorized into a set of slots. Slots are important units of information within a frame. The slots which are used will depend on the context. In the context of environmental pollution *pollutant*, *source*, *organism*, *medium* and *location* are slots. The asterisk notation (e.g., *pollutant*) is used here to indicate a slot within the environmental pollution context. The member of each slot (category) that occurs in the document (frame) is referred to as the value of the slot. In this example, the value of the *location* slot is actually a list. Sublists within this list specify three rivers and a country. The sublists within the value list of the slot are referred to as the slot fillers for that slot. Thus Wales is a slot filler for the *location* slot in document 705. The three rivers (Gain, Mawdach and Wen) are also *location* slot fillers.

A relational database can be simulated in a frame system when the same set of slots is used for all the documents referred to in a particular relational table (see also the discussion of relational databases and frames in Chapter 4). Figure 6.20 shows an example of a relational database with four slots (*pollutants*, *location*, *organism*, and *medium*). However, relational databases also allow a variety of operators to be

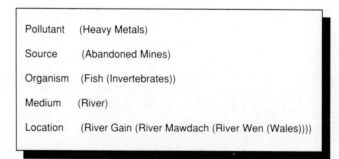

Pollutant	(Heavy Metals)
Source	(Abandoned Mines)
Organism	(Fish (Invertebrates))
Medium	(River)
Location	(River Gain (River Mawdach (River Wen (Wales))))

Figure 6.19 Categorization of the information shown in Figure 6.18 into a set of slots.

Document #	Pollutant	Location	Organism	Medium
11	DDT	Great Lakes	Fish	Lake
18	Heavy Metals	Wales	Fish	River
25	DDT	Ohio	---	---
27	DDT	France	---	---
41	Lindane	Japan	Crab	---
52	Detergent	England	---	Estuary
55	Lead	---	Shrimp	---
59	Cadmium	---	Birds	---
63	Lead		Cormorant	---
68	Pesticides	---	---	Ocean
71	Mercury	---	Gannet	---
89	Mercury	---	Shrimp	---
94	Heavy Metals	Canada	---	River

Figure 6.20 Documents on pollution represented as tuples within a pollution database.

applied in accessing the information within documents (Maier, 1983), as discussed in Chapter 2. We will focus below on the development and use of a frame hierarchy which then forms a front end to a relational database.

The first task in the development of a text interpretation system is the translation of database information into usable knowledge. Ideally, much of this translation is done during the indexing process. This is true for CAS Online where the information traditionally stored in databases (bibliographic data, keywords, abstract) is supplemented with knowledge statements (the controlled vocabulary terms with their associated text modifications). This is shown in Figure 6.21, where the controlled vocabulary terms are preceded by the letters 'IT' (e.g., Pesticides) and followed by a text modification

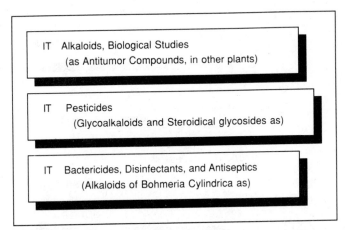

Figure 6.21 Examples of index terms supplemented with knowledge statements.

(in parentheses). The knowledge statement contained in an index term can be converted into an entry in a relational database in a straightforward fashion, as Figure 6.22 shows. The highly structured nature of index entries suggests the use of scripts (Schank & Abelson, 1977) as an appropriate method of knowledge representation. A script is a description of a class of events in terms of contexts, participants and subevents (Rich, 1983). An example of a sketchy script is

<substance> is produced by <anatomical structure> under <condition>

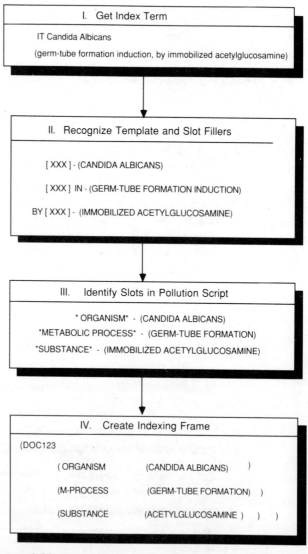

Figure 6.22 The conversion of an index term into an index frame.

A complete representation of the knowledge contained in a sketchy script such as this would require a more detailed analysis (cf. Schank, 1975). Such an analysis is not appropriate here because the possible meanings are constrained by the syntax and semantics of the sketchy script. In text management applications, the goal of the system is not to understand completely the knowledge in the relational database, but only to understand as much as is necessary to retrieve relevant information during online search.

Sketchy scripts, as used here, are frames that represent collections of predicates. Each frame (sketchy script) contains an ordered set of slots. Each slot has associated with it a set of information units (slot fillers) which can fill (instantiate) that slot. The slot fillers may be primitives or they may themselves be frames. Thus the use of sketchy scripts can both encode information and organize that information into knowledge structures. Consider as an example the sketchy script which refers to "uses of alkaloids." Some of the surface structures (index terms) in the database that represent uses of alkaloids are shown below.

> IT Alkaloids, Biological Studies (as Antitumor Compds., in higher plants)
> IT Pesticides (Glycoalkaloids and steroidal glycosides as)
> IT Bactericides, Disinfectants, and Antiseptics (Alkaloids of Boehmeria Cylindrica as)

These surface structures can be transformed into sketchy scripts. Thus a sketchy script representation might be

> *Substance* is used as *Use*.

A corresponding surface structure is

> GLYCOALKALOIDS are used as PESTICIDES.

In the structured indexing method used in Chemical Abstracts, this sketchy script can be represented as a surface structure in a number of syntactic forms, some of which are shown below.

> IT S, XXX (as U, XXX)
> IT U (S as, XXX)
> IT U (S)
> IT S (XXX, XXX U Activity of)

(where XXX stands for an arbitrary word or phrase, U stands for a particular use, and S stands for a substance).

Knowledge of the surface structure to deep structure mappings of the type illustrated above permits automated translation of the index terms of the Chemical Abstracts into a relational database representation. The parsing process outlined below allows these mappings to be inferred automatically, augmenting this syntactic knowledge with semantic understanding as required.

6.4.4.1 Templates: The Basic Syntactic Unit

The surface structures outlined above are basic patterns which can be used to guide the parsing process. Most of the early natural language systems in artificial intelligence used a simple pattern matcher to interpret their inputs (Winograd, 1983). By avoiding the need for the type of deeper conceptual analysis used in more recent natural-language systems we can simplify the parsing process and increase its computational efficiency. The term parsing is used here loosely, since the program for translating the database-constructed templates out of the index terms and matched these templates against previously stored patterns and its semantic knowledge. A more detailed account of the translation process (including listings of the LISP/FRL functions) is given elsewhere (Chignell, 1984).

The template construction process consisted of identifying phrases within the text modification (using commas as phrase boundary markers) and building templates for each phrase. In the constructed template, the keywords (OF CONTG IN FOR FROM RELATION BY AT WITH TO ON BETWEEN EFFECT REMOVAL OVER) were retained from the original phrase, while intervening words were replaced by "xxx." A list used in this way is generally referred to as a "Stop list." Figure 6.23 shows an example of the template construction process.

For the 874 water pollution index terms in our sample database, 114 distinct templates were constructed using this method. Each of these templates had one or more slots, signified by "xxx" where a variety of word phrases could be inserted.

Slots in a template are referred to as template slots, whereas slots in a frame are referred to as frame slots. In many cases a template slot will be closely related to a particular frame slot as is the case with (by xxx) and *pollutant* but it is important to maintain the distinction between uninterpreted syntactic template slots and meaningful frame slots.

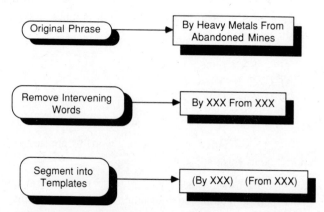

Figure 6.23 An example of the template construction process.

The major goal of the translation process is to identify each template slot filler as a frame slot filler and update the relational database accordingly. Preprocessing methods are used on the template slot fillers to assist this process. Stemming is used to reduce multiple entries of a slot filler. In the system developed here removal of the plural form is the only stemming process used. Thus "metal" and "metals" are both stored as metal. Segmentation is the second preprocessing step used in our system. (Ammonia and chlorides) are translated to the separate template slot fillers (ammonia), (chloride). The current version of the system does not distribute meaning across the conjunction. Thus (chem and smelting industry) becomes (chem), (smelting industry).

The creation of the relational database is an iterative process and postprocessing of the relational database is used to correct wrong frame slot allocations as well as problems arising from nondistributive conjunctions and the like.

During the translation process, all the information known about a particular template slot is stored in a frame. This frame is assigned a name which identifies uniquely the template slot. Further information about frame naming conventions and other details of the database translation not covered in this chapter are given elsewhere (Chignell, 1984, Appendix B).

6.4.4.2 *Semantic Interpretation*

Translation from the original index terms into the relational database is a learning process where successful translation results in the modification of data structures. The template slot frames store a combination of syntactic and semantic information and are a basic part of database translation. In some situations, however, information in the template slot frames will not be sufficient in identifying a slot filler. The slot filler may have been recognized in another template previously. Keeping a global list of all the fillers assigned to a particular slot allows us to identify the current slot filler in this case.

Aside from the design of appropriate data structures that can store the knowledge obtained during database translation, it is important to define a set of frame slots which will classify adequately the knowledge required in the relational database. *pollutant* is a useful slot in environmental chemistry, for instance, but is not very useful as a slot in pharmacology. The set of frame slots for environmental chemistry currently used by the system is given below. The set of frame slots used in this version of the system was derived from consultation with several indexing experts at Chemical Abstracts Services. One expert was asked to sort 200 controlled vocabulary terms into clusters of related terms. One of the clusters that he produced he labeled environmental chemistry/pollution. It included a number of sub-clusters, such as:

1. FLUE WASTE GASES
   EXHAUST GASES
   TOBACCO SMOKE
2. COATING MATERIALS
   CERAMICS
   BAKERY PRODUCTS

CEMENT
ADHESIVES
BRICKS
BINDING MATERIALS
FLOURS
3. SINTERING
BREWING
FERMENTATION
4. SLAGS
FIRE RESISTANT MATERIALS
INSECTICIDES
FIRE PROOFING AGENTS
FUNGICIDES
5. DISPERSING AGENTS
FOULING CONTROL AGENTS
WASTEWATER TREATMENT

These clusters were labeled

1. Offending effluents
2. Products that, when used or produced, pollute the environment
3. Processes that could affect the environment
4. Ground pollution
5. Processes related to wastewater treatment

Similar clusters were produced for topics such as "Pharmacology" and "naturally occurring plant components."

This expert also indicated relationships among terms that crossed these cluster boundaries, such as

SINTERING is a process used in manufacturing BRICKS.
ANALGESICS are used to treat HEADACHES.

An analysis of the sorting data from two experts led to the development of a model of the observed relationships, that is, a knowledge representation that accounted for all of the observed relationships. This knowledge representation suggests that controlled vocabulary terms can be related to one another in terms of scripts. The data from the sorting task implied the existence of the following script for Environmental Pollution (the terms shown in parentheses are examples of fillers for each slot).

_____ are pollutants. (SOLVENTS) (SLAGS)
They are found as _____ (AIR POLLUTION) (WATER POLLUTION)
in the form of _____ . (DUST) (FUMES)

These pollutants are produced during the use/manufacture of
_____ (ADHESIVES) (INSECTICIDES)
in the _____ industry. (PHARMACEUTICALS) (AGRICUL-
TURE) by the process of _____. (FERMENTATION) (SIN-
TERING)
This polutant can be controlled with _____.
(DISPERSING AGENTS) (WASTEWATER TREATMENT)

There was a similarity between the scripts implicit in the text modifications and
the scripts derived from having experts sort the controlled vocabulary terms. This
similarity means that controlled vocabulary terms and terms within the text modifications can all be assigned to the same slots in the same sets of scripts. In order to
cross-validate the sorting results, we consulted an expert indexer whose specialty
is Environmental Chemistry. She suggested that the documents in the Chemical
Abstracts dealing with environmental pollution could be described in terms of nine
major slots:

1. Pollutant
2. Physical state of pollutant
3. Source of pollutant
4. Kinetics (reactions and processes that modify the pollutant)
5. Geographical location
6. Polluted medium
7. Removal or control
8. Analysis
9. Transmission (pollutant transport processes)

During construction of the relational database it was found that some additional slots
were required, namely *organism*, *effect* (e.g., the effect of a pollutant on the
scale morphology of fish) and *control* (e.g., maximum permissible levels of a
pollutant).

6.4.4.3 *Translating the Templates*

Given the set of 12 slots into which document information could be classified and the
syntactic constraints provided by the templates, a straightforward translation method
was developed. The translation method for each template slot filler consisted of trying
each of the following four strategies in turn until translation was achieved.

> *Strategy A:* Syntactic/Semantic Analysis—This strategy assumes that the
> template is familiar and that a frame has already been constructed for the
> template slot. The strategy requires a search for the current phrase within
> the template slot frame. If successful, the relational database is updated by
> assigning the current phrase to the slot where it was found in the template
> slot frame.

Strategy B: Syntactic Analysis—This strategy also assumes that a template frame already exists for the template slot. It attempts to guess the frame slot on the basis of the predominant slot in the template slot frame. For instance, if nine out of ten of the previous fillers in the template slot frame have been pollutants it would assume that the current phrase is also a pollutant. If successful, the relational database is updated. The template slot frame is also updated, since the current phrase was not already in the template slot frame and the relevant frame slot had to be guessed on the basis of slots assigned previously to phrases within that syntactic form.

Strategy C: Semantic Analysis—When a phrase cannot be interpreted on the basis of the information contained in a syntactic knowledge structure (the template slot frame) it may still be possible to classify it if its meaning is already known, without the aid of a syntactic analysis. Strategy C searches for the current phrase in the global list of known pollutants, known locations, and on through all 12 slots if necessary. If this strategy is successful, the relational database and template slot frame are updated.

Strategy D: Ask an Expert—This strategy is used when the other three strategies fail. Strategy D asks the expert to identify the slot to which the current phrase belongs. After the expert makes the classification, the relational database, template slot frame, and the global list of slot fillers for the chosen slot are all updated.

The operation of the four strategies can be illustrated with an example. Figure 6.24 shows the conditions under which each strategy is called upon and the effect that each strategy has on the data structures. In this example, phrases within the template (by xxx) are being translated. At the beginning of the example the template has not been encountered before and a template slot frame (BY-SLOT-1) is constructed after the first phrase is analyzed. Prior to the example, the system knows of only three pollutants (mercury, lead, and DDT) which are stored in the global list of pollutants. Since the first phrase is analyzed prior to the construction of the template slot frame, Strategies A and B cannot be used. Strategy C also fails because CADMIUM has not been encountered previously. Thus Strategy D (ask-expert) is used. Since the expert classifies cadmium as a pollutant (for document 1) CADMIUM is entered as a *pollutant* in the template slot frame. CADMIUM is also added to the list of pollutants known by the system and the fact that document 1 talks about cadmium as a pollutant is entered into the relational database.

Document 2 in the example has MERCURY as the phrase in the template. Strategy A fails since only CADMIUM has been stored in the template slot frame so far. Strategy B is inappropriate because there is not yet enough information to guess on the basis of syntax (there is only one phrase stored in the frame so far). Mercury is a known pollutant, however, and thus semantic analysis (Strategy C) succeeds. The fact that mercury is a pollutant of interest in document 2 is added to the relational database, and mercury as a pollutant is also added to the template slot frame (BY-SLOT-1). Document 3 has the phrase MERCURY in the template as well. Since mercury is a known pollutant in the template slot frame, Strategy A is appropriate and the syntactic/semantic analysis succeeds. Only the relational database needs to be updated here.

By the time document N is analyzed the number of pollutants stored in the template slot frame and in the global list of pollutants has grown considerably. Nevertheless, BROMIDES is a pollutant term that has not been seen before by the system, and Strategies A and C will fail accordingly. Strategy B is appropriate now, since a consistent mapping has been established between the template and the pollutant slot. The vast majority of the phrases in the template (by xxx) are pollutants with high confidence. The present version of the system has confidence in its guesses and updates the relational database, global list of pollutants, and template slot frame in light of the fact that BROMIDES refers to a pollutant. At times this confidence can be misplaced. In translating the database, syntactic analysis soon established that phrases in the templates (in xxx) were locations which led to ground-waters being classified as locations in a few documents. This type of problem is relatively minor and can be overcome either by relying more on expert consultation, or else by guessing more than one slot (e.g., *location* and *organism*) on the basis of syntax and waiting until more knowledge is accumulated before making a final decision.

Learning consisted of the modification of the data structures (relational database, template slot frame, global list of slot fillers) after the translation of each template slot filler. This learning process was illustrated in Figure 6.24. Each filler that is allocated to a slot will be placed in the global list of fillers for that slot, the appropriate slot of the template slot frame, and in the document frame within the relational database.

In essence, a system such as this learns semantic information from the expert and infers syntactic and additional semantic information from the structure of the templates. There is a tradeoff between learning from the expert and learning by inference. Learning from the expert is time-consuming and subject to human errors such as inconsistency and forgetfulness. Learning by inference uses educated guesses which will sometimes be wrong, and is also computationally expensive. Further empirical analysis is required to determine the best mix of expert training and learning by inference. The amount of training versus inference in the translation procedure can be manipulated by changing the confidence level required for guessing. The present version makes a commitment to a single meaning when learning how to translate the phrases in the database. More sophisticated interactive indexing systems might adopt a "wait and see" attitude where several meanings are assigned to a phrase provisionally, and superfluous meanings are discarded as more evidence accumulates.

6.4.4.4 Hierarchical Indexing

Organization of information is necessary for efficient retrieval of that information. Classification of information into basic classes has been a preferred method of organizing information in areas as diverse as taxonomy (Sneath & Sokal, 1973), psychiatry (Strauss, Bartko, and Carpenter, 1973), and library science (Foskett, 1977).

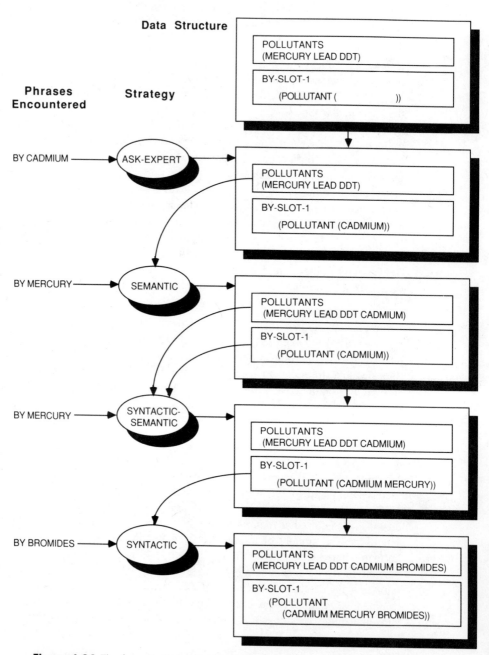

Figure 6.24 The four strategies for template translation in operation, showing their effects on relevant data structures.

Figure 6.25 Representation of the mercury node.

Each unit of information can be represented as a node in the hierarchy. Part of the meaning of a node will be given by its position in the hierarchy. Figure 6.15 shows fragments of concept hierarchies. The position of mercury in the pollutant hierarchy, for instance, tells us that mercury is a polluting heavy metal. Additional information may also be attached to the mercury node, as shown in Figure 6.25. The mercury node is a frame in the hierarchical knowledge structure and extra information is provided by the *ambiguous* and *organism* slots in that frame. The first slot indicates that mercury is an ambiguous word that can refer to a pollutant, a planet, or a useful substance. The second slot indicates that mercury often appears as a pollutant in fish.

As discussed earlier, the form of indexing required in a database depends to a great extent on the types of query that are anticipated. In the system described here we require the user to form a query in terms of keyword phrases. Thus, during the retrieval process it will be necessary to map the user's keyword phrases and the relational database's slot fillers onto nodes in the hierarchy. This mapping will be facilitated during the indexing process by constructing a node in the hierarchy for each new keyword phrase and slot filler that is seen. (Heavy metals), for instance, is a slot filler that appears in the database and it is mapped onto the HEAVY-METAL node. (Primary Treatment), on the other hand, is a term that appears in user's keyword phrases, but not in the current version of the relational database. It too is mapped onto a node, in this case the PRIMARY-TREATMENT node. These nodes are inserted into the hierarchy with the assistance of an expert. LISP/FRL functions which run these node insertion procedures (CLASSIFY-RDB-FILLERS, CLASSIFY-NEWFILLER, PUT-NODE-IN-TREE) are listed elsewhere (Chignell, 1984). The essential feature of both procedures is that when an unfamiliar slot filler or keyword phrase is encountered, the system consults the expert who moves down the tree until the nearest superordinate of the new concept is found.

Simple node insertion is not always sufficient when building the tree. In some cases a new filler may necessitate rebuilding a portion of the tree. With larger hierarchies it may be necessary to make more radical changes in the tree structure, in which case a switch operator would be useful. This operator switches the positions of a parent and its child (making the parent the child and the child the parent) and also allows changes to other nodes affected by the switch, as necessary. Insertion and

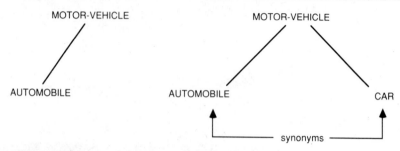

Figure 6.26 Mapping the user's vocabulary onto the database vocabulary.

rebuilding (and, possibly, switching) allow flexible and interactive construction of the concept hierarchy, which grows and evolves as the system learns about the database and experiences user queries.

6.4.4.5 Functions of the Index Hierarchy

The index (or concept) hierarchy has four main functions in the system described here.

1. It acts as a long-term memory. The hierarchy stores all the slot fillers in the relational database along with all the keyword phrases input by expert users.

2. The concept hierarchy also functions as an organized form of the relational database information.

3. The concept hierarchy provides a mapping of the user's vocabulary of keyword phrases onto the database's vocabulary of slot fillers. Figure 6.26 illustrates how this mapping works. In this example, the user's keyword phrase refers to "car" while the database slot filler refers to "automobile." After node insertion, automobile is nested under motor vehicle. When car is inserted into the tree, it is also nested under motor vehicle and the synonymous relationship between car and automobile is observed. This synonymous relationship is now captured in the CAR and AUTOMOBILE frames, as Figure 6.27 shows. Car, as a keyword phrase, can be mapped into the equivalent database term available via the synonym slot.

4. The concept hierarchy functions as a blackboard (Section 4.4.4) for information about the current search. Nodes in the hierarchy are activated in response to user queries. Each activated node is a concept that is hypothesized to be relevant to the search. The state of a search at a given point in time is indicated by the set of nodes that are active. The set of active nodes is available to all the system processes and thus node activation within the concept hierarchy is equivalent to having a blackboard where the knowledge accumulated during the search is written.

These functions complement the general associativity of the hypermedia network, and the logical structure of relational databases, permitting the development of flexible

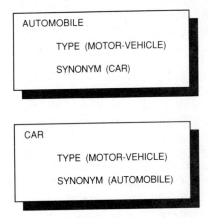

Figure 6.27 Representation of a synonymous relationship within frames.

storage and retrieval strategies within an intelligent database that capitalizes on a combination of these different storage and organization techniques.

6.4.5 Queries in Text Retrieval

The first task of a comprehensive text management and retrieval system is that of understanding the initial query. The demonstration system described above requires the user to input the query as a set of keyword phrases. This restriction on input simplifies parsing enormously and will be compensated for by flexible query negotiation once the initial query has been understood. If the user were interested in the contamination of fish in the Great Lakes by mercury, an appropriate set of keyword phrases would be:

(mercury) (fish) (Great Lakes).

with each phrase being set off from the others by parentheses. In processing each phrase in the query, the first strategy of the system is to look for a node in the concept hierarchy that corresponds to the phrase. Thus (Great Lakes) would be recognized as the node GREAT-LAKE (the addition of the hyphen and removal of the plural results from a frame naming convention used by the system). If the phrase is not recognized, the user is asked to insert the unfamiliar phrase into the tree using operators such as those described above.

After the phrase is recognized (or inserted), the corresponding node is activated. This may be done by putting the value "yes" in the *active* slot of the node frame. The descendents of this node are also activated. Thus activation of HEAVY-METALS leads to the activation of MERCURY, LEAD, CADMIUM.

The set of all documents attached to active nodes in the hierarchy represents a pool of possibly relevant documents. A variety of operations can be carried out on this pool of documents. Boolean ANDs can be used to find the documents that are relevant for a particular subset of active nodes. Thus, a provisional set of documents relevant to mercury and fish could be found by ANDing the sets of documents attached to the two nodes.

The relational database is a second component of long term memory. Learning can also be used to update and improve the knowledge within the relational database. During translation of the database, syntactic analysis may lead to some errors. One example is that of putting Galway Bay as an organism. As the system learns, there are a couple of ways in which an error such as this could be detected. Firstly, when Galway Bay is entered as a phrase in a query, wrong inferences might be made on the assumption that Galway Bay is an organism and interaction with the user may establish that Galway Bay is a location (although the system might lose face in finding out). Secondly, a smart inferencing system might infer facts that are normally a part of the general knowledge that people have. Thus the system might recognize that "bay" usually refers to a body of water or geographical location, or, by knowing that Galway is a part of Ireland, may suggest that Galway Bay is a location rather than an organism.

6.4.5.1 Query Contexts

A query consists of more than keyword phrases taken one at a time. The particular combination of phrases in a query establishes a context (cf., Gestalt Psychology) that is more than the sum of the separate effects of each phrase taken alone. The keyword phrases (fish) (North America) (mercury) when combined in a query suggest that there are fish in North America and that those fish may contain mercury (assuming that the user's query is based on factual knowledge that the phrases in the query can occur together). This type of information is not trivial to a system that does not have access to the general knowledge and common sense that humans take for granted. Thus the presence of (fish) (North America) as a query, but the absence of queries such as (fish) (Sahara) are a potentially useful source of implicit knowledge.

One method for representing the information in a query is to create local contexts in concept frames which correspond to information merged from all the previous queries. The creation and updating of contexts is demonstrated using an example containing three successive queries.

> First Query: (fish) (mercury) (Great Lakes)
> Second Query: (fish) (lead)
> Third Query: (crab) (mercury) (Great Lakes)

The process of context formation for each query consists of three steps.

1. Find the appropriate slot in the pollution script for each keyword phrase, that is

> (fish) - *organism*
> (mercury) - *pollutant*
> (Great Lakes) - *location*

2. For each phrase in the query establish a context comprised of the pollution slots of the other phrases in the query, i.e.:

(FISH (CONTEXT1 (LOCATION POLLUTANT)))
(MERCURY (CONTEXT1 (ORGANISM LOCATION)))
(GREAT LAKES (CONTEXT1 (ORGANISM POLLUTANT)))

3. For each pollutant slot in the context of a phrase, add that slot to the phrase's frame and fill that slot with the appropriate phrase. This process is repeated for each of the phrases.

(FISH (LOCATION (GREAT-LAKES)) (POLLUTANT (MERCURY)))
(MERCURY (ORGANISM (FISH)) (LOCATION (GREAT-LAKES)))
(GREAT-LAKES (ORGANISM (FISH)) (POLLUTANT (MERCURY)))

There is an analogy between the context formation method used in this demonstration system and the process of schematization in human cognition (Bartlett, 1932), where a succession of specific instances is merged into a single schema that captures the essence of those instances. Thus, someone interested in pollutants in fish could look at the pollutants slot in the fish frame and find that lead and mercury were pollutants found in fish. Other knowledge could be derived by comparing contexts for different phrases. Locations where fish were polluted with cadmium would be suggested by intersecting the location slots for FISH and for CADMIUM. Contexts keep track of the prevailing interests of users. This knowledge may be used to trigger expectations about what else a user might be interested in, given a set of keyword phrases that were input.

In the system described here, human experts are called upon only for the classification of unfamiliar phrases and slot fillers. The system is designed so as to capitalize on the knowledge already contained in the database and the user's knowledge as much as possible. There is little explicit input of knowledge into the system, with training occurring interactively and at the discretion of the system. The performance of this text interpretation system may then be enhanced in a number of ways. For instance, production rules attached to nodes represent a good method of storing explicit expert knowledge. Examples of such rules might be

If the user is from the Environmental Protection Agency consider documents referring to legal standards.
If the user refers to primary or secondary treatment he may be interested in wastewater treatment.
If a freshwater organism is referred to, the user may only be interested in inland bodies of water such as lakes and rivers.

This querying method may be extended to a constrained natural language querying system where the database query parser specifically translates statements into collections of keyword phrases that form a query context.

6.4.6 Evaluative Summary

Many aspects of the associative knowledge used by indexers appear to be largely idiosyncratic. In the EP-X system (Section 6.6.1), a basic hierarchy was formed using reference texts, but it soon became clear that many of the concepts in the reference texts might not be relevant to the documents actually in the CAS Online database (this finding that "textbook" hierarchies had to be modified for practical use was also found in Project Jefferson). As a result, the hierarchy was built interactively, with new nodes being added only as they were found to be necessary, on the basis of experience with users' queries and knowledge about the documents in the database.

Scripts were found to be a convenient way of representing concepts that appeared in the database. Thus, much of the intermediary's expertise could be expressed in terms of knowledge about the types of script that could appear in the database.

For instance, an example of a water pollution script is

"The effect of water pollution caused by heavy metals from abandoned mines on fish and invertebrates in the rivers Gain, Mawddach and Wen, in Wales."

The representation of complete scripts requires a causal analysis of the way in which certain slots influence other slots. In general, it is much simpler, both computationally and conceptually, to break the text modifications of the controlled vocabulary terms into phrases and identify slots one at a time, rather than the whole script. Thus the statement mentioned above is represented in EP-X as follows:

pollutant - heavy metals
source - abandoned mine
organism - fish, invertebrate
location - River Gain, . . . , Wales
medium - river

Little, if any, information is lost in using the frame/slot representation since the context of environmental pollution allows one to determine the script on the basis of a set of slots and their fillers. It is obvious, for instance, that a pollutant comes from a source rather than vice versa. This fundamental insight (that a script is implied by a set of slots within a constrained context) allowed us to reduce the database translation problem to one of classification, rather than textual understanding.

■ 6.5 ONLINE DATABASES AND RETRIEVAL SERVICES

There are estimated to be over 2 billion documents in electronic form around the world. Databases differ according to factors such as their scope and chronological coverage, and the subjects that they address. Reference databases carry citations to information rather than the complete text of the document. In contrast, source databases contain original source data such as the full text of the original document.

In general the availability of information in online databases is the result of a two stage process

1. Database producers develop the databases.
2. Online services provide access to databases.

Database producers get the raw information and filter it, index it, and possibly add abstracts and summary material. Most database producers then license their databases to online services who then make them generally available along with databases from other database producers. Thus large online services act like information supermarkets, allowing users to carry out "one-stop shopping" for information. However, some database producers (e.g., Chemical Abstracts Services) provide their own online service, which then competes with the use of their database on other online services to which it has been licensed. We will now describe a representative set of databases.

6.5.1 LEXIS and NEXIS

Lexis is an electronic legal service produced by Mead Data Central. Mead Data Central is a company that is known for its full text databases, Lexis, and Nexis. The Law is, of course, a naturally information-intensive profession because of the emphasis on precedent and previous cases. Frequently, information can make the difference in a legal case. Lexis provides the full text of federal cases along with the case law of all 50 U.S. states. The effect of Lexis on the legal profession is so strong that some law schools require their students to learn to search online.

Lexis tracks U. S. Federal and state law, as well as British and French law. The Federal information covers topics such as tax, patents, trademarks and copyrights, communications, energy, public contracts, trade regulations, and labor. When searching Lexis, one can find a case based on who the judge was, which court the case was heard before, by counsel, by section of statute or regulation, or by keywords or keyword phrases used in the decision.

Nexis is the other major full text database from Mead Data Central. Nexis has been described as the publishing industry's answer to the great library of Alexandria. Nexis provides information from a large number of newspapers, magazines, wire services, and newsletters, along with sources such as the New York Times Information Bank (Infobank) and the *Encyclopedia Britannica*. Not surprisingly, Nexis is a particularly popular database among journalists.

As of 1987, Nexis was made up of four main databases

    Nexis Magazines
    Nexis Newsletters
    Nexis Newspapers
    Nexis Wire Services

Topics covered by Nexis include

> Administration and Management
> Advertising and Advertising Industry
> Aerospace Industry
> Biotechnology
> Business and Industry
> Chemical Industry
> Chemistry
> Commodities
> Communications and Telecommunications
> Computers and Computer Industry
> Defense and Defense Industry
> Economics
> Electrical and Electronics Industry
> Energy Industry
> Engineering
> Financial Investments
> Financial Services Industry
> General Interest
> Health Care
> International Affairs
> Legal and Regulatory—U. S. Federal
> Mining
> Physics
> Science and Technology
> Sports

Nexis was introduced by Mead Data Central in 1979. It was originally designed as a follow-on product to Lexis that would offer attorneys access to general news and information. However, Nexis now has a broader appeal that stems from making full text available to a wide variety of sources. In addition to the full text of *The New York Times*, for instance, Nexis provides the complete transcripts of "The MacNeil/Lehrer NewsHour" since 1982, along with a large number of full-text magazines such as *Aviation Week* and *Space Technology*, and *U.S. News and World Report*.

Nexis is both a retrieval system and a collection of text databases. As a retrieval system, it offers a number of features that are helpful to those who are not trained in library science. For instance, the system automatically searches for the single and plural possessives (e.g., company, companies, company's) of a noun so that users don't have to worry about including these variations in their original query. Nexis also has a practice database that is billed only at basic connect rates and a comprehensive online help system.

6.5.2 Medline

While Lexis may appeal to lawyers, and Nexis to journalists, Medline is well suited to physicians and those interested in biomedical technology. Medline is produced by the National Library of Medicine and is one of the major sources of biomedical literature. It is generally recognized as the most comprehensive resource for medical literature and covers diverse health fields such as biomedicine, veterinary medicine, biological and physical sciences, and other topics that relate to medicine and health care. Medline contains information that otherwise appears in three printed indexes

> Index Medicus
> Index to Dental Literature
> International Nursing Index

MEDLINE (MEDLARS onLINE) indexes articles from over 3,000 journals published in the United States and 70 other countries. Over 250,000 records are added per year, of which over 70% are English-language. Medline also appears as the MESH and MESZ databases in the BRS system.

6.5.3 SCISEARCH

SCISEARCH is produced by the Institute for Scientific Information (ISI). It indexes a number of disciplines in science and technology. SCISEARCH is somewhat unique in that it claims to include 90% of the world's significant scientific and technical literature. It also has a citation indexing feature that allows one to retrieve a newly published article through the subject relationship established by an author's reference to prior articles. Consider, for example, that one is interested in finding recent articles on chunking in human memory and the limits of short term memory span. You know that a landmark article was written in 1956 by George Miller with the abbreviated title "The Magical Number Seven Plus or Minus Two." Using citation indexing, one can then find those articles in the present year which referenced this article. Citation indexing is particularly useful when one is not sure what index terms to use in a query but one does know about a few key articles that have appeared on the topic.

SCISEARCH includes all the records published in the Science Citation Index, plus additional citations published in the Current Contents. In producing SCISEARCH, significant items are indexed from over 2600 major scientific and technical journals.

6.5.4 Dialog

Dialog is the granddaddy of online services. It is also the largest. Although there is some overlap with the coverage of BRS (Section 6.5.5) and other online services,

Dialog has the most comprehensive coverage of databases. Dialog covers databases in science, business, technology, chemistry, law, medicine, engineering, social sciences, business, economics, and current events, to name just some of the topics covered. The Dialog system contains close to 200 million records, but even then it probably has just 10% of the world's online information. Dialog has well over 200 databases that reference more than 60,000 publications from around the world. Dialog began in the 1960's as an offshoot of the Lockheed Missiles and Space Company. What began as an in-house project to index company files and store them in an online database turned into a contract to design and implement a bibliographic retrieval service for the National Aeronautics and Space Administration. Lockheed then won similar contracts from the Atomic Energy Commission and other government agencies. In 1972, Dialog Information Retrieval Services was formed as a subsidiary that would market databases produced by private and government organizations. Dialog grew rapidly to become the dominant supplier of online databases. In 1988, Dialog was purchased from Lockheed by Knight Ridder.

6.5.5 BRS

BRS is an online service that was established in 1976. It now contains over a hundred databases. The BRS databases cover areas such as business and finance, education, reference, science and medicine, and the social sciences. BRS has a particularly strong representation of databases in the areas of health care and medicine. BRS also includes some full text databases such as Medline.

BRS was one of the first database services to introduce flexible price structuring. For instance, BRS After Dark was a system that allowed users to access information after business hours relatively cheaply. This contributed greatly to the increased use of information services and encouraged other services to follow suit. More recently, BRS has experimented with leasing its databases to Universities. In this format, the university mounts a selection of the BRS databases and search software on a local mainframe and pays a usage fee to BRS. In turn it is provided with regular database updates. For instance, this arrangement is currently in place at the University of Southern California, and the electronic notebook in Project Jefferson uses the BRS databases as a source of online information.

6.5.6 Dow Jones News/Retrieval Service

The Dow Jones News/Retrieval Service (DJNS) combines financial, business, and general information within a single online service. DJNS provides quotes, financial and investment services, business and economic news, and general information services. DJNS offers quotes in real-time, as they appear on the floor of the exchanges. DJNS provides composite prices of common and preferred stocks, and warrants from the New York, American, Midwest, and Pacific exchanges. It also provides composite options from the Chicago Board Operations Exchange and the American, Philadelphia, Midwest, and Pacific exchanges. DJNS provides further information on futures, and historical quotes and averages.

DJNS contains profile information on thousands of publicly owned companies in the United States. These profiles include:

> corporate profile
> balance sheets for two years
> income statements for three years
> the current fiscal year's quarterly income statements
> sales and operating income for up to 10 lines of business
> five year summary data
> owners and directors
> ownership and subsidiaries
> other corporate events
> Two-year list of reports on file with the SEC
> Management discussion

In terms of the financial and investment category, DJNS also contains the Money Market Service's Economic and Foreign Exchange Survey, Zacks Investment Research's Corporate Earnings Estimator, and Standard and Poor's Online. Aside from all this financial information, DJNS also contains a wide range of business and economic news, and general news and information.

DJNS began in 1974 by offering a condensed version of *The Wall Street Journal*, *Barron's*, and *The Dow Jones Wire*. In 1981, DJNS began an aggressive marketing campaign that boosted its number of subscribers from 15,000 in 1980 to 60,000 in 1984. At the same time it began to expand its coverage of information to today's impressive level.

■ 6.6 THE ROLE OF EXPERT SYSTEMS AND INFERENCE IN INFORMATION RETRIEVAL

One answer to the problems identified above is to incorporate components of these classes of knowledge in an expert system search intermediary for online retrieval. Expert systems are generally defined as computer programs that solve problems of commercial and scientific importance using knowledge and inference procedures. The development of an expert system requires that there be a human expert who can act as a source of the expertise that will be built into the program. Some have objected to this narrow view of expert systems and have used the alternative term "knowledge based systems" to reflect the fact that the same general methods can be used to create intelligent behavior whether or not the rules and inference procedures are explicitly modeled on those of a corresponding human expert (e.g., Davis and Lenat, 1982).

In the case of information retrieval, the question arises as to whether it is appropriate to mimic exclusively the methods used by human search intermediaries in expert systems. The memory intensive nature of the information retrieval task may favor computer representations of the task that avoid at least some aspects of search expertise designed to ameliorate deficiencies in human memory.

In addition to the question of what search expertise should be incorporated within an expert system search intermediary (c.f., Kinnell and Chignell, 1987), there is the prior question of whether or not it is appropriate to try and build expert system search intermediaries. There are a number of features of expert systems that seem ill-suited to applications in online information retrieval. These include the following:

An expert system is restricted to a narrow knowledge domain.
Expert systems are interactive and should have a relatively fast response time.
Expert systems are knowledge-intensive and the task of constructing expert systems (known as knowledge engineering) is fairly onerous.

Online information retrieval systems typically deal with vast amounts of knowledge that are spread diffusely across different knowledge domains. Furthermore, given current computer technology, operating the huge number of rules necessary to deal with a large amount of diffuse knowledge would not be possible in an interactive environment with adequate response times.

It is clearly inappropriate to build expert system search intermediaries that attempt to deal with all possible knowledge domains. By their nature, expert systems utilize the expertise of one, or a few, experts in a *limited* domain. Thus in applying expert systems techniques to the online retrieval task it is necessary to target specific knowledge domains such as environmental pollution or the U.S. Constitution. Even with a narrow domain, the concept of an expert system must be tailored further to meet the needs of online information retrieval. Whereas conventional expert systems work with facts directly, information retrieval is concerned with indirect access to information. As Paice (1986) has pointed out, search intermediaries do not generally have expert knowledge in the fields for which they are responsible. Yet it seems to be this domain knowledge, expressed in both the language of the user and the language of the database, that is the most important element of online retrieval.

The three major components of an expert system are the knowledge base and inference engine, plus a user interface. As we discussed above, it is probably not appropriate to construct the knowledge base for an expert system search intermediary based on rules of search expertise. Instead the knowledge-based system should represent and organize the domain knowledge in a way that allows users to express queries accurately and efficiently. Thus the knowledge base for an online retrieval intermediary will not consist of rules in the form of a production system such as OPS5 (e.g., Waterman, Hayes-Roth and Lenat, 1983), but will instead be a concept hierarchy (similar to the architecture used in the MDX system, Chandrasekaran and Mittal, 1983). The inference engine, too, will be modified with the user having more control of the reasoning process than typically occurs with expert systems. While the system may make suggestions about broadening or narrowing the topic, or point out ambiguities and errors, it is the user who has to be in charge of where to go next during query formulation because it is his information need that is being discussed. This again creates an unusual situation for expert systems because the user has critical information upon which the success of the interaction depends and the expert system can only get that information by interacting with the user. Thus knowledge based search intermediaries are not going to be expert systems in the usual sense. Instead they are going to be like roadmaps of knowledge, with signposts about where to go next and hints about what to do.

6.6.1 EP-X: A Knowledge-Based Search Intermediary

We can illustrate the development of knowledge-based search intermediaries using frame hierarchies with the case study introduced earlier. EP-X was built after careful study of the *Chemical Abstracts* database and after observing the performances of indexers and searchers (e.g., Chignell, 1984; Smith, Chignell and Krawczak, 1985).

Although not a natural language understanding system per se, EP-X assumes that the user initially represents her topic internally as a natural language request, then asks the user to map her topic into a list of keywords or keyword phrases and enter them using an alphanumeric keyboard. EP-X then displays a natural language interpretation of the user's topic. The interaction with EP-X creates a mapping of a topic of interest into a set of appropriate keywords, with iterative keyword entry and interpretation as the means toward obtaining agreement between what the user believes her topic to be, and how the system interprets it.

The architecture of EP-X is based on a "divide-and-conquer" strategy for online retrieval which was inspired by prior studies of expert human searchers. The documents are indexed by concept frames, and a separate hierarchical organization of frames is then used as a retrieval front end. A search in EP-X consists of two parts, first the user finds the neighborhood of interest, and then the user interacts with the system in increasing recall and precision (Figure 6.28, redrawn after Shute, Smith, Krawczak, Chignell and Sater, 1986, Figure 1).

The first task for EP-X is to negotiate with the user in finding the neighborhood of documents that is likely to contain the relevant set. The user finds the neighborhood by inputting keyword phrases which are then linked using a Boolean AND operation and matched against the database. The important innovation that EP-X uses, however, is that the keyword phrases activate frames within the frame hierarchy. Thus the neighborhood is not just a set of documents that must then be sorted through, but is instead a location in conceptual space specified by activated nodes in the frame hierarchy. During the Find Neighborhood phase of the search, the user may continue to add or delete phrases to or from the keyword list until a satisfactory neighborhood is found.

Increased recall and precision is achieved in EP-X by allowing the user to move up (generalizing the search) or down (focusing the search) the frame hierarchy. This process can be illustrated with an example (extracted from Krawczak, Smith, and Shute, 1987).

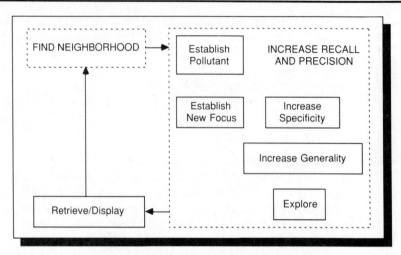

Figure 6.28 The EP-X system search strategy.

ENTER KEYWORD LIST

Your keyword list currently consists of the following:

POLLUTION

NATURAL WATERS

RADON-222

CESIUM-137

STRONTIUM-90

- Type your next keyword or keyword phrase and press RETURN.

- If you're done entering your keyword list, just press the RETURN key.

ENTER KEYWORD:

- if you want to get further explanation, type HELP and press RETURN.
- if you want to start a new search, type RESTART and press RETURN.
- if you want to stop the search, type STOP and press RETURN.

Figure 6.29 Entering keywords in EP-X.

Suppose that a user is interested in the topic "pollution of natural waters including lakes, rivers, and so on, by radioactive substances such as Radon-222, Cesium-137, or Strontium-90."

As the user enters each new keyword phrase, EP-X places it in the box at the top of the screen (Figure 6.29). During this transaction EP-X must infer that

a. The term pollution is too general since all the documents in the database discuss pollution.
b. The semantic interpretation of the concept NATURAL WATERS includes subconcepts such as lakes, rivers, oceans, and bays.

EP-X gives the user a chance to review his keyword list and make any necessary changes. In this example the user elects to make no changes. EP-X then produces an interpretation screen (Figure 6.30) which translates the users's list of keywords into an English interpretation of the topic. In making this interpretation EP-X infers that

CHECK INTERPRETATION

14 documents are available on the occurrence of radon-222, cesium-137 or strontium-90 as pollutants in natural bodies of water.

Do you want to:

1 CHANGE   your keyword list to clarify your topic
2 DISPLAY   your current document set
3 BROADEN   your topic
4 NARROW   your topic (HIERARCHIES will be shown)

Type a 1, 2, 3, or 4 and press RETURN to indicate your choice.

ENTER CHOICE: 3

When appropriate type either HELP, RESTART or STOP and press RETURN.

Figure 6.30 Checking an interpretation of a query.

    a. NATURAL WATERS is a member of the general class *polluted media*.

    b. RADON-222, CESIUM-137, and STRONTIUM-90 are all members of the general class *chemical pollutants*.

    c. The relationship between the classes *polluted media* and *chemical pollutants* is that pollutants occur in polluted media.

The user wants more than 14 documents and chooses the BROADEN option. Before giving the user a chance to select a keyword to broaden, EP-X makes any reasonable suggestions based on its knowledge (Figure 6.31). In this case, EP-X notices that RADON-222, CESIUM-137, and STRONTIUM-90 are all specific concepts that fall under the more general term RADIOACTIVE SUBSTANCES.

In addition to suggesting that the search be broadened to include all radioactive substances, EP-X tells the user the implications of taking this step, i.e., that 73 documents will be added to the current document set. In this example the user elects to go with this suggestion, replacing the specific radioactive substances with the more general term.

BROADEN TOPIC

Do you want to consider broadening concepts dealing with:

    1 CHEMICAL POLLUTANTS - Radioactive Substances
    2 POLLUTED MEDIA - Water
    3 BROADEN NO MORE CONCEPTS

ENTER CHOICE: 3

When appropriate type either HELP, RESTART or STOP and press RETURN.

Figure 6.31 Broadening a topic.

CHECK INTERPRETATION

> 87 documents are available on the occurrence of radioactive substances as pollutants in natural bodies of water.

Do you want to:

    1 CHANGE   your keyword list to clarify your topic
    2 DISPLAY   your current document set
    3 BROADEN   your topic
    4 NARROW   your topic (HIERARCHIES will be shown)

Type a 1, 2, 3, or 4 and press RETURN to indicate your choice.

ENTER CHOICE: 4

When appropriate type either HELP, RESTART or STOP and press RETURN.

Figure 6.32 Checking a revised interpretation of a query.

The user now decides that the topic is, if anything, too broad and decides to end the broadening process. EP-X then tells the user its new interpretation of the topic based on the broader concept RADIOACTIVE SUBSTANCES (Figure 6.32). The user elects to try to narrow this topic. EP-X then gives the user a choice of hierarchies to view. Each hierarchy represents one of the general classes of information about environmental pollution that are identified in EP-X, such as *polluted media, chemical pollutants, organisms, geographic locations, sources,* and *removal processes.* Each class is represented by a hierarchy of all semantic primitives in that class. The user chooses the hierarchy representing polluted media. EP-X then displays the portion of the polluted media hierarchy (Figure 6.33) that shows its understanding of the concept NATURAL WATERS. It does this by displaying all of the subconcepts that go into creating the semantic definition. At this point the user can delete specific subconcepts to refine his definition of NATURAL WATERS.

In order to support the type of interaction shown in the foregoing example, EP-X needs knowledge about

1. Semantic primitives (concepts).
2. Class membership.

3. Relationships between classes (topics).

4. Miscellaneous relationships not captured in the first three categories of knowledge.

A system such as EP-X must contain an unambiguous set of semantic primitives or else it will jump to erroneous conclusions when making suggestions or interpretations. Ambiguous words such as PRECIPITATION are handled by creating separate semantic primitives for each word sense or usage. Thus, there are distinct concepts representing RAIN, SNOW, and so on, versus REMOVAL PROCESS for the other major sense of the term. The second step in describing semantic primitives is to define each primitive or concept in terms of its subconcepts. These "parent-child" relationships are then represented in hierarchies. Knowledge about class membership is used to infer what role the primitive plays in environmental pollution. Thus EP-X can infer that FISH plays the role of an organism in environmental pollution since FISH is a member of the *organism* hierarchy.

To capture the stereotypic relationships that exist between the classes in a topic, each

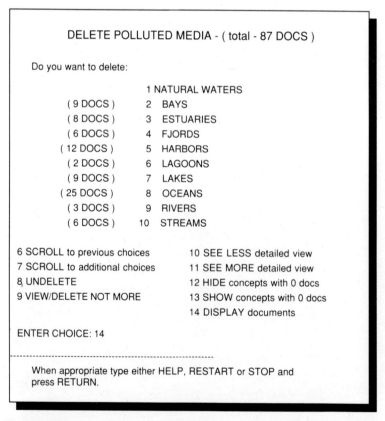

Figure 6.33 The subconcepts of natural waters shown as options for deletion.

general topic is represented in EP-X as a frame. The slots in the frame represent the classes involved in the topic. Valid slot fillers are any semantic primitives that belong to the class.

EP-X uses this knowledge to infer the user's specific topic. For example, if the user enters HEAVY METALS, a *pollutant*, and FISH, an *organism*, EP-X looks for a frame describing a relationship between these two classes. Filling in each slot in the frame with the appropriate semantic primitive produces the specific topic

the uptake of HEAVY METALS AND THEIR COMPOUNDS in FISH.

To retrieve the appropriate set of documents for a specific topic, EP-X views each of the documents in its database as an instance of a particular frame. That is, each document represents a topic (frame) that describes relationships between specific semantic primitives (slot fillers). It then retrieves all documents that match the user's topic.

Each document in EP-X's database is indexed according to the topics that EP-X knows about. Consider, for instance, a document on environmental pollution which describes the effects of heavy metals from industrial waste on trout populations in Lake Erie. Using a keyword indexing strategy, the following frame entry is placed in the database in addition to the standard bibliographic information:

```
Document XXX
Type of Pollution: Water
Pollutant: Heavy Metals
Source: Industry
Transportation Process: Unknown (suspect Leaching)
Medium: Lake
Location: Lake Erie
Effect: Unknown
Entity: Trout
Concentration: Unknown
Response: Unknown
```

This frame is then an instance of the following general topic:

<Type of Pollution> where <Pollutant> from <Source> is transported by <Transportation Process> to <Medium> in <Location> and results in <Effect> on <Entity> with level of <Concentration> and is counteracted by <Response>

Frames represent a method for describing concepts such as instances of water pollution. They allow one to deduce what information is missing (such as the concentration of the pollutant in the above example) and the underlying script indicates the cause and effect relationships that exist between keywords. It is not suprising then that frames have been a focus of attention in recent research on new online retrieval methods (e.g., Monarch and Carbonnel, 1987; Croft, 1987). Further description of the current version of the system, including an evaluation of its performance, is provided by Krawczak, Smith, and Shute (1987).

In summary, we do not expect the development of stand-alone expert systems for information retrieval. Instead, we expect information retrieval to be subsumed within a more powerful intelligent database environment that includes the capabilities of knowledge-based indexing and deductive retrieval that would otherwise have been handled by a stand-alone expert system.

6.6.2   Inference on Large Databases

As we pointed out in Chapter 4, the role of expert systems as high level programming environments has been overlooked in the past. While the development of knowledge-based search intermediaries has received some attention, we expect that expert systems will have their major impact on information technology in carrying out deductive retrieval and inferencing.

It seems natural to carry out inference on large databases. Consider, for instance, the role of inference in querying. Query languages allow one to describe the information that one needs in some way. In a relational database, the query is expressed as a collection of terms and relational operators. In a textual database the query is typically expressed as a Boolean string composed of relevant terms connected by the Boolean operators AND, OR, NOT. However, in the same way that inference acts as a high level programming language (Kowalski, 1979), inference may also be used to carry out more sophisticated querying.

For instance, an inferencing capability, combined with a profile of research interests might be used to sort information into the following classes

    i. Directly pertinent—need full text

    ii. Interesting—need abstract

    iii. Possibly relevant—need citation

in much the same way that a medical diagnostic system may attempt to classify incoming patients into different disease categories.

Inference can assist information retrieval in a number of ways. For now we will express some generic rules that typify different types or styles of inferential information retrieval. Using the notation introduced in Chapter 4, where predicates are underlined, variables are indicated by surrounding single quotes, and rules are terminated with a semi-colon, we can formulate the following:

    Retrieve 'information-XX'

      If   'information-X' matches the current query

    and   'information-X' is within the current context

    and   'information-X' filtered is 'information-XX' ;

This generic rule retrieves information on the basis of three criteria. The first clause tests that the content of the information matches the content of the query. The second clause checks that the information makes sense within the current context of the search, where context may be broadly defined and may differ somewhat from a strict interpretation of the query. The third clause then applies a filter to the information before it is displayed to the user. Depending on the situation, different filters might be applied to reflect the user's background and interests.

We can then formulate two additional generic rules. The first rule specifies how information may match the current query, and the second rule defines what it means for a given piece of information to be within the current context.

> 'information-X' <u>matches</u> the current query
> If   'information-X' <u>keyword-matches</u> the current query
> or   'information-X' <u>associative matches</u> the current query
> or   <u>further negotiate</u> the current query;
>
> 'information-X' <u>is within</u> the current context
> If   'information-X' <u>related</u> to Subject
> and   Subject <u>is relevant</u>;

The generic rules listed above are designed to be evocative and somewhat self explanatory. The ways in which these generic rules are actually specified in a retrieval system will lead to different types of retrieval behavior. For instance, the ways in which further query negotiations are carried out or the relevance of subject topics is determined will reflect design decisions that are made for particular retrieval systems.

More generally, inference may be used not only as a retrieval aid but as a method for converting large databases into decision support or expert systems environments. In this book, we will focus on intelligent databases for information retrieval and utilization.

6.6.3 Information Retrieval and Instruction

Modern approaches to instruction have generally presupposed an orderly transfer of information from instructor and texts to the student. Yet the natural way to learn is to question and to discover. However, consider how learning occurs in a modern university. The modern university can be viewed as little changed from the medieval university in terms of the ways in which it is organized and the way in which learning is assumed to take place. While books have become plentiful, and relatively cheap compared with the overall cost of education, the lecture has changed surprisingly little. Lecturing permits relatively large numbers of students to interact with one teacher. In spite of its cost effectiveness, the lecture is certainly not a complete learning environment. Even under the best of circumstances, there is relatively little opportunity to explore ideas and interact with the instructor during a lecture. Lectures are often viewed as forums to motivate students and set learning goals, whereas most of the real learning occurs in laboratories, libraries, and through homework assignments and discussions with other students.

Tutorials provide more of the interactive component that is missing from lectures. In one form of tutorial format that is commonly used, the student pursues a course of readings under the guidance of the tutor and then submits periodic written reports. These in turn are the subject of tutorial discussion sessions (singly or in small groups).

The tutor/mentor is an attractive model for learning with intelligent databases. Here the user/student is encouraged to explore knowledge directly and to ask questions. The lecture seems more like conventional information retrieval systems and databases where information is provided without a great deal of interaction. When a student asks a question, further information is provided. The social and environmental constraints typically prevent a more active exploration of knowledge.

It seems desirable to allow users to interact with and explore knowledge directly. To do so, however, might overwhelm them with a mass of information that they are simply unable to deal with effectively. What is the amount of material that a human can deal with when interacting with an information retrieval system or intelligent database? We can get some clues by considering other types of information intensive tasks (Wheeler, 1987). The length of text that can be comfortably focused upon when reading is different from the corresponding comfortable spans when writing or editing. Editors can often keep in mind the compositional logistics of a typed document of some 60 or more pages as they search for redundancies and inconsistencies. Readers can, by flipping backwards and forwards through the text, keep track of roughly 10 or 20 pages of material, knowing where to refer to earlier portions of the argument. In creative writing, however, the focus tends to be much more immediate with an immediate focus on just a page or two around the current insertion point.

We can liken the user of an information system to a reader. However, since one cannot flip through screens as one can through the pages of a book, it is probably optimistic to expect people to keep track of more than 10 screens in an information system, even with the assistance of maps and navigational devices. Thus part of the specification of an intelligent database should be to keep track of the relationships between, and structure of, informational concepts. Ideally, the user should only have to express intentions, and read and understand concepts. Learning can then occur as a process of discovery.

In more structured searching, the process of learning is secondary to the goal of retrieving specific information. Here the focus is on the formulation of an adequate query and the subsequent retrieval of relevant information rather than on the process of discovery through direct exploration of information.

■ 6.7 FORECASTING THE FUTURE IN INFORMATION RETRIEVAL

Recently there has been a renewed interested in new information technologies. This interest has been stimulated by the explosion in mass storage capability, the continuing development of artifical intelligence technology, and the increasing power of microcomputer workstations. In this book, we outline a framework for coordinating these technologies within intelligent databases. In this section, we explicitly consider questions based on issues judged to be important in forecasting the future of intelligent information retrieval (cf., Porter, Wiederholt, Coberly, and Weaver, 1988). Relevant questions, and our answers to the questions, are as follows:

1. Does the key to improving information retrieval capability lie in developments in AI-based technologies?

   In Chapter 4 we outlined some of the contributions that expert systems can make in the development of intelligent databases. In the near term, constrained natural language interfaces that conform to a reasonably natural, but constrained, grammar may prove useful in querying. However, while AI-based technologies will certainly help, we expect that hypermedia will also have a great impact on intelligent information retrieval.

2. What are the institutional issues to be addressed in the development of IIR?

   Legal and social issues such as royalties and copyrights need to be carefully considered, along with other issues such as networking, communications, and cost generally. Several questions need to be clarified in order to incorporate intelligent databases into existing social and economic structures. It seems likely that new methods will need to be developed for assigning ownership to, and paying for the use of, information.

3. When, and to what extent, will widespread implementation of online, full-text databases be achieved?

   The widespread implementation of full-text databases requires modification of existing environments so that the information available in online databases is integrated smoothly with useful tasks. Methods are needed for treating full text databases as if they were indexed. This may require an extension to the concept indexing approach discussed earlier in this chapter.

4. What are the major conceptual and technological milestones that will have the most impact on the development of Intelligent Information Retrieval (IIR)?

   Following on from our answers to previous questions we see conceptual indexing as representing one such technological milestone. More generally, we expect that intelligent database technology, along the lines discussed in this book, will have a major impact on information retrieval technology.

   However, our research with intelligent databases has pointed out a need for an underlying object-oriented concept dictionary in large applications. This would remove the need for document content formalization in IIR, while maintaining a consistent indexing policy. Improvements in knowledge acquisition and machine learning will also facilitate the processes of knowledge engineering required in building intelligent databases.

5. What are the main tools and methodologies needed to implement IIR?

   Perhaps the two tools that are most needed are automated and interactive indexing, and new methods of browsing and of building browsing tools. At the moment there are too few ways of searching for, or browsing through, information.

6. How will local, corporate, and engineering databases be merged into the evolving IIR environment?

In addition to automated or interactive indexing, extended applications need to embed text retrieval within other tasks, such as online documentation, computer-based instruction, advice and explanation, decision support, and the like. Numerical and graphical databases should not be treated as special cases. Statistical routines and machine induction should be incorporated within the IIR framework. We don't expect that graphical interpretation will be the basis for retrieval in the near term.

Eventually we expect that different information sources will be handled by dispersed data storage and local retrieval in such a way that users do not have to worry about where information comes from unless they are particularly interested in that topic. Much of the information will be available "virtually" with very fast access from centralized file servers.

7. Who will develop the IIR capability?

R & D funding is growing at an accelerating pace in both industry and academia as the size and importance of the problem becomes obvious. We expect a combination of academics, software developers, and large database companies to combine in developing intelligent database technology. Innovative projects such as Intermedia at Brown University, Project Jefferson at USC, Project Perseus at Harvard, as well as proprietary commercial projects, provide clues as to the kind of organizational structures that will produce the innovations of the future.

8. What will IIR look like in the near term?

This is a difficult question to answer, but here are three scenarios sketched out very briefly:

Most likely system. A full hypermedia workstation networked to a variety of databases, including a standard interface that will uniformly query any electronic information in a transparent fashion. The information browsing and retrieval capabilities will be smoothly integrated with other workstation tasks. This is essentially the system described in Chapter 7 of this book.

Conservative system. Standard DBMS environments extended to include inference engines that allow deductive retrieval, along with transparent access to multimedia peripheral devices.

Optimistic System. Multi-windowing system using integrated voice and pointing device input, in the style of the "knowledge navigator" simulated in recent Apple videos and demonstrations. Smooth integration of physical simulation, concept indexing, and graphical reasoning within a consistent object-oriented data model. Distributed sites are tied in to an evolving world-brain or central encyclopedia/dictionary. While we see this type of system as a laudable goal, we don't expect it any time soon.

■ 6.8 SUMMARY

In the past thirty years, two technologies have developed which are leading to a new paradigm (cf. Kuhn, 1971) for the library and information sciences. First, the development of the computer, with its processing and mass storage capabilities, has allowed online storage of text, with resulting increased accessibility and availability of text. As a result, online information retrieval systems have developed. Artificial intelligence (AI) is the second technology of major importance to information science. AI has the potential to revolutionize the indexing strategies (and ultimately the retrieval methods) used in online retrieval by representing documents in terms of concepts rather than keywords. Frames in particular are an effective way of representing the concepts expressed in documents.

The technologies of information retrieval and text management are in a state of transition. This dynamic process of change has been characteristic of information technology ever since the invention of writing. Initially, the emphasis was on the materials used to produce text, i.e., paper and pens. With printing, mass production of texts became possible, and the emphasis shifted to that of making the printing process cheaper and more efficient. As the number of books available increased exponentially with the improved printing technology, the necessity to organize and classify the information became apparent, and library science and indexing schemes developed to meet the need. Information tools such as card catalogs, photocopying, and microfiche allowed people to access information through a combination of keywords and citation data. The development of online databases created new opportunities and challenges for information science.

The current paradigm of information retrieval refers to documents as collections of keywords, reflective of the information within the document. The available indexing methods require a great deal of expertise when it comes time to carry out a search. Several classes of expertise are required to conduct online searches. Procedural, domain, and strategic expertise, as well as knowledge of database-specific construction and practices, are all used actively by skilled searchers. But what of the user who wishes to conduct online searches, yet lacks some of this requisite expertise? We have shown how knowledge-based systems can be developed that allow the user to build his query directly, thus permitting searchers who lack some knowledge to conduct searches unaided by human intermediaries. The ultimate goal of systems such as EP-X and Jefferson is to remove the emphasis on search strategy and replace it with emphasis on subject knowledge. This gives more control to the subject specialist (or student) who is the information seeker.

The indexing strategy used constrains the inherent possibilities of the information retrieval system. It is clear that keywords do not fully index the knowledge contained within a document. On the other hand, natural language understanding is not yet at the stage where the document can serve as its own index entry and retrieval can be done on the basis of full-text analysis. Further, given current and near future computing capabilities, it is likely that full-text analysis in information retrieval will be too burdensome computationally to merit extensive implementation. Thus information science appears to be confronted by the two extremes of keyword and full-text indexing. In this chapter we have examined a third alternative lying between these two extremes which we refer to as concept indexing.

Text management and retrieval systems, and the associated indexing and search methods are a major part of the new information retrieval paradigm. This paradigm shift will change the way in which online retrieval systems function. The most obvious change for users will be in the nature of the interface between them and the information retrieval system. To compensate for the increased burden on the user, the system will know more about the subject matter and will be able to respond to errors better, both on operational levels and subject levels. Syntax will become transparent. Users will take on a more active role as they search through the relevant domain knowledge in formulating queries rather than handing over much of the search activity to an intermediary. Development and implementation of a new paradigm for information retrieval will be a difficult and costly task, requiring new methods of indexing documents. Aside from the need for concept indexing to support the new paradigm, user interfaces for information retrieval will have to be much improved if the goal of effective end user direct access is to be achieved.

Specifications for knowledge-based search intermediaries of the future include the following guidelines. A knowledge-based search intermediary should encourage the development of simple, veridical, user-conceptual models of system function. It should display and accept information in ways which are compatible with human cognitive processes (Shute, Smith, Krawczak, Chignell, and Sater, 1986), and concurrently provide context-sensitive, multi-layered error handling and on-line HELP facilities. Domain knowledge should be represented in such a way that semantic associations among concepts are preserved. Logical operations, search heuristics, and database-specific policies may also be integrated into the intelligent system's control regime, to reduce the cognitive burden on end-users. The omission of any of these classes of expertise from a knowledge-based interface may make the use of that system ineffective for some users. To provide non-expert end-users the capability to conduct successful searches on their own, knowledge-based systems must integrate components of *all* of these classes of expertise.

The reader may notice that many of the features of this new information retrieval paradigm are shared with intelligent databases, as characterized in this book. In particular, concept (knowledge-based) indexing is critical to the functionality of intelligent databases. We expect that the task of information search and retrieval will be carried out by intelligent databases in the future as the emphasis moves from retrieval of secondary sources (documents) to information management, question answering, and decision support.

7

INTELLIGENT DATABASES

■ **7.1 INTRODUCTION**

In Chapter 1 we motivated the development of intelligent databases, while Chapters 2 to 6 discussed the components of the technologies needed for building intelligent databases. This chapter discusses the integration of the technologies reviewed in the previous chapters.

We begin by reviewing the stepwise, three-layer architecture of an intelligent database introduced in Chapter 1. This architecture consisted of the high-level tools, the high-level interface level, and the database support level. Building on the material introduced in the previous chapters, we now elaborate on the structure of these layers.

In Section 2 we present FORM (Formal Object Representation Model) as a general model of intelligent databases. FORM draws on the discussions of the previous chapters in the sense that it is an object-oriented, deductive, hypermedia model specifically suited to database applications. We discuss the structure of FORM and illustrate one of its applications—an intelligent information management workstation.

Then in Sections 7.3, 7.4 and 7.5 we focus on the structure of each of the three layers of the intelligent database; that is, high-level tools, the user interface, and the database engine. We begin the discussion from the base level upwards (i.e., with the intelligent database engine) and use it as a foundation for the high-level interface and the high-level intelligent tools.

In Section 7.6 we discuss an example application, Fortune Finder, which is developed within FORM and which fully utilizes the technology of intelligent databases discussed in the previous chapters.

7.1.1 The Architecture of an Intelligent Database

As discussed in Chapter 1, the top-level architecture of the intelligent database consists of three levels.

High-level Tools, High-level Interface, and Intelligent Database Engine as shown in Figure 7.1.

The high-level tools provide the user with a number of facilities such as intelligent search, data quality and integrity control, and discovery. They are object-oriented, deductive, and their basic structure mirrors the representation methods of the intelligent database model.

The high-level user interface is the level that users directly interact with. As such, it has to deal as much with how the user wants to think about databases and information management as it has to do with how the database engine actually operates. Associated with this level are a set of representation tools that enhance the functionality of the intelligent database.

The user interface is presented in two aspects. There is a core model that is presented to the user. This core incorporates a hypermedia object-oriented representation of information, along with a set of integrated tools for browsing, searching, and asking questions. In addition, there are a set of high-level tools, which although not an essential part of the core model, nevertheless enhance the functionality of the intelligent database system for certain classes of user.

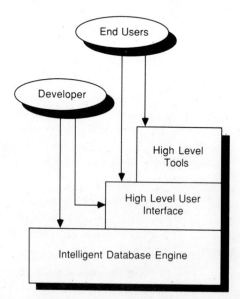

Figure 7.1 The architecture of an intelligent database.

The base (third) level of the system is the intelligent database engine. The intelligent database engine incorporates a model that allows for deductive object-oriented representation of information that can be expressed and operated on in a variety of ways. In this chapter we present the semantics of this model. We shall not attempt to define a syntax for this model, thereby avoiding a bias towards a specific implementation. The engine includes backward and forward chaining inference procedures as well as drivers for the external media devices, version handlers, optimizing compilers, and the like. Many of the features of this integrated engine will depend on the specifics of the hardware and software environment in which an intelligent database is implemented.

We formalize the model for the intelligent database engine and the user interface within FORM and show how the high-level tools may be easily built within this framework. To motivate the specific constructs involved in developing FORM, we shall delineate the requirements for an intelligent database.

7.1.2 Requirements for an Intelligent Database

A traditional database developer may legitimately ask, *"How does an intelligent database improve upon what I am using today?"* To answer this question, we show how intelligent databases extend traditional database paradigms. Thus we pose and answer the following four questions:

a. How do intelligent databases improve upon the current generation of end-user database languages—i.e., What comes after QBE?

b. How do intelligent databases improve upon the current generation of database programming systems—i.e., What comes after SQL?

c. How do intelligent databases and expert systems allow both programmers and nonprogrammers to build application interfaces and graphic objects—i.e., What comes after fourth-generation languages?

d. How can this technology and hypertext be combined to deal with the information overload problem especially in the area of textual databases—i.e., Where do we go after Xanadu?

These questions may be answered in the following manner:

a. An intuitive visual model involving a deductive and object-oriented visual system can be used to create a pattern-matching QBE-like system that performs deductive queries and expert database consultations with a great deal of ease (Figure 7.2).

The resulting system may be defined by the equation

$$\text{End-User System} = \text{Hypermedia} + \text{QBE} + \text{Inference} \\ + \text{Object Orientation}$$

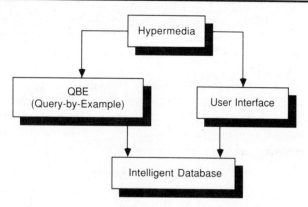

Figure 7.2 Overall architecture of a QBE-like system for deductive querying and expert database consultations.

The appeal of the visual nature of both hypermedia and QBE is well known. However, this can then be easily extended to inference and object orientation. This system thus provides more power and user friendliness than the traditional QBE interface.

b. Traditional SQL based systems rely on interfaces with cursors and programming languages such as C and Cobol. In an intelligent database SQL is extended in two distinct directions

  1. *Unification Based SQL.* Queries are obtained by merging SQL with pattern matching rules. This uses the rule-based paradigm as a powerful and natural extension of the control structures involved in performing SQL queries.

  2. *Object-oriented SQL.* Object-oriented extensions to SQL are provided. This not only facilitates the formation of queries, but improves the data definition process. Further the object-oriented and the rule-based extensions to SQL are themselves uniformly merged.

The resulting system (Figure 7.3) may then be defined by the equation

$$\text{Programming System} = \text{SQL} + \text{Logic} + \text{Object Orientation}$$

Again, these components may be merged in a seamless and uniform manner.

c. We introduce a deductive object-oriented *Dialog Language* that naturally extends concepts involved in systems such as Microsoft Windows™, the Macintosh Finder™ and Open Look™ with deductive inheritance and attached predicates. This language may either be viewed as a "deductive and object-

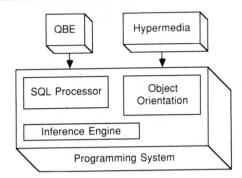

Figure 7.3 A programming system for an intelligent database.

oriented version" of a hypermedia system or as a "hypertext version" of an expert-system language. The key point here is to use a *declarative* approach to dialog specification, rather than the procedural (or event-driven) approach used in the Macintosh Finder (Desktop), Microsoft Windows, OS/2™, New Wave™, and so on. Here, objects are used as the basic building blocks for dialogs, and rules and unification are used as the firing mechanisms for invoking dialogs.

The structure of the dialog language (Figure 7.4) is then defined by

Dialog Language = Screen Primitives + Dynamic icons
+ Object orientation + Inference + Hypermedia

One of the most attractive features of the approach presented here is that it is *seamless* and *extensible*. Thus, although end users may use a small section

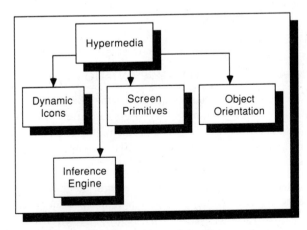

Figure 7.4 The structure of the dialog system.

of the dialog language to build dialogs, programmers may use a larger set of features. Moreover, this approach will prove extremely powerful in the context of *object-oriented spreadsheets,* which combine logical and object-oriented "rippling" with the traditional arithmetic method of value propagation used in systems such as Lotus 123. This then naturally leads to a full framework for decision support systems.

d. Later in this chapter we present a design for an Intelligent Information Retrieval Workstation (IIRW), which combines the features described in (a), (b), and (c) to provide a *dynamic* hypermedia system whose links and data are dynamically updated as the information content of the system changes.

Due to its reliance on dynamic links, this system has distinct advantages over traditional systems, both for authoring hypermedia systems and in the flexibility it provides to end-users.

Thus, our intelligent information retrieval workstation uses dynamic hypertext, object-oriented programming, knowledge representation, concept structures, and logic. The workstation is distinguished by several novel features integrated within a powerful retrieval facility.

A typical application for such a workstation lies in the field of financial research for corporations and is demonstrated by the Fortune Finder system. In this application, new information becomes available all the time and values in databases (e.g. current stock prices, etc.) rapidly change.

In the next section we present a formal model that satisfies the equations above. In Sections 7.3 to 7.5 we show how this model realizes the layered stepwise architecture of intelligent databases. The model has wide-scale availability in a number of fields. For instance in the field of *decision support,* which is now emerging as a more formal discipline that extends spread-sheets and databases. The impact of expert databases on decision support will be very important. After all, why do we access data if not for making decisions?

■ 7.2 FORM: A FORMAL OBJECT REPRESENTATION MODEL

The goals formulated in Section 7.1 may be achieved within a single uniform framework: FORM (Formal Object Representation Model). This model may be used at different levels of detail as a programming and system design tool for both programmers and end users. Thus the model is seamless in the sense that there is no dramatic change between the end-user and the programmer mode.

FORM captures the *conceptual* model of the underlying integrated database and inference engine. The underlying engine thus provides "native support" for the constructs, in FORM. Moreover, the user interface system itself is written in FORM, providing a great deal of portability.

Not surprisingly, FORM integrates the technologies discussed in Chapters 2 through 6. The basic idea behind FORM is quite intuitive and easy to grasp.

a. We use object orientation as a basic paradigm in all data and knowledge representations. This is naturally achieved by viewing all concepts, databases, objects, and so on with an object-oriented point of view. This builds on the material in Chapter 3.

b. We use an integrated database and inference engine that uses a uniform approach to forward, backward, and inexact inference with unification. Further, the inference engine can simultaneously deal with logical and object-oriented views of the same database. Rule based and object-oriented features are thus seamlessly integrated within the engine, based on the discussion presented in Chapter 4.

c. We use the technology developed in (a) and (b) above to support a dynamic hypermedia system. Here all presentable objects (be they cards, folders, forms, pictures, etc.) are treated as objects stored in the object-oriented deductive database. The dynamic links are then implemented with explicit database assertions and deductive rules, as suggested in Chapter 5.

d. Finally, most of the high-level tools such as Automatic Discovery and Data Quality Control tools are themselves written in FORM, providing both a very uniform user interface and a high degree of portability.

The overall integration of these concepts is then performed in terms of the uniform model—FORM.

7.2.1 The Basic Concepts of FORM

The basic structuring concept in FORM is an object. FORM objects generally correspond to objects within an object-oriented system or elements within a hypermedia system. A FORM object has the following manifestations in the different contexts:

- It is a *frame* in an expert-system context.
- It is an *object* in an object-oriented system.
- It is a *relation* in a relational database.
- It is a *text fragment* in a hypertext system.
- It is a *diagram*, a *picture*, or a *sound* in a hypermedia system.

One of the features of the FORM model is that it unifies these apparently diverse entities in terms of a conceptual structure (the object) that emphasizes the common function of packaging and presenting information.

Objects, regardless of their use, have *attributes* that are generally characterized according to the context in which the object appears. *Attributes* appear as

- *slots* in frames.
- *attributes* in objects.
- *fields* in relations.

- *key words* in text fragments.
- *labels* or *tags* in diagrams, pictures, etc.

Objects described in any of these ways then enjoy the same type of inheritance properties as frames and objects (as described earlier in Chapters 3 and 4) and may be involved in various forms of reasoning through unification and rule-based inference (Figure 7.5).

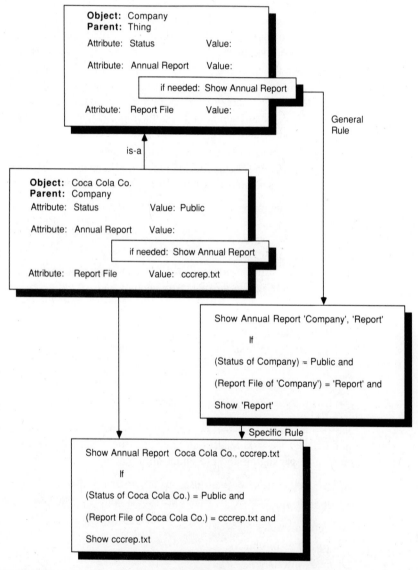

Figure 7.5 An example of the use of objects and rules to integrate reasoning and retrieval.

Each attribute has a name that is local to the object. Attributes can have *values*, which may be assigned by assignment operations. The value of an attribute may be another object. Thus, FORM supports the strong notion of object identity discussed in Chapter 3. Hence, the same object can be the attribute value of more than one object. In other words, objects may be shared within a graph-structured object space, providing a great deal of generality.

Each attribute may have a set of *attached predicates*. Attached predicates are fired whenever the attribute is accessed, as discussed in Chapter 4. There are two types of attached predicates.

> *if-needed*—fired when the value of the attribute is accessed.

> *if-added*—fired when the value of the attribute is modified.

This provides objects with dynamic data storage capabilities.

7.2.2 Methods and Facts

To use objects, we need to operate on them. Thus with each object a specific set of *methods* (also called *operations*) may be associated. Each method is *local* with respect to the object.

A method (operation) may cause a change in the value of the object's attributes, assert facts, print, and so on. A method may be defined by backward, forward, or inexact rules with unification. The collection attributes and methods associated with an object capture the behavior of the object. Thus, objects are abstract data types.

Moreover, each object has a local *factbase* which may hold a number of assertions. These facts are fully local to the object, that is, they are not considered part of other factbases. Each operation/method simply accesses the facts available within the object. Facts within the object's local (i.e., private) factbase may thus be modified to change the internal state of the object, providing the capability for information hiding.

Methods access attributes simply by naming them, for example

> method1 Attribute1

applies the predicate method1 to the value of Attribute1. The attributes of an object are "public" and may be directly accessed and updated. Thus, if the object Person has the attribute Age, then

> (Age of Person)

provides us with the value of the attribute Age wherever it is used. This is in contrast to the local factbase of an object which is *hidden* from other objects and may be only accessed by the object's methods.

Special naming conventions are used to facilitate the use of methods. For instance the term "Object-Name" always refers to the name of the object from which the method is *invoked*. This will become particularly useful when methods are inherited, as discussed in the next section.

A number of specific predicates facilitate communication between objects. For instance, the predicate

> send-message 'Object' , 'Method', 'Arg1', . . . , 'Arg N'

sends a message to 'Object' that results in the invocation of the predicate 'Method' with the given arguments. This provides the obvious advantages associated with data abstraction, as discussed in Chapter 3. The send-message predicate naturally accepts an indeterminate number of arguments. For instance, to raise an employee's salary, we prove the goal

> send-message John Smith, Raise Salary, 10%

where Raise Salary is a method defined within the object Employee, which is a parent of John Smith.

7.2.3   Parents, Instances, and Inheritance

Each object has at least one *parent object*. A specific object called *Thing* is the parent of all other objects, that is "Everything is a Thing." An object may have more than one parent, that is *multiple inheritance* is also allowed.

Each object inherits the attributes and methods of each of its parents. Obviously, all objects have access to the attributes and rules associated with the object *Thing*. Thus, Thing acts as a global factbase and rulebase.

When proving a method for an object, we search the inheritance graph if the method may not be locally found within the object. This has very powerful implications. For instance, consider the object Scenario which is gradually "enriched" with the addition of sub-scenarios. This allows for the execution of logical what-if scenarios in a very natural way.

Each object may have a set of *instances*. Each instance inherits from its parent object. Thus instances are "generic replicas" of the *structure* of an object, as discussed in Chapters 3 and 4. Object instances may naturally be stored within databases as records. Instances may be accessed either with the predicate model or the object model, as discussed in Chapter 4.

Thus, the full power of attached predicates, methods and predicates is available for use with instances. For example, we may monitor the integrity of updates to the database with an attached if-added predicate, as discussed in Section 4.7.2.

Note that the inheritance mechanism here is very general and supports both delegation and object inheritance as described in Chapters 3 and 4. It is convenient to "group" objects which have the same structure together in sets, tables, stacks, or relations.

This is exactly what is done in record-oriented models. The inheritance mechanism in FORM is "complete" in the sense that it provides a general mechanism for inheriting or sharing structure, values, rules, and methods.

We can create instances of objects with the <u>new-object</u> predicate, as in

<u>new-object</u> John Smith, Employee

An instance of the object Employee then inherits the structure and methods of the Employee object.

7.2.4 Presentations and Links

Attributes and methods allow us to use objects as a knowledge representation technique. Each object also has a *presentation* which defines the way in which it may be viewed by the user (Figure 7.6).

For instance, an object may be presented at a specific location on a screen, or may be presented in a number of forms (e.g., pie-chart, bar-chart). In early programming languages, presentation issues concerned the way in which information was formatted on various output devices. In the FORM model, the presentations for an object are naturally determined by inheritance, that is, once we have an object called "personal computer market share," which is a child of "market share," then it may be displayed in a variety of formats that are particularly suited to information concerning market share.

Each object presentation may also have a set of *links*. The links are references to other objects from within an object's presentation. A link may be either

- A direct link which is specifically stated.
- A dynamic link which is obtained by inference.

Links naturally allow for hypermedia operations on objects. Various types of links are discussed below in Section 7.4.1.1.

7.2.5 Dialogs: The Building Blocks of User Interfaces

Within FORM, all information is displayed to the user in terms of *dialogs*. A dialog is an object which has as parent a special object called DIALOG (IntelligenceWare 1988b).

Using Dialogs allows us to have a uniform representation mechanism for building user interfaces. Using Dialogs has three distinct and orthogonal advantages.

a. It provides data abstraction; for example, one can port software far more easily. It also allows for good software development, and so on.

b. It makes it unnecessary to be an "expert" programmer to build user interfaces. For instance, (without HyperCard) one has to be a Macintosh expert to build

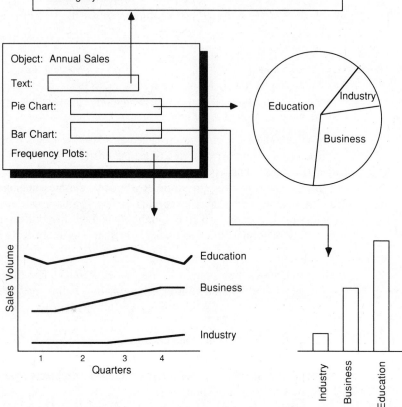

Sales in the business market were up considerably with that market accounting for 35% of our Widget/2 model. There were also some growth in the engineering / industrial sector, which accounted for 8% of sales in the past financial year. Although volume remained fairly constant in the educational market, the proportion of current Widget/2 sales that went to education fell slightly to 57%.

Object: Annual Sales

Text:

Pie Chart:

Bar Chart:

Frequency Plots:

Education
Industry
Business

Sales Volume

Education
Business
Industry

1 2 3 4
Quarters

Industry
Business
Education

Figure 7.6 Different representations of objects.

Macintosh programs. But HyperCard makes this unnecessary. However, we go beyond HyperCard in FORM dialogs.

c. Our approach allows for the use of rules in building dialogs. This allows us to use a far more powerful programming paradigm than traditional programming.

Each dialog has a set of "participating objects" of which it is composed. In traditional terms, these participating terms are generally referred to as "buttons," "editable items," etc.

The parent object "DIALOG" has specific information about the type of hardware and visual display being used. This results in high levels of portability.

The participating objects have specific "relative locations" with respect to each other. The presence of these relative locations again ensures portability.

Each participating object in a dialog has a set of dependencies which propagate changes made to that object throughout the dialog. For example by changing a specific element changes may ripple through dialogs.

The Dialog System provides two orthogonal facilities:

    i. Data abstraction for event and agent based environments.
    ii. The use of rules as well as procedural languages for dialog management.

Item (i) in itself is very important. It allows applications to be distinct from the hardware and the operating environments in which they are executed. Data abstraction provides a great deal of flexibility and portability in software development.

Item (ii) achieves a next level of expressive power by using rules and object-orientation as a very high-level programming paradigm. This results in far shorter programs and allows end-users to easily build dialogs.

7.2.5.1　Basic Concepts of Dialogs

The basic concepts involved in a Dialog are as follows:

> _Window:_ A distinct area of a screen to which input or output may be sent.

> _Item:_ A specific marker or editing area within a window which can be acted upon by the user or the dialog application.

> _Menu:_ A method of choosing among a number of selections.

> _Event:_ A change in a state of a dialog, initiated by the user or the system.

> _Action:_ A set of programs or procedures which are initiated upon the occurrence of an event.

> _Dependency:_ A link between some event or item and others which conditionally specifies a "trigger."

> _Input Device:_ A device for inputting data or actions (e.g. keystroke, mouse click).

A Dialog is thus a window with a set of items (and possibly menus) which performs a set of actions upon the occurrence of some events. Windows may be overlapped and be used as pop-up windows, and so on. Each window has a specific set of attributes such as background and text color.

This easily allows for the development of a QBE system, either for use within a hypermedia system or in stand-alone mode. The QBE paradigm is extended by the use of rules, expressed as a sequence of clauses. Since each clause can itself be viewed as a card, rules and queries are naturally merged within a uniform environment.

Moreover, by using the technologies of intelligent databases, the user may input rules by example, and, piece by piece discover rules by incremental induction. This provides an unprecedented level of functionality.

The Dialog System provides a number of built-in item types as follows:

> *Editable:* These are items that accept editable input from the keyboard. Each editable item has a maximum length. Types are separately enforced by triggering dependencies. Editables are similar to the Macintosh "Text-edit" items.

> *Message:* These are items that are for display only. A message has a maximum length after which the text is word-wrapped to the next line.

> *Button:* These are items that upon activation trigger a specific dependency.

> *Slide Bar:* A slide bar is a way to graphically input a numeric value (such as a confidence level) in an intuitive way.

> *Choice:* A choice item presents to the user a group of options, one of which can be selected by the user. If all the options cannot be displayed in the screen space allocated, the options may be "scrolled."

> *Set:* A set item presents to the user a group of options, many of which can be selected by the user. If all the options cannot be displayed in the screen space allocated, the options may be "scrolled."

> *List Box:* A list box allows the user to create or edit related data "records" as a group. A list box may have multiple columns. A list box can be used to edit a list, a relation, or a spreadsheet.

A number of attributes are associated with each item. These determine color, background, etc. In the case of listboxes, these attributes determine whether or not the user can add elements to the listbox, and so on.

These basic types may be easily extended for different environments by using data abstraction. For instance, the types "Fuel Gauge" or "Temperature Gauge" may be easily added to work like curved slidebars.

The Dialog System uses a top level event dispatcher. This event handler manages keystroke events, etc. and allows for the interception of events. An action is a procedure or predicate which is invoked by a trigger. Actions help establish conditions and constraints.

The concept of nested transactions, as discussed in Chapter 2, is important in dialogs. This means that changes made to the objects in a dialog are not permanent until the user has explicitly committed them. The transactions need to be nested since the user may invoke another dialog from within the current dialog. These may be thought of as "pop-up" or "parenthetical" dialogs.

The issue of nested transactions has widespread implications in a variety of applications, such as cooperative authoring and maintaining of large software environments (CASE and version maintenance). In such applications, changes need to be made provisionally on a nested transaction basis (combined with the possibility for backtracking if necessary). The application of the concepts of nested transactions illustrates the viability of applying database methodology and formalisms within a wide variety of instances.

7.2.6 An Example of FORM

We will illustrate the FORM model with a particular type of intelligent database application, namely an intelligent information retrieval workstation (IIRW). Other variants of the FORM model may be constructed for different intelligent database applications such as intelligent tutoring systems, CASE, and computer integrated manufacturing (CIM).

The ultimate goal of an IIRW is to present information to the user. At each point in time, there are three questions involved here.

    i. What is the context for the display?
    ii. What is to be displayed?
    iii. How is it to be displayed?

Question iii refers to the form of presentation of each object used in the display. In the FORM model, a display is a collection of objects presented simultaneously. Each display is constructed dynamically from the set of objects that are inferred to be the most relevant in the current context. Question ii above addresses the issue of which objects are to be displayed. This question can only be reasonably answered if some account is taken of the current context, which is what question (i) considers. The context is important because it establishes the relevance of objects. The judged relevance of the objects is then used to answer question (ii) by selecting those objects which are most relevant given the current context.

The dynamic nature of the FORM model is evidenced not only in the way in which displays are constructed "on the fly" but also, as we show later, by the creation of dynamic links. In addition, each object may have a number of representations. The multiple representations of each object are linked to a single concept represented by a unique object name. Consider, for instance, the object Coca-Cola. Representation of this object begins by attaching a definition to it:

> *Coca-Cola is a specific soft drink as well as the name of a company that manufactures and sells Coca-Cola as one of its major activities.*

We then describe the major properties of the Coca-Cola Company. First, it will have a set of properties that are shared with large corporations in general. Second, it will have a set of properties that are shared with its competitor soft drink companies (e.g., Pepsi Cola) and with the beverage industry in general, such as seasonal variation in demand for its product, and a high advertising budget. Third, there will be a set of properties that are fairly unique, such as the effect that the introduction of the new Coca-Cola formula had on the company a few years ago. These properties themselves define the concept of Coca-Cola in terms of a complex set of subconcepts. In the current model, we view these subconcepts as nodes that are linked in various ways to the general concept of Coca-Cola.

Part of the description of Coca-Cola will revolve around the organization of the beverage industry and of large corporations in general. In the FORM model, this organizational information is described in terms of inheritance hierarchies.

Coca-Cola may also be described in terms of the relations that it has to other concepts. Soft drinks with high caffeine content, for instance, are frequently used as stimulants. With regard to this usage, Coca-Cola (the soft drink) is related to coffee, although there is no direct corporate connection between the soft drink and coffee industries that we are aware of. This type of relationship may be represented with a hypermedia link.

7.2.6.1 Combining Objects

In addition to defining the nature of individual objects, the FORM model also provides methods for combining objects. These methods are

a. The linear path (or stack). In this method, the objects are linked sequentially, much as the pages in a book or the records in a sequential file.

b. The hierarchy. Hierarchies allow objects to be nested within categories and subcategories. Hierarchies also permit properties or characteristics to be inherited across parent-child links.

c. Links. The FORM model also specifies a standard set of link types. The link types used in FORM are related to the set of link types discussed earlier in Chapter 5. The FORM link types will be introduced in Section 7.4.2.

7.2.6.2 Logical Deduction

The browsing capabilities provided by the FORM model link types may be augmented by allowing a series of operations to be performed on an object. These operations are dynamically determined with a set of rules based on context, the user, data available, and so on. To seek further information, the user must first "select" an object (or enter information about an object). The user is then provided with a number of choices about how to find more information about the object itself or about related objects. Some of the choices will be static or fixed and generally available whenever the object is displayed. Other choices will be context sensitive, or determined at runtime.

These inferentially controlled choices are determined by rules, for example

> 'X' is a choice for operator, 'Object'

If   'Object' <u>is-a</u> 'Parent' and
           'X' is a choice for operator, 'Parent';
or,
           Stock is a choice for operator, 'Object'
If

           'Object' <u>is-a</u> Company and
           (Status of 'Object') = Public;

In the second rule shown above, stock will be a choice if the company is public. Similarly, the information that is actually displayed will change according to the interests of the IIRW's user.

Logical deduction is also used to select objects to be displayed and to update the information within objects before it is displayed.

7.2.6.3 Querying

In contrast to browsing, querying involves a more structured form of search where the nature of the desired information is specified a priori. Instead of recognizing interesting information from a selection of choices (as in browsing), the user has to construct a query that will take him to the relevant information. However, the existing model of querying, such as is observed in SQL or QBE systems, or even in large online retrieval services such as DIALOG and BRS, was developed before the widespread use of hypermedia. Thus there is an opportunity to integrate browsing functions into more effective querying systems. The effectiveness of such querying systems may be further enhanced by extending the nature of hypertext to include dynamically-defined, as well as static, links.

The equation

> hypertext = packaged text

applies to most hypertext systems today. However, by using an object-oriented and rule-based paradigm, the IIRW envisioned here goes beyond this by allowing

    i. The dynamic calculation and updating of information.
    ii. The dynamic adjustment of links and associations (i.e., the structure of information).

This dynamic view of hypertext and hypermedia stems from a revised conception of the traditional relationship between queries and information structures. This revised approach has been necessitated by the sheer volume of changing information that must now be dealt with in many applications, since managing physical links manually in a large hypertext system in which information changes frequently will be virtually impossible.

We envision four major tasks within a Dynamic Hypermedia Information Retrieval system (the basis for the IIRW).

1. Knowledge representation.
2. Inference and reasoning.
3. Browsing.
4. Structured information retrieval.

In structured information retrieval, new methods of querying are needed to take advantage of the properties of dynamic hypermedia. The FORM model may be used to create a seamless and natural relationship between browsing tools and structured queries. This is done by viewing querying as a side effect of the browsing process. Thus, as users browse, they come across interesting concepts and terms. When they feel it to be appropriate, they may access a tool which constructs a query (structured information search) which then returns a set of relevant information. This information may consist of documents, citations, or indexed hypertext fragments. The only requirement for structured search is that information be indexed.

In the FORM model, the indexing is achieved through specialized ATTRIBUTES which are then searchable. Once a set of information has been retrieved in a structured search it may then be read through sequentially, or automatically linked into a hypertext network, based on the sharing of index terms between the documents or text fragments. However, the details of this linking process and its use are not an integral part the FORM model.

FORM may be viewed as a model for describing the objects within an intelligent database. Thus we may think of FORM as a data model for intelligent databases. In addition to this data model, we need to formulate the structure of each of the three components of an intelligent database discussed earlier. We begin with the intelligent database engine and use it as a foundation for the high-level interface and the high-level intelligent tools.

■ **7.3 THE INTEGRATED INTELLIGENT DATABASE ENGINE**

The intelligent database engine implements the features of the intelligent database model (FORM) discussed above. Many of the features of the engine will be shared with database engines, inference engines, and software systems in general.

The key features of the architecture of the intelligent database engine are:

a. Native support for the FORM model through complex object storage support and optimization of complex object accesses.

b. Close integration of data access and the inference engine.

c. Based on (b) above, the global optimization of FORM queries and programs resulting in very efficient performance.

d. Efficient support of multimedia storage and display that is built into the engine.

The major components of the integrated intelligent database engine are as follows.

The Compiler/Optimizer—The Compiler/Optimizer is a module which will accept an intelligent database program and generate optimized internal code using metadata information on the physical database structures as well as the rule manager to perform optimization.

The Rule Manager—The rule manager encapsulates all the algorithms that are used in performing forward and backward chaining on the rules. It invokes the access module for performing matches and searches on the persistent object space.

The Explanation Manager—The rule manager tells the explanation manager about its searches and the explanation manager records these in data structures that are passed to the user who then requests explanations on goals that succeed or fail.

The Transaction Manager—The transaction manager encapsulates all the algorithms that are needed to perform concurrency control and recovery, ensuring atomicity of transactions.

The Meta-data Manager—The meta-data manager contains all the meta-data information associated with the persistent database, including schemata, inheritance hierarchies for the classes of the persistent objects, methods and operators associated with the classes, and access method information also associated with class instances.

The Access Module—The access module contains all the access method codes for performing efficient searches on records, image data, long text data, as well as clustering algorithms for complex objects. It incorporates single and multidimensional index structures such as B-trees.

The Multi-Media Manager—The multi-media manager incorporates routines to handle peripherals such as scanners and digitizers as well as efficient management of multi-media devices such as write once optical disks, CD-ROMS and so on. For instance, write once optical disks would need special algorithms to allocate sectors in order to have more efficient storage utilization.

The two main ideas here are

a. Connectivity to peripheral multimedia devices.

b. Efficient management of these peripheral devices through software techniques.

The memory manager—The memory manager performs caching of persistent database objects and provides memory chunks to all the other modules; it also incorporates garbage collection operations.

The intelligent database model is the second level of the entire system. It consists of an object-oriented representation of information that acts as a bridge between the user interface level above it and the intelligent database engine below it (Figure 7.7). The intelligent database model should not be confused with the FORM model which is a functional description of the major structural objects and operations of an intelligent database. The features of the FORM model are represented at the system level by the intelligent database model that enforces them within an object-oriented framework. We now consider the way in which information is represented in this object-oriented intelligent database model.

7.3.1 Abstract Data Types

Much of the functionality of the intelligent database derives from the use of abstract data types that allow the equivalence of information to be recognized and transmitted across diverse representations of that information. For instance, an employee of a company might be represented as a record in a relational employee database for that company. A biography of that person may also appear within a hypermedia document, or that employee may be referred to as an instance of the general class of Person elsewhere in the system. However, in the intelligent database model, no matter where the information about the employee is stored, the descriptions, rules, and so on are referring to a common object (i.e., the instance of that person) that is being described. As with other object-oriented representation systems, collections of objects correspond to classes. The system is also extensible with new classes or subclasses being defined as needed. Generally one defines an initial hierarchy of built in data types in the intelligent database model and the user can then extend or customize this hierarchy to fit his own information manipulation and management needs.

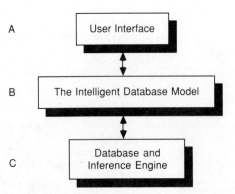

A   User Interface

B   The Intelligent Database Model

C   Database and Inference Engine

Figure 7.7 The bridge between the user-interface level and the intelligent database engine.

7.3.2 Object Identity

The notion of object identity is central to the development of the intelligent-database model. Since the underlying representation is a network of objects (nodes) and links and since this underlying object representation is used to link disparate pieces of information pertaining to a particular object, it is necessary to detect and preserve the identity of objects.

Object identity is a complex topic that can be handled with a variety of strategies. Figure 7.8 (after Khoshafian and Copeland, 1986) shows how different languages can be characterized in terms of a two-dimensional space where one dimension refers to the way that object names (identities) are generated and the other dimension refers to the temporal extent of object identity.

At one extreme, a language like Smalltalk-80 has object identity built into the language. In order to maintain this strong notion of identity, Smalltalk must maintain its representation of identity during updates, in addition to using identity in the semantics of its operators, and providing operators to manipulate identity.

However, although Smalltalk-80 creates strong object identities, these identities are transient in that once a program stops running, the identities are lost. In contrast, a language like OPAL (Copeland and Maier, 1984) not only maintains a strong version of object identity, but it also maintains these identities over time so that data are persistent.

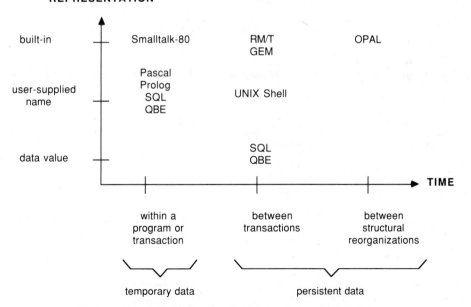

Figure 7.8 A two-dimensional characterization of languages.

Languages also differ in the way that they implement important constructs that have direct bearing on the identity of objects. Specifically, the power of each implementation technique can be measured by the degree of value, structure and location independence it provides. Figure 7.9 provides a schematic representation of a taxonomy for distinguishing different levels of data independence and location independence.

The simplest implementation of the identity of an object may well be the physical address of that object (which could be real or virtual). In such an implementation,

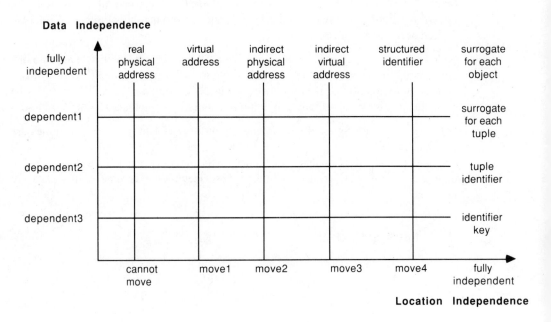

Data Independence

	real physical address	virtual address	indirect physical address	indirect virtual address	structured identifier	surrogate for each object
fully independent						
						surrogate for each tuple
dependent1						
						tuple identifier
dependent2						
						identifier key
dependent3						
	cannot move	move1	move2	move3	move4	fully independent

Location Independence

dependent1	*dependent2*	*dependent 3*	
value independent somewhat structure dependent	value independent structure dependent	value and structure dependent	

move1	*move2*	*move3*	*move4*
move page within one virtual address space	move object within one physical address space	move object within one virtual address space	move object within one disk or server

Figure 7.9 Analysis of implementation techniques in terms of data independence and location independence.

there would be no location independence since physical address implementation does not permit an object to be moved between address spaces.

Object identity may also be implemented indirectly, as in the case of Smalltalk-80, where identity is maintained through entries in object tables. Each entity is referred to as an object-oriented pointer (OOP).

In the intelligent database model described here, object identity is maintained by use of an object dictionary. Object names are unique and no distinction is made between the names of a single object that are used in different versions. Needless to say, the complexity of maintaining object identity increases greatly when the model is modified to include versioning and related issues.

7.3.3 Inheritance

The third component of object orientation in an intelligent database is inheritance. Inheritance allows sharing of structure as well as behavior of objects. It provides a most natural mechanism for organizing information. The intelligent database data model allows both class (abstract data types) and instance (object) inheritance. Delegation is also supported. In FORM the conflict between encapsulation and inheritance is minimal since it is up to the designer to decide whether the data is represented in the interface or local factbase.

7.3.4 Built-in Data Types

The intelligent database model also includes a rich collection of built-in data types, including integers, character strings, as well as voice, animation, motion. It is important to note the distinction between abstract data types that allow the same concept to be recognized in different contexts, and specific data types which allow the concept to be implemented in a particular context or medium. Thus "person" may be an abstract data type which subsumes a number of specific data types such as the way that person speaks (the voice data type), the way that person walks (animation), the age of that person (integer) and so on. With a piece of information like a person's age, there may be both an abstract and a specific data type associated with it. In abstract terms the age is the output of a rule that measures the temporal duration between a person's birthdate and the current time, whereas in specific terms the age is an integer number of years corresponding to that duration.

7.3.5 Declarative Predicates and Rules

The basic object representation of the intelligent database model is supplemented with declarative predicates and rules that permit the use of inference. In our version of the intelligent database model these predicates include Horn-clause semantics along with a number of logical and extra-logical quantifiers. These declarative predicates and rules implement a number of the features of the FORM model, including conditional links, the calculation of view information, and the use of attached procedures (with text objects, for instance).

Rules are handled uniformly throughout the intelligent database environment because the entire intelligent database is controlled by a combined rule-based inference

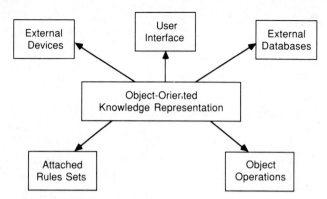

Figure 7.10a The intelligent database control architecture.

engine—object system operating on an object-oriented representation of knowledge linked to external devices and databases. This is illustrated in Figure 7.10 which shows how an interaction within an intelligent database is handled by rule firings and object operations.

7.3.6 Certainty Factors

Like other knowledge-based systems, intelligent-database environments must handle the issue of uncertain knowledge and how it should be dealt with. Our recommendation

A Sample Interaction

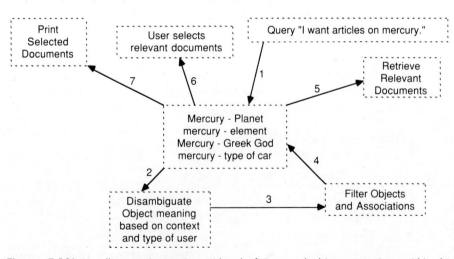

Figure 7.10b Handling an interaction with rule firings and object operations within the intelligent database architecture shown in Figure 7.10a. The numbers 1 through 7 in the figure indicate the order in which the steps in the transaction are made.

is that inexact reasoning be avoided in browsing, since the user may not be goal-oriented in a conventional sense and the calculation of uncertainties in the face of user-defined information utility is extremely problematic. On the other hand, inexactness will need to be dealt with in some advice-giving and question-answering environments. Since the underlying operations of the intelligent database shell are rule-based, certainty factors and inexact inference can be employed as they would be in expert systems generally.

7.3.7 Distribution, Concurrency, Resiliency, Versions, and MultiProcessing

This architecture of FORM naturally allows for the introduction of a multi-blackboard architecture. Here each *agent* is simply an object which has Agent as a parent and has a specific slot called "Blackboard Name" which names the blackboard to which the agent belongs. A named blackboard is then an object with parent Blackboard. Each Blackboard then has a specific slot called Scheduler which names a special scheduler.

A final feature that the intelligent database model needs is version management. This is necessary because of the vast amount of dynamically changing information. To the extent that information imported into the system may be faulty, or distributed authoring processes may occur simultaneously at different sites, version management is necessary. The classic example of a version management problem is when two authors independently work on the same file. It later becomes extremely difficult to merge these two divergent versions of the file into a single version that captures the best features of both. In the model proposed here version management is implemented by attaching properties to objects according to the date at which they were created or modified and the author who carried out the modification. Rules and other information are similarly tagged. Earlier versions of modified information are then cached according to date of modification. Depending on the type of intelligent database operation, the period between updates and archiving of modified information may vary between hours and months.

Thus FORM allows for distributed processing with blackboards and messages. Indeed, a distributed fail-safe version of such a system may be implemented with a suitable concurrency and resiliency algorithm based on the work of Minoura and Parsaye (1984). This algorithm may be easily extended to deal with version management for group data processing.

■ 7.4 THE INTELLIGENT DATABASE USER INTERFACE

It is a commonly accepted truism that the user interface is critical to any application or environment. Thus much of the functionality of intelligent databases depends on the intelligence and the naturalness of the user-interface level. The functionality of the intelligent database user interface is provided both by a core user-interface model and by a set of high-level tools that provide supplementary capabilities. We shall discuss each of these in turn.

An intelligent information retrieval system should allow for rapid and up to date research in this environment.

At a minimum, this requires that the workstation has the following characteristics:

a. It has an integrated database and knowledgebase management system to support its retrieval mechanism, allowing concepts and rules to be embedded within a browsing environment by the developer.

b. It uses dynamic hypermedia in which both the links and the contents of associations are dynamically adjusted based on a set of criteria such as user interest, context, database entries, and so on.

7.4.1 User-Interface Core Model

The user-interface core model drives the functionality of the user interface. The model consists of objects (objects) connected by links. The entire functionality of intelligent databases proceeds from this model.

An object consists of a name and a set of attributes. The representation of an object is shown in Figure 7.11. An object belongs to a class, and has one or more methods associated with it either directly, or through the class that it belongs to. Objects and classes may be linked to other objects and classes. The user sees the interface in

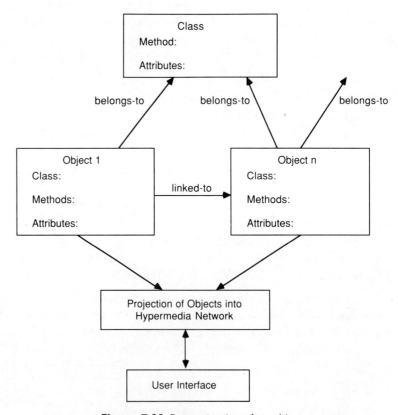

Figure 7.11 Representation of an object.

terms of these objects connected by links into a network. The user interacts with this network of objects in a few fundamental ways, however the most basic concept within the core model of the user interface is that of movement and navigation. At each point in the interaction, the user is somewhere, that is, at a particular object or node in the system. The following choices are then available to the user:

- move to a different object
- find out more about the current object
- answer a question (which may or may not be related to the current object)
- modify the current object
- take notes on the current object
- transfer information about the current object or a search topic into a personal database

The users' understanding of this model and awareness of where they are in the midst of this potentially complex structure is enhanced by the use of a set of standard forms to represent objects and operations within the interface, as shown in Figures 7.12 and 7.13. These standard forms are meant to be illustrative and are not intended to be a graphical standard for intelligent databases. Much empirical research is necessary to find out which set of graphical forms will work best with typical user populations.

Figure 7.13 shows a form for an object in the system in browse mode. The form includes a number of fields, buttons, and tools. In general, fields display information, buttons navigate through the information, or execute functions, and the tools carry

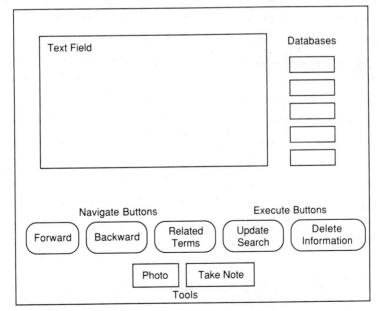

Figure 7.12 Example of an object form during browse mode.

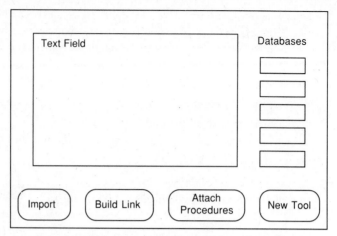

Figure 7.13 Example of object form during edit mode.

out interactive tasks. The difference between buttons and tools is that tools require the user to interact with the system in performing the task whereas buttons may execute functions autonomously.

A form may also be constructed for times when the system is in edit mode. Here the user (author) may import new information into a field, link information to the contents of a different object, attach a procedure to a button, or construct a new tool.

A further, and more complex, editing (authoring) function involves writing an inference procedure that will govern the creation of dynamic links at run time. In similar fashion to the way in which methods may be attached to objects or classes, FORM inferential procedures may apply to a single form, to sets of forms, or to an entire hypermedia network.

Other forms may be used to initiate search queries in the system. These forms have an associated set of tools that govern the type of search query being expressed. SQL, verbal Boolean, and graphic Boolean operations are available.

Views represent particular perspectives on information. Views are implemented as collections of inference procedures that govern the display of dynamic links. As such, views have to be authored and the number and type of views will generally vary from one intelligent database to another.

7.4.2 Link Types within the Core Model

The functionality of the user interface is provided by links implemented as special (where to go next) properties attached to objects. These links fall under a number of different types, as explained below. Our discussion of links here modifies the earlier treatment given in Chapter 5 and distills the most important of the link types within the context of intelligent database applications.

Navigation links were introduced in our discussion on hypermedia in Chapter 5. We have revised the concept of navigation links here to provide the functionality required by intelligent databases.

1. *Move to links* simply move to a related node. They allow one to move around or navigate through hypermedia.

2a. *Zoom-in links* expand the current node into a more detailed account of the information. The effect is similar to moving from an abstract to a complete view of the document in text, or to zooming to a magnified view of a small part of the complete picture, much as one might move from a map of an entire city to a map of the downtown area enlarged to fit the same page area as the city map. These links work with multilevel objects that may be described at different levels of description.

2b. *Zoom-out pan links* return to a higher level view of the current object (these links are particularly useful in browsing facilities). Zoom-out links are normally the inverse of zoom-in links so that every zoom-out link will have a corresponding zoom-in link and vice versa.

The following set of view links are generally used in browsing. They provide views of where one is currently and where one can go from this point. As such, they represent a powerful form of navigation. Although there are a large number of views that conceivably could be used, we suggest the use of the following view links in the core intelligent database definition.

3. *Hierarchy links* allow the user to view any hierarchies that the current object is embedded in. If more than one hierarchy is involved, the user chooses which context is appropriate. The tree is then displayed and the user may move directly to a new object by clicking on the corresponding node in the tree structure.

4a. *Broaden links* display the parents of the current object for the hierarchies that it is embedded within.

4b. *Specialize links* display the children of the current object as defined by the hierarchies that it is embedded within. The relationship between the broaden and specialize links is somewhat analogous to the relationship between the zoom-in and zoom-out links.

5. *Landmark view links.* Fisheye views and their construction were described in Chapter 5. Fisheye views are especially useful in that they display highly salient (landmark) objects that may be reached from the current node. Landmark views are a generalization of the fisheye approach that makes no assumptions about the relative distribution of near and far landmarks in the field of view. Thus a landmark view may show a high density of both near and far objects, whereas a fisheye view tends to use a distance-density gradient where there are progressively fewer objects as one moves into the distance (Figure 7.14). In the FORM model, landmarks are organized into three categories, that is, closely related landmarks, moderately related landmarks, and landmarks that bear no known conceptual relationship to the current

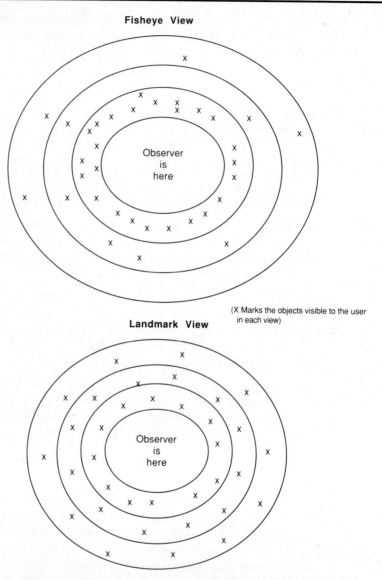

Figure 7.14 The difference between landmark and fisheye views.

object. This last category of landmarks allows the user to jump quickly over different regions in a hypermedia network.

6. *Serendipity links* allow the user to jump to a new piece of information at random. Successful people sometimes claim that information is often retrieved or located by serendipity. Or, when a user is having a mental block, it may be useful to jump to a completely unexpected and novel region of the network so as to snap out of an unproductive or circular thought process.

7. *Reward links* are another class of links that may be difficult to justify in terms of logical functionality, but nevertheless prove useful for motivating the user and maintaining involvement with the system. Reward links provide an interaction which is not directly ·task-relevant but which increases motivation and improves subsequent performance on the task. Obviously, the type of links which prove to be rewarding may vary widely from user to user.

Serendipity links may be implemented using a pseudorandom number generation approach. The proper construction of reward links will generally require more thought. Reward links are a reflection of a recent trend towards more motivational interfaces where the user interface provides an enjoyable and motivating task environment. One example of a reward link that the authors observed is a hypermedia interface for teaching users about library services. Here an ice cream cone was used to symbolize the reward. Each time the user clicked on the ice cream cone, they received a different reward, such as a sequence of animation or a piece of music.

Another class of links are filtering links. Filtering links are used to customize the interface. Normally users are not aware of link filtering, since it will be carried out in the intelligent database engine level. However, link filters may be viewed and modified by sophisticated users. In the intelligent database model proposed here, filtering links are implemented as conditional links.

8. *Conditional links.* The availability or activation of these links is conditional upon the stated interests or purposes of the user. They may also be used for security purposes. Conditional links are hidden unless they are of interest or a particular user has access or has been cleared to use them. As an example, there may be a conditional link between mercury and planet nodes which is active for astronomers but suppressed for environmental chemists and meteorologists. Under some conditions, conditional restrictions could be disabled so that hidden links were seen. Conditionals provide the fundamental mechanism for customizing hypermedia to the needs and interests of different users. They also help prevent hypermedia from becoming unnecessarily complex with users being bombarded by information that is not relevant to their needs. Conditional links are implemented by methods attached to objects. These methods dynamically determine the conditional links that are relevant in the current context.

Conditional links may interpret the user's interests autonomously, or they may let the user interpret which choice is appropriate in an ambiguous context by displaying a type of dialog box.

Searching is an important activity within the intelligent database. One of the tasks in defining the core user interface model is to provide a clean integration of browsing and searching functions. This is handled by defining search as part of the browsing process. At any point in the hypermedia network, the user may initiate a database search. Index links provide the bridge between browsable hypermedia and searchable databases.

> **9.** *Index links* move the user from an indexed node to the corresponding index entry for that node. The index can then be used to enter the relational database or to find documents which share a particular index term. Indexing hypertext is a good way of controlling the proliferation of links between nodes.

Other links are used to organize the objects within the hypermedia network. While these links are already implicit in the object definitions, these links make them explicit and available to the user, so that objects and their attributes may be viewed directly.

> **10.** *Is-a links* are similar to corresponding links used in semantic networks and frame systems to indicate membership of a category. Is-a links permit nodes to be organized.
>
> **11.** *Has-a links* are used to describe the properties of nodes. They will generally be used by objects, although they can also be used to implement object-like capabilities within hypermedia.

Explanation is a feature that is necessitated by the inference capability built into intelligent databases. Inference occurs either because inference is being used to build links dynamically or because inference is being used to answer a question. In either case, the inference process may be captured in an inference tree which can be viewed by the user through the implication links.

> **12.** *Implication links* are used to connect facts in inference trees. They are generally equivalent to rules that are being, or have been, fired. The use of implication links will generally be confined to inferential hypermedia.

The final type of link in our model is used for programming and for providing the ability to run applications or carry out actions from within the intelligent database environment.

> **13.** *Execute links (buttons)* allow hypermedia to be a high-level programming interface. Buttons cause actions to be carried out; typically, the execution of some code. In the HyperCard implementation, execute links correspond to buttons with Hypertalk scripts attached to them. These scripts may then include hooks into more conventional programming languages such as C or Pascal (XCMDs and XFCNs in HyperCard).

7.4.3 The Structure of the Core Model

We mentioned earlier how forms can be used to represent objects in the core model. These objects can generally be represented as nodes within a hypermedia network.

This approach extends earlier models of information that were introduced in the NoteCards and HyperCard systems which utilize card and stack metaphors for building information structures.

A form is the basic display unit. In physical appearance, a form may be thought of as a resizable card. In multi-windowing systems, each window represents a different form, and forms may be overlapped and repositioned on the screen. A form contains fields, attributes, and buttons, and will generally be surrounded by a number of tools that are relevant in the current context. Buttons may be either icons or highlighted text. Buttons may also be embedded within fields, and a special tool may be used to highlight or hide the embedded buttons. Attributes represent information that may be dynamically modified. Thus the current price of a company's stock would be an example of an attribute. In general, attributes will be filled with highlighted (and changeable) text or visual information, while fields represent information that is designed to be viewed by the user rather than modified dynamically or used by a reasoning process.

Fields that contain text and embedded attributes may be referred to as text objects. Text objects represent a fundamental unit of text presentation within an intelligent database. As well as providing a method of text presentation, they also constitute fully-functioned object objects where one attribute refers to the text template, that is, the text of the field minus the attributes (Figure 7.15), and the remaining attributes function like the attributes in a conventional object where the information they contain may be stored and retrieved in a variety of ways. Text objects may also be linked in inheritance hierarchies, as shown in Figure 7.16. Procedures may be attached to the attributes of a text object, just as they may be attached to any other object.

As with a text object, a field may contain embedded buttons and slots. A field normally represents a single text object, graphic object, or the like. When a field contains text

Presentation View of Text Object

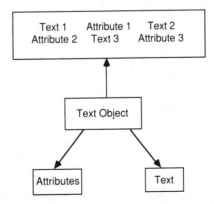

Figure 7.15 The components of text objects.

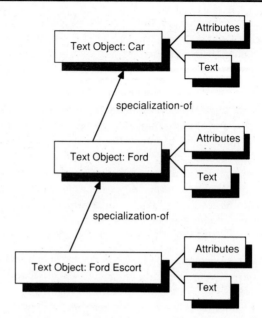

Figure 7.16 Text objects linked within inheritance hierarchies.

with embedded attributes, and the field is embedded within an inheritance hierarchy, it is referred to as a text object. Often, text objects will correspond to objects.

Since forms may contain more than one field, more than one object may be displayed on the same form. In the user-interface model, forms are dynamic, that is, the information is selected and pasted on to them at run time. Thus the display process will generally consist of selecting the static information to be displayed in the current context and overlaying it with the appropriate dynamic information.

The use of forms is an extension of the notecard metaphor used in HyperCard and NoteCards. Forms may be organized into stacks. At first glance, this would appear to be a rather sequential notion that does not fit easily with the hypermedia concept of associatively structured information. However, even in an intelligent database, there is a place for both sequenced and associative information. Some objects have an inherently sequential organization, such as the entries in a dictionary, or an address book. Thus stacks represent the stored or archived information. In dynamic interaction, the stack is no longer relevant as an organizing construct, though, as the definition of "next screen" is constantly updated according to the changing context and the user's choices.

The notion of forms and stacks can be extended to include database tables. Thus the user interface model provides a number of methods for interacting with information, each consistent with one or more information management tasks such as browsing, searching, editing, notetaking, and question answering. Database tables are particularly useful for representing information in relational databases and for editing the attribute descriptions of objects. In this formulation, objects may be represented as rows in tables where the columns are attributes. Entries within cells of these database tables may then be handles to underlying objects, or they may be numerical or other values.

The core model may be used in a number of ways for designing and developing intelligent databases. In general, the use of the model should be consistent with sound interface design practice. Intelligent databases should be designed for easy use, and should conform to the specifications of an intelligent interface (Chignell and Hancock, 1988).

One of the first tasks of the intelligent database developer involves splitting the relevant knowledge and information into manageable chunks (objects). Although information objects are often complex, related research suggests that a few complex objects are easier to deal with than a larger number of simpler objects due to the properties of human attention. Thus the development environment is modular and allows the developer to deal with the definition of one object at a time. Each task involved in building the dynamic hypermedia environment for an application is presented as an object description task, so that the developer is not faced with the burden of "programming" a complex application and dealing with the procedural details of how links are used during information retrieval. Thus intelligent database development environments will generally utilize direct manipulation and declarative programming techniques.

Developers and other "power users" may operate directly on the hypermedia representation using operators such as "add", "delete", and so on. This allows them to select and delete or select and establish links during the development process. These operators may be implemented in a tool palette reminiscent of the one used in the HyperCard environment.

7.4.4 Interface Operations

Conventional models of information retrieval were discussed in Chapter 6. Dynamic hypermedia within the FORM model greatly expands the capabilities for information retrieval.

Since not all information may be displayed to the user at once, the user should be able to seek more information. This may be done by

a. Referring to an object in a display and performing an operation.

b. Specifically asking for information on a subject and then performing (a) once the information is displayed.

Various studies (summarized in Gazzaniga, 1988) of human memory have shown that there are two basic information retrieval operations.

    i. Selection (recognition).

    ii. Recall.

They have dramatically different costs in terms of brain activity. Thus, as may seem intuitively obvious, it is much easier to select something by pointing to it, rather than remembering it. Traditional hypertext allows for this form of point and seek operation as the recall of information is replaced by browsing.

The IIRW offers browsing facilities which are characteristic of hypermedia systems such as Intermedia (e.g., Yankelovich, Haan, and Meyrowitz, 1988). However, in the IIRW these browsing facilities are enhanced with inferential mechanisms that make links dynamically defined and context sensitive.

For instance, consider a display of text

The main competitor to Pepsi Co. is the Coca-Cola Company.

The user selects the word Coca-Cola Company by highlighting it. The user may at other times type the word "Coca-Cola Company" and ask about information relating to it.

Now the system displays a set of possible choices for information about the object (i.e. Coca-Cola Company)

Annual Report
Subsidiaries
Summary of Business Activities
Stock Analysis
Investment Outlook

The user may now select Subsidiaries and a list of the company's subsidiaries will appear. The user may then select Columbia Pictures and continue on to get an annual report for that company.

From within the annual report, the information may then be displayed in a variety of forms. The user may also get the same information by typing Coca-Cola and then being shown a set of contexts in which the object Coca-Cola may be interpreted, (e.g., company, soft drink). Thus the same information may be retrieved either by unstructured browsing or through structured (query-based) searches.

The complexity and power of information retrieval is also enhanced through the inheritance of object descriptors. An example of this type of inheritance process is:

The term Coca-Cola Company is recognized as an object. Of course, to begin with, a disambiguation may take place (e.g. each object name may have a set of synonyms,). After identification, a set of possible choices for the company is calculated. The object has parent company so, a set of choices apply there and may be interpreted using an inheritance rule such as:

'X' <u>is a choice for</u> operator, 'Object'
If
'Object' <u>is-a</u> 'Parent' and
'X' <u>is a choice for</u> operator, 'Parent' ;

The linkage of hypermedia nodes to corresponding hierarchical representations provides a powerful form of indexing. Conventional information retrieval capability can then be achieved by having selection operators which allow users to identify terms within the hierarchical structures which should be added to an information retrieval query. Thus, like inference, information retrieval is a separate process that may be linked to the hypermedia representation. Our solution here is to achieve inference in hypermedia through the link predicates while providing an information retrieval capability by attaching a retrieval engine to the hierarchical index. Thus our hypermedia model does not replace conventional information retrieval, but incorporates it within a broader model of information access and utilization.

One of the features of the FORM model is that it describes text in terms of objects or text objects. In bibliographic information retrieval systems, text is generally treated in terms of unanalyzable documents that have index terms attached to them. Search is carried out on the basis of the index terms and documents judged to be relevant are then passed back to the user in toto. In an IIRW, there is more emphasis on the softcopy representation of information. Here the unit of information is the screen, or even a window within a screen. Thus FORM defines the object of text as a text object.

A text object is a collection of text strings, buttons, and attributes linked within a list. In the visual representation of this list, the items of the list are printed sequentially, with the buttons and slots being highlighted or colored so as to indicate their special functionality. Buttons serve two functions. First, they serve as embedded index terms. Thus, in structured search, interesting button labels can be accumulated and added to the search query. Buttons are also the means by which the user can initiate the ACTIONS described earlier.

OPERATIONS that can be initiated by the user are indicated by attributes within the text object. Normally, attributes may be updated by the IIRW system in the same way that object attributes generally may be updated as information is propagated through a knowledge base. However, the user may also update attributes within a text object directly. This implicit operation may then lead to propagated changes to related objects.

▪ 7.5 HIGH-LEVEL TOOLS

As discussed in Chapter 1, high-level tools are provided in a tool box consisting of distinct tools, reflecting the facts that different applications have different needs and it is unnecessary to burden all applications and users with tools which they may not need.

In Chapter 1 we distinguished seven types of high-level tools:

1. Knowledge discovery tools
2. Data integrity and quality control tools
3. Hypermedia management tools
4. Data presentation and display tools
5. Decision support and scenario analysis tools
6. Data-format management tools (reformat data, etc.)
7. Intelligent system design tools

It is these tools which deliver the power of intelligent databases to end users and developers. We now discuss the features of each category of tools.

7.5.1 Knowledge Discovery Tools

Integrating databases and expert systems is one method of capitalizing on the information available in databases. Machine learning and discovery represent a second method. In this method we rely on *induction* rather than deduction and inference.

These tools represent a new and exciting frontier in intelligent database technology which allows us to extract knowledge from data. They allow a user to automatically discover hidden (and often totally unexpected) relationships which exist in a large database.

Thus here the goal is to extract knowledge from the database in the form of rules by observing patterns in the data. With the widespread use of databases, there is no real shortage of data or examples. If anything, many organizations have more data than they can deal with. The proliferation of laser disks will merely accelerate this trend. What is needed are intelligent programs which analyze data to discover patterns, regularities and knowledge (Parsaye 1987).

Of course such tools require CPU cycles and in many environments today there is an abundance of unused CPU cycles. As Tukey (1986) points out, with the widespread availability of personal computers and workstations, a million CPU cycles are now less expensive than a second of a professional's time spent on analyzing data.

Many professionals use some form of personal computer or workstation. The typical workstation stores a lot of data which requires analysis. However, the workstation is usually switched off for about 16 hours a day, that is close to 70% of its lifetime. Thus most professionals possess two commodities in excess:

i. Data that require analysis.
ii. Processing power that is not used.

With suitable software technology, we may apply (ii) to (i) in order to produce interesting results by intelligent data analysis. In this way, workstations can be left on to analyze data and discover useful information. This is important since the number and size of available databases is growing so fast that there will never be enough human analysts to analyze all the data.

From an evolutionary point of view, machine learning may be viewed as an important step in the development of intelligent databases. There are three basic levels in dealing with a database (Figure 7.17):

i. We collect data, for example we maintain records on clients, products, sales, and so on.

ii. We query data, for example we ask "which products had increasing sales last month?"

iii. We try to understand data, for example, "what makes a product successful?"

When using a query language we need to know what to ask about. If we ask a relevant question, we will get an interesting answer. However, often there is so much data that we may not know what the relevant questions are. In a machine learning system, the program discovers the relevant questions by performing an intelligent analysis of the data. Often this points out totally unexpected relationships which may be further pursued with queries.

Machine learning may be viewed as a layer on top of the database query system. A query language such as SQL can deal with step (ii), but it cannot automatically answer questions posed in (iii), since we do not know what to ask for. All we may have are hypotheses which may be tested with repeated queries. But we need to form the hypothesis, SQL will not form it for us.

The answers to questions posed in step (iii) are often unexpected. To deal with step (iii), an analyst needs to:

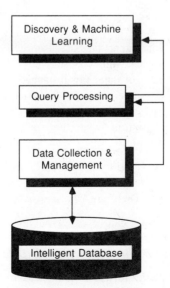

Figure 7.17 Three basic levels in dealing with a database.

a. Form hypotheses.

b. Make some queries.

c. View the results and perhaps modify the hypotheses.

d. Continue this cycle until a pattern emerges.

This task can, however, be automated with a machine learning program that tirelessly queries the database until knowledge is discovered. Such a program forms the hypotheses itself in order to discover unexpected knowledge, finding what queries should be asked and building the mechanisms to ask those queries. This, in effect, provides an intelligent layer on top of a database and its query language.

For instance, by using the machine learning tool IXL (IntelligenceWare 1988c), a car manufacturer discovered the reasons for wiring problems in a database of car trouble reports, while a computer manufacturer discovered that a large number of disk drive problems were due to one specific error repeatedly performed by one operator in one process (MIS Week, 1988). Thus these tools discover relationships that users would not have even expected. Since today's oceans of data are abundant with these relationships, these tools will dramatically increase our ability to distill knowledge from databases.

7.5.1.1 Statistics and Machine Learning

For many years, statistical techniques have been the basic tools for viewing and understanding large amounts of data. Statistical techniques emerged as methods of analyzing numeric data, and in the right hands, they can be very useful in providing insight into the overall structure of data. There is no doubt that statistics should play an important role in any program that tries to learn from data. However, with few exceptions, statistical techniques in general have been oriented towards numbers, not knowledge.

Statistical analyses allow the user to summarize the numerical properties of information. Intelligent database users will sometimes require summary statistics or inferential statistics. Summary statistics allow the user to get a quick overview of the general properties of data. For instance, given all the employees in a database, what is the average number of years that each employee has worked in the MIS department versus the marketing department. This then allows an assessment of information relative to the question "where are we having turnover problems in the company?"

Inferential statistics are much more varied and complex than summary statistics and are poorly understood by the general public. The title of the book "How to Lie with Statistics" reflects the somewhat seedy reputation that users of statistics have. Then there is the line "There are lies, there are damned lies, and then there are statistics."

Inferential statistics can be dangerous in the wrong hands, but they allow one to get valuable insights into patterns that exist in data, and they complement the rule-based reasoning provided by the logical inference tools.

Inferential statistics rely on a mathematical model of the distribution of data, which is compared with a set of observed values. Then, in one way or another, the discrepancy between the model and the observed values is captured in the inferential statistics, or a representation of the data is formulated which best fits the assumptions of the model.

One of the main operations of multivariate statistics is reification. Here one takes a set of descriptors (fields) for objects and collapses them into a subset of descriptors that best describe the key attributes of the object.

The most popular reification techniques are factor analysis, principal components analysis, and cluster analysis. More extensive discussion of these topics lies outside the scope of this book. The reader should consult a standard text on multivariate statistics.

Another class of statistical question concerns the discovery of different groups within data. Given a set of data about cars produced from different manufacturing plants one might ask the question, "How do the cars produced at Nashville differ from those produced at Detroit?" given a set of descriptors such as the frequency of mechanical failures and so on. Discrimination may then be made using a rule-based or a statistical approach.

One of the cornerstones of statistical theory is hypothesis testing. Here the goal is to ascertain whether or not two or more groups of data are different. Common techniques for doing this include t-tests and analysis of variance (both univariate and multivariate).

Multivariate analysis can also be used to visualize data. Thus the techniques of factor analysis and principal components analysis not only reify data, they also provide a coordinate representation of the data. Another technique for spatial mapping is multidimensional scaling.

The final class of statistical techniques we will mention here is trend analysis. This is useful in the analysis of chronologically sequenced information. Long sequences are generally handled using time series analysis based either on the correlation of data collected at different time points, or on what is known as spectral analysis of data. Even within statistics, time series analysis is particularly poorly understood. However, the ability to observe trends is obviously a very useful tool for users of intelligent databases to have access to.

Statistical techniques may be used in this endeavor to gain insight into the underlying trends that exist in data. However, while statistical techniques are useful, conventional statistics should not be viewed as the only available tool for data analysis. To date statistical techniques have been used by statisticians rather than "average users" since:

    a. Their use requires an understanding of statistics.
    b. Their results require "interpretation" by a statistician.

There will never be enough human statisticians to analyze all the data in all the databases. Thus there is a great deal of scope for intelligent user interface technology combined with statistics and artificial intelligence. Statistical techniques are now evolving and merging with artificial intelligence. A good example of this form of evolution is the Rex system at AT&T Bell Laboratories (Gale, 1986) which is a front end to a regression analysis system.

There are at least two basic ways in which current statistical methods should be extended before they can be widely used for data analysis. To begin with, due to their roots in numeric processing, statistical techniques almost always provide their conclusions in terms of "mathematical equations." To capture knowledge, we need to use machine learning techniques to discover "logical relationships," which are expressed in terms of rules rather than equations.

Rules are more readable than mathematical equations.

Secondly, statistical programs generally need "interpretation" after they have been executed since they use the language of applied math. They produce curves, equations and matrices, instead of logical relationships such as rules which use the language of logic. Many people who have databases do not really know statistics in detail and will not be able to interpret the results, but can easily read through a set of rules. To make statistics widely available, we need to have an "expert" statistician built into a data discovery program.

The output from such a system is usually easy to read and comprehend. For example, by examining a database of client information for telemarketing bonds, a machine-learning system may discover the rule

> Rule 131
> Confidence = 65%
> If
>   Portfolio size = medium
> and
>   Age < 55
> and
>   Credit rating > B
> and
>   Purchase activity = high
> Then
>   Purchases of further low price products = likely ;

This form of rule is better understood by most users than a statistical correlation matrix. Thus to make data analysis widely available, we need to

a. Extend statistics and combine it with artificial intelligence to discover logical relationships and knowledge—i.e., a machine-learning system.

b. Use intelligent interfaces which deliver the underlying power of machine-learning technology to large numbers of users with ease.

7.5.1.2   *Approaches to Machine Learning*

The term *machine learning* has been used in a variety of artificial intelligence applications. It generally refers to the ability of a program to discover or learn information by itself. A variety of programs that aim to "learn" have been developed. Samuel's highly successful checker's program was such an example (Samuel, 1963). John McCarthy actually defined "intelligence" in a program in terms of its ability to learn (McCarthy, 1968).

One of the early ideas for programs which discover knowledge from data was the CLS algorithm developed by Hunt et al. (1966). In this system, a decision tree was generated by repeatedly separating a set of examples into smaller subsets, characterized by the values of attributes for each example. CLS eventually evolved to the ID3 (Iterative Dichotamizing 3rd) algorithm (Quinlan, 1979). Today, ID3 is the most popular method of decision tree generation, mostly because it is easy to implement and it produces simple decision trees effectively. However, if unguided, ID3 can easily go astray and generate monstrous decision trees that make little sense (Michie, 1984). For several years now, Quinlan, Michie, and others have experimented with a variety of heuristics based on cost functions, information theoretic ($-$ p log p) measures, chi squared tests, and so on in attempts to tame ID3.

Quinlan and Michie's work on the ID3 algorithm has been very important in initiating activity in the field of knowledge discovery and has undoubtedly had a positive effect on the commercialization of decision tree generation systems. For instance, a variant of ID3 was successfully used to discover new chess end-game tactics previously unknown to any chess master (Quinlan, 1983).

However, our own research has shown the basic ID3 algorithm to have at least five major limitations (Parsaye and Hansson 1988). First, it is extremely brittle, i.e., small changes in the database of examples can produce large changes in the resulting decision trees. Second, unlike the AQ family of algorithms (Michalski et al., 1983), ID3 produces no "generalizations" on the data presented to it, i.e., it only produces decision trees, not general rules. Third, unlike the INDUCE or CLUSTER algorithms (Michalski et al., 1983; Stepp, 1984), ID3 cannot handle structured data. Fourth, the original algorithm has no provisions for dealing with inexact data or producing inexact recommendations. Finally, heuristic classification measures for ID3 are as brittle as general-purpose GPS-like heuristics (Parsaye & Chignell, 1988).

An alternative approach to rule generation has been pursued by Michalski's group at the University of Illinois at Urbana, resulting in a series of algorithms such as AQ, INDUCE and CLUSTER (Michalski et al., 1983). In much of this approach, the basic language of expression is GVL (Generalized Variable-valued Logic) capable of representing predicate calculus forms.

The heart of the AQ family of algorithms is Michalski's STAR procedure, which uses type and structure information to generalize a single given example based on a set of constraints. The basic idea in AQ is to select one example, generalize it as long as it does not conflict with counter examples, then apply STAR repeatedly, until all examples in the example set have been generalized.

From a historical perspective, Michalski's work may well be considered as the first original "knowledge generalization" system and is indeed a very effective induction and generalization method on constrained example sets. These algorithms appear to be much more powerful than ID3 in generalization power. The main problem with using the unguided AQ algorithm on large databases is that far too many generalizations are produced. Thus when presented with a great deal of data, the AQ family of algorithms tends to be too liberal, in the sense that they jump to conclusions too quickly.

The AQ/11 and the more recent AQ/15 algorithms include some basic methods of limiting generalizations, but given a large database the heuristics may go astray since the induction method has no "knowledge" of the induction domain. Thus, while original AQ works well on constrained example sets, its application to large databases will result in far too many generalizations. There are, however, a number of ways in which AQ can be modified to restrict its generalization method and to produce meaningful generalizations even on large amounts of data. The AQ algorithm does not, however, deal with inexact data, or produce inexact results.

The RX and the Radix projects at Stanford University (Blum, 1982, 1986) are good examples of pioneering work in distilling information from large databases. The basic approach used in RX relies on statistical techniques for determining correlations between time oriented events recorded in the American Rheumatism Association database. In its first phase of operation, RX's Discovery Module uses lagged correlations to generate a set of tentative relationships. In the second phase, the Study Module uses a knowledge of medicine and statistics to create a study design. The study design is then executed by a conventional statistical package.

What distinguishes the RX approach is that it assumes that it is dealing with a large database and combines statistical observations with model analysis. This approach has shown its viability in dealing with the effects of the steroid drug prednisone (Blum, 1986).

Another approach to inexact induction and relationship identification has been proposed by Gaines and Shaw in the ENTAIL system (Gaines & Shaw, 1986). This approach does not correspond to either the ID3 or the AQ/11 systems, but produces inexact measure based either on fuzzy (Zadeh, 1965) minimum/maximum measures or distance measures. This approach has not been designed for application to large databases, but is suitable for inducing relationships between sets of items presented with inexact values.

Holland's method of classification takes a different view from the systems we have described so far. In this approach a series of inputs is classified by a set of classifiers (i.e., rules) with weights. However, during the learning process, the premises of the rules may change in response to deficiencies in learning. Although this method is very interesting, it has been hard to judge its practicality since few implementations of it exist. The system PI (Process of Induction) proposes to implement such a classification system and is well described by Holland et al. (1986).

Thus machine learning covers a wide spectrum of topics (e.g., Michalski et al., 1983; Holland et al., 1986; Quinlan 1983; Langley et al., 1986; Gaines & Shaw 1986; Lenat 1976; Blum 1982). Our use of the term generally refers to algorithms which discover rules and patterns by analyzing a set of examples. Well-known machine learning and discovery techniques include

ID3: which generates decision trees to classify data.
AQ: which generalizes rules more powerful than decision trees.
INDUCE: which generates rules for structural descriptions.
CLUSTER: which clusters data and discovers structure.
RX and RADIX: which statistically deal with time oriented data.
ENTAIL: which generates inexact rules from inexact data.
Holland's Classifier: which classifies patterns based on features.
IXL: which combines statistics and machine learning techniques.

Figure 7.18 depicts the lineage of some machine learning systems.

7.5.1.3 *IXL (Induction on eXtremely Large databases)*

In this section we describe IXL (Induction on eXtremely Large databases), a system that unites machine learning and statistics to distill knowledge from large databases (IntelligenceWare 1988c).

IXL first subjects data to comprehensive statistical analysis and then uses machine learning algorithms to find patterns and rules which distill the information or "expertise" in the database. The architecture of IXL is shown in Figure 7.19. IXL consists of five modules.

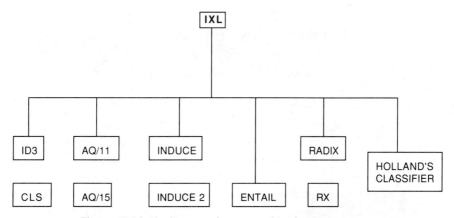

Figure 7.18 The lineage of some machine learning systems.

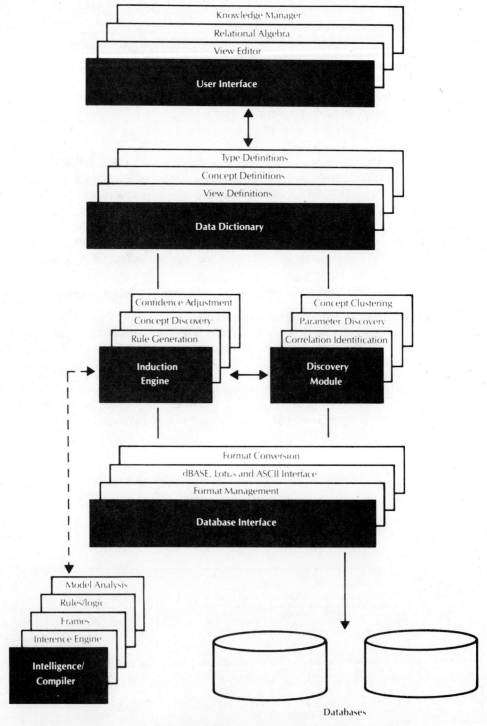

Figure 7.19 The architecture of IXL.

- The user interface.
- The data dictionary.
- The discovery module.
- The induction engine.
- The database interface.

The user interface relies on windows, pop-up menus, and context sensitive help to allow a user to specify which databases should be dealt with and how they should be searched. The data dictionary stores and manages the concepts provided by the user. Relational algebra operations are supported by using database views, i.e., schema structures of databases. The discovery module searches the database for interesting patterns and relationships. It may be guided by specifying the criteria to focus on, or it may be set to roam freely through the database. The induction engine uses correlations identified by the discovery module to generate rules of knowledge, expressed in terms of user defined concepts and criteria. The database interface reads data from a variety of databases and file formats. The system includes its own data manager and database editor, so that data from other sources, for example public databases, bulletin boards, mainObjects, and so on may be ported in ASCII form for analysis. This affords the opportunity to analyze large amounts of readily available data.

The user interface supports the relational algebra with an intuitive set of commands, providing the user with control over schema structures. Further, the user may define concepts such as large or young with *virtual attributes* expressed as rules. For instance, a user may define a view with the attribute "large" which takes on values between 0 and 100, as confidence factors calculated with an inexact rule. For instance, given many patients, the concept "critical" may be expressed by a number of attributes such as

> Confidence = 80
> 'Patient' <u>is</u> critical
>
> If
>
> 'Patient' <u>has</u> Internal Bleeding
>
> and
>
> 'Patient' <u>is</u> old ;

The predicate 'Patient' *is* old is itself again expressed by an inexact rule. So we may ask IXL: "What can you say about patients who are critical?" The user may also define a set of new virtual attributes, in terms of which the induction should take place. The system will then create a virtual relation for "critical" and perform induction on it.

The discovery process can be focused on knowledge that the user will find most useful by setting discovery parameters and defining concepts. Forms of discovery used in IXL include

- Correlations.
- Clusters.
- Logical relationships.
- Time-oriented relationships.
- Structural relationships.

The data in the database is analyzed for these criteria and measures of proximity are used to define such relationships. For instance, from a database of people, we may discover that

> If Person <u>is</u> young
> Then Age <u>is related to</u> Height.

Several conventional statistical techniques are used to identify relationships, correlations and structure. However, these techniques are combined with logical analysis in order to guide search and interpret results automatically. For instance, why is there no correlation between two attributes? Is it because the symbolic values are rank ordered incorrectly, or is there really no correlation? The system also expects missing or erroneous values. These are treated as the user sees fit (i.e., the user may specify the level of error to expect in the database).

The results of the discovery phase are provided to the induction system for generalization. Thus the discovery phase provides heuristics for induction. Induction and deduction are combined in two ways:

a. The central part of the discovery system is rule-based and performs deduction to perform discovery.

b. The user may deductively specify concepts in terms of rules and objects and induce on these concepts.

IXL has been used in a very diverse number of application areas and has discovered a significant number of previously unknown rules of knowledge. For instance, by applying IXL to databases of failure reports, a number of manufacturers have discovered previously unknown reasons for product failures; contractors for the U.S. government have applied IXL to crime databases; financial analysts have applied it to financial data, medical researchers have used it on patient data, and so on. The key point here is that there are often more application areas for machine learning than we may have anticipated.

7.5.1.4 *Benefits and Applications of Machine Learning*

The risk/benefit ratio for machine learning is very attractive. A machine learning system has to discover just a few unexpected relationships to pay for itself. And since the discoveries may always be rechecked with queries, there is little chance of loss due to errors, but great potential for gain. This is in contrast to expert systems which mimic human experts. If an expert system errs, the consequences may be serious.

Machine learning systems are easy to utilize, since they require minimal programming. While it takes time and effort to encode knowledge in an expert system, a machine learning system may often be simply "added on top" of the database. It does not require knowledge, but discovers knowledge.

In many corporations, multiuser VAXes are idle almost every night. The information discovered by utilizing these processors during their "off-hours" can be of significant use in decision making. Corporations which use intelligent tools to understand their data will be able to make more effective decisions.

Thus, with machine learning, data glut should be viewed as an "opportunity" and not as a problem. The pay-offs from machine learning are likely to be significant. Even if we manage to provide a fraction of database users with hidden knowledge from their databases, we will achieve a substantial level of productivity increase within society as a whole. Thus the use of machine learning tools to discover knowledge from large databases signals the beginning of a new era in the application of artificial intelligence.

7.5.2 Data Integrity and Quality Control Tools

The tools in category 2 are needed due to the unwanted side effects of the increasing number and size of databases. In particular, two conflicting side effects are:

a. We are becoming extremely dependent on data stored in databases.

b. There are an increasing number of errors appearing in databases.

Thus as the size and number of databases increases, so does the the chance of errors within the data. In many cases, errors in databases go undetected, causing serious problems later. It is thus imperative to have tools which automatically detect or signal errors in databases. These range from tools which use the encoded knowledge of an expert to detect errors in data to tools which signal statistically deviant records.

Database Supervisor (Parsaye and Lee, 1989) is an example of a system which enforces integrity on the data in a database and measures the quality of data. The system relies on both statistical and deductive methods for testing hypotheses provided by the user and for enforcing integrity constraints.

Traditionally database systems have enforced even simple integrity constraints such as range checking, and so on. Database Supervisor allows comprehensive integrity constraints to be expressed much more easily in terms of pattern-matching rules. This allows the user to change the integrity constraints without changing the application program. The system automatically checks for anomalies and deviations in values based on a set of criteria provided by the user.

In most applications integrity is encoded in terms of procedural programs when the application is developed. Often, integrity constraints are "spread-over" a program, with each constraint being coded as a specific set of instructions. As the constraints (inevitably) change, the program needs to be "reopened" for further surgery.

Although most constraints take the form of "should not be allowed" rules, their implementation is often not obvious, since the rules have to be "coded" into procedures. Sometimes, the constraints are not those that you want, since their meaning is lost in the translation to procedures.

With the database supervisor, constraints are expressed in terms of a set of rules which are "separate" from the program. Then as the constraints change, the rules are changed without "re-opening" the program. This has two advantages:

- The chance that the constraints are accurate increases.
- The ability to change the constraints improves.

The database supervisor may also provide a set of statistical features for measuring data quality. For instance, deviation from the standard deviation and deviation from typical correlations are detected. These feature should be particularly useful for users and developers with large databases.

7.5.3   Hypermedia Management Tools

In many ways, the intelligent database is a shell in which disparate sources of information and data can be accessed, manipulated, and displayed. Not all users will want to see all the information that is potentially available to the system, in the same way that different people tend to gravitate towards different sections of a public library. So, hypermedia documents will generally be available as external tools that can be accessed when needed by particular users. For the foreseeable future at least, the sum total of the world's information will not be available in a single massive hypermedia document, instead, hypermedia documents will be available for sets of users with interests in particular types. Thus one hypermedia document might be concerned with English literature, another with business information, and so on. Each of these hypermedia documents may be loaded into the intelligent database environment as needed.

Hypermedia documents allow a number of tasks to be performed, including:

> knowledge representation
> linkage to inference systems
> information retrieval
> browsing

In Chapter 5, we broke each of these tasks down further into subtasks. For knowledge representation, these subtasks included:

1. Representing text and graphics.
2. Representing concepts.
3. Representing organizational structures.
4. Representing relations between concepts.

Each of the representational subtasks require an authoring process. Thus as with building an expert system, constructing an intelligent database application requires a complex knowledge engineering process. Figure 7.20 illustrates the analogy between knowledge engineering in developing an expert system and knowledge engineering-authoring in developing an intelligent database application.

Much of the knowledge engineering required to build facts, rules, and objects will correspond to the process described in texts on expert systems (e.g., Parsaye and Chignell, 1988). In addition, however, there is a complex authoring task associated with linking large amounts of information and building hypermedia networks.

Contexts may be used to provide perspectives or partitions in hypermedia (Delisle and Schwartz, 1987). A single object can have multiple instances in different contexts, and an object may be described by a global identifier (which identifies all instances of that object in all contexts) and a local identifier which identifies the instance of that object in a given context. Within the intelligent database model, users may browse information objects of a variety of forms, including traditional "text units" that

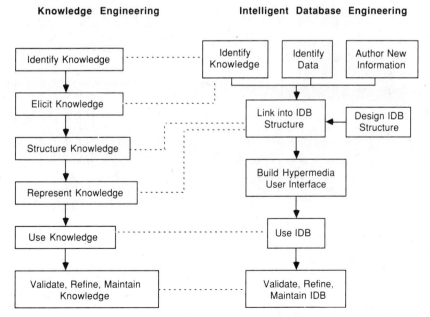

Figure 7.20 Knowledge engineering in expert systems and intelligent database (IDB) development.

would normally be encountered as the paragraphs of documents. The objects of the hypermedia can be related either pragmatically or semantically. Semantic relations reflect the meanings that are normally assigned to the objects independent of context.

Pragmatic relations between objects reflect the situational context in which the dialog between user and hypertext system takes place and can be defined on an "as-needed" basis. Some types of relation that may prove generally useful include:

a. Informational smoothing. Relations that overcome apparent inconsistencies.

b. Concept references (e.g., this concept appears in this object). Concept references allow users to explore the usage of a concept in different documents or nodes.

c. Analogy and similarity. In instructional settings, these nodes can act to compare and contrast concepts, thereby sharpening and clarifying their definitions in the minds of users.

d. Details. These relations act like replacement buttons in Guide, moving down a level of detail. These relations are particularly useful in text processing.

e. Generalization. These relations are the obverse of detail relations in that they are used to guide the user up an abstraction hierarchy that is embedded in hypermedia.

f. Implication. These relations were defined earlier in Section 4.4.2.

The treatment of pragmatic relations is an important topic that lies outside the scope of this discussion. Instead, we view hypermedia in terms of input and output operations. The input operations of authoring a hypermedia system involve describing and linking the objects. In hypermedia output (browsing), the hypermedia consists as a set of linked dialogs.

Experience with the development of hypermedia systems such as Project Jefferson (Chignell and Lacy, 1988) has shown just how difficult the hypermedia authoring can be. At first, it would seem that the process of linking all the information objects would be the most difficult and time consuming authoring task. However, our experience has shown that indexing is the most critical authoring task. Once objects have been thoroughly indexed, it is then possible to create static links based on observed correlations between the usage of index terms, and to create dynamic links based on a set of rules. Typically, it is possible to create a large number of well-behaved dynamic links with a proportionately much smaller set of rules.

One strategy that has proven successful for creating a large number of relevant static links from a set of well-indexed information objects is as follows:

1. Collect a large set of secondary information sources (books, articles, etc) that refer to the information objects.

2. Index these secondary information sources using the primary information objects.

3. Calculate the link strength between information object pairs based on the number of secondary sources (documents) that each pair co-occurs in.

4. Set a threshold (this may be defined differently for different user populations) and create static links for those object pairs that co-occur as index terms for more than a certain number or proportion of the secondary sources.

This strategy has the useful property of converting the authoring process into an indexing process, which is a far better understood, and possibly simpler, process. Furthermore, there is a great deal of indexed secondary source information already available which may be utilized in constructing hypermedia networks.

The automated, or semi-automated process of inferring links on the basis of indexing practice seems preferable to, or at least far more efficient than, the process of trailblazing that Bush (1945) originally thought would be necessary to construct hypertext links.

Many of the problems of authoring hypermedia are common to indexing in general. For instance, a limited amount of uniqueness should be enforced within the vocabulary of objects. This may be carried out using an online thesaurus of see also links. Thus, although each concept is represented only once, it is attached to alternative usage terms through which it may be accessed. However, it should be noted that although each object name is unique, these synonymous terms may be shared with other objects. Thus when synonyms, rather than standard object names are used, the system requires disambiguation.

7.5.4 Data Presentation and Display Tools

Given a large database, most users wish to see and display some of the data (or summaries thereof). Thus the presentation and display tools provide graphics, forms and other methods of data presentation. While this category is logically separate from the previous one, in practice the display tools will often be an extension of the hypermedia management tools.

Graphics summarize information in a visual form. Graphic representation tools take on many forms, including bar and pie charts, scattergrams, frequency polygons and maps. Some of the most compelling examples of graphic representation utilize the projection of numerical information on a visual model or map. The famous graphic showing the fate of Napoleon's army in Russia is an example of this (Tufte, 1983). That graphic succeeds in plotting the values of six variables: the size of the army; it's location on a two-dimensional surface (two variables); direction of the army's movement; and temperature on various dates during the retreat from Moscow (the two variables of time and temperature). Another example is the type of map that uses special graphics to visualize demographic data associated with cities.

We illustrate the use of graphics in an intelligent database representation tool with the example of an object-oriented interactive data graphics tool (Young, 1987). This tool (Ida) has five basic objects: presentations, assemblies, data sources, data displays, and scales.

The layout of the graphical displays is controlled by presentations and assemblies. An assembly is a set of data displays and a presentation is a set of independent assemblies collected for display. Data sources are responsible for drawing while data displays are image managers. Scales represent coordinate transformations.

Data displays are built up in layers and control the appearance of windows. Each data display has attributes such as the window which will receive its output, the visibility of the current layer, and the scrollability of the current layer. Each layer of a data display is represented by an object. Each data display has at least one layer, and the first layer is represented by an object directly referenced by the data display's assembly. Additional layers are then connected to the first layer.

In Ida, a data source is a graphic object which represents visual information in a "virtual plot." A portion of the virtual plot may be imported into a layer of a data display. The appearance of this plot once it has been imported will depend on a number of attribute values for the data source.

Young illustrates the concept of a data source with the example of single index curves. A single index curve's attributes include the following:

- the data points (in some coordinate system)
- data sampling interval
- line width and pattern
- drawing operation
- data point marking symbol
- data point coordinates to display
- current curve visibility
- destination data display layer

This curve may then be drawn onto a data display layer. The data points, sampled at the specified sampling interval, define the plot. The line description details the type of curve to be drawn, with a specified drawing operation. Each data point may also be annotated by its coordinates.

Scales are defined on the X and Y dimensions. They define the current transformation between the world coordinates (the device independent representation of the object) and the device coordinates (the view of the object that will be displayed in the layer of the window).

Ida has six basic graphic operations:

1. Clear window.
2. Erase data display buffer.
3. Draw image.
4. Show drawn image.

5. Adjust world coordinate clipping region.
6. Update (respond to scrolling).

We discussed the Ida system here to illustrate how an interactive graphics display system may be described in an object-oriented fashion. Features that enable graphics systems such as Ida to be linked to an intelligent database as representation tools include:

a. A taxonomic hierarchy of graphic classes.

b. Composition of graphic displays represented as hierarchically organized class instances.

c. Message passing is used to implement graphic operations on composite structures.

d. Binding of the graphic attributes of instances is postponed until needed.

e. Methods for graphic operations are provided over a diverse set of classes.

f. The graphic display tools may be extended by the user through method specialization.

Another popular representation tool is the form. Forms can be thought of as information templates or receptacles and can be used to input information into databases or output information from databases. The FORM model capitalizes on the intuitive nature and widespread use of forms by making them the central metaphor for intelligent databases.

Citation card forms (Figure 7.21), for instance, can be used to catalog library books. Such forms hide the underlying data structures from the user, by instead presenting the key concepts of the data model. In this case, the key concepts are the major fields in the citation. Giving these fields the familiar appearance of a standard 3 by 5 card catalog entry makes their meaning immediate and obvious. Many potentially useful forms are not included as part of the core model here because they tend to be application specific. Those forms that are included address the general tasks of information manipulation and management that occur in all intelligent databases.

7.5.5 Decision Support and Scenario Analysis Tools

Tools for decision support and scenario analysis allow for a uniform merger between spread-sheets, databases, financial modeling systems, etc. This stems from a view of decision support as a special kind of information management, retrieval, and utilization, where the information is tailored towards particular decision making activities.

Spreadsheets are an extremely popular class of software, partly we suspect because they are relatively easy to use, but also because they allow people to ask a variety of "what if?" questions concerning a set of data. There are many books on spreadsheets and their use. We will focus here on illustrating the formulation of a spreadsheet within

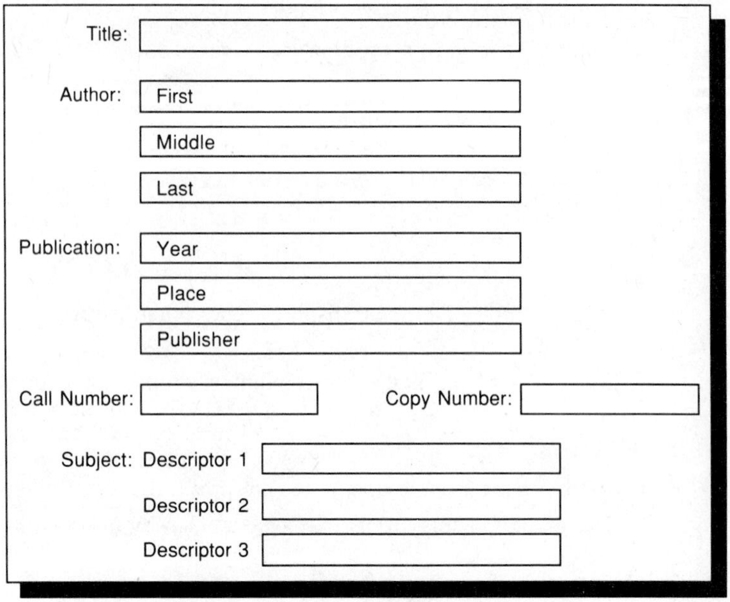

Figure 7.21 Citation card form describing a library book.

an object-oriented model in such a way that it may then be linked as a representation tool for an intelligent database.

A spreadsheet can be thought of as a special tool that has a corresponding model represented in the interface. In the case of the spreadsheet, there is a close mapping between the underlying data manipulations and storage, and the physical operations performed by the user on the interface's model of the task. In other cases this mapping may not be so immediate or apparent. A simplified version of the spreadsheet model outlined here is implemented as the HyperCalc example distributed as part of the HyperCard package on the Apple Macintosh microcomputer.

Figure 7.22 shows the basic HyperCalc structure consisting of six fields. The entire card may be viewed as an object. This object then has six fields or attributes, namely, miles per year, gallons per year, miles per gallon, cost per mile, price per gallon, and cost per year. The values for three of the attributes are dependent on the values of other attributes. The relevant equations are as follows:

gallons per year = miles per year / miles per gallon
cost per mile = price per gallon / miles per gallon
cost per year = gallons per year * price per gallon

Each of these equations is then implemented by a method attached to the object. These methods act like "if-needed" attached predicates during object access.

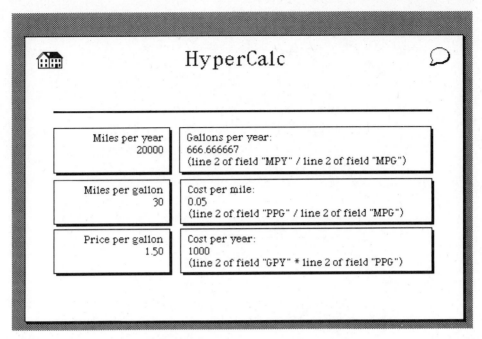

Figure 7.22 The basic Hypercalc structure.

Figure 7.23 shows the extended HyperCalc structure. Each spreadsheet is defined as a class. Columns within the spreadsheet are attributes and rows of the spreadsheet are objects. The functionality of the spreadsheet is then implemented by permitting the user to select a subset of objects within a class and to update attribute values. The modification of an attribute value then triggers updating of all the dependent attribute values via the appropriate methods. In this case the spreadsheet updating is analogous to the operation of an "if-changed" attached procedure in a object system.

Ideally, representation tools present operations at the database modeling level to the user in a natural and obvious way. One of the most "natural" ways of viewing information is in terms of objects that can be manipulated. The spreadsheet is one representation tool that embodies these three features of visuality, familiarity, and manipulability. The "extended HyperCalc" spreadsheet is a tool for representing, at the interface level, what is occurring at the level of the database model in such a way that the user can operate on the representation and thereby have the desired actions occur at the level of the database model.

7.5.6 Data-Format Management Tools

Data never seems to be in the format that it is needed in. The tools in Category 6 allow users to transform data between formats, for example, to merge an Ascii file with data in dBASE format and data obtained from IBM's DB2 with an automatically generated SQL query. These tools are indispensable for real data analysis applications.

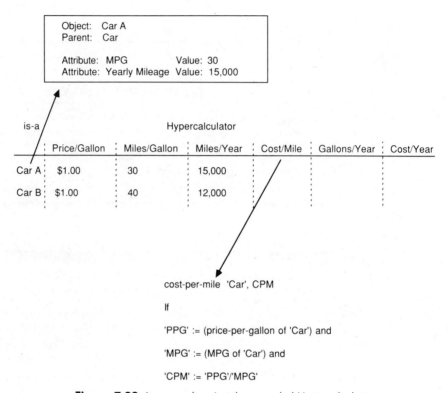

Figure 7.23 An example using the extended Hypercalculator.

These tools are often too machine dependent to be described in great detail here, but in general they perform the following functions:

Reformatting—They transform data from one format to another.

Relational algebra—They operate on tables with the relational algebra.

Query generation—They generate queries to external databases to obtain data.

Concept construction—They build virtual fields from database tables.

Here concept construction means that we build a new column in a table, based on a given set of rules. For instance, given the column "Date of Birth" in a table, we may define a new column "Age," based on the current date.

7.5.7 Intelligent System Design Tools

These tools provide facilities for designing intelligent databases. Although the fields of database design, information system design, and expert system design have maintained a separate existence in the past, their integration in an intelligent database is essential. Thus these tools allow system developers and administrators to better design and maintain intelligent databases. However, a full discussion of these tools is beyond the scope of this chapter.

■ 7.6 FORTUNE FINDER: AN INTELLIGENT DATABASE APPLICATION

There is plenty of evidence that much of human information retrieval is strongly associative. In contrast, information science has focused on structured search rather than browsing or associative retrieval of information.

We illustrate the use of intelligent databases with an example which indicates the breadth of the intelligent database approach, and which ranges in scope from information retrieval to high-level programming environments and complex decision support systems.

A financial analyst is using an intelligent database to find information relevant to a stock purchasing decision. The system being used is called Fortune Finder. Fortune Finder illustrates some of the functionality of the intelligent database, where the database is acting as a sophisticated decision support environment.

The fundamental aim of Fortune Finder is to facilitate the access and use of information pertaining to the Fortune 1000 companies. Fortune Finder was chosen as a demonstration of intelligent database technology because of its commercial value, the inherent nature of financial analysis as an information browsing task, and the ready availability of information on the financial status of the Fortune 1000 companies.

The implementation of the stock investment task required some knowledge engineering in order to determine what information was most relevant. Based on the recommendations of texts on stock investment, the following information was determined to be important:

- the number of institutional investors in a company
- the price-to-earnings ratio of a company
- the size of dividends paid by a company relative to the rest of the industry
- the price of the stock
- the long-term debt relative to capitalization
- the long-term debt relative to sales
- annual sales
- total assets of the company
- current liabilities of the company

It is assumed that the potential investor will use Fortune Finder to browse through information on different companies, focusing on those aspects of a company's financial performance that are most relevant to stock investment decisions.

In Fortune Finder the options available to the user are generally presented as a set of pull down menus attached to a main menu bar. The user selects a menu, and then an item from the resulting pull down menu. At each point in a Fortune Finder session, input from the user determines where the system should go next. There are a number of situations in Fortune Finder where a transaction has just been completed and a set of general choices has to be provided to the user. The intelligent selection of the choices in such cases is handled by the Activity Manager which corresponds to a set of rules controlling the overall interaction with the user. The selections made available by the Activity Manager will generally depend on where one is in the information structure, who the user is, what their task is, and so on. Inference is used to tailor the choices to the current context. In the case where a node has just been explored, the choices selected for presentation by the Activity Manager might be:

- link to a new node
- explore this node further
- search the database
- take a note

The main components of the Fortune Finder architecture are shown in Figure 7.24. These include the Browser, the Note Taker, the Activity Manager, the ObjectBase (FrameBase), and the Rule Base.

Figure 7.25 shows an implementation of Fortune Finder using a CD-ROM drive to provide basic information about the Fortune 1000 companies (e.g. the Compact Dis-

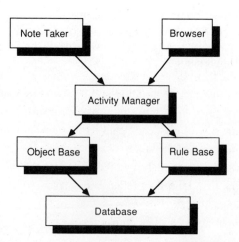

Figure 7.24 The main components of the Fortune Finder architecture.

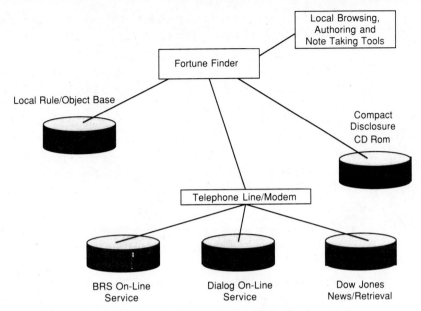

Figure 7.25 An example of a Fortune Finder implementation.

closure system), an online encyclopedia to provide general knowledge, connection to a mainframe database for current quotes and information (e.g., Dow Jones News/Retrieval Service), and connection to local or corporate databases.

The first functionality that we consider is the browser, which is at the heart of Fortune Finder.

7.6.1 Browsing

In spite of the variety of operations and activities that are available, the major activity in Fortune Finder is browsing. Database searching and notetaking are tasks that are performed while one is browsing and the fundamental task for Fortune Finder is always determining an answer to the question "where does the user want to go next?" Thus Fortune Finder is organized as an information browsing system with nested tools that perform database searches, note taking, and other useful activities along the way. Report generating is a separate tool that acts upon the personal information structures generated by browsing and searching within Fortune Finder.

Thus one of the major tasks in Fortune Finder is to choose which node to move to next in the information network. Fortune Finder uses inference to determine which of the related nodes are most likely to be of interest to the user in the context of the current task.

The process of selecting what further information to show about the current node, or which node to move to next is normally not visible to the user. However, in cases where aspects of the current context are ambiguous as far as the Activity Manager is concerned, Fortune Finder may request additional information from the user about his interests or the nature of the current task.

The browser has three main functions:

- marking a node so that you can return to it later
- exploring the current node
- moving to a new node

The purpose of marking a node is to enable the user to return to the same point in the information network at a later time. Note that this does not restore the entire Fortune Finder environment at that time, only the position of the current node in the network.

The mark is set by the user and then labeled. This allows the user to select the restart node at a later time using the label which might include text such as the date when the node was marked and the reason for marking it. Once the node has been marked, it is available for later re-entry.

When the explore node option is selected, the system uses inference based on the current context and user model to determine what information about the node should be available to the user. The different elements of information are then presented as choices in the "explore" pull down menu available under the menu bar.

Fortune Finder is organized as an information browsing tool with nested tools that perform note taking along the way. One of the major tasks is to choose which node to move to next in the information network. Inference is used to determine which of the related nodes are most likely to be of interest to the user in the context of the current task. In addition to these dynamic links that are available under the "NewNode" pull down menu, static links may be embedded within the current information screen. These static links can then be selected from the "Button" menu.

The process of selecting link options to appear in the NewNode pull down menu is normally not visible to the user. However, in cases where aspects of the current context is ambiguous as far as the link selection process is concerned, Fortune Finder may request additional information from the user about his interests and the nature of the current task.

Selection of link options is carried out by a set of rules operating on the information provided by the object system.

Options are displayed within a popup menu. The user selects an option by pointing with mouse or selecting with the arrow keys.

Dynamic links between companies are determined using a set of rules such as:

Company X <u>is related to</u> Company Y

if

X <u>is a subsidiary of</u> Y

and

Company X <u>is related to</u> Company Y

and

X , Y <u>share the same</u> SIC code (that is, they belong to the same general industry or activity)

or

Company X <u>is related to</u> Company Y

if

X , Y <u>have the same</u> parent company.

7.6.2   The Note Taker

The use of a note taker in Fortune Finder reflects the fact that people look for information with a task in mind, or for a reason, whether or not that reason can be completely verbalized. The ability to write a note which can then be integrated with the retrieved information is an essential part of many tasks.

To the user, the process of writing a note is much like using a simplified word processor. However, once written, the note may be indexed, appended to other information, and later be made available for retrieval as part of the overall intelligent database.

Anyone who has jotted down lots of notes on scraps of paper will recall problems in finding a particular note when it was needed. Sometimes the act of looking for the note takes longer than it took to write down the note in the first place. Labeling notes makes them easier to find. When labeling a note, the user is prompted for the name of the note after he finishes writing it. The system ensures that the label for each note is unique.

Notes are stored as objects within a special objectbase allocated to notes. Labels are assigned as the names of the text object corresponding to the notes. Each note object contains a special attribute called note-text. When this attribute is accessed, the text of the note is written out by an attached procedure.

Labels are helpful, but sometimes one wants to collect all the notes that refer to a particular topic. This can be done by indexing notes and allowing the stack of notes in a particular environment to be searched by their index terms. Searching through notes is a specialized type of database search operation.

In keeping with the word processing capability of notes they may be edited simply by calling up the note and selecting the editing tool. The user may build a template for the report. This corresponds to an outline into which the information in the notes and information screens may be inserted. The template builder is a primitive outlining tool.

In generating a report or written document on the basis of an information browsing/searching episode, the user can refer back to notes previously written. Some of these notes may be linked to information screens.

Riffling through notes is controlled by the Activity Manager and corresponds to presenting the notes in the current package in order, one at a time. Note searching is also available. Note searching is carried out in analogous fashion to database searching, with Boolean queries being admissible. Tagging the notes corresponds to creating special facts indicating that particular notes will be included in the report.

Once tagged, the notes and the linked screens must be placed in a linear order for the report. The user sees a menu containing the labels of the selected notes. As the user clicks on each note the user is prompted to indicate the appropriate insertion point in the report template. Notes that are not selected for the report are retained in the note package, along with notes that are selected.

Many information searches require some output, ranging from a set of brief notes to a full-scale report. Normally the creation of the text file occurs at the end of a session. Here the user labels the text file that is to be created and the system links the text objects attached to the report template and outputs them to a text file.

7.6.3   The Photo Feature

Every information screen in Fortune Finder may be photographed. A photograph consists of linear text output of all the text fields that were shown to the user in the current display. The user is asked to annotate this *photo* so that it is easier to retrieve at a later time and possibly use in writing subsequent reports. If the user does not supply a label (name) for the photo, then a default system name is provided for it. The user is also able to choose to write index terms for the photo (or have default system index terms for the screen attached to the photo). These default index terms are typically inherited from the index terms assigned to the main object or element that the screen describes.

Photo annotation occurs after the user selects the photo tool. The system then prompts for a label. If the user simply presses enter, the default label is applied.

The use of the photo tool creates a special note object within the note objectbase. This note object is named according to the assigned label and the fact that it is a photo is recorded in the note-type slot.

Fortune Finder assumes that there is a natural relationship between notes and photos. Although it is not mandatory, a user may link a photo to a note or vice versa. After a photo has been taken and annotated, the user is prompted for a possible note. If the user chooses he may either write a new note that will be linked to the photo, or he may link an existing note to the photo. In either case, the user is taken to the note taking tools to select or write the note, after which he is returned to the current node and given a menu of further options. The nesting of notes within photos or vice versa is an example of the more general process of nesting notes that occurs during note organization.

After taking the photo the user sees a prompt asking if he wants to link a note to it. If so he then enters the note taking environment. After the new note is completed (or an old note is selected for linking), it is linked to the photo and the user returns to the current node and the previous information screen is shown along with the standard menu bar.

7.6.4 Note Organization

Like a photo, a note is stored as a special object within the note objectbase. If the user wants to select a particular note this may be done by providing the name of the note or the name of the topic (index term) that is relevant after choosing the select note option from the note taking pull down menu.

After the note selection function is chosen, the user is asked to submit the label for the note desired. The note is then available for linking or nesting. The note may also be viewed, but the resulting note screen may not be edited.

The Note Organizer provides a rudimentary outlining facility. A note may be organized as a child of another note. Through successive organizing steps, the user is able to build a hierarchical structure for the notes which can then be output as draft sections and subsections of a report.

The user chooses the note organizing selection from the note taking pull down menu. The user is then prompted for the names of the parent note and the child note. An additional choice under the note taking menu is view outline. This option shows the current organization of the notes with nesting indicated by indented note labels. Notes that have not been explicitly organized are automatically entered into the outline in the order that they were written.

7.6.5 Structured Searching

Database searching is another tool that can be activated at almost any time from within Fortune Finder by selecting from the main menu bar. Terms to be included in the query may be selected from a factbase of relevant terms, or new interesting terms may be input directly by the user.

Terms are combined according to the type of database search function being used. Database search function is a toggle that can be varied by the user. In addition to Boolean retrieval, relational and other database querying methods may be used.

The user builds a search query hierarchically. This eliminates the ambiguity experienced by most human searchers when the search query is built up in linear left-to-right order. The process of building the search query is carried out in steps with each step involving the application of a Boolean operator to one or more relevant terms. Thus "not PepsiCola" would be a query formulation step as would be "PepsiCola and Coca-Cola." The user is then permitted to let the Boolean string stand for each search step or supply a new label which will be used in later steps. For instance the user may supply the label "colas" for "PepsiCola or Coca-Cola." The user may then add an additional step such as "colas or beverages," and so on.

Boolean query formulation is carried out by specialized rules. Each step in the query formulation process results in a set of documents stored in a package (c.f. a citation stack in Project Jefferson). Subsequent Boolean operations that refer to that step are carried out directly on the package. The documents in the package may be information screens, citations, or even notes. The user may modify the search parameters to determine which types of document will be available to the current search.

The search query provides structured information search within Fortune Finder. It allows users to retrieve documents relating to a particular subject without having to browse each document directly. A summary of the search results are provided to the user. The documents retrieved may also be viewed by the user one by one as if they were information screens. These documents may then be either photographed or deleted from the package. If photographed the normal operation of the photo tool will occur and the user will be asked if he wants to annotate the photo or link it to a note.

7.6.6 The Questioner and Adviser

Other features of Fortune Finder include the Questioner, a system that permits specific searches that include selection operations. Examples of questions that might be asked include "How many companies have a price to earnings ratio of less than 15?" or "What are the 10 largest institutional shareholders for Eastern Airlines?"

Another component is the Adviser. This contains embedded expert systems. Thus if a user was searching through information and asked the question "Advise me on which food industry stock I should buy today," Fortune Finder would then act as an advisory expert system and after some interaction with the user provide its advice.

It might be argued that many expert systems are actually forms of deductive retrieval and thus it makes sense to allow the capability to embed expert systems within an intelligent database system such as Fortune Finder. More generally, this embedding of expert systems within Fortune Finder illustrates the synergistic relationship between expert system inference and databases. In a database system, where some of the information is represented in terms of objects and rules, the database can act as an extension of the knowledge base of the expert system in finding the information that the expert system needs as it reasons. Similarly, when searching for information, an expert system may be used to infer information not directly available or to assist in making a number of decisions relating to what information to show the user next at different points in a session.

7.6.7 Fortune Finder in Retrospect

Thus, Fortune Finder is designed as a complete environment for information seeking, note taking, and deductive retrieval. Inference in Fortune Finder occurs during browsing. Inference determines what nodes (companies) will be offered as dynamically selected choices when the user wants to change his position in the database. These "links" are created on the fly by inference. Static links are displayed as buttons embedded within text. These buttons are indicated by highlighting.

One of the design decisions made in Fortune Finder was to distinguish between other company names or descriptors that are embedded within text and corresponding names and descriptions determined to be related to the current node by inference. Embedded buttons are available as choices within one pull-down menu, while links that are inferred dynamically to also be relevant are available in a second pull-down menu. A third pull-down menu then shows additional information that can be viewed about the current company. The choices in this third menu are also determined dynamically through inference. Note that the choices in the first pull-down menu, which reflect the embedded buttons in the text, may refer both to other companies (link to a different node) or to further information about the current company (explore the current node).

The fundamental aim of Fortune Finder is to facilitate the access and use of information. Thus, it is a good demonstration of the intelligent database approach. In the browse feature, exploration allows the user to move between topics or nodes. When the user is at a particular node, they may choose to explore that node in more detail using the explore node option. Exploration choices are determined dynamically on the basis of the user's interests and the task being performed. For instance, the stock information option would be displayed if the user was interested in looking at companies in terms of possible stock investments. The stock investment case study considered in the Fortune Finder prototype can be extended to provide a complete information management tool for financial and investment analysis of the Fortune 1000 companies.

Fortune Finder combines conventional hypertext browsing, the use of dynamic hypertext with inference, and notetaking, within an integrated information management environment. Since it is written within an expert system shell that includes hypertext tools and links to relational databases, it is relatively easy to extend the functionality and to develop authoring tools that simplify the conversion of information into the Fortune Finder format.

■ 7.7. SUMMARY

In this chapter we have shown how the structure of an intelligent database may be formulated in a single uniform framework: FORM (Formal Object Representation Model). This model may be used at different levels of detail as a programming and system design tool for both programmers and end users. Thus the model is *seamless*, in the sense that there is no dramatic change between the end user and the programmer mode.

FORM integrates the technologies discussed in Chapters 2 through 6. It uses object orientation as a basic paradigm in all data and knowledge representations It relies on an integrated database and inference engine which uses a uniform approach to forward, backward, and inexact inference with unification. Further, the inference engine can simultaneously deal with logical and object-oriented views of the same database. FORM uses these underlying technologies to support a dialog manager and a dynamic hypermedia system at the user-interface level. These are then used to support a number of high-level tools which dramatically increase our ability to utilize the data in an intelligent database.

8

SUMMARY

The preceding seven chapters have described intelligent databases and the technologies that support their development. It should be obvious by now that intelligent databases cover a range of topics that are not typically considered in combination. This has made it necessary for us to introduce each topic (expert systems, databases, etc.) in some detail, so that readers may become acquainted with the relevant topics that they were previously unfamiliar with. If the previous chapters have been read, the reader should now have a good sense of what intelligent databases are and how they may be developed. In this chapter we reinforce this knowledge by reviewing the material covered in the previous chapters and outlining the key points as we see them.

■ 8.1 THE NATURE OF INTELLIGENT DATABASES

In our initial definition of intelligent databases we characterized them as *databases that manage information in a natural way, making that information easy to store, access, and use*. We did not attempt to rigorously define the concepts of "ease" and "naturalness." Instead, we provided criteria for what makes a database intelligent. In terms of a performance criterion, intelligent databases should allow users to perform tasks involving large amounts of information that otherwise could not possibly be performed.

We defined three levels of database intelligence.

1. Intelligence of the high level tools provided by the database.
2. Intelligence at the user interface level.
3. Intelligence of the underlying database engine.

and we discussed how intelligent databases represent a new technology for information management that has evolved as a result of the integration of traditional approaches to databases with more recent fields such as

- Object-oriented programming
- Expert systems
- Hypermedia
- Online information retrieval

Until recently these technologies were treated in isolation, partly due to the fact that because of the phenomenal growth in each field, the connections and correspondences to the other fields did not have time to form. However, it is our view that these technologies have now reached a stage of maturity where it is possible to define an overall unifying structure for viewing all of these fields as parts of a blueprint for intelligent databases.

Our discussion of intelligent databases throughout this book was motivated by several goals.

- to manage large volumes of information
- to make information easily and meaningfully available
- to provide mechanisms that will augment human capabilities
- to make the information in online databases almost as available as if it were already inside the memory of the user

In addition to these overall goals, the essential characteristics of an intelligent database are that it is easy and natural to use, can handle large amounts of information in a seamless and transparent fashion, and that it allows people to carry out their tasks using an appropriate set of information management tools. Such information management tools are essential in a world of information glut where the capability to store massive amounts of information exceeds our capability to effectively retrieve that information.

In our view, the solution to the problem of information glut requires the development of intelligent databases. In itself, electronic access does not answer the problem of ready access to information, since having billions of words of text is not much use to one if there is no way of knowing which particular documents address the current information need.

In developing an intelligent database technology as a solution to the problem of information glut, we began by establishing a context for the technology in terms of the information society. Perhaps the central fact and assumption of the information society is that *the world of concrete objects is being controlled more and more by a parallel, but separate, world of abstract objects and concepts.*

The modern information society has arisen out of the ability to store information and data in electronic databases. The first step toward the modern database was the representation of information in written form. We showed how there was a series of revolutions in hard-copy information technology that preceded the development of electronic databases.

Intelligent databases represent the latest step in the evolution of database technology. All databases typically include a data model, an indexing system, and a querying language among other components. However, conventional databases are generally static in the sense that they are updated with new information from time to time, and this updating process is carried out externally instead of being an intrinsic task carried out by the database system itself.

Knowledge-based systems enhance the dynamism of databases by providing the capability for reasoning and inferring new information on the fly. This creates the capability for self-modifying databases *(metastorage)*, as well as the ability to reason about what information a user might be interested in, even if the user's information need was not originally expressed that way.

One of the features of intelligent databases is that due to the intelligent processes that they embody, they are more easily linked to human intelligence. Most of human behavior can be interpreted in terms of people processing information in order to select activities and achieve their goals. We can distinguish between the senses and muscles, which act as a person's interface with the outside world, and the mind, which internally processes information and accordingly plans actions. This distinction between senses and muscles on the one hand, and mind on the other, is roughly equivalent to the user interface level and database support level of information systems. This equivalence creates a potential for making databases intelligent and providing them with powerful interfaces.

The construction of intelligent databases has only recently become possible with advances in computing technology. The ability to create networks of computers makes vast distributed databases possible and removes physical barriers to information. Similarly, the removal of memory limitations in mass storage allows one to store a great deal of information in ways that make it easy to use, even if they are fairly profligate in terms of the space that they consume on the storage device. Thus it is conceivable to have multiple representations of information at different points in information networks or hierarchies.

■ 8.2 OVERVIEW OF DATABASES

Our discussion of databases began by considering the history and evolution of databases from the early development of file structures on mainframe computers. The hierarchical, network, and relational data models were introduced, along with a distinction between the conceptual, logical, and physical levels of database architecture.

Because of the relational model's theoretical purity, popularity, and close relationship to logic, the focus of Chapter 2 was on relational DBMSs. Methods of querying relational databases were examined, with emphasis on the SQL and QBE querying languages. A practical database design methodology based on forms specification techniques was then outlined with a simple example, generating a relational database definition along with other information that is useful for application development.

Like most technologies, the directions that databases pursued were determined not only by improving hardware and software capability, but also by the socioeconomic needs of the organizations that used computers. In the 1960s, the use of mainframes became widespread in many companies. These companies often had a great deal of data that they stored on disks. It soon became apparent that a large amount of information was common to different applications and that there was a need to share access to data. As a result, scattered files and data were integrated into centralized databases.

The basis of database technology consists of methods for structuring and organizing data. Data needs to be organized if it is to be useful, and data models specify how separate pieces of information are related in a database. Information is generally broken down into data structures such as records and fields. At the file level, records are the basic units of data storage.

The conceptual view of a database is a somewhat abstract representation of the physical data and the way that it is stored. The same conceptual model of the database can apply to a variety of different physical implementations. In contrast, the logical level of database description consists of the definition of the logical structure of a database, written as logical schemas within a data definition language. At present, most databases only have a limited understanding of what the data that they contain really means. This is a major motivation behind the development of intelligent and active databases. Semantic data models are designed to overcome the problem of limited understanding by incorporating more meaning into the database. In essence, intelligent databases use knowledge representation and inference methods to implement powerful semantic models.

In our discussion of databases, we introduced the network and hierarchical models in addition to the relational model. However, the relational model was our major emphasis in Chapter 2 and it is the relational model, combined with object-oriented approaches, that we believe will be most useful in building intelligent databases.

The relational database model offers the simple notion of tables as the only data structure for user interaction. Its close relationship to set theory and first-order logic allows the relational model to inherit many elegant properties and operators since it is based on a well-defined logical structure, namely, the relational algebra.

Formally, the representation of relational data consists of lists of relations and their attributes, along with the description of existence constraints. Data retrieval within the relational model is handled by using the relational algebra to manipulate relations.

However, in practical use, features of the relational model are often modified. Thus we reviewed the rules that Codd offered in defining what really constitutes a relational DBMS. These rules are a helpful tool in database product evaluation.

In our discussion of relational databases, we also included an introduction to two well-known commercial systems, SQL and QBE. SQL is rapidly emerging as the standard database language for all platforms and has been adopted as an ANSI standard. SQL is, in fact, more than merely a database query language. It includes features for defining the structure of the data, modifying the data, and specifying security constraints within the database.

Query-by-example (QBE) is a query language that incorporates a number of the features of the relational model and is expressed in a table format, but it does not conform as closely to the relational model as does the SQL query language. QBE is designed to build queries interactively. The idea of querying by example is that instead of describing the procedure to be followed in obtaining the desired information, the user gives an example of what is required.

∎ 8.3 OBJECT ORIENTATION

Chapter 2 reviewed some of the steps by which early views of data as disconnected numbers and strings of text have developed into sophisticated database management issues. In Chapter 3 we considered a new philosophy and implementation for storing information and data, that is, object-oriented databases. We should stress that the object-oriented approach supplements the relational approach, and well-designed object-oriented systems may be integrated with more conventional relational databases.

One fundamental feature of an intelligent database is that the abstract data model of the database provided to the user closely resembles the user's model of the real world. What should be some of the characteristics of the model of the data that structures intelligent databases? Our belief is that the most powerful and expressive feature that must be incorporated in an intelligent database is object orientation. In Chapter 3 we introduced, explained, and illustrated the elements of object orientation and object-oriented databases.

Fundamental concepts of object orientation include abstract data typing (encapsulation), inheritance, and object identity. When these concepts are coupled with persistency and transaction support, the result is extremely powerful systems called object-oriented databases. We described object-oriented databases in Section 3.6.

Section 3.7 presents three main applications of object orientation in addition to knowledge representation: discrete-event simulation, design engineering, and software engineering. However, to begin with we trace back the history of object-oriented databases by reviewing the history of object orientation.

However, software engineering as a whole and data modeling more specifically has also progressed as a self-contained discipline. In other words, although some of these changes were due to the availability of high-performance hardware components, the software engineering "science" itself is starting to acquire its own characteristics and progress at a rapid pace. In fact, we are seeing more and more a *decoupling* of the hardware and software components of computation. The support of the same language, operating system, or application on different platforms is a simple example of this.

We also identified four areas in database data modeling and programming in general that have progressed towards more expressive paradigms; namely, representation of the object space, use of declarative and navigational programming styles, abstraction and modularization, and inheritance.

We found a certain amount of confusion and controversy regarding the overloaded term *object-oriented*. We presented a particular characterization of object orientation that emphasized the three most fundamental aspects of the paradigm: abstract data typing or encapsulation, inheritance, and object identity. These concepts were explained in detail.

We described the minimal database capabilities that an object-oriented database should have including: (i) a "high-level" query language with query optimization capabilities in the underlying system; (ii) support of atomic transactions (concurrency control and recovery); and (iii) support of indexes and access methods for fast associative retrieval.

We also described GemStone, the first commercially available object-oriented database. We showed how the OPAL language, which constitutes both the data definition and data manipulation (conceptual) database languages of GemStone, is very similar to the programming language Smalltalk. We described the GemStone architecture and showed how OPAL allows users to commit or abort their transactions, create indexes, and express queries.

Chapter 3 closed by illustrating the viability of the object-oriented style of programming to a number of application domains including discrete-event simulation, and software and design engineering.

■ 8.4. EXPERT SYSTEMS AND DATABASES

One of the central problems in developing intelligent databases involves how one should extend database models and systems so as to construct intelligent databases. The solution that we proposed was to add extra knowledge representation and inferencing capability. The tools for knowledge representation and inferencing were provided by the technology of expert systems.

In Chapter 4 we introduced the essential elements of expert systems that assist in making databases more intelligent. We found that expert systems provided two types of support: (a) higher level programming capabilities and (b) a knowledge representation formalism.

We defined an expert system as a computer program that relies on knowledge and reasoning to perform a difficult task usually performed only by a human expert. We showed that not only do expert systems provide the machine reasoning capability that can make databases intelligent, but they may be viewed as higher level methods of database programming.

The *architecture* of expert systems was broken up into three major components: the knowledge base, the inference engine, and the user interface. We showed how the task of representing knowledge in the knowledge base involves describing knowledge in terms of five elementary components: naming, describing, organizing, relating, and constraining.

Frames and objects were used as the major methods for representing knowledge in a form that could be used by an inference engine. It was shown how objects could be represented in hierarchies, which then made inheritance possible. These basic representations could also be supplemented with attached procedures (methods) that provided additional links between the knowledge representation and inferencing systems.

We discussed inference as the process of combining facts and rules to deduce new facts. Inference trees were used as a diagrammatic way of representing the structure of knowledge and as helpful tools in visualizing inference. Rules were presented as combinations of premises and conclusions and it was shown how rules could be applied in both backward chaining and forward chaining methods of inference. The use of two-valued logic in inference was then extended to include inexact inference.

After the basic exposition on expert systems, we addressed the problem of applying expert systems to the development of intelligent databases where it is necessary not only to represent the knowledge about a database in a form that can be used for deductive retrieval, but also to build a software interface between database management systems and expert systems.

We emphasized an approach to expert systems where they are primarily seen as high-level programming environments for information and knowledge intensive tasks. We showed how a relational database may be closely integrated with a reasoning system using relational predicates and objects. Thus the integration between expert systems and relational databases relied on two interchangeable models for representing database relations within a knowledge base: the predicate model and the object model.

These two models were shown to be fully interchangeable, thereby providing a great deal of flexibility. The predicate model represents relations within a "virtual" (disk-based) factbase. Data is added using the assert predicate, removed with the retract predicate, and retrieved with standard predicate matching from within the expert-system shell.

The integration of expert systems and database systems within the framework of intelligent databases is particularly appealing because the user can directly manipulate the semantics of the database in a straightforward fashion, in contrast to approaches where the semantics are "hardwired" into the data model. This removes the need to predefine complex semantic constructs within the basic language of the database.

Expert systems not only provide a way of archiving expertise and making it available when it is needed, but provide higher level language constructs that are useful for database programming. These constructs include backward and forward rules, attached predicates, knowledge representation, and relational predicates. Expert database systems seem to offer a way of combining the best features of database systems and expert systems.

Facts, rules, objects, and inference engines are basic tools for knowledge representation and inference within intelligent databases. These basic components of expert systems are also useful in constructing computational models of conventional databases, hypertext systems, and in building the more advanced systems for text interpretation and retrieval that intelligent databases require.

■ 8.5 THE ROLE OF HYPERMEDIA

Hypertext was defined as a tool for building and using associative structures. Although a normal document is linear and one tends to read it from beginning to end, reading hypertext is open-ended and one can jump from idea to idea depending on one's interests.

Hypertext can be thought of as an enriched thesaurus where, instead of links between words, links between documents and text fragments are available. Thus hypertext is simultaneously a method for storing and retrieving data. From an intelligent database perspective, hypertext can be thought of as a database system with unrestricted links among records and files.

We extended the notion of hypertext to hypermedia where information could be represented in alternative media such as graphics and sound, as well as text. Networks of information linked within hypermedia form new types of document that we referred to as hypermedia documents. These documents serve as systems for knowledge representation, linkage to inference systems, information retrieval, and browsing.

The model of hypermedia presented in Chapter 5 consisted of a basic set of node and link types that permit multiple and interlinked representations of knowledge. This model was then supplemented with ancillary tools and processes to provide the capabilities of browsing, knowledge representation, inference, and information retrieval that are critical to the performance of an intelligent database.

It was recognized that hypermedia systems are more flexible than traditional information structuring methods in that they allow information in a variety of forms (media) to be attached to nodes. Nodes in hypertext (hypermedia) will generally include buttons that provide links (send messages) to other nodes. The variety of nodes that can be defined in hypertext make it an extremely flexible knowledge representation tool. This flexibility is further enhanced by providing a variety of link types. Links define the structure of hypermedia and provide the capability for browsing and exploring the nodes.

There are many different types of links that can be defined, one of which is navigational links. Node and link types may also be constructed that are inferential or organizational in nature.

Because of the way in which it has evolved and the emphasis that has been placed on its unstructured nature, hypermedia has generally been regarded as an informal way of providing information that can be browsed. One of our goals was to show that hypermedia is in fact an extremely flexible knowledge representation environment that is analogous in many ways to semantic networks. Different types of knowledge representation formalism can be implemented in hypermedia by structuring and defining the basic types of nodes and links in different ways. We defined a set of node and link types for using hypermedia in intelligent databases and we refined this set further in Chapter 7.

The strengths of hypermedia arise from its flexibility in storing and retrieving knowledge. However, this flexibility may also lead to problems where it is difficult to maintain a sense of where things are in a relatively unstructured network of information. Browsing tools are a way of getting round these problems. We described two closely related browsing approaches: the fisheye model and the landmark model.

The fisheye lens model is built on the observation that humans often represent their own neighborhood in great detail, yet only indicate major landmarks for more distant regions. The landmark model was introduced as a modification of the fisheye view approach to browsing that designates certain nodes in the hypermedia as landmarks, because of their familiarity, memorability, or salience. These landmarks act like the familiar landmarks in a city, giving the user a chance to orient themselves around objects that have known locations. It was shown how one could provide views of these landmarks where users have a chance to view landmarks that are at different sets of conceptual distances from the current location.

We also discussed the issue of information filtering in hypermedia that corresponds to the process of making queries and retrieving information in databases and conventional information retrieval systems. In our view, hypermedia-based information retrieval systems should filter information to suit the needs of the user. The success of query languages in database applications also strongly suggests the need for some type of querying mechanism in hypermedia.

The linkage of hypermedia nodes to corresponding hierarchical representations provides a powerful form of indexing. Like inferencing, information retrieval is a separate process that may be linked to the hypermedia representation. Thus our hypermedia model does not replace conventional information retrieval but incorporates it within a broader model of information access and utilization.

We also discussed how hypermedia holds a great deal of promise as a query formulation aid. Hypermedia documents can be used to create sophisticated online thesauri where words are linked to their definitions, to synonyms and related terms, and so on. Thus query formulation will be greatly assisted as the hypermedia allows the vocabularies of the user and the system to converge prior to carrying out search.

In the evolving technology of intelligent databases that is presented in this book, hypermedia may also be used as a user interface to the powerful information management capability available in an intelligent database. We showed how hypermedia may be used in this fashion in our discussion of the intelligent database user interface in Chapter 7.

■ 8.6 TEXT MANAGEMENT AND INTELLIGENT DATABASES

Text databases represent a critical component of intelligent database technology. Much of human knowledge is stored in the form of text and we face the issue of linking this text-based knowledge to knowledge-based representations that can be used in reasoning. Thus Chapter 6 was concerned not only with outlining the principles and methods of information science and online text retrieval, but also with the processes of converting textual information into a knowledge representation that could be understood by an inferencing system.

Although information is a familiar concept, it can be defined in a number of different ways depending on one's perspective. We informally defined the amount of information that one has received in terms of the amount of surprise that one experiences after hearing the information. Similarly, we may define the value of information in terms of what we learn after receiving the information and the benefit derived from that new knowledge.

Information retrieval is concerned with the representation, storage, organization, and accessing of information items. Current capabilities for storing information far exceed the amount of information that can be efficiently organized and retrieved. The basic model of information retrieval is very simple. Information is stored, and later when it is needed it is retrieved.

Specialized expertise is usually required to understand the indexing policies employed in databases and to formulate search queries in the language of the database. Since most end users do not have this expertise, they require the aid of a search intermediary in carrying out a search. However, even though an intermediary is often used in online information retrieval, at some point the information needs of the user must be compared with the information that is available. Most commonly, the matching paradigm of information retrieval is used where the information need is represented as a query, and the potential information (i.e., documents) is represented as a collection of index terms which can be matched against the query. Those documents whose index representations most closely match the query are then assumed to be relevant and their citations are passed to the user.

Since the process of constructing queries is fairly difficult, it makes sense to consider how the old query can be refined based on the judged relevance of the documents obtained with it. This idea is the basis of relevance feedback. Relevance feedback is based on a scoring algorithm where the weights associated with terms that appear in relevant documents are increased, while terms that appear more often in irrelevant documents are either removed from the query or have their importance weights reduced.

We discussed how information retrieval performance is generally assessed using two measures, namely recall and precision. These measures are typically based on subjective judgments of relevance made by users as they inspect document citations and abstracts. We suggested adding the third evaluation criterion of utilization, which can be thought of as the number of documents obtained in the search that were actually used by the user.

After reviewing the topic of information retrieval, we then addressed a fundamental problem in text management, namely, how to index text according to the concepts that it discusses. We proposed that this concept indexing process be built on concept hierarchies, which can be constructed in a number of ways. We described one method where experts are asked to sort a collection of terms (typically obtained from standard reference sources) into a hierarchy directly.

Concept indexing is one version of the general process of indexing documents that may be carried out manually or automatically. Manual indexing is a difficult task and consequently database companies frequently apply rules to assist indexers and to enforce indexing consistency. In addition to representing concepts within frame hierarchies, we also showed how index terms may sometimes be translated into a relational database representation using a learning process.

Our discussion of online databases reviewed the large amount of information available with well over 2 billion documents stored in thousands of databases. Databases differ according to factors such as their scope, chronological coverage, and the subjects that they address. A few illustrative database services were reviewed. We explained how database producers get the raw information and filter it and index it, sometimes adding abstracts and summary material.

We closed the chapter by considering some questions that have been judged to be important in forecasting the future of intelligent information retrieval. Our answers to these questions were framed from the perspective of intelligent databases.

We do not see a sharp distinction between text databases and other types of databases, although they have often been treated as separate problems in the past. Many of the features of information retrieval as discussed in Chapter 6 are shared with intelligent databases as characterized in this book. In particular, concept (knowledge-based) indexing is critical to the functionality of intelligent databases. We expect that the task of information search and retrieval will be carried out by intelligent databases in the future as the emphasis moves from retrieval of secondary sources (documents) to information management, question answering, and decision support.

■ 8.7 THE INTELLIGENT DATABASE MODEL

We formalized the requirements for an intelligent database by presenting FORM (Formal Object Representation Model) in Chapter 7. This included an intuitive visual model involving a deductive and object-oriented visual system that was used to create a pattern-matching QBE-like system which performs deductive queries and expert database consultations with a great deal of ease.

The resulting system was defined by the equation

End-User System = Hypermedia + QBE + Inference + Object Orientation

Traditional SQL based systems were extended in two ways.

1. *Unification-Based SQL*. Queries are obtained by merging SQL with pattern matching rules. This uses the rule-based paradigm as a powerful and natural extension of the control structures involved in performing SQL queries.

2. *Object-oriented SQL*. Object-orientated extensions to SQL are provided. This not only facilitates the formation of queries, but improves the data definition process. Further, the object-oriented and the rule-based extensions to SQL are themselves uniformly merged.

The resulting system was defined by the equation

Programming System = SQL + Cursors + Logic + Object orientation

We also introduced a deductive object-oriented *Dialog Language* that extends concepts involved in systems such as Microsoft Windows and the Macintosh Finder with deductive inheritance and attached predicates. This language may either be viewed as a "deductive and object-oriented version" of a hypermedia system or as a "hypertext version" of an expert-system language.

The structure of the dialog language was defined by

Dialog Language = Screen Primitives + Dynamic icons + Object orientation + Inference + Hypermedia

Later we presented a design for an *Intelligent Information Retrieval Workstation* (IIRW), which combines the features described earlier to provide a *dynamic* hypermedia system whose links and data are dynamically updated as the information content of the system changes.

We then presented a formal model and showed how this model realizes the layered stepwise architecture of intelligent databases. The FORM model may be used at different levels of detail as a programming and system design tool for both programmers and end users. Thus the model is *seamless*, in the sense that there is no dramatic change between the end user and the programmer mode.

We also discussed high-level tools and the user interface to the intelligent database, along with the database engine. We illustrated the use of the intelligent database technology with the example of Fortune Finder, a system for managing and utilizing information relating to financial analysis of the Fortune 1000 companies.

The implementation of intelligent databases was inconceivable prior to the development of hypermedia systems, advanced microcomputer workstations and expert systems. Now that these technologies have matured, intelligent databases can be used to respond to the needs of data rich and information poor users.

With the rapidly increasing pace of technology development, in the near future intelligent databases will transform our view of *information* to the same dramatic extent that computer technology itself has transformed our view of *computation* in this century.

BIBLIOGRAPHY

Abarbanel, R.; Tou, F.; and Gilbert, V. (1988). KEE Connection: A bridge between databases and knowledge bases. In M. Yazdani and M. Richer (eds.), *AI Tools and Techniques*. Norwood, NJ: Ablex.

Abiteboul, S., and Bidoit, N. (1984). An algebra for non normalized relations. *ACM International Symposium on PODS*, March.

Abiteboul, S., and Hull, R. (1984). IFO: A formal semantic database model. *Proceedings of the ACM SIGACT-SIGMOD Symposium on Principles of Database Systems*.

Ackerman, W. B. (1982). Dataflow languages. *Computer* (February).

Agha, G., and Hewitt, C. (1987). Concurrent programming using actors. In A. Yonezawa and M. Tokoro (eds.), *Object-Oriented Concurrent Programming*. Cambridge, MA: The MIT Press.

Akscyn, R., and McCracken, D. L. (1984). The ZOG approach to database management. *Proceedings of the Trends and Applications Conference: Making Database Work*, Gaithersburg, MD.

Akscyn, R.; McCracken, D. L.; and Yoder, E. (1987). KMS: A distributed hypertext system for sharing knowledge in organizations. *Proceedings of Hypertext '87*, Chapel Hill, NC.

Albano, A.; Cardelli, L.; and Orsini, R. (1985). Galileo: A strongly-typed interactive conceptual language. *ACM Transactions on Database Systems, 10* (June).

Allen, T.; Nix, R.; and Perlis, A. (1981). A hierarchical document editor. *Proceedings of the ACM SIGPLAN/SIGOA Conference on Text Manipulation*. Portland, OR.

Ambron, S., and Hooper, K. (1988). *Interactive Multimedia*. Redmond, WA: Microsoft Press.

Anderson, J. R. (1983). *The Architecture of Cognition*. Cambridge, MA: Harvard University Press.

Andrews, T., and Harris, C. (1987). Combining language and database advances in an object-oriented environment. *Proceedings of OOPSLA-87*.

449

Arbib, M.; Conklin, J.; and Hill, J. (1987). *From Schema Theory to Language*. London: Oxford University Press.

Astrahan, M. M., et al. (1976). System R: A relational approach to data management. *ACM Transactions on Database Systems, 1*, 97–137.

Atkinson, M. P.; Bailey, P. J.; Cockshott, W. P.; Chisholm, K. J.; and Morrison, R. (1983). An approach to persistent programming. *Computer Journal, 26* (November).

Atkinson, M.; Buneman, P.; and Morrison, R. (eds.) (1985). *Persistence and Data Types Papers from the Appin Workshop*, University of Glasgow.

Attneave, F. (1957). *Applications of Information Theory to Psychology: A Summary of Basic Concepts, Methods, and Results*. New York: Holt, Rinehart & Winston.

Bancilhon, F., and Khoshafian, S. (1986). A calculus for complex objects. *ACM International Symposium on PODS*.

Bancilhon, F.; Briggs, T.; Khoshafian, S.; and Valduriez, P. (1987). FAD- a simple and powerful database language. *Proceedings of VLDB 1987*.

Bartlett, F. C. (1932). *Remembering: A Study in Experimental and Social Psychology*. London: Cambridge University Press.

Baskin, A. B. (1980). Logic nets: Variable-valued logic plus semantic networks. *International Journal on Policy Analysis and Information Systems, 4*, 269.

Bates, M. J. (1986). Subject access in online catalogs: A design model. *Journal of the American Society for Information Science, 37*, 357–376.

Batory, D. S., and Kim, W. (1985). Modeling concepts for VLSI CAD objects. *ACM Transactions on Database Systems, 10* (September).

Beeman, W. O.; Anderson, K. T.; Bader, G.; Larkin, J.; McClard, A. P.; McQuillan, P. J.; and Shields, M. (1987). Hypertext and pluralism: From lineal to non-lineal thinking. *Proceedings of Hypertext '87*, Chapel Hill, NC.

Begeman, M. L.; Cook, P.; Ellis, C.; Graf, M.; Rein, G.; and Smith, T. (1986). PROJECT NICK: Meetings augmentation and analysis. *Proceedings of Computer-Supported Cooperative Work (CSCW '86)*, Austin, TX.

Belkin, N. J., and Vickery, A. (1985). *Interaction in Information Systems: A Review of Research from Document Retrieval to Knowledge-Based Systems*. The British Library Board.

Bell, D. (1979). The social framework of the information society. In M. L. Dertouzos and J. Moses (eds.), *The Computer Age: A Twenty-Year View*. Cambridge, MA: The MIT Press.

Bigelow, J., and Riley, V. (1987). Manipulating source code in dynamic design. *Proceedings of Hypertext '87*, Chapel Hill, NC.

Biggerstaff, T.; Ellis, C.; Halasz, F. G.; Kellog, C.; Richter, C.; and Webster, D. (1987). *Information Management Challenges in the Software Design Process*. MCC Technical Report STP-039-87.

Blair, D. C., and Maron, M. E. (1985). An evaluation of retrieval effectiveness for a full-text document-retrieval system. *Communications of the ACM, 28*, 289–299.

Blum, R. (1982). Discovery, confirmation and incorporation of causal relationships from a large time oriented clinical database: The RX project. *Computers and Biomedical Research*.

Blum, R. (1986). Computer assisted design of studies using routine clinical data: Analyzing the association of prednisone and serum cholesterol. *Annals of Internal Medicine*.

Bobrow, D. G., et al. (1986). Common loops merging lisp and object-oriented programming. *Proceedings of OOPSLA-86*.

Bolt, R. A. (1980). Put-that-there: Voice and gesture at the graphics interface. *Computer Graphics, 15,* 262–270.

Bolt, R. A. (1985). Conversing with computers. *Technology Review, 88,* 35–43.

Bolter, J. D. (1987). Hypertext and creative writing. *Proceedings of Hypertext '87,* Chapel Hill, NC.

Booch, G. (1986). Object-oriented development. *IEEE Transactions on Software Engineering, SE-12(2),* February 1986.

Borgman, C. L. (1986). Why are online catalogs so hard to use? Lessons learned from information-retrieval studies. *Journal of the American Society for Information Science, 37,* 387–400.

Borko, H., and Bernier, C. L. (1978). *Indexing Concepts and Methods.* New York: Academic Press.

Borning, A.; Lenat, D. B.; McDonald, D.; Taylor, C.; and Weyer, S. A. (1983). Knoesphere: Toward a searcher's guide to encyclopedic knowledge. *Proceedings of IJCAI-83.*

Brachman, R. J. (1977). What's in a concept: Structural foundations for semantic networks. *International Journal of Man-Machine Studies, 9,* 127–152.

Brachman, R. J. (1979). On the epistemological status of semantic networks. In N. V. Findler (ed.), *Associative Networks: Representation and Use of Knowledge by Computers.* New York Academic Press.

Bradshaw, J. L., and Nettleton, N. C. (1981). The nature of hemispheric specialization in man. *The Behavioral and Brain Sciences, 4,* 51–92.

Braine, M. D. S. (1978). On the relationship between natural logic of reasoning and standard logic. *Psychological Review, 85,* 1–21.

Broadbent, D. E., and Broadbent, M. H. P. (1978). The allocation of descriptor terms by individuals in a simulated retrieval system. *Ergonomics, 10,* 343–354.

Brodie, M. L., and Mylopoulos, J. (eds.) (1986). *On Knowledge Base Management Systems.* New York: Springer-Verlag.

Brooks, H. M. (1987). Expert systems and intelligent information retrieval. *Information Processing and Management, 23,* 367–382.

Brown, P. J. (1986). A simple mechanism for authorship of dynamic documents. In J. C. von Vliet (ed.), *Text Processing and Document Manipulation.* London: Cambridge University Press.

Brown, P. J. (1987). Turning ideas into products: The guide system. *Proceedings of Hypertext '87,* Chapel Hill, NC.

Buell, D. A. (1981). A general model of query processing in information retrieval systems. *Information Processing and Management, 17,* 249–262.

Burstall, R. M., and Goguen, J. A. (1977). Putting theories together to make specifications. *Proceedings of IJCAI-77.*

Bush, V. (1945). As we may think. *Atlantic Monthly, 176,* 101–108.

Buzzard, G. D., and Mudge, T. N. (1985). Object-based computing and the Ada programming language. *Computer* (March).

Campbell, B., and Goodman, J. M. (1987). HAM: A general purpose hypertext abstract machine. *Proceedings of Hypertext '87,* Chapel Hill, NC.

Cardelli, L., (1984). *Amber.* AT&T Bell Labs Technical Memorandum 11271-840924-10TM.

Cardelli, L., and Wagner, P. (1985). On understanding types, data abstraction, and polymorphism. *Computing Surveys, 17.*

Cardenas, A. F. (1979). *Data Base Management Systems.* Boston, MA: Allyn and Bacon.

Cerri, S., and Pelagatti, G. (1984). *Distributed Databases: Principles and Systems.* New York: McGraw-Hill.

Chamberlin, D. D.; Astrahan, M. M.; Eswaran, K. P.; Griffiths, P. P.; Lorie, R. A.; Mehl, J. W.; Reisner, T.; and Wade, B. W. (1976). SEQUEL 2: A unified approach to data definition, manipulation, and control. *IBM Journal of Research and Development, 20,* 560–575.

Chandrasekaran, B., and Mittal, S. (1983). Conceptual representation of medical knowledge for diagnosis by computer: MDX and related systems. *Advances in Computers, 22,* 217–293.

Charney, D. (1987). Comprehending non-linear text: The role of discourse cues and reading strategies. *Proceedings of Hypertext '87,* Chapel Hill, NC.

Chen, P. P. (1976). The entity-relationship model—toward a unified view of data. *ACM Transactions on Database Systems, 1(1).*

Chiaramella, Y., and Defude, B. (1987). A prototype of an intelligent system for information retrieval: IOTA. *Information Processing and Management, 23,* 285–303.

Chignell, M. H. (1981). *Cognitive Mechanisms of Categorization.* Ph.D. Dissertation. Department of Psychology, University of Canterbury, New Zealand.

Chignell, M. H. (1984). *Knowledge-Based Information Retrieval.* Masters Thesis. Department of Industrial and Systems Engineering, Ohio State University.

Chignell, M. H., and Hancock, P. A. (1988). Intelligent Interfaces. In M. Helander (ed.), *The Handbook of Human-Computer Interaction.* Amsterdam: North-Holland.

Chignell, M. H.; Hancock, P. A.; Smith, P. J.; and Shute, S. J. (1986). Information retrieval: An intelligent interface perspective. *Proceedings of the IEEE International Conference on Systems, Man, and Cybernetics,* 372–377.

Chignell, M. H., and Higgins, T. J. (1987). Intelligent warning systems for instrument landings. *International Journal of Industrial Ergonomics* (November), 2, 77–89.

Chignell, M. H., and Lacy, R. M. (1988). Integrating research and instruction: Project Jefferson. *Academic Computing* (September).

Chignell, M. H., and Parsaye, K. (1989). A componential foundation for knowledge engineering. *IEEE Expert.*

Chignell, M. H., and Patty, B. W. (1987). Unidimensional scaling with efficient ranking methods. *Psychological Bulletin, 101,* 304–311.

Chignell, M. H., and Peterson, J. G. (1988). Strategic issues in knowledge engineering. *Human Factors, 30,* 427–440.

Cleverdon, C. (1984). Optimizing convenient online access to bibliographic databases. *Information Services and Use, 4,* 37–47.

Clifford, J., and Warren, D. S. (1983). Formal semantics for time in databases. *ACM Transactions on Database Systems, 8(2).*

Codd, E. F. (1970). A relational model for large shared data banks. *Communications of the ACM, 13,* 377–387.

Codd, E. F. (1979). Extending the database relational model to capture more meaning. *ACM Transactions on Database Systems, 4,* 397–434.

Codd, E. F. (1985). Is your DBMS really relational? *Computer World* (October 14).

Cohen, P. R. and Kjeldsen, R. (1987). Information retrieval by constrained spreading activation in semantic networks. *Information Processing and Management, 23,* 255–268.

Collier, G. H. (1987). Thoth-II: Hypertext with explicit semantics. *Proceedings of Hypertext '87,* Chapel Hill, NC.

Collins, A. M., and Loftus, E. F. (1975). A spreading-activation theory of semantic processing. *Psychological Review, 82,* 407–428.

Conklin, J., and Richter, C. (1985). Support for exploratory design. *Proceedings of the AIAAACM/NASA/IEEE Computers in Aerospace Conference,* American Institute of Aeronautics and Astronautics, Also MCC TR #STP-117-85.

Conklin, J. (1986). *A Theory and Tool for Coordination of Design Conversations.* MCC TR No. STP-236-86, MCC, Austin, TX.

Conklin, J. (1987). Hypertext: A survey and introduction. *IEEE Computer, 20(9),* 17–41.

Conklin, J., and Begeman, M. L. (1987). gIBIS: A hypertext tool for team design deliberation. *Proceedings of Hypertext '87,* Chapel Hill, NC.

Copeland, G. P. (1980). What if mass storage were free? *Proceedings of the Fifth Workshop on Computer Architecture for Non-Numeric Processing.* Pacific Grove, CA.

Copeland, G. P., and Khoshafian, S. (1987). Identity and versions for complex objects. *Proceedings of Persistent Object Systems: Their Design, Implementation, and Use.* University of St. Andrews, Scotland, Research Report No. 44.

Copeland, G. P. and Maier, D. (1984). Making smalltalk a database system. *Proceedings of the SIGMOD Conference,* ACM, Boston.

Corda, U., and Facchetti, G. (1986). Concept browser: A system for interactive creation of dynamic documentation. In J. C. van Vliet (ed.), *Text Processing and Document Manipulation.* London: Cambridge University Press.

Cox, B. (1984). Message/object programming: An evolutionary change in programming technology. *IEEE Software* (January) 50–61.

Cox, B. (1986). *Object-Oriented Programming: An Evolutionary Approach.* Reading, MA: Addison-Wesley.

Cox, B., and Hunt, B. (1986). Objects, icons, and software ICs. *BYTE* (August).

Crane, G. (1987). From the old to the new: Integrating hypertexts into traditional scholarship. *Proceedings of Hypertext '87,* Chapel Hill, NC.

Croft, W. B. (1987). Approaches to intelligent information retrieval. *Information Processing and Management, 23,* 249–254.

Cuadra, J. (1987). *Directory of Online Databases, Volume 8.* New York: Elsevier.

Dahl, O-J., and Nygaard, K. (1966). SIMULA - An ALGOL-based simulation language. *Communications of the ACM, 9,* 671–678.

Dahl, O-J.; Myhrhaug, B.; and Nygaard, K. (1970). *The SIMULA 67 Common Base Language.* Publication S22, Norwegian Computing Centre, Oslo.

Dahl, V. (1983). Logic programming as a representation of knowledge. *IEEE Computer, 16,* 106–113.

Danserau, D. F., and Holley, C. D. (1982). Development and evaluation of a text mapping strategy. In Flammer and Kintsch (eds.), *Discourse Processing.* Amsterdam: North Holland, pp. 536–554.

Date, C. J. (1986). *An Introduction to Database Systems* (two volumes). Reading, MA: Addison-Wesley.

Date, C. J. (1987). *A Guide to SQL Standards*. Reading, MA: Addison-Wesley.

Davis, R., and Lenat, D. B. (1982). *Knowledge-Based Systems in Artificial Intelligence*. New York: McGraw-Hill.

Dawes, R. M. (1979). The robust beauty of improper linear models in decision making. *American Psychologist, 34*, 571–582.

Dayal, U.; Goodman, N.; and Katz, R. (1982). An extended relational algebra with control over duplicate elimination. *Proceedings of PODS*.

DeJong, G. (1979). Artificial intelligence implications for information retrieval. *Proceedings of the Sixth International ACM SIGIR Conference on Information Retrieval*. pp. 10–17.

Delisle, N., and Schwartz, M. (1986). Neptune: a hypertext system for CAD applications. *Proceedings of ACM SIGMOD '86*, Washington, DC, pp. 132–142.

Delisle, N., and Schwartz, M. (1987). Contexts: a partitioning concept for hypertexts. *Proceedings of the Computer Supported Work Conference*.

Deppsich, U.; Paul, H. B.; and Schek, H. J. (1986). A storage system for complex object. *Proceedings of 1986 International Workshop on Object-Oriented Database Systems*. Pacific Grove, CA.

Diettrich, K. R. (1986). Object-oriented database systems: The notion and the issues. *Proceedings of the International Workshop on Object-Oriented Database Systems*. Pacific Grove, CA.

Dillon, M., and McDonald, K. (1983). Fully automatic book indexing. *Journal of Documentation, 39*, 135–154.

di Sessa, A. (1985). A principled design for an integrated computational environment. *Human-Computer Interaction, 1*, 1–47.

di Sessa, A., and Abelson, H. (1986). Boxer: A reconstructable computational medium. *Communications of the ACM, 29*, 859–868.

Donelson, W. C. (1978). Spatial management of information. *ACM SIGGRAPH*.

Durding, D. M.; Becker, C. A.; and Gould, J. D. (1977). Data organization. *Human Factors, 19*, 1–14.

Dyer, M. G. (1983). *In-Depth Understanding*. Cambridge, MA: MIT Press.

Ehrig, H.; Kreowski, H.; and Padawiz, P. (1978). Stepwise specification and implementation of abstract data types. *Proceedings of the 5th ICALP*.

Eich, J. M. (1982). A composite holographic associative recall model. *Psychological Review, 89*, 627–661.

Engelbart, D. (1963). A conceptual framework for the augmentation of man's intellect. In P. D. Howerton and D. C. Weeks (eds.), *Vistas in Information Handling, Vol. 1*. Washington, DC: Spartan Books.

Engelbart, D. C., and English, W. K. (1968). A research center for augmenting human intellect. *AFIPS Proceedings, Fall Joint Computer Conference*.

Engelbart, D. C. (1984a). Authorship provisions in augment. *IEEE 1984 COMPCON Proceedings*, Spring.

Engelbart, D. C. (1984b). Collaboration support provisions in augment. *Proceedings of the AFIPS Office Automation Conference*.

Engelbart, D., and Hooper, K. (1988). The augmentation system framework. In S. Ambron and K. Hooper (eds.), *Interactive Multimedia*. Reading, MA: Addison-Wesley.

Erman, L. D.; Hayes-Roth, F.; Lesser, V.; and Reddy, D. (1980). The Hearsay-II speech understanding system. *ACM Computing Surveys, 12 (3)*.

Erman, L. D.; London, P. E.; and Fickas, S. F. (1981). The design and an example use of HEARSAY-III. *Proceedings of IJCAI-81*, pp. 409–415.

Eswaran, K. P.; Gray, J. N.; Lorie, R. A.; and Traiger, I. L. (1976). The notions of consistency and predicate locks in a database system. *Communications of the ACM, 19*, 624–633.

Everitt, B. S. (1974). *Cluster Analysis*. London: Heinemann.

Fagin, R. (1980). Horn clauses as relational dependencies. *Proceedings of the ACM Conference on Foundations of Computer Science*, Los Angeles.

Fairchild, K. F.; Poltrock, S. E.; and Furnas, G. W. (1988). SemNet: Three-dimensional graphic representations of large knowledge bases. In R. Guindon (ed.), *Cognitive Science and its Applications for Human-Computer Interaction*. Hillsdale, NJ: Lawrence Erlbaum Associates.

Fenichel, C. (1980). Online searching: Measures that discriminate among users with different types of experience. *Journal of the American Society for Information Science, 32*, 23–32.

Fishman, D., et al. (1987). Iris: An object oriented database management system. *ACM Transactions on Database Systems, 5(1)*.

Forester, T. (1987). *High-Tech Society: The Story of the Information Technology Revolution*. Cambridge, MA: MIT Press.

Foskett, A. C. (1977). The subject approach to information. In the *Library of Congress Classification, 3rd Edition*, Chapter 21. Hamden Connecticut: Linnet Books.

Foskett, D. J. (1963). *Classification and Indexing in the Social Sciences*. Washington, DC: Butterworths.

Foster, G., and Stefik, M. (1986). Cognoter, theory and practice of a collaborative tool. *Proceedings of the Computer-Supported Cooperative Work (CSCW '86) Conference*, Austin, TX.

Frisse, M. E. (1987). Searching for information in a hypertext medical handbook. *Communications of the ACM, 31*. 880–886.

Furnas, G. W. (1986). Generalized fisheye views. *CHI'86 Proceedings*, Boston, MA, pp. 16–23.

Furnas, G. W.; Landauer, T. K.; Gomez, L. M.; and Dumais, S. T. (1983). Statistical semantics: Analysis of the potential performance of keyword information systems. *Bell System Technical Journal, 62*, 1753–1806.

Furnas, G. W.; Landauer, T. K.; Gomez, L. M.; and Dumais, S. T. (1987). The vocabulary problem in human system communication. *Communications of the ACM, 30*, 964–971.

Furtado, A. L., and Kerschberg, L. (1977). An algebra of quotient relations. *Proceedings of the ACM SIGMOD International Conference*, Toronto.

Gale, W. (ed.) (1986). *Artificial Intelligence and Statistics*. Reading, MA: Addison-Wesley.

Gaines, B., and Shaw, M. (1986). Induction of inference rules for expert systems. *Journal of Fuzzy Sets and Systems*.

Garg, P. K. (1987). Abstraction mechanisms in hypertext. *Proceedings of Hypertext '87*, Chapel Hill, NC, pp. 375–395.

Garrett, L. N., and Smith, K. E. (1986). Building a timeline editor from prefab parts: The architecture of an object-oriented application. *Proceedings of OOPSLA '86*, Portland, OR.

Gazzaniga, J. (1988). *Mind Matters*. New York: Basic Books.

Giroux, L., and Belleau, R. (1986). What's on the menu? The influence of menu content on the selection process. *Behaviour and Information Technology, 5,* 169–172.

Glossbrenner, A. (1983). *The Complete Handbook of Personal Computer Communications*. New York: St. Martin's Press.

Glossbrenner, A. (1987). *How to Look it up Online*. New York: St. Martin's Press.

Goguen, J. A.; Thatcher, J. W.; Wegner, E. G.; and Wright, J. B. (1975). Abstract data types as initial algebras and correctness of data representation. *Proceedings of the Conference on Computer Graphics, Pattern Recognition, and Data Structures.*

Goldberg, A. (ed.) (1988). *A History of Personal Workstations*. New York: ACM Press.

Goldberg, A., and Robson, D. (1983). *Smalltalk-80: The Language and its Implementation*. Reading, MA: Addison-Wesley.

Goldstein, I. P., and Bobrow, D. G. (1984). A layered approach to software design. In D. Barstow, H. Shrobe, and E. Sandewall (eds.), *Interactive Programming Environments*. New York: McGraw-Hill, pp. 387–413.

Good, M. D.; Whiteside, J. A.; Wixon, D. R.; and Jones, S. J. (1984). Building a user-derived interface. *Communications of the ACM, 27,* 1032–1043.

Goodman, D. (1987). *The Complete HyperCard Handbook*. New York: Bantam Books.

Greene, S. L.; Gomez, L. M.; and Devlin, S. J. (1986). A cognitive analysis of database query production. *Proceedings of the Human Factors Society 30th Annual Meeting*, Dayton, OH, pp. 9–13.

Gregory, R. (1983). Xanadu—Hypertext from the future. *Dr. Dobb's Journal, 75.* (January), 28–35.

Gregson, R. A. M. (1975). *Psychometrics of Similarity*. New York: Academic Press.

Greif, I. (1988). *Computer-Supported Cooperative Work: A Book of Readings*. San Mateo, CA: Morgan Kaufman.

Guida, G., and Tasso, C. (1982). A robust interface for natural language person-machine communication. *International Journal of Man-machine Studies, 17,* 417–433.

Guttag, J. (1977). Abstract data types and the development of data structures. *Communications of the ACM, 20.*

Halasz, F. (1988). Reflections on NoteCards: Seven issues for the next generation of hypermedia systems. *Communications of the ACM* (July).

Halasz, F. G.; Moran, T. P.; and Trigg, R. H. (1987). NoteCards in a nutshell. *Proceedings of CHI+GI 1987.*

Hammwohner, R., and Thiel, U. (1987). Content oriented relations between text units— A structural model for hypertexts. *Proceedings of Hypertext '87*, 155–173.

Hancock, P. A., and Chignell, M. H. (eds.) (1989). *Intelligent Interfaces: Theory, Research, and Design*. Amsterdam: North Holland.

Hawkins, D., and Wagers, R. (1982). Online bibliographic search strategy development. *Online, 6,* 12–19.

Hayes-Roth, B. (1984). *BB1: An Architecture for Black Board Systems that Control, Explain, and Learn About Their Own Behavior*. Technical report HPP-84-16, Stanford University.

Hayes-Roth, B. (1985). A blackboard architecture for control. *Artificial Intelligence, 26,* 251–321.

Hayes-Roth, F.; Waterman, D. A.; and Lenat, D. B. (1983). *Building Expert Systems*. Reading, MA: Addison-Wesley.

Heisenberg, W. (1970). *The Physicist's Conception of Nature*. New York: Harper & Row.

Herot, C. F. (1980). Spatial management of data. *ACM Transactions on Database Systems, 5,* 493–514.

Hershey, W. (1984). ThinkTank. *BYTE* (May), p. 189.

Hershey, W. (1985). Idea processors. *BYTE* (June).

Hewitt, C. (1977). Viewing control structures as patterns of passing messages. *Artificial Intelligence, 8(3)*.

Hirsch, E. D. (1987). *Cultural Literacy*. New York: Houghton Mifflin.

Hirtle, S. C., and Mascolo, M. F. (1986). Effect of semantic clustering on the memory of spatial locations. *Journal of Experimental Psychology: Learning, Memory, and Cognition, 12,* 182–189.

Hjerppe, R. (1986). Project HYPERCATalog: Visions and preliminary conceptions of an extended and enhanced catalog. In B. C. Brookes (ed.), *Intelligent Information Systems for the Information Society*. Amsterdam: Elsevier.

Holland, J.; Holyoak, K. J.; Nisbett, R. E.; and Thagard, P. R. (1986). *Induction: Processes of Inference, Learning, and Discovery*. Cambridge, MA: MIT Press.

Hollands, J. G., and Merikle, P. M. (1987). Menu organization and user expertise in information search tasks. *Human Factors, 29,* 577–586.

Horowitz, E., and Williamson, R. (1986). SODOS: A software documentation support environment—its definition. *IEEE Transactions on Software Engineering, SE-12(8)* (August).

Howard, H. (1982). Measures that discriminate among online searchers with different training and experience. *Online Review, 6,* 315–327.

Howe, G. R., and Lindsay, J. (1981). A generalized iterative record linkage computer system for use in medical follow-up studies. *Computers and Biomedical Research, 14*.

Hull, R., and Yap, C. K. (1984). The format model: A theory of database organization. *Journal of the ACM, 31(3)* (July).

Humphrey, S. (1987). Illustrative description of an interactive knowledge based indexing system. *Proceedings of the ACM SIGIR Conference*, New Orleans, LA, 73–90.

Hunt, E., et al. (1966). *Experiments in Induction*. New York: Academic Press.

Ichikawa, T., and Hirakawa, M. (1986). ARES: A relational database with the capacity of performing flexible interpretations of queries. *IEEE Transactions on Software Engineering, SE-12,* 624–634.

IntelligenceWare (1988a). *The Intelligence/Compiler*. IntelligenceWare, Los Angeles.

IntelligenceWare (1988b). *Database Supervisor*. IntelligenceWare, Los Angeles.

IntelligenceWare (1988c). *IXL: The Machine Learning System*. IntelligenceWare, Los Angeles.

Jacobs, B. E. (1982). On database logic. *Journal of the ACM, 29(2)* (April).

Jaeschke, G., and Schek, H. (1982). Remarks on the algebra of non first normal form relations. *Proceedings of the ACM International Symposium on PODS*, Los Angeles, pp. 124–138.

Jagannathan, D.; Guck, R. L.; Fritchman, B. L.; Thompson, J. P.; and Tolbert, D. M. (1988). SIM: A database system based on the semantic data model. *Proceedings of ACM SIGMOD*.

Jarke, M., and Vassiliou, Y. (1985). A framework for choosing a database query language. *Computer Surveys, 17,* 313–340.

Johansen, R. (1988). *Groupware: Computer Support for Business Teams*. New York: Free Press.

Johnson-Laird, P. N. (1975). Models of deduction. In R. Falmagne (ed.), *Reasoning: Representation and Process in Children and Adults*. Hillsdale, NJ: Erlbaum.

Jonassen, D. H. (1986). Hypertext principles for text and courseware design. *Educational Psychologist, 21*, 269–292.

Jones, W. P. (1986). *The Memory Extender Personal Filing System*. HI-138-85, MCC, Austin, TX.

Jones, W. P., and Dumais, S. T. (1986). The spatial metaphor for user interfaces: Experimental tests of reference by name versus location. *ACM Transactions on Office Information Systems, 4*, 42–63.

Kahneman, D.; Slovic, P.; and Tversky, A. (1982). *Judgment under Uncertainty: Heuristics and Biases*. London: Cambridge University Press.

Karlgren, H., and Walker, D. E. (1983). The polytext system- A new design for a text retrieval system. In F. Kiefer (ed.), *Questions \Answers*, Berlin: D.Reidel Publishing, pp. 273–294.

Katz, R. H. (1987). *Information Management for Engineering Design*. Berlin: Springer-Verlag.

Katz, R. H., and Lehman, T. J. (1984). Database support for versions and alternatives of large design files. *IEEE Transactions on Software Engineering, SE-10*.

Kay, A. C. (1977). Microelectronics and the personal computer. *Scientific American* (September).

Kay, A. C. (1984). Computer software. *Scientific American, 251*, 53–59.

Kay, A. C., and Goldberg, A. (1987). Personal dynamic media. *IEEE Computer, 10(3)*, 31–43.

Khoshafian, S., and Briggs, T. (1988). Schema design and mapping strategies for persistent object models. *Information and Software Technology* (December).

Khoshafian, S., and Copeland, G. (1986). Object identity. *Proceedings of OOPSLA-86*, Portland, OR.

Khoshafian, S., and Frank, D. (1988). Implementation techniques for object oriented databases. *Proceedings of the Second International Workshop on Object-Oriented Database Systems*.

Khoshafian, S., and Valduriez, P. (1987). Persistence, sharing, and object orientation: a database perspective. *Proceedings of the Workshop on Database Programming Languages*, Roscoff, France.

Khoshafian, S.; Franklin, M. J.; and Carey, M. J. (1988). *Storage Management for Persistent Complex Objects*. MCC Technical Report ACA-ST-118-88.

Khoshafian, S.; Valduriez, P.; and Copeland, G. (1988). Parallel processing for complex objects. *Proceedings of the Fourth International Conference on Data Engineering*.

Kimura, G. D. (1986). A structure editor for abstract document objects. *IEEE Transactions on Software Engineering, SE-12(3)*, 417–435.

King, R., and McLeod, D. (1984). A unified model and methodology for conceptual database design. In M. L. Brodie, J. Mylopoulos, and J. W. Schmidt (eds.), *On Conceptual Modeling: Perspectives from Artificial Intelligence, Databases, and Programming Language*. New York: Springer-Verlag.

King, R., and McLeod, D. (1985). Semantic database models. In S. B. Yao (ed.), *Database Design*. New York: Springer-Verlag.

Kinnell, S. K., and Chignell, M. H. (1987). Who's the expert? Conceptual representation of knowledge for end user searching. *Proceedings of the Eighth National Online Meeting*, New York, pp. 237–243.

Klatzky, R. L. (1980). *Human Memory*. San Francisco: Freeman.

Klausner, A., and Goodman, N. (1985). Multi-relations: Semantics and languages. *Proceedings of VLDB 1985*.

Knuth, D. (1984). Literate programming. *Computer Journal, 27(2)*, 97–111.

Kohonen, T. (1977). *Associative Memory: A System-Theoretical Approach*. Berlin: Springer-Verlag.

Kolodner, J. L. (1983). *Retrieval and Organizational Strategies in Conceptual Memory: A Computer Model*. Hillsdale, NJ: Erlbaum.

Kowalski, R. (1979). *Logic for Problem Solving*. New York: North-Holland.

Kraft, D. H. (1985). Advances in information retrieval: Where is that /#*&@ record? *Advances in Computers*, 24, 277–318.

Krawczak, D.; Smith, P. J.; and Shute, S. J. (1987). EP-X: A demonstration of semantically-based search of bibliographic databases. *Proceedings of the ACM SIGIR Conference*, New Orleans, pp. 263–271.

Kruskal, J. B., and Wish, M. (1978). *Multidimensional Scaling*. Beverly Hills: Sage.

Kuhn, T. S. (1970). *The Structure of Scientific Revolutions*, second edition. Chicago: The University of Chicago Press.

Kulkarni, K. G., and Atkinson, M. P. (1986), EFDM: Extended functional data model. *The Computer Journal, 29(1)*.

Kuper, G. M., and Vardi, M. Y. (1984). A new approach to database logic. *Proceedings of the ACM International Symposium on PODS*, Waterloo, Canada.

Kuper, G. M., and Vardi, M. Y. (1985). On the expressive power of the logic data model. *Proceedings of the ACM SIGMOD*, Austin, TX, pp. 180–187.

Lacy, R. M.; Chignell, M. H.; and Kinnell, S. K. (1988). Authoring hypermedia for computer based instruction. *Proceedings of the Annual Meeting of the Human Factors Society*, Anaheim, CA.

Lambert, S., and Ropiequet, S. (1986). *CD ROM: The New Papyrus*. Redmond, WA: Microsoft Press.

Lancaster, F. (1968). *Information Retrieval Systems*. New York: Wiley.

Landauer, T. K.; Dumais, S. T.; Gomez, L. M.; and Furnas, G. W. (1982). Human factors in data access. *Bell System Technical Journal*, 61, 2487–2509.

Landauer, T. K.; Galotti, K. A.; and Hartwell, S. (1983). Natural command names and initial learning: A study of text-editing terms. *Communications of the ACM*, 26, 495–503.

Landow, G. P. (1987). Relationally encoded links and the rhetoric of hypertext. *Proceedings of Hypertext '87*, Chapel Hill, NC.

Langley, P., et al. (1986). *Scientific Discovery*. Cambridge, MA: MIT Press.

Lansdale, M. W.; Simpson, M.; and Stroud, T. R. M. (1987). Comparing words and icons as cue enrichers in an information retrieval system. *Proceedings of Human Computer Interaction, Interact '87*, 911–916.

Larson, J. (1986). A visual approach to browsing in a database environment. *IEEE Computer* (June).

Ledbetter, L., and Cox, B. (1985). Software-IC's, *BYTE* (June).

Lee, E. S., and McGregor, J. N. (1985). Minimizing menu search time in menu retrieval systems. *Human Factors, 27,* 157–162.

Lehnert, W. (1979). *Text Processing Effects and Recall Memory.* Technical Report 157. Yale University, Department of Computer Science.

Lenat, D. (1976). *An AI Approach to Discovery in Mathematics.* Ph.D. Dissertation, Department of Computer Science, Stanford University, 1976.

Lenat, D. B.; Borning, A.; McDonald, D.; Taylor, C.; and Weyer, S. A. (1983). Knoesphere: Building expert systems with encyclopedic knowledge. *Proceedings of IJCAI-83,* Karlsruhe, West Germany.

Lenat, D. B.; Borning, A.; McDonald, D.; Taylor, C.; and Weyer, S. A. (1985). A prototype electronic encyclopedia. *ACM Transactions on Office Information Systems, 3,* 63–88.

Lieberman, H. (1981). *A Preview of Act 1.* MIT AI Lab Memo No. 625.

Lieberman, H. (1986). Using prototypical objects to implement shared behavior in object-oriented systems. *Proceedings of OOPSLA-86,* Portland, OR.

Lieberman, H., and Hewitt, C. (1983). A real-time garbage collector based on the lifetimes of objects. *Communications of the ACM, 26(6).*

Lindsay, R. K.; Buchanan, B.; Feigenbaum, E. A.; and Lederberg, J. (1980). *Applications of Artificial Intelligence to Chemistry: The DENDRAL Project.* New York: McGraw-Hill.

Liskov, B. H., and Zilles, S. M. (1975). Specification techniques for data abstractions. *IEEE Transactions on Software Engineering, SE-1.*

Litwin, W. (1980). Linear hashing: A new tool for file and table addressing. *Proceedings of VLDB 1980,* pp. 212–223.

Lowe, D. G. (1985). Cooperative structuring of information: The representation of reasoning and debate. *International Journal of Man-Machine Studies, 23,* 97–111.

Lynch, K. (1960). *The Image of the City.* Cambridge, MA: MIT Press.

Maier, D. (1983). *The Theory of Relational Databases.* Rockville, MD: Computer Science Press.

Maier, D., and Stein, J. (1986). Indexing in an object-oriented DMBS. *Proceedings of 1986 International Workshop on Object-Oriented Database Systems,* Pacific Grove, CA.

Maier, D.; Stein, J.; Ottis, A.; and Purdy, A. (1986). Development of an object-oriented DBMS. *Proceedings of OOPSLA-86,* Portland, OR.

Malone, T. W.; Grant, K. R.; Turbak, F. A.; Brobst, S. A.; and Cohen, M. D. (1987). Intelligent information-sharing systems. *Communications of the ACM, 30,* 390–402.

Marchionini, G., and Shneiderman, B. (1988). Finding facts vs. browsing knowledge in hypertext systems. *IEEE Computer* (January), 70–80.

Marcus, R. S. (1983). An experimental comparison of the effectiveness of computers versus humans as search intermediaries. *Journal of the American Society for Information Science, 34,* 381–404.

Marriott, F. (1974). *The Interpretation of Multiple Observations.* New York: Academic Press.

Marshall, C. C. (1987). Exploring representation problems using hypertext. *Proceedings of Hypertext '87,* Chapel Hill, NC, pp. 253–268.

Maxemchuck, N. F., and Wilder, H. A. (1982). Virtual editing: I. The concept. *Proceedings of the Second International Workshop on Office Information Systems.* Couvent Royal de St. Maximin, October 13–15.

McCarthy, J. (1968). Programs with common sense. In M. Minsky (ed.), *Semantic Information Processing*. Cambridge, MA: MIT Press.

McCracken, D. L., and Akscyn, R. (1984). Experience with the ZOG human-computer interface system. *International Journal of Man-Machine Studies, 21* (2), 293–310.

McGregor, J. N.; Lee, E. S.; and Lam, N. (1986). Optimizing the structure of database menu indices: A decision model of menu search. *Human Factors, 28,* 387–399.

McNamara, T. P. (1986). Mental representations of spatial relations. *Cognitive Psychology, 18,* 87–121.

McQuillan, P. J. (1987). Computers and pedagogy: The invisible presence. *Journal of Computer-Based Educational Research*.

Menger, K. (1953). *Topology Without Points*. The Karl Menger Lectures, American Mathematical Society.

Meyer, B. (1988). *Object-Oriented Software Construction*. Englewood Cliffs, NJ: Prentice-Hall.

Meyrowitz, N. (1986). Intermedia: The architecture and construction of an object-oriented hypertext/hypermedia system and applications framework. *Proceedings of OOPSLA '86,* Portland, OR.

Michalski, R., and Chilauski, R. (1980). Learning by being told and learning from examples. *Journal of Policy Analysis and Information Systems, 4,* 1980.

Michalski, R. S.; Carbonell, J. G.; and Mitchell, T. M. (eds.) (1983). *Machine Learning, Volume I*. Palo Alto, CA: Tioga Books.

Michalski, R. S.; Carbonell, J. G.; and Mitchell, T. M. (eds.) (1986). *Machine Learning, Volume II*. Los Altos, CA: Morgan Kaufman Publishers.

Michie, D. (1984). Automating the synthesis of expert knowledge. *ASLIB Proceedings*, London.

Miller, G. A. (1956). The magic number seven, plus or minus two: Some limits on our capacity for processing. *Psychological Review, 63,* 81–97.

Mills, J. (1963). *Guide to the Use of the UDC, Part 1 of B.S. 1000C*. London: British Standards Institution.

Minoura, T., and Parsaye, K. (1984). Version based concurrency control of a database system. *Proceedings of the 1984 ACM/IEEE Conference on Data Engineering,* Los Angeles.

Minsky, M. (ed.) (1968). *Semantic Information Processing*. Cambridge, MA: MIT Press.

Minsky, M. (1975). A framework for representing knowledge. In P. H. Winston (ed.), *The Psychology of Computer Vision*. New York: McGraw-Hill.

Mohl, R. F. (1982). *Cognitive Space in the Interactive Movie Map: An Investigation of Spatial Learning in Virtual Environments*. Department of Architecture, Massachussetts Institute of Technology.

Monarch, I., and Carbonell, J. (1987). CoalSORT: A knowledge-based interface. *IEEE Expert* (Spring), 39–53.

Monty, M. L. (1986). Temporal context and memory for notes stored in the computer. *ACM SIGCHI Bulletin, 18,* 50–51.

Monty, M. L., and Moran, T. P. (1986). A longitudinal study of authoring using NoteCards. *ACM SIGCHI Bulletin, 18,* 59–60.

Moon, D. A. (1986). Object-oriented programming with flavors. *Proceedings of OOPSLA-86,* Portland, OR.

Murdock, B. J. (1982). A theory for the storage and retrieval of item and associative information. *Psychological Review, 89,* 609–626.

Mylopoulos, J.; Bernstein, P. A.; and Wong, H. K. T. (1980). A language facility for designing database-intensive applications. *ACM Transactions on Database Systems, 5(2).*

Mylopoulos, J., and Wong, H. K. T. (1980). Some features of the taxis data model. *Proceedings of the 6th VLDB Conference.*

Negroponte, N. (1979). Books without pages. *Proceedings of the IEEE International Conference on Communications IV.*

Nelson, N. M. (1987). *CD-ROMS in Print 1987.* Meckler Corporation.

Nelson, T. H. (1965). The hypertext. *Proceedings of the World Documentation Federation.*

Nelson, T. H. (1981). *Literary Machines.* Swathmore, PA: T. H. Nelson.

Nelson, T. H. (1988). Managing Immense Storage. *BYTE* (January).

Newell, A., and Simon, H. (1972). *Human Problem Solving.* Englewood Cliffs, NJ: Prentice-Hall.

Nicod, J. (1930). *Foundations of Geometry and Induction.* New York: Harcourt Brace.

Nii, P. (1980). *An Introduction to Knowledge Engineering, Blackboards, and AGE.* Report HPP-80-29, Stanford University.

Norman, D. A.; Rumelhart, D.; and the LNR Research Group (1975). *Explorations in Cognition.* San Francisco: Freeman.

Noyce, R. N. (1977). Microelectronics. *Scientific American, 237(3).*

O'Brien (1985). *Trellis Object-Oriented Environment Language Tutorial.* DEC Eastern Research Lab Report, DEC-TR-373, November 1985.

Oldroyd, B., and Schroder, J. J. (1982). Study of strategies used in online searching: 2. Positional logic—an example of the importance of selecting the right boolean operator. *Online Review, 6,* 127–133.

Oren, T. (1987). The architecture of hypertexts. *Proceedings of Hypertext '87,* Chapel Hill, NC.

Osborn, S. L., and Heaven, T. E. (1986). The design of a relational database system with abstract data types. *ACM Transactions on Database Systems, 11(3).*

Owl International (1986). *Guide: Hypertext for the Macintosh.* Bellevue, WA: OWL International.

Ozsoyoglu, M. Z., and Ozsoyoglu, G. (1983). An extension of relational algebra for summary tables. *Proceedings of the 2nd International Conference on Statistical Database Management,* Los Angeles, pp. 202–211.

Paice, C. (1986). Expert systems for information retrieval? *Aslib Proceedings,* October, 343–353.

Palay, A. J., and Fox, M. S. (1981). Browsing through databases. In Oddy, R. N., et al. (eds.) *Information Retrieval Research.* London: Butterworth.

Papadimitriou, C. H. (1979). The serializability of concurrent database updates. *Journal of the ACM, 26,* 631–653.

Parker, D., and Parsaye, K. (1980). Inferences involving embedded multi-valued dependencies and transitive dependencies. *Proceedings of the ACM SIGMOD Conference,* Los Angeles.

Parnas, D. L. (1972). On the criteria to be used in decomposing systems into modules. *Communications of the ACM, 12* (December).

Parsaye, K. (1982). *Higher Order Abstract Data Types*. Ph.D. Dissertation, Department of Computer Science, University of California at Los Angeles, Report No. CSD-820112.

Parsaye, K. (1983a). Logic programming and relational databases. IEEE Transactions on Database Engineering, December 1983.

Parsaye, K. (1983b). Database management, knowledge base management and expert system development in prolog. *Proceedings of the ACM SIGMOD Database Week Conference*, San Jose, CA.

Parsaye, K. (1985a). The next 700 expert system languages. *Proceedings of the IEEE COMP-CON Conference*, San Francisco.

Parsaye, K. (1985b). The evolutionary road to expert systems. *Proceedings of the Expert Systems in Government Conference*, Washington, DC.

Parsaye, K. (1987). Machine learning: The next step. *Computer World*.

Parsaye, K., and Chignell, M. (1988). *Expert Systems for Experts*. New York: Wiley.

Parsaye, K., and Hansson, O. (1988). *Discovering Knowledge from Large Databases*. Technical Report, IntelligenceWare, Los Angeles.

Parsaye, K., and Lee, R. (1989). *Database Supervisor Reference Manual*. IntelligenceWare, Los Angeles.

Parsaye, K., and Lin, K. Y. (1987). An expert system structure for automatic fault tree generation for emergency feedwater systems for nuclear power plants. *Proceedings of the Second IEEE WESTEX Conference*, Anaheim, CA.

Parsaye, K., and Murphree, S. (1987). Automating the knowledge acquisition process. *Proceedings of the AI Conference*, Long Beach, CA.

Pasquier, J. (1986). *The Method and Model Base of the Electronic Book: Markov Chains and Reliability Modeling*. Institute for Automation and Operations Research, University of Fribourg (Switzerland).

Peterson, L. R., and Peterson, M. J. (1959). Short-term retention of individual verbal items. *Journal of Experimental Psychology, 58*, 193–198.

Pitman, K. M. (1985). *CREF: An Editing Facility for Managing Structured Text*. A.I. Memo No.829, M.I.T. A.I. Laboratory, Cambridge, MA.

Pollit, S. (1987). An expert systems approach to document retrieval: A summary of the CANSEARCH research project. *Information Processing and Management, 16*, 73–90.

Pontecorvo, M. S. (1987). A hypermedia multiple perspective mechanism. *Proceedings of Hypertext '87*, Chapel Hill, NC.

Porter, A. L.; Wiederholt, B. J.; Coberly, J. V.; and Weaver, M. D. (1988). *Intelligent Information Retrieval: An Assessment of the State of the Art and Future Prospects*. Technical Report, Search Technology, Norcross, Georgia.

Postin, T. (1974). *Fuzzy Topology*. Technical Report, Battelle Research Institute, Geneva.

Proctor, R. W. (1981). A unified theory for matching-task phenomena. *Psychological Review, 88*, 291–326.

Quillian, M. R. (1968). Semantic memory. In M. Minsky (ed.), *Semantic Information Processing*. Cambridge, MA: MIT Press, pp. 227–270.

Quinlan, R. (1979). Discovering rules from large collections of examples. In D. Michie (ed.), *Expert Systems in the Micro Electronic Age*. Edinburgh: Edinburgh University Press.

Quinlan, R. (1983). Learning efficient classifications. In R. Michalski, et al. (eds.), *Machine Learning, Volume I*. Palo Alto, CA: Tioga Books.

Quinlan, R. (1986). Induction of decision trees. In R. Michalski, et al. (eds.), *Machine Learning, Volume II*. Los Altos, CA: Morgan Kaufmann.

Raskin, J. (1987). The hype in hypertext: A critique. *Proceedings of Hypertext '87*, Chapel Hill, NC.

Rau, L. F. (1987). Knowledge organization and access in a conceptual information system. *Information Processing and Management, 23*, 269–284.

Raymond, D. R., and Tompa, F. W. (1987). Hypertext and the New Oxford English Dictionary. *Proceedings of Hypertext '87*, Chapel Hill, NC.

Reisner, P. (1981). Human factors studies of database query languages: A survey and assessment. *Computing Surveys, 13*, 13–31.

Remde, J. R.; Gomez, L. M.; and Landauer, T. K. (1987). SuperBook: An automatic tool for information exploration-hypertext? *Proceedings of Hypertext '87*, Chapel Hill, NC.

Rentsch, T. (1982). Object-oriented programming. *SIGPLAN Notices* (September).

Rich, E. (1983). *Artificial Intelligence*. New York: McGraw-Hill.

Risch, T.; Reboh, R.; Hart, P.; and Duda, R. A. (1988). Functional approach to integrating database and expert systems. *Communications of the ACM, 31*, 1424–1437.

Roberts, R. B., and Goldstein, I. P. (1977). *The FRL Primer*. MIT AI Lab Memo No. 408. Cambridge, MA.

Rosch, E., and Mervis, C.B. (1975). Family resemblances: Studies in the internal structure of categories. *Cognitive Psychology, 7*, 573–605.

Rosch, E.; Mervis, C. B.; Gray, W. D.; Johnson, D. M.; and Boyes-Braem, P. (1976). Basic objects in natural categories. *Cognitive Psychology, 8*, 382–439.

Roth, M.; Korth, H.; and Siberschatz, A. (1984). *Theory of Non-First-Normal-Form Relational Databases*. TR-84-36, Department of Computer Science, University of Texas at Austin.

Russell, D. M.; Moran, T. P.; and Jordan, D. S. (1988). The instructional design environment. In J. Psotka, L. D. Massey, and S. A. Mutter (eds.), *Intelligent Tutoring Systems: Lessons Learned*. Hillsdale, NJ: Erlbaum.

Salton, G. (1987). Another look at automatic text-retrieval system. *Communications of the ACM, 29*, 648–656.

Salton, G., and McGill, M.J. (1983). *An Introduction to Modern Information Retrieval*. New York: McGraw-Hill.

Saltzer, J. H. (1978). *Naming and Binding of Objects*. In Goos and Harman (eds.), Lecture Notes in Computer Science. Berlin: Springer-Verlag.

Samuel, A. (1963). Some studies in machine learning using the game of checkers. In A. Feigenbaum (ed.), *Computers and Thought*. New York: McGraw-Hill.

Scacchi, W. (1989). On the power of domain-specific hypertext environments. *Journal of the American Society for Information Science*.

Schank, R. (1975). *Conceptual Information Processing*. Amsterdam: North-Holland.

Schank, R. C., and Abelson, R. P. (1977). *Scripts, Plans, Goals and Understanding*. Hillsdale, NJ: Erlbaum.

Schek, H. J., and Scholl, M. H. (1986). The relational model with relational valued attributes. *Information Systems, 11(2)*.

Servio Logic (1986). *Programming in OPAL.* Servio Logic Development Corporation. Beaverton, OR.

Shafer, D. (1988). *Hypertalk Programming.* Indianapolis: Hayden Books.

Shaffert, C., Cooper, T., Bullis, B., Kilian, M., and Wilpolt, C. (1986). An Introduction to Trellis/Owl. *OOPSLA-86 Proceedings,* pp. 9–16.

Shasha, D. (1985). Netbook: A data model for text exploration. *VLDB Proceedings.*

Shibayama, E., and Yonezawa, A. (1987). Distributed computing in ABCL/1. In A. Yonezawa and M. Tokoro (eds.), *Object-Oriented Concurrent Programming.* Cambridge, MA: MIT Press.

Shipman, J. (1981). The functional data model and the data language DAPLEX. *ACM Transactions on Database Systems, 6(1).*

Shneiderman, B. (1983). Direct manipulation: A step beyond programming languages. *IEEE Computer, 16(8),* 57–69.

Shneiderman, B., and Morariu, J. (1986). *The Interactive Encyclopedia System (TIES),* Department of Computer Science, University of Maryland.

Shneiderman, B. (1986). *Designing User Interfaces.* Reading, MA: Addison-Wesley.

Shneiderman, B. (1987). User interface design for the hyperties electronic encyclopedia. *Proceedings of Hypertext '87,* Chapel Hill, NC.

Shu, N. C.; Wong, H. K. T.; and Lum, V. Y. (1983). Forms approach to requirements specification for database design. *Proceedings of SIGMOD 1983.*

Shute, S. J.; Smith, P. J.; Krawczak, D.; Chignell, M. H.; and Sater, M. (1986). Enhancing cognitive compatibility in a knowledge-based information retrieval system. *1986 Fall Industrial Engineering Conference Proceedings,* pp. 111–115.

Siegel, A. W., and White, S. H. (1975). The development of spatial representations of large-scale environments. In H. W. Reese (ed.), *Advances in Child Development and Behavior.* New York: Academic Press.

Smith, J. B.; Weiss, S. P.; and Ferguson, G. J. (1987). A hypertext writing environment and its cognitive basis. *Proceedings of Hypertext '87,* Chapel Hill, NC.

Smith, J. M., and Smith, D. C. P. (1977). Database abstractions: Aggregations and generalizations. *ACM Transactions on Database Systems, 2,* 105–133.

Smith, K. E., and Zdonik, S. B. (1987). Intermedia: A case study of the differences between relational and object-oriented database systems. *Proceedings of OOPSLA '87,* Orlando, FL.

Smith, P. J.; Chignell, M. H.; and Krawczak, D. (1985). Development of a knowledge-based bibliographic information retrieval system. *Proceedings of the IEEE International Conference on Cybernetics and Society,* Halifax, Nova Scotia.

Smolensky, P.; Bell, B.; Fox, B.; King, R.; and Lewis, C. (1987). Constraint-based hypertext for argumentation. *Proceedings of Hypertext '87,* Chapel Hill, NC.

Sneath, P. H. A., and Sokal, R. R. (1973). *Numerical Taxonomy.* San Francisco: Freeman.

Snyder, A. (1985). *Object-Oriented Programming for CommonLisp.* Hewlett-Packard Technical Report ATC-85-1.

Snyder, A. (1986). Encapsulation and inheritance in object-oriented programming languages. *Proceedings of OOPSLA '86,* Portland, OR.

Spezzano, C. (1986). Unconventional outliners. *PC World* (March), p. 168.

Stanfill, C., and Brewster, K. (1986). Parallel free-text search on the connection machine system. *Communications of the ACM, 29,* 1229–1239.

Stanfill, C., and Waltz, D. (1986). Toward memory-based reasoning. *Communications of the ACM, 29,* 1213–1228.

Stefik, M., and Bobrow, D. G. (1986). Object-oriented programming: Themes and variations. *AI Magazine, 6(4).*

Stefik, M.; Foster, G.; Bobrow, D. G.; Kahn, K. M.; Lanning, S.; and Suchman, L. (1986). Beyond the chalkboard: Using computers to support collaboration and problem solving in meetings. *Communications of the ACM, 30(1).*

Stein, L. A. (1987). Delegation is inheritance. *Proceedings of OOPSLA-87.*

Stepp, R. (1984). *Conjunctive Conceptual Clustering.* Ph.D. Dissertation, University of Illinois, Urbana, 1984.

Stonebraker, M. (1986). Triggers and inference in database systems. In M. L. Brodie and J. Mylopoulos (eds.), *On Knowledge Base Management Systems.* New York: Springer-Verlag.

Stonebraker, M.; Wong, E.; Kreps, P.; and Held, G. (1976). The design and implementation of INGRES. *ACM Transactions on Database Systems, 1,* 189–222.

Strauss, J. S.; Bartko, J. J.; and Carpenter, W. T. (1973). The use of clustering techniques for the classification of psychiatric patients. *British Journal of Psychiatry, 122,* 531–540.

Streeter, L. A., and Lochbaum, K. E. (1988). An expert/expert-locating system based on automatic representation of semantic structure. *Proceedings of IEEE Conference on AI Applications,* San Diego.

Stroustrup, J. (1986). *The C++ Programming Language.* Reading, MA: Addison-Wesley.

Takane, Y.; Young, F. W.; and de Leeuw, J. (1977). Nonmetric individual differences multidimensional scaling: An alternating least squares method with optimal scaling features. *Psychometrika, 42,* 7–67.

Tanaka, M., and Ichikawa, T. (1988). A visual user interface for map information retrieval based on semantic significance. *IEEE Transactions on Software Engineering, SE-14,* 666–671.

Tanguay, D. A. (1986). *A General System for Managing Videotex Information Structures.* University of Waterloo, Department of Computer Science Technology RID:CS-86-23.

Teshiba, K., and Chignell, M. H. (1988). Development of a user model evaluation technique for hypermedia based interfaces. *Proceedings of the Annual Meeting of the Human Factors Society,* Anaheim, CA.

Thomas, S. (1982). *A Non-First-Normal-Form Relational Database Model.* Ph.D. Dissertation, Vanderbilt University.

Thompson, B., and Thompson, B. (1987). Hyping text: Hypertext and knowledge representation. *AI Expert* (August), pp. 25–28.

Thompson, D. A. (1971). Interface design for an interactive information retrieval system: A literature survey and a research system description. *Journal of the American Society for Information Science, 23,* 361–373.

Thorndyke, P. W., and Hayes-Roth, B. (1982). Differences in spatial knowledge acquired from maps and navigation. *Cognitive Psychology, 14,* 560–589.

Tichy, W. (1982). Design, implementation, and evaluation of a revision control system. *Proceedings of the 6th International Conference on Software Engineering,* Tokyo, Japan, pp. 58–67.

Tou, F.; Williams, M.; Fikes, R.; Henderson, D. A.; and Malone, T. (1982). RABBIT: An intelligent database assistant. *Proceedings of the American Association for Artificial Intelligence,* Pittsburgh.

Tou, J. T. (1980). Knowledge engineering. *International Journal of Computer and Information Sciences, 9,* 275–285.

Trigg, R. H. (1983). *A Network-Based Approach to Text Handling for the Online Scientific Community.* TR-1346, Department of Computer Science, University of Maryland.

Trigg, R. H., and Irish, P. M. (1987). Hypertext habitats: Experiences of writers in NoteCards. *Proceedings of Hypertext '87,* Chapel Hill, NC.

Trigg, R. H.; Moran, T. P.; and Halasz, F. G. (1987). Adaptability and tailorability in NoteCards. *Proceedings of INTERACT '87,* Stuttgart, West Germany.

Tsur, S., and Zaniolo, C. (1986). LDL: A logic based data language. *Proceedings of VLDB '86.*

Tufte, W. (1983). *The Visual Display of Quantitative Information.* Cheshire, CT: Graphics Press.

Tukey, J. (1977). *Exploratory Data Analysis.* Reading, MA: Addison Wesley.

Tukey, J. (1986). Statistician's expert systems. In W. Gale (ed.), *Artificial Intelligence and Statistics.* Reading, MA: Addison-Wesley.

Ullman, J. (1980). *Principles of Relational Database Systems.* New York: Computer Science Press.

Ullman, J. D. (1987). Database theory—Past and future. *Proceedings of 6th PODS,* San Diego.

Ullman, J. D. (1988). *Principles of Database and Knowledge-Base Systems.* Rockville, MD: Computer Science Press.

Ungar, D. (1984). Generation scavenging: A non-disruptive high performance storage reclamation algorithm. *Proceedings of the ACM Software Engineering Symposium on Practical Software Development Environments,* Pittsburgh.

Valdez, J. F.; Chignell, M. H.; and Glenn, B. G. (1988). Browsing models for hypermedia databases. *Proceedings of the Human Factors Society.*

Valduriez, P. (1987). Join indices. *ACM Transactions on Database Systems, 12(2).*

Valduriez, P.; Khoshafian, S.; and Copeland, G. (1986). Implementation techniques of complex objects. *Proceedings of VLDB,* Kyoto, Japan.

van Rijsbergen, C. J. (1979). *Information Retrieval.* London: Butterworth.

Walker, J. H. (1987). Document examiner: Delivery interface for hypertext documents. *Proceedings of Hypertext '87,* Chapel Hill, NC, pp. 307–324.

Walker, J. H. (1988). Supporting development documents with concordia. *IEEE Computer* (January).

Wanger, J.; McDonald, D.; and Berger, M. C. (1980). *Evaluation of the Online Search Process: A Final Report.* Springfield, NTIS.

Wason, P. C., and Johnson-Laird, P. N. (1972). *Psychology of Reasoning: Structure and Content.* Cambridge, MA: Harvard University Press.

Wegner, P. (1987). Dimensions of object-oriented language design. *Proceedings of OOPSLA-87,* Orlando.

Weiskamp, K., and Shammas, N. (1988). *Mastering HyperTalk.* New York: Wiley.

Weyer, S. A. (1982). The design of a dynamic book for information search. *International Journal of Man-Machine Studies, 17,* 87–107.

Weyer, S. A., and Borning, A. (1985). A prototype electronic encyclopedia. *ACM Transactions on Office Information Systems, 3,(1),* 66–88.

Weyer, S. A. (1987). As we may learn. Multimedia in education: Interfaces to knowledge. *Proceedings of the Education Advisory Council Conference.*

Wheeler, H. (1987). *The Virtual Library.* University of Southern California.

Wiederhold, G. (1983). *Database Design.* New York: McGraw-Hill.

Wilder, H. A., and Maxemchuck, N. F. (1982). Virtual editing: II. The user interface. *Proceedings of SIGOA Conference Office Automation Systems,* Philadelphia.

Williams, M. D. (1984). What makes RABBIT run? *International Journal of Man-Machine Studies, 21,* 333–352.

Williams, M. W. (1987). *Proceedings of the National Online Meeting.* Learned Information.

Winograd, T. (1983). *Language as a Cognitive Process. Vol. 1:* Syntax. Reading, MA: Addison-Wesley.

Wirth, N. (1984). Data structures and algorithms. *Scientific American* (September), 60.

Wong, H. K. T. (1983). *Design and Verification of Information Systems.* Ph.D. Thesis, University of Toronto.

Wrigley, E. A. (ed.) (1973). *Identifying People in the Past.* London: Edward Arnold.

Wulf, W. A.; London, R. L.; and Shaw, M. (1976). An introduction to the construction and verification of alphard programs. *IEEE Transactions on Software Engineering, SE-2.*

Wurman, R. S. (1989). *Information Anxiety.* New York: Doubleday.

Yankelovich, N.; Haan, B.; and Meyrowitz, N. (1988). Intermedia: The concept and the construction of a seamless information environment. *IEEE Computer* (January).

Yokote, Y., and Tokoro, M. (1987). Concurrent programming in concurrent smalltalk. In A. Yonezawa and M. Tokoro (eds.), *Object-Oriented Concurrent Programming.* Cambridge, MA: MIT Press.

Yonezawa, A., et al. (1987). Modeling and programming in an object-oriented concurrent language ABCL/1. In A. Yonezawa and M. Tokoro (eds.), *Object-Oriented Concurrent Programming.* Cambridge, MA: MIT Press.

Young, R. L. (1987). An object-oriented framework for interactive data graphics. *OOPSLA '87 Proceedings,* pp. 78–90.

Zadeh, L. (1965). *Fuzzy Sets, Information and Control, Vol. 8.*

Zaniolo, C. (1983). The database language GEM. *Proceedings of the ACM SIGMOD Conference,* San Jose, CA.

Zaniolo, C. (1985). The representation and deductive retrieval of complex objects. *Proceedings of VLDB '85.*

Zdonik, S. (1984). Object management system concepts. *Proceedings of the Conference on Office Information Systems, ACM/SIGOA,* Toronto.

Zdonik, S., and Wegener (1986). Language and methodology for object-oriented database environments. *Proceedings of the Nineteenth Annual Hawaii International Conference on System Sciences.*

Zemankova, M., and Kandel, A. (1985). Implementing imprecision in information systems. *Information Science, 37,* 107–141.

Zloof, M. M. (1975). *Query-by-Example: Operations on the Transitive Closure.* IBM RC 5526. Yorktown Heights, NY.

Zloof, M. M. (1977). Query-by-example: A data base language. *IBM Systems Journal, 16,* 324–343.

INDEX